American Civilization Since World War II

Readings on its Character,
Style, and Quality

American Civilization Since World War II

Readings on its Character, Style, and Quality

Edited by

**Albert Karson and
Perry E. Gianakos**

Michigan State University

Wadsworth Publishing Company, Inc.
Belmont, California

iv

L. C. Cat. Card No.:
68-29158
Printed in the
United States of America

Second printing: July 1969

Dedicated
to those scions of
the new America
Craig and Eric
and
Nick, Tom and Paul

The readings in this collection examine and evaluate various aspects of American society since World War II—its ideas, its institutions, its arts, its technology, its people—in short, many of those components that go to make up what we call American Civilization. We have two purposes in this book. First, we explore a new way of gauging the American character, through what American civilization has created. It does not seem unreasonable to judge a pragmatic people by its own standards. Second, we want to help students recognize and understand the radical transformation that has taken place in our society since World War II. The selections, therefore, focus directly on many of the most important aspects of this development in American civilization.

A number of recent books attempt to deal with the question first raised by Crèvecoeur almost two hundred years ago: "What then is the American, this new man"? Now that the United States is the richest, most powerful nation in the world, Crèvecoeur's question reappears with increasing frequency and intensity. Answers have been sought through investigations of the American identity, character, and personality. Such studies have literary parallels in the works of novelists and playwrights who are concerned with the American, the person, and his search for identity. But such direct examination of "the American," with emphasis on personal, psychological, and subjective approaches, needs to be supplemented by the insights and analyses of a wider variety of observers.

This collection aims, therefore, at the broader question: What have the Americans created? Ultimately, an investigation into what Americans have done and are doing should shed light on what Americans *are*. It should also provide important insights into the nature and dynamics of American culture.

The significance of these insights is suggested by Henry Bamford Parkes in *Gods and Men: The Origins of Western Culture*. In his preface, he writes:

> I have concentrated on describing those cultural creations that still have power to shape our thinking and stir our emotions. . . . I believe that the main factors in the political and economic development of any society are its general view of life and system of values, that these are reflected in its philosophy, literature and art.

We adopt Professor Parkes' view and go beyond his primary concern with philosophy, literature, and art to include the factors that make up a total society in the twentieth century. In an industrial, technological society such as ours these factors encompass a wide range—from the urban environment through teenage culture to "the American way of death."

The basis on which we made our selections can be stated simply. We have chosen the most authoritative, interesting and well-written pieces we could find dealing with the most significant aspects of recent American civilization. Since Americans are notoriously self-critical, there is a great deal of material from which to choose. The tone of the various selections ranges from the reasoned and objective to the scolding and polemical.

The readings are arranged in two parts. "Panoramas, Perspectives, and Broadsides" is made up of articles that are broad in scope and attempt an overview of American civilization as an integrated whole. The second part, "Particulars, Specifics, and Potshots," contains selections dealing generally with narrower aspects of American civilization. The readings in each section are arranged chronologically. Each selection is introduced by a headnote which, in addition to providing biographical information, also gives cross-references to the other selections in the book which deal with the same or similar ideas. Many articles in Part Two provide documentary evidence for some of the general views in Part One. This cross-referencing should help the student acquire a more integrated picture of American civilization. For the same reason, we have included an index of subjects, in which selections are listed under broad topical headings by author.

Our introduction is not meant to synthesize the ideas presented in the readings. Rather it is an attempt to identify certain elements that seem to differentiate the postwar period from the era before the war. We hope to provide, therefore, not historical context but a practical description of the postwar milieu and, thus, enable the student to view the ideas of the various writers against a broad backdrop. Although we suggest some conclusions about the American—his character and the civilization he has produced—we have by no means foreclosed other, independent conclusions.

Acknowledgments

We wish to thank our colleagues in the Department of American Thought and Language, Michigan State University, for their helpful suggestions: Henry Silverman, Bernard Engel, Nora Landmark, Thomas Kishler, Joseph Lee, John Appel, Heyward Ehrlich, and George Landon; thanks are due also to Lawrence H. Battistini of the Social Science Department and to our colleagues in the University, Russel Nye, Walter Adams, and Charles Larrowe.

Thanks also to John Cary, Carl Withers, Robert K. Reddy and John Cain, who also contributed. We are grateful for the help of Jean Houghton in the MSU Library Reference Division and Julia Thompson of the Library's Catalog Department and Opal E. Peterson and Isabel Butterfield of the Library's Documents Room. Mrs. Jeanette Aldrich was our patient, painstaking typist. The contributions of Milton Cantor, University of Massachusetts, Roderick Nash, University of California at Santa Barbara, and Robert Woodward, San Jose State College, who reviewed the manuscript, are gratefully acknowledged.

To Martha A. Karson a special thank you for suggestions and advice about the social-psychological aspects. We are also grateful for the MSU All-University Research Grant, which provided partial financing.

Finally, we acknowledge contributions of the following Honors College students in the Fall 1966, class of American Thought and Language in University College: Thomas S. Assiff, Pauline G. Bailey, Garrey L. Callihan, John B. Chapman, Stephen E. Cramer, Gregg H. Downey, Eleanor M. Farrell, Helene B. Goldstein, Susan A. Holyoke, John D. Hopkins, Bruce W. Irwin, Paul F. Kelly, Frank S. Kessler, Judith L. King, Harold D. Laycock, Helen M. Lyons, John J. Malouin, Wallace P. McMartin, Mary A. Saranen, James A. Sheehan, Paula F. Sikes, Susan M. Smolinske, Gregory S. Whitney.

Contents

xi

introduction

I

During the last twenty-five years, the period with which this book is concerned, change has been so profound and so all-pervasive that few if any aspects of American life have gone untouched. The spectra of changes—as the readings in this book will document—range from the problem of the individual's identity to the character of the mass society; from the present disorder of the American landscape to the redesign of cities; from the role of the hero in contemporary fiction to the role of the female in American society. John E. Brooks, who is concerned with the quantitative differences between life in America in 1939 and the present, terms this era "the great leap." (16)[1] Others refer to this period as the beginning of the "post-industrial age." America thus continues to be, as Henry Bamford Parkes has said, not just a place; in its continuing state of becoming, it is also a "state of mind." (1)

To what can we trace the radical transformation of these last twenty-five years, and what has been its effect on the American character—that is, on the *typical and dominant modes of behavior and attitudes which distinguish Americans from other national groups?* It seems to us that there are at least four major interrelated elements that constitute the change-producing ambience of these postwar years. And the interrelation and interaction of these elements has determined their total significance in shaping postwar American society. There is, first of all, what has been termed "a creative federalism," which uses Keynesian economics to achieve material abundance. Second, is the international involvement of America making it the focus of world politics. Third, is a movement which—to use the current ecumenical expression—we term "the American democratic *aggiornamento,*" in effect an updating of historic American democratic ideals and their institutionalization in positive law. Finally, the roles of science and technology have expanded so continually and so pervasively that they can properly be said to be "meta-functioning"—that is, functioning far beyond what was once considered their normal bounds.

1 Numbers following book titles and names designate readings in this text.

1

II

The first of these four far-reaching elements, the implementation of Keynesian economics, resulted from the decision to use the federal government in a new, creative way. John Brooks, in *The Great Leap,* calls John Maynard Keynes's economic theory "a profound transformation of basic economic ideas." Keynesianism, according to Brooks, is a belief that capitalism's "apparent built-in cycle of inflation and depression, of boom and bust, must be interrupted by the leveling hand of government action." More specifically, Brooks says, Keynes believed that "the economy of a free country had to be government-managed through correctly timed deficit spending and control of demand through tax-rate changes." John Kenneth Galbraith (25), who calls the change from conventional economic theory to Keynesian theory "the rejection of automaticity," goes on to discuss the social advantages of the deficit spending recommended by Keynes. Galbraith has developed the notion of a welfare capitalism concerned with furthering the public weal. The economic innovations of Keynes and Galbraith break radically with the conventional economic wisdom of the past, which invariably demanded balanced budgets, a convertible gold standard, and a "free" market in which government played little or no part. In another context, John F. Kennedy has described a recital of this traditional economic litany as an "incantation to the past."

The "new economics" was introduced to America during President Franklin D. Roosevelt's New Deal. According to Galbraith, Keynes himself "urged his ideas directly on President Roosevelt" in 1933. It is doubtful if Roosevelt fully understood Keynes, but some New Deal policies, especially the resort to deficit financing, coincided with Keynes's ideas. It was not until the Full Employment Act of 1946, passed during President Harry Truman's administration, that the government explicitly supported Keynesian theory by law. Even though President Eisenhower's economic homilies to the nation were generously sprinkled with obeisances to "fiscal responsibility," his administration also employed Keynesian ideas. Subsequently, both Presidents Kennedy and Johnson have been more candid in stating the positive benefits that can accrue from planned unbalanced budgets, deficit spending, and tax cuts. The relative success of these programs has demonstrated the efficacy of the "new economics."

The United States government's use of these new economic ideas, combined, of course, with our industrial capacity, has changed the fundamental economic facts of life. We are the first nation in history to be faced with a problem of abundance. However, although many Americans have developed what amounts to a "credit-card way of life," not all serious difficulties have been overcome. For, as Michael Harrington points out in *The Other America* (33), affluence has not reached all sectors of the population. The exploding Negro urban ghettos are violent manifestos of that fact.

Affluence has introduced other new problems into American life. Meaningful work, for example, is disappearing. And, while affluence has meant superhighways, they are, as John Kouwenhoven points out in *The Beer Can by the Highway*, littered with the debris of affluence—junkyards, billboards, and honky-tonk strips. Although, affluence means more "things" for more people, it also means greater pollution of the air and water. And, finally, affluence has taken a toll on the American personality, for we are now faced with the problems of anomie, alienation, and, as Allen Wheelis (26) tells us, a loss of identity.

But whatever the disadvantages, the benefits of abundance are also apparent, as evidenced by the increasing attention to the quality of American life and more leisure, which hopefully means more time for the arts, amusement, entertainment, and fun. These developments may have resulted in the substitution of what Bernard Iddings Bell (2) calls "crowd culture" for high art or what Dwight MacDonald calls "kitsch" for *kultur*. But such developments have released the average man from the harshness of necessity. Perhaps the new American civilization has "museumized" the traditional art forms in the new culture palaces—such as New York City's Lincoln Center—and treated paintings, for example, as investments, tax gimmicks in the art game. But there seems to be no doubt that abundance enhances the dignity of human life.

In sum, we have been transformed from a producing society to a consuming one. We are the pioneer nation in human history to "suffer" that change, and the full consequences have yet to be realized. We have yet to overcome the agony of our search for a substitute for the Puritan ethic in which work and success have made up the primary motivation in America. But the process, as John M. Blum (31) puts it, is already under way.

III

The second factor relates to the expanded role in international affairs that has forced the United States to operate as one of the world's two superpowers. Before entering World War II, America was largely isolationist, frequently anti-foreign, and provincial. She emerged from that conflict as an international leader fully committed to a global outlook. For the first time in her history, she began to play the role for which her wealth and power had equipped her as early as the turn of the century. Today there is, as Raymond Aron has put it, "no area on earth to which American diplomacy is indifferent."[2] Recognition of this fact has resulted in the stationing of American troops in every quarter of the globe and the expenditure of many billions of dollars.

2 "The Thankless Role of a Great Power," *The United States* by P. O'Donovan *et al.* (*Life* World Library, 1965), pp. 169–176.

The United States commitment in the postwar world involved first such obvious things as providing food, medicine, and clothing to relieve the human suffering left in the war's wake; second, furnishing money and material for the rebuilding of the war-ravaged areas of Europe, Asia, and Oceania. But, further, since American occupation armies required occupation governments in the former enemy territory, Americans had to start from scratch to build an international apparatus to meet this need. Also, America was committed to the goal of international cooperation through the United Nations. All of these developments were accepted in the normal course of events, and, in themselves, would have been sufficient to commit the nation to a new world stance. But it was the abnormal — the beginning of the cold war between the United States and the USSR — which fixed America irrevocably as the focus of all world politics.

A whole new set of domestic problems arose as a result of the United States' greatly expanded international role, and, more specifically, as a direct consequence of the cold war. There is, for example, the threat of a military-industrial-political complex, described by C. Wright Mills in his book *The Power Elite* (23) and cautioned against by President Eisenhower in his last presidential address. There is the threat of a society mobilized for war, which Fred J. Cook and others have described and from which Karl Shapiro's poem, in the epigraph for Part 2, derives its theme. There is also increasing concern that the large amounts of money poured into federally sponsored research at universities may influence greatly the scope and direction of American scholarly enterprise. So great has been the flood of government largess that some critics are suggesting that some of our most respected institutions may already have been compromised. There is also mounting concern that we cannot support domestic reform and social innovation while increasing amounts of money are devoted to our extensive international undertakings. Particularly strong have been the complaints about the "financial drain" of the Vietnam war, which cost about 3 per cent of the Gross National Product, some 24 billion dollars, in 1966 and which yearly takes an increasing percentage.

Attitudes abroad toward America also have changed considerably since the early days of the postwar era, when the help of the United States was welcomed. As the leading world power, today we are suspected, envied, criticized, and damned. Raymond Aron attempts to comfort us with the knowledge that we have a "thankless role." Paraphrasing a French revolutionary, he reminds us that "one does not reign innocently," that "the most powerful state never seems innocent," and that "everything has a price, especially power and wealth." Consequently, in his view, "the richest and most powerful country in the world cannot be popular, and the United States in this century must be even more unpopular than Great Britain was in the last century, both for what it is and for what it does. The ruling state is denied what it most wants, and above all the Americans want to be liked." [3] On the other hand, the pessimistic view of Arnold Toynbee (11) may be truer than we choose to believe. Our immaturity in world politics may have made us so fearful of revolutionary change that we have become proponents of the status quo where once America was the source of revolutionary ideals. President John F. Kennedy used to derive some comfort from the fact that, as he put it, "African mothers are still naming their babies after Abraham Lincoln and George Washington." If Toynbee's analysis is true, then we can expect future African mothers to find other names for their babies.

The United States' involvement in international affairs has been most successful in Europe. Europe's postwar prosperity, stability, and security resulted in part from a series of American commitments—the Truman Doctrine (1947), the Marshall Plan (1947), and the North Atlantic Treaty (1949). The general aim of all these programs was to contain Russian expansionist tendencies and to guarantee the uninterrupted recovery of war-devastated Europe within a free and democratic framework. In fact, the difficulties that NATO experienced in the late 1960's were the result not of failures but of successes. The apparent *détente* between the United States and Russia at the same time has been attributed in part to these commitments. The Sino-Soviet split and the increasing affluence of the countries of the Eastern bloc are also important contributing factors in the present relaxation of tension. In the Far East (where the United States could not prevent the fall of Nationalist China), the democratization of Japan and the rebuilding of her economy were begun. So great has been the success of that program that today the Japanese economy ranks among the top five (USA, USSR, West Germany, United Kingdom, Japan). In 1966, the Japanese GNP topped 95 billion. As a democratic model for other Asian economies, an alternative to totalitarian regimes, Japan sets a valuable example for United States policy.

The United States has played a large role in a number of other specific international accomplishments, which include freer trade, greater scientific cooperation, the decolonization of most of Africa and Asia, a greater American appreciation of the problem of world population with a consequent change in traditional attitudes toward its solution, and the export of American business know-how and technology, as described in *U.S. News and World Report* (27). In sum, America's role as the focus of international politics, while it has not accomplished everything that might have been hoped for, has been accepted as a major occupation of the American government in the postwar period. It is a central fact in contemporary American civilization, although in the late 1960's, a number of influential voices were calling for a re-evaluation of American military and political commitments overseas.

3 *Ibid.*

IV

In his book *Expanding Liberties,* Milton R. Konvitz says: "The last twenty-five years have seemed eminently to be such a time, in which millions of men everywhere seemed to be moved by a spirit greater than themselves— men who demanded more liberty, more and better education, a bigger share of the fruits of nature and of their own labor, more responsibility for the direction of their lives and destinies."[4] In effect, this embodies what we mean by "the American democratic *aggiornamento*" (a word borrowed from Italian literally translated as *bringing up to date),* the third element in the postwar ambience. To put it another way, we could say that the period since the war has seen a general updating of American democratic practices to make them more closely approximate American democratic ideals. American life, with some important exceptions, has been increasingly democratized in the light of the new needs and demands which have evolved out of experience. This is especially true in the wider range of choice provided for the young, the freer expression permitted in litera- ture and the arts, and the broadening of the permissible range of dissent from official government policy—both at home and abroad.

All kinds of evidence exist to which one could point for substantiation. Most important is what has been termed "the civil rights revolution." From President Truman's executive directive desegregating the armed forces in 1948, to the Supreme Court's decision in 1954 outlawing segregation in the public schools, up to the Voting Rights Act of 1965, pressure has been mounting to obtain for Negro Americans their full social, econom- ic, and political rights. The methods Negro Americans have used to for- ward these rights, the sit-ins and nonviolent demonstrations, have been pro- tected by Supreme Court decisions and by legislation. All of these acts have enhanced the Negro American's pride and dignity, as evidenced in a very bitter way by *The Autobiography of Malcolm X* (45). The half- and heavy-hearted belief on the part of some Negro Americans in the white man's myths about Negro inferiority is being discarded. This new aware- ness and pride has had a revolutionary effect on many young Negroes— now better educated and now more determined to gain their full rights as human beings. Negro creativity—long established in music and now en- couraged by wider opportunity for expression—is to be seen on all sides: in literature, in drama, and in painting. The Negro's emergence in other hitherto all-white areas of American life is attested to by the many Negroes who have joined the middle and upper echelons of management. As we shall indicate further on, however, forward momentum seems to be thwarted for the present.

The post-World-War-II period has also been marked by an increasing concern with the unequal status of women in American society. The social-

4 (New York, 1966), p. xv.

psychological aspects are described, in part, in Betty Friedan's *The Feminine Mystique* (37) and Morton Hunt's *Her Infinite Variety* (34). Legislation ending job and wage discrimination against women has helped correct some economic abuses, although great areas of economic and social discrimination still exist. Finally, for better or worse, the double standard appears to be waning.

In addition, the opportunities for young people have been expanded. Many states have extended the voting franchise to 18-year-olds, and others are considering it. Extensions of the original G.I. Bill and other educational programs financed by federal aid have greatly broadened opportunities for higher education. More than that, as *Newsweek* (53) points out, a whole youth subculture has been developed in this country, handsomely financed by parents, greatly extending the freedom of the adolescent. Youth represents, perhaps, a new kind of aristocracy, excused from work and encouraged to consume. While this extension of freedom is a positive value, because it provides young people with a wider area for exploration, an undesirable consequence may be what Eric Hoffer terms "the juvenilization of society."

Numerous other examples can be cited to support the notion of the American democratic *aggiornamento:* the Supreme Court's decision ordering more representative legislatures (based on the one-man, one-vote principle); the reinforcement of constitutional guarantees protecting the rights of accused persons and restraining illegal police practices; the decision on prayer in the public schools to maintain their religious neutrality; and, finally, an updating of the definition of the general welfare to include the right to clean air, to clean water, to good health, to safe cars, to truthful advertising, and to a more beautiful environment. All of these events of the past twenty-five years give evidence of a concern for and expansion of the rights and liberties of all people.

Unfortunately, opposition has been able to frustrate the forward movement of the democratic *aggiornamento* in a number of areas. The leaders of the civil rights movement are bitter about American society's failure to support the Negro's war for freedom while open-handedly supporting the South Vietnamese's struggle for independence. The ghetto riots in American cities in the late sixties revealed a group of people which Daniel Moynihan terms a subclass untouched by the recent civil rights and economic advances. Moreover, a new, alienated, revolutionary leadership has appeared which believes that American society will never become integrated. Ironically, the Negro American sees his individual worth and dignity more readily acknowledged in the military service than in civilian life—as if only in an authoritarian situation can he hope to get equal rights. The report of the National Advisory Commission on Civil Disorders, issued in the spring of 1968, went further than affirming the validity of the Negro protest. For the first time in American history, a governmental body acknowledged the root problem to be "white racism." Solemnly warning the nation of the dangerous drift toward an apartheid society, and setting no price tag on costs, the commission set forth the most far-reaching program ever formulated to eliminate racial discrimination and poverty. Failing this, the commission warned, the nation would continue to be racked by periodic riots, with all their attendant death and destruction.

Looking at the society at large, we find liberty constricted by emerging aberrations. These are seen in the "other-directed" personality that David Riesman (19) describes, in the "organization man" of William Whyte (24), and in the status-seeker who wants to prove that he is "more equal than others." Such aberrations result from the increased structuring and bureaucratization of the mass, urbanized, industrial society. Their study by social scientists signifies a new awareness of both the threats to and the opportunities for the expansion of the democratic ideal.

To sum up, despite some significant failures and unforeseen constrictions, on balance we see forward movement in the field of civil rights and civil liberties. Konvitz calls ours an era of "expanding liberties." Corporate collectivism—what Adolph Berle calls "nonstate collectivism," with its demand for conforming behavior—has now been offset by a series of Supreme Court decisions opening new vistas for free action. At the least, the past twenty-five years of history have allayed the fears of many that the centralized government represents a threat to the liberties of the citizens. Actually, through the use of "matching funds" in a new and creative way, the federal government has been engaged in a process of ending privilege and extending liberty.

V

By our final "ground factor"—a meta-functioning science and technology—we mean to suggest that science and technology have now assumed the crucial role in American society. They are the fundamental and pervasive operational modes. The ultimate significance of this fact has yet to be grasped. In addition, much of the wealth of the nation—both private and public—is invested in the scientific-technological enterprise. The results are both good and bad. Without tracing the history of science and technology and their relation to industrialism, we can point, at least, to some of the crucial effects of the scientific-technological enterprise upon America since World War II.

Ironically, the new American civilization began with the explosion of the atomic bomb. The force that threatened the end of the world also heralded the beginning of a new world, thus making the Bomb, paradoxically, a symbol of both destruction and creation. For energy which can destroy can also create. The new physics inspired all branches of science to develop new scientific disciplines. Astrophysics and the space program, biochemistry and biophysics, the new genetics, cybernetics, among others, resulted from this inspiration. Not only is there an ever-expanding technology, there is also a rapid incorporation of that technology into the society. Steven Dedijer (15) sums up this development and its social effect by saying: "Because more research of the most modern kind is done and more of its results are used in the United States than in any other country of the world, the interactions of science and society there are stronger and the resulting social changes are more rapid and intense than anywhere else I have been."

Some unfortunate consequences of the scientific-technological progress of the last twenty-five years should be noted. First, these fields of knowledge have become more and more incomprehensible to large sectors of the American public. This fact, coupled with the rise of a scientific elite, which Jules Henry (40) describes, represents a threat to democratic society. Decision making in a number of important areas has now become the function of a specialized group; furthermore, the representatives elected by the people to make decisions are often ill-equipped to make them in these vital areas. They, too, must go along with the experts. It was a special group, for instance, and not the people's representatives who decided to put a man on the moon in the 1960's. The significance of this decision is indicated by the amount of the nation's resources dedicated to its accomplishment. The consequence of such developments to the nation's political life, therefore, has been the concentration of power in the hands of a few specialists.

In addition, the postwar emphasis on science and technology may have perverted the function of American education and scholarship. The humanistic areas have been seriously neglected, while billions of dollars have been poured, perhaps indiscriminately, into every aspect of the scientific-technological enterprise. This disproportionate commitment of resources has created a serious imbalance of values and social priorities.

Science, of course, has done much on the positive side, and will do more. Eric Hoffer says that today science makes possible an "ultimate Sabbath." He calls the new intense interaction of science and society "the second creation." Simply put, man now has the power totally to reshape himself, and his biological and physical environment. He can undoubtedly wage a successful war against man's age-old enemies — famine, pestilence, disease, and war. In short, the new meta-functioning science and technology have contributed mightily to the genesis of a new American civilization.

VI

What then is the American, this new man — and what is the character of the society he has produced? To answer, in part, the second half of this question we find ourselves in agreement with Henry Bamford Parkes when he suggests that Americans have not yet developed the sense of order, form, and style which is characteristic of what he calls high civilization. In that sense, it can be said that American society has changed little from the days in which Crevecoeur and Tocqueville wrote. However, as many of the readings in this book indicate, there is apparent a dominant style, form, or order which interprets freedom narrowly in economic terms. The modern corporation, as an American invention, has left its impact in a number of ways upon American society. Such great production (GNP 739 billions) requires vast consumption. To foster the accelerating rate of consumption, the principles of marketing are employed. This, in turn, has had a pervasive effect on everything from education to politics. Affluence, to a great many Americans, appears to have become a good in and of itself. One result is that democracy is vulgarized by the devices of consumer research.

The United States, in the first flush of a pervasive affluence, seems to have departed from the earlier vision of Thomas Jefferson, that the chief end of any political economy should be to produce human happiness and that it should improve the cultural and moral well-being of its citizens.

The activities of American youth suggest — perhaps in a more exaggerated and less disguised way — what the difficulties are in the larger society. In general, two groups among the youth stand out. Some pursue a larger ideal of service, as in the Peace Corps, Vista, and the many voluntary individual movements. These groups recognize that we live in an age of suffering that demands concern and self-sacrifice. Others, however, pursue the ultimate economic values set by the adult culture: fun and stylishness, of which "camp" and "mod" fashions are a result; excitement and sensation, of which sexual and drug experimentation, sky-diving, motor-cycling, surfing, and hot-rodding are refinements of contemporary consumerism. The mass media too, as part of the marketing operation, are systematically engaged in transmitting the values of such basically economic goals. One might say that affluence in post-industrial America has democratized what were formerly aristocratic privileges, although it should be pointed out that traditional aristocracies of the past were also builders of high civilization. If, then, there is a "problem of youth," it may be a reflection of the aberrations of the adult population.

Hopefully, there is a recognition in society that great material achievements are but means to an end. President Johnson's Great Society speech (13) reflects such an awareness. It may be that the President's vision of a great society represents a movement away from mere sterile consumerism toward the distant goal of "high civilization," to use Parkes's terms. But it will, of course, depend on more than Presidential exhortations; it will ultimately depend on a host of people and institutions dedicated to the realization of spiritual goals — both cultural and moral — to match America's fantastic material achievement.

As to the American character, we would describe it as still energetic, creative, practical, and intelligent in its attempt to master the physical environment. It is disconcerted, however, by concerns of quality. The development of the "interior" life in the United States has not been nearly so successful as the conquest of the frontier. Perhaps postwar drama and literature, describing, as they do, lunatic characters in a lunatic environment, are subtle revelations of this fact.

Further, we believe that the humanitarian nature of the American has been demonstrated beyond doubt in the aftermath of World War II. And for all of the country's power, it still retains a strong self-image based upon older, outmoded myths. Accordingly, the development and use of America's vast military power is interpreted by many as the self-defensive reflex of a fundamentally harmless, well-intentioned nation. To some foreign observers, such attitudes appear smug and self-righteous.

As most European writers observe, Americans are still cheerful and optimistic. But these characteristics have been tempered during the postwar years by an awareness of unresolved menacing evils, such as The Bomb and "police actions." This tempered optimism is perhaps more sophisticated and more desirable than the old Can-Do approach, which took as its slogan: the difficult we do immediately; the impossible takes a little longer. Still reinforcing this tempered optimism, though, are those old frontier styles of exaggeration and braggadocio.

Where Crevecoeur saw this new man, the American, as one who had abandoned the religious and national allegiances that were part of his European heritage, we find that Americans, in the main, have retained certain of these allegiances and modified them, adding them to the American culture, attempting to achieve a genuine pluralism that will move beyond toleration toward an esteem for difference. Events of the last few years support the belief that American society has, in many respects, been made safer for diversity.

Finally, we believe that Americans still reject an overt class structure and still see themselves as middle-class. And, while they do favor the white collar over the blue, Americans still cherish meaningful work and individual achievement.

More and more, though, it seems to us, as we try to understand the American in his society, the most pertinent, recurring question becomes: Beyond economic abundance, beyond affluence, beyond material accumulation, what does the new American civilization stand for? Are the traditional values still a vital, directing force?

part one

Panoramas,
Perspectives,
and Broadsides

Lawrence Ferlinghetti   **Sailing thru the Straits of Demos**

Sailing thru the straits of Demos
we saw symbolic birds
shrieking over us
while eager eagles hovered
and elephants in bathtubs
floated past us out to sea
strumming bent mandolins
and bailing for old glory with their ears
while patriotic maidens
wearing paper poppies
and eating bonbons
ran along the shores
wailing after us
and while we lashed ourselves to masts
and stopt our ears with chewing gum
dying donkeys on high hills
sang low songs
and gay cows flew away
chanting Athenian anthems
as their pods turned to tulips
and heliocopters from Helios
flew over us
dropping free railway tickets
from Lost Angeles to Heaven
and promising Free Elections
So that
we set up mast and sail
on that swart ship once more
and so set forth once more
forth upon the gobbly sea
loaded with liberated vestal virgins
and discus throwers reading *Walden*
but
shortly after reaching
the strange suburban shores
of that great American
demi-democracy
looked at each other
with a mild surprise
silent upon a peak
in Darien

Henry Bamford Parkes   **The American Experience**   1

Henry Bamford Parkes, one of the foremost contemporary interpreters of American civilization, was born in Sheffield, England, in 1904. He received a classical education from Oxford and, in 1929, he was awarded a Ph.D. in history from the University of Michigan. Since then he has taught history at New York University, where he is Professor of History and head of the Department of American Civilization. His works include Jonathan Edwards, Fiery Puritan *(1930),* The Pragmatic Test *(1941),* A History of Mexico *(1938),* The United States of America, A History *(1953), and* Gods and Men: The Origins of Western Culture *(1959). In the selection that follows, Professor Parkes discusses certain contradictions in American society, which, though tolerable in the agrarian past, now—in the 20th century—demand resolution. Rejecting both European capitalistic and Marxist ideas, Parkes finds the meaning of America in an indigenous agrarian tradition which made it possible for individuals to possess their own means of production. This philosophy of an earlier America, deduced from the American experience and best expressed in the thought of Thomas Jefferson and John Taylor of Caroline, must be adapted to 20th century American industrial life. Only in this way can the demands of freedom and order be reconciled with a minimum of coercion and enable the authentic democratic ideal to win the voluntary allegiance of Americans. For related ideas, see Gabriel; Schlesinger, Sr.; Berle; Cox.*

What does it mean to be an American? What are the special characteristics of American civilization, and in what ways does it differ from the civilization of other nations? In order to answer these questions it is necessary to turn to American history. For the character of a nation, like that of an individual, is the product of its past experience and is revealed best in its actions. . . .

I have written this book in the belief that American civilization has certain unique features that differentiate it from that of any European country. The culture of the United States has been the product of two main factors:

of the impulses and aspirations that caused men and women to leave their European homes and cross the Atlantic; and of the influences of the American natural environment. As a result of these factors the Americans have acquired, not only certain characteristic political ideals and beliefs, but also a distinctive view of life and code of values. This view of life and code of values guide the behavior of individual Americans and are reflected in American philosophy and in American literature and art. I believe that these distinctive qualities of American culture have not been sufficiently appreciated, and that American intellectuals and political theorists have frequently been too much influenced by European concepts that have little relevance to American realities . . .

I believe that once these essential tendencies of American culture have been defined, then the political and economic development of the American people, their religion and philosophy, and their literature and art can all be regarded as reflections of the same basic attitudes. The history of America can thus be interpreted as the working out of certain basic cultural drives that are exhibited both in American thought and in American action. And the problems of present-day America are due largely to certain contradictions that were always inherent in the American cultural pattern but that did not become acute until the twentieth century. These contradictions cannot be resolved unless they are understood; and they can best be understood through a study of their origin and development in the American past.

In dealing with the early political and economic development of America, I have emphasized chiefly the drive toward an agrarian democracy: toward a society, in other words, in which almost all men would be independent property owners. The product partly of the desire for independence that caused the Atlantic migration and partly of the abundance of cheap land in the American continent, the agrarian ideal took shape during the colonial period, was asserted during the Revolution, and remained a dominating factor in American politics down to the Civil War. And in spite of the growth of industrial capitalism, it has continued to have a most important influence on the attitudes of the American people down to the present day. I believe that one cannot appreciate the special qualities of American civilization unless one understands the agrarian tradition (which cannot be duplicated in the history of any important European country); yet as a result of European preconceptions (both capitalistic and Marxist), the true meaning and importance of this tradition have not been sufficiently recognized . . . I have interpreted American political and economic history mainly in terms of the rise and decline of agrarianism, of the contradictions and limitations of the agrarian attitude, and of the conflict between American agrarianism and European doctrines of capitalism and socialism. Although the agrarian economy of eighteenth-century America has now disappeared, I believe it is only by understanding and redefining their agrarian tradition and adapting it to an industrial economy that twentieth-century Americans can create the kind of society that will fulfill their national ideals.

Those American qualities that were expressed, on the political level, by such spokesmen of agrarian democracy as Jefferson, Jackson, and Lincoln, can be traced also in the development of American religion, in the philosophy of such men as William James, and in the literature both of the pre-Civil War period and of the twentieth century. The intellectual and aesthetic manifestations of the American mind exhibit the same aspirations and the same inner contradictions as its political theory. In discussing these subjects I have tried to show what they have in common with each other and to present all of them as different manifestations of the same basic cultural tendencies. As long as the works of different American writers and thinkers are approached on the superficial level of the ideas they consciously inculcate, and are judged by their political beliefs (as in the three volumes of Parrington), they appear to be very diverse and no common pattern can be discovered. It seems to me that when they are explored more deeply and are examined for their implicit assumptions, then even intellectual creations that appear to run counter to the main stream of American development can be interpreted as significant expressions of the American spirit.

The New Man

The central theme in the history of the Americas can be stated very simply. During the four and a half centuries that have elapsed since the first voyage of Columbus, a stream of migration has been flowing from Europe westward across the Atlantic and into the two American continents. Relatively small during the first three hundred years, it increased during the nineteenth century and did not reach its peak until shortly before the First World War. In all, between fifty and sixty million persons left their European homes and established themselves in the New World. During the same period another five or ten millions were brought to the Americas by force from Africa. This is by far the largest movement of peoples in all history. There was no comparable process at any earlier epoch, and nothing like it is likely to happen again in the future. Whether one judges it by the number of individuals involved in it or by its results and implications, it is the most important single factor in the recent history of the human race.

That this movement of the European races into the New World should be regarded as the essential substance of American history is not difficult to understand. The explorer, the conquistador, the pioneer, and the liberator are the primary symbols of the American cultures. But the full implications, political and psychological, of this migration are not so

easy to define. Establishing himself in the New World, the American repudiated a part of his European inheritance. In certain respects, though
not in all, he ceased to be a European and became a new subspecies of
humanity. It is only by understanding the qualities of this new man, the
American, that we can interpret much that may otherwise seem puzzling
or disturbing in his achievements and his behavior. We must, above all,
avoid the error of regarding the civilization of America as a mere extension, without significant changes, of that of Europe. The differences between them should, in fact, be emphasized, since otherwise the American
peoples will be unable either to form a sound evaluation of their own
institutions or to avoid misunderstandings with those European nations
with whom they must be associated. . . .

Both the North and the South Americans have displayed certain common American characteristics, but these developed more fully in the north.
The imprint of European institutions, of monarchy, aristocracy, and cleri-
calism, and of the view of life and habits of thought associated with them,
was much deeper and more lasting in the southern countries than it was
in the United States. This was owing partly to the authoritarian policies
of Spanish imperialism and partly to the presence of large Indian populations who could be reduced to a servitude resembling that of the peasants
of feudal Europe. To a large degree Latin America became an extension
of Latin Europe. The migration to the United States, on the other hand,
created a new way of life that quickly acquired certain unique qualities.

The impulse of migration may be described, negatively, as an impulse
of escape. The American fled from a Europe where he could find no
satisfying fulfillment of his energies and was confronted by conflicts and
dilemmas that had no easy solution. The groups who came to all parts
of the New World were, in general, those who were most acutely discontented with their status in European society and who had the least hope
of being able to improve it. The Hispanic colonies were settled mainly
by impoverished members of the lower nobility and by adventurers from
the lower classes. Unable to achieve aristocratic status at home, they
hoped to win riches, land, and glory for themselves in America. Most
of the early immigrants to the United States came from the petty bourgeoisie in the English cities or from the yeoman farmers; a few were
motivated primarily by the desire to put into practice novel religious or
political ideas, but the majority expected to improve their economic condition. The later migration from the other European countries into both
North and South America was similar in character, including some religious and political refugees, but consisting mainly of ambitious younger
sons of the bourgeoisie and of oppressed and land-hungry peasants from
Ireland, Germany, Scandinavia, Italy, and the Austrian and Russian empires. All sought in the New World an environment where they could

act more freely, without being restricted by traditional forms of authority and discipline or by a scarcity of land and natural resources.

Of the various factors that caused men to come to America, the economic was no doubt the most important. Throughout the period of the migrations, there was no free land in Europe; natural resources were limited; and the population was always in danger of increasing faster than the means of subsistence. Migration always occurred chiefly from areas of Europe where agriculture was still the chief occupation and where (owing to the growth of big estates or to genuine overcrowding) the demand for land was in excess of the supply. This was true of Spain in the sixteenth century, of England in the early seventeenth, and of Ireland, Germany, Scandinavia, Italy, and the Slavic countries of the east in the nineteenth.

An almost equally influential stimulus to migration was the European class system. This was, in fact, perhaps the chief cause of European economic privation, since the big estates of the aristocracy diminished the supply of land available for the peasants. Before the discovery of America, European society had been molded by feudalism into a tightly knit organic structure in which every individual, from the king at the top to the humblest peasant at the bottom, was expected to know his place and to perform the duties appropriate to it. These class differences had become a deeply rooted part of the European consciousness. Ambitious and enterprising members of the middle and lower classes could sometimes improve their position, either individually or in groups, but the battle against aristocratic privilege was always difficult, and never reached a conclusion. For such persons the opening of the New World beyond the Atlantic promised an easier escape from frustration and the sense of inferiority.

Privation and inequality weighed upon all underprivileged persons in Europe, but did not cause all of them to come to America. Human behavior is conditioned by economic and social factors in the sense that these establish the problems to be solved, but it is not determined by them: how particular individuals choose to act in a given situation depends upon deeper, more intangible, and more mysterious forces. Confronted by the same difficulties, some individuals preferred to submit to them or to continue struggling with them, while others, generally the more restless and adventurous, decided to come to the New World. Thus the settlement of America was a selective process that attracted those members of the European middle and lower classes who had the appropriate bent and disposition; it appealed not necessarily to the ablest or strongest, but usually to the most enterprising. In a sense it may be said that America was from the beginning a state of mind and not merely a place.

In the New World, at least during the earlier period of colonization, this selective process continued. Those who had the requisite energy, adaptability, and capacity for endurance survived and prospered; others died of starvation or in battle with the Indians. In the course of centuries certain qualities became established as suitable to the new environment and as characteristically American. Men born in the New World were disposed, both by inheritance and by conditioning, to develop them, and later immigrant groups found it necessary to acquire them. Thus the civilizations of the New World promoted certain special psychic configurations that differentiated the American from the European.

In the Hispanic countries the presence of Indian labor and the importation of Negro slaves enabled many of the early immigrants to achieve the aristrocratic status to which they aspired. But in the United States there were no Indian peoples who could be made to work for white overlords; and though the institution of Negro slavery was adopted during the colonial period, its influence was restricted to one section of the country. There were in the United States, on the other hand, enormous stretches of fertile land and vast mineral resources of all kinds. Immigrants could find, in this undeveloped and almost empty country, opportunities for self-advancement that have never been equaled in the whole of human history. The individual had to display industry, courage, and resourcefulness; but if he possessed these qualities, then security, independence, and prosperity were within his reach. This unexampled abundance of land and resources was the cardinal factor in the development of American civilization. It molded the character of the American people, and was the chief reason for the unique qualities of their way of life. It facilitated the growth of individual freedom and social equality, and it promoted attitudes of optimism and self-assurance.

The society that developed under these conditions differed from that of Europe not only in its political and economic characteristics but also in some of its animating beliefs and views of life. The American acquired new attitudes and learned to see the world in a new way. And the nationality he created became a vast experiment in new social principles and new modes of living.

The European mind had been dominated by a hierarchical sense of order. This sense was embodied most completely in the philosophical and political theory of the Middle Ages; but even after the breakdown of feudalism and the repudiation of the scholastic philosophy, it continued, in one form or another, to permeate the consciousness of most Europeans. Human society was regarded as the reflection of an ideal order derived from the will of God and fully embodied in the cosmos. And the life of the individual acquired meaning and value insofar as he conformed with the order of the society to which he belonged. Yet the Europeans believed also that the attempt to realize this ideal order in concrete forms must always be incomplete. Evil was an inherent element in human experience, and both in nature and in the human spirit there were anarchical and rebellious forces that conflicted with the ideal order and that could never be wholly controlled. This belief in the reality of evil led to the European doctrine of original sin and was the basis of the European sense of tragedy.

The first immigrants to America brought with them this sense of order, but in the American world it gradually grew weaker; it did not remain a permanent part of the American consciousness. Coming to a country where there was no elaborate social organization, and where the individual must constantly do battle with the forces of nature, the American came to see life not as an attempt to realize an ideal order, but as a struggle between the human will and the environment. And he believed that if men were victorious in this struggle, they could hope that evil might gradually be conquered and eliminated. What appeared as evil was not a fundamental and permanent element in the nature of things, but should be regarded merely as a problem to which the correct solution would one day be discovered. The American was therefore a voluntarist and an optimist. He did not believe in the devil, nor did he accept the dogma of original sin.

The most obvious result of this American attitude was the fostering of an extraordinary energy and confidence of will. The American came to believe that nothing was beyond his power to accomplish, provided that he could muster the necessary moral and material resources, and that any obstacle could be mastered by means of the appropriate methods and technology. A failure was the result either of weakness or of an incorrect technique. By contrast with the European, the American was more extroverted, quicker and more spontaneous in action, more self-confident, and psychologically simpler. His character was molded not by the complex moral and social obligations of an ordered hierarchical system, but by the struggle to achieve victory over nature.

Rejecting both the belief in a fixed social order and the belief in the depravity of human beings, the American created a society whose special characteristic was the freedom enjoyed by its individual members. Respect for the freedom of every individual and confidence that he would use his freedom wisely and constructively became the formative principles of the new American nationality. By crossing the Atlantic, the American had asserted a demand to be himself; he had repudiated the disciplines of the class hierarchy, of long-established tradition, and of authoritarian religion. And in the society that took shape in the New World it was by his natural and inherent quality that the individual was measured, rather than by rank or status or conformity to convention. To a much greater degree than elsewhere, society in America was based on the natural man rather than on man as molded by social rituals and restraints. The mores of America were less rigid and less formalized than those of any earlier community, and the individual was less inhibited. The American did not believe that men needed to be coerced, intimidated, or indoctrinated into good behavior.

By European standards this American attitude often seemed unrealistic, Utopian, and naive. The American appeared to be deficient in the recognition of evil and in the sense of tragedy. Yet as long as he was engaged primarily in the conquest of the wilderness, he had good reasons for his optimism. His naiveté was, in fact, an expression of a genuine innocence. He was simpler than the European because his life was freer, more spontaneous, and less frustrated. In Europe, with its economic privation, its hierarchy of classes, and its traditional disciplines and rituals, emotional drives were more inhibited; and it is when aggressive energies are thrown back upon themselves and can find no satisfying outlet in action that they become evil. The European was psychologically much more complex than the American, and therefore capable of deeper and more subtle insights and of profounder spiritual and aesthetic achievements; but he was also more corrupt, with a greater propensity toward the negative emotions of fear and avarice and hatred. He believed in the depravity of human nature because he knew it in his own experience.

In social organization and in practical activity the American confidence in human nature was abundantly justified by its results. The tone of American society was more generous and hospitable, more warmhearted and more genuinely kindly, than that of other peoples. And by encouraging individuals to develop latent talents and to prefer versatility and adaptability to professional specialization, it promoted an astonishing activity and ingenuity. The genius of American life lay in its unprecedented capacity to release for constructive purposes the energies and abilities of common men and women. In consequence, the material achievements of the Americans were stupendous. And though they hated the authoritarian discipline of warfare, they displayed when they went to war an inventiveness and a resourcefulness that no other people could equal.

Yet though the civilization of the Americans had remarkable virtues, it also had grave deficiencies. The conditions that produced their material achievements did not result in any corresponding intellectual efflorescence. Their bent was toward the conquest of nature rather than toward metaphysical speculation or aesthetic creation. And though their suspicion of professional pretensions and their trust in the abilities of the common man had astonishing results in politics, technology, and warfare, the effect upon intellectual life was less desirable; for the common man has usually valued material progress above the difficult and apparently useless disciplines of abstract thought. In consequence, the more formal intellectual activities of the Americans often appeared to be timid, conventional, and derivative. They frequently used ideas that had been borrowed from Europe, and that had little relevance or vital connection with their own society. Their practice was usually bolder and more original than their theory. Outside the fields of practical activity, America developed no living system of general ideas and no continuing intellectual tradition, so that each generation of writers and thinkers had a tendency to start afresh, with little guidance or encouragement from the past.

Whether the American civilization was capable not only of rapid material growth but also of stability was, moreover, open to question. For the conditions under which it had acquired its unique qualities were transitory and not permanent. The land and the natural resources of the New World were not inexhaustible. Before the end of the nineteenth century every part of the United States had been settled; and most of its resources had become the private property of individuals. There was no longer an open frontier inviting the restless, the dissatisfied, and the ambitious. And though an expanding capitalism continued to offer opportunities for the exercise of initiative, it was only the exceptionally enterprising and the exceptionally lucky, not the average American citizen, who could take advantage of them. Under such circumstances, certain contradictions that had always been inherent in the American view of life became more manifest and more dangerous. For while the Americans had believed in a universal freedom and equality, they had also encouraged and applauded the competitive drive of individuals toward wealth and power. And in a complex industrial society this drive was directed less against nature and more against other human beings. Those individuals who succeeded in acquiring economic privileges did so by restricting the freedom of others; and the competitive struggle for power and prestige threatened to destroy the human warmth and openheartedness that had hitherto been the special virtues of American society.

How far and by what methods could the qualities of the American way of life be preserved after the conditions under which they first developed had disappeared? These questions began to confront the American people in the twentieth century. As long as they had been engaged in conquering and settling an empty continent, material conditions had in themselves promoted freedom, equality, and a spirit of co-operation. But after this process had been completed, the Americans could remain a democratic people only by conscious choice and deliberate effort. If they wished to remain American, they must now acquire a more critical understanding of their way of life, of the historical experience by which it had been shaped, and of the contradictions within it which must be eliminated or transcended. They had to establish a cultural and intellectual tradition matching their material achievements and growing out of the American experience instead of being borrowed from Europe. Otherwise the American experiment in democracy could have no happy outcome.

And upon the results of this American experiment depended, in large measure, the future not only of the Americans themselves but of the whole human race. For the movement toward individual liberation and towards the mastery of nature, which was represented in its purest and completest form in the United States, was of world-wide extent, so that the whole world seemed to be gradually becoming Americanized. During the entire period from the voyage of Columbus to the present day, while some persons sought a greater freedom by crossing the Atlantic, others fought for it at home; the same forces of social protest that caused the Atlantic migration brought about profound changes in the society, first of Europe, and afterwards of the Orient; and the rise, first of the bourgeoisie, and afterwards of the proletariat, caused a slow disintegration of traditional concepts of social hierarchy. During the nineteenth century the rapid expansion of capitalism in Europe and Asia created opportunities comparable to those existing in America, while the achievements of American democracy exerted a magnetic influence and attraction upon the peoples of other countries. Thus the civilizations of the Old World were moving in the same direction as the new civilization of America. There was no complete transformation of European society, and still less of the society of the Orient. Europe never forgot the feudal emphasis on rank, status, and authority or the belief in individual subordination to the order of the whole; nor did the European acquire the simplicity and the optimism characteristic of the American. In Europe the struggle between the principles of freedom and those of authority was unending and reached no decisive conclusion. Yet the problem that confronted the Americans — the problem of reconciling the freedom of individuals with the welfare and stability of society — had universal implications. Would the achievements of American civilization continue to attract the peoples of other countries? Or would the Americans themselves end by abandoning American principles and reverting to earlier traditions of authority and social hierarchy?

For these reasons the history of America, considered as a state of mind and not merely as a place, presented a series of problems of immense spiritual and practical importance. . . .

Conclusion

The main animating principle of American nationality has been the belief that the average man can be trusted with freedom, that he does not require the guidance of an authoritarian church or of a privileged aristocracy or bureaucracy, and that whenever he finds adequate opportunity for exercising initiative, hidden talents and energies will be released for constructive purposes. This belief, derived from European religious and philosophical sources, but brought for the first time to full fruition in the open spaces of the American continent, has justified itself again and again in American history from the first settlements in Virginia and Massachusetts down to the Second World War. Throughout the history of America, moreover, it has exercised a magnetic influence upon the development of Europe. The revolutionary doctrine of equality, preached by European radicals but most fully exemplified in the American world, has been the chief provocation of European internal conflicts; and the inability of some European countries to make the necessary adaptation of their institutions has been the main underlying cause of twentieth-century totalitarianism.

But while the Americans have believed in the right of all men to freedom and opportunity, they have also exalted the drive of the individual will toward wealth and power; they have adopted a morality of personal (and largely material) success; and as a result of both their economic system and their Calvinist heritage, they have exalted activity above contemplation and material accumulation above aesthetic, intellectual, and spiritual development. The animating standards of American civilization have been predominantly acquisitive and competitive, while more important values have received little social sanction or encouragement. This emphasis on the will, on conquest, and on a kind of materialistic asceticism was the natural and appropriate accompaniment of the pioneering process; and as long as there was still empty land to be settled, it was possible to reconcile it with democratic ideals. Yet there has always been conflict between the ideal of freedom for all and the drive of power-hungry individuals for privilege and success. And since the settlement of the West and the growth of capitalism, the continued emphasis on material conquest has become a cultural lag that is no longer appropriate to the social environment. It is a main cause of the sense of frustration and maladjustment that is so pervasive a characteristic of the American mind in the twentieth century.

In the last resort, as all the early spokesmen of American democracy recognized, faith in the human capacity for freedom depends on religious and philosophical affirmations. It is derived, as Jefferson declared, from the belief in an innate moral sense and, as Emerson proclaimed, from the belief that man has the lawgiver within himself and can trust his own deepest intuitions. But while the history of America confirms in many ways this trust in human nature, it also suggests that confidence in the individual is not enough. Man's moral sense and spiritual intuitions require the objective support of a general view of life and of appropriate social institutions. And the creation of spiritual values and social forms that will give support to American democratic aspirations is a task that has remained unfinished. There is still much truth in Whitman's gloomy suggestion that Americans were "somehow being endowed with a vast and more and more thoroughly-appointed body, and then left with little or no soul."

Every high civilization is imbued with a sense of form, style, and order. The individual feels himself to be part of a social unity and harmony, which is regarded as the embodiment of universal and objective ideals and as a reflection of an ultimate harmony in nature. He finds emotional security and personal fulfilment, not through the assertion of his will against the natural and social environment, but through participation in the processes of nature and in the collective enterprise of society. Yet in subordinating himself to the social order, he does not deify it or endow it with absolute and final authority (as in the totalitarian states). He is loyal to it only because, and insofar as, it is an attempt to realize ideals to which he himself gives spontaneous allegiance and by which he himself can achieve the full development of his own personality; and he recognizes that evil is an inherent element in human life, that concrete social institutions must always fall short of ideals, and that the struggle to realize them more fully is unending. It is only in these terms that concrete social institutions must always fall short of ideals, and that the struggle to realize them more fully is unending. It is only in these terms that the apparent polarity of freedom and order can be transcended. The synthesis of individual will and social discipline, without which there can be no high civilization, is to be found not in intellectual formulas, but in the sentiment of patriotism, in moral and religious idealism, and (as Whitman declared) in "the manly love of comrades."

American civilization has never sufficiently developed this sense of form, order, and underlying harmony, as its literature, its philosophy, and its economic development abundantly make manifest. Without a deeper and more comprehensive sense of order, the United States cannot become a high and stable civilization, nor can the Americans as individuals find emotional security and fulfilment. But this sense cannot be borrowed from elsewhere, as American intellectuals have sometimes been tempted to believe. As Whitman insisted, any American order must be a native product, accepting the concept of human equality and developed through a deeper understanding of American society and the needs and aspirations of American man.

This growth of a more vital sense of order is indispensable if the Americans are to retain their freedom. The United States was able to flourish without it for three hundred years chiefly because of its unique situation — its open frontier and rapidly expanding economy. But when its society became less mobile and more static, both a greater restraint on individual ambition and a fuller individual participation in social enterprises became necessary. If this problem is not solved through the growth of a genuine social idealism, then it can be predicted that America will finally become totalitarian. For totalitarianism is a method of enforcing order upon a people who have lost any genuine sense of unity. Either the Americans will achieve an organic order based on the free participation of individuals or they will succumb to a mechanistic order imposed by an absolute state. Either they will give a free allegiance to their society as an attempt to realize common rational values and liberal ideals, or they will become merged on a subhuman level in a mass movement of emotionalism and fanaticism.

Ever since the time of Alexander Hamilton, Americans who have felt a need for order have often turned back to European traditions of authority and class hierarchy in the belief that a democracy must necessarily be anarchical and hostile to cultural standards. But according to the evidence of history there is no necessary connection between high civilization and any particular political and social system. Civilization flourishes when society is permeated with humane values, and at different periods this has occurred under the rule of kings, of aristocracies, and of popular majorities. If the American faith in the possibilities of a democratic civilization has not so far come to full fruition, it is not because of any inherent incompatibility between high cultural attainment and popular government, but because, as a result of certain specific factors in their historical experience, Americans have been too narrowly intent on the production and consumption of goods. But there are other resources in the American heritage which have been insufficiently explored. In particular, there is the whole agrarian tradition of the eighteenth and early nineteenth centuries. The spokesmen of agrarianism believed that the proper standard for judging an economic system was not whether it produced as much wealth as possible, but how far it maintained the freedom of individuals and promoted their moral and cultural development. In spite of their fears of strong government they were by no means averse to legislation designed to bring about a wide distribution of private property, maintain economic security, and prevent that "accumulation of wealth by law without industry" which John Taylor regarded as the essence of aristocracy. The agrarian economy has now disappeared, but the underlying principles of agrarian thought have not lost their validity. Thomas Jefferson and John Taylor can be quoted on both sides of virtually every current controversy, but their lasting importance is that they judged political and economic questions by humane standards combined with a faith in the possibilities of popular government.

2

Bernard Iddings Bell   Crowd Culture

Bernard Iddings Bell, theologian and scholar, is a graduate of the University of Chicago. He served as a chaplain during World War II and later served as head of St. Stephen's College for fourteen years. He has lectured widely and published extensively. In the selection that follows, Bell criticizes the common man and the culture he has produced. It is a criticism frequently made of American democracy that the lowest common denominator most often prevails. Democracy is thus viewed as a leveling down instead of a leveling up. For related ideas, see Brogan, Barzun, Kouwenhoven, Roper.

The chief threat to America comes from within America.

It comes from our prevailing self-admiration, from indisposition to listen to adverse criticism of our way of life, disinclination to see ourselves as we are, an unwillingness to confess our sins which has come dangerously near to being an inability to see that there are serious faults to admit and remedy. Most Americans regard an insistence on national self-criticism as traitorous or near it. In consequence, our people as a whole have acquired and retain a false optimism about the ability of our way of life to survive and flower. Most of us have a juvenile trust in the permanence of an America whose people forget the transitoriness of the immediate and the superficiality of the obvious, pay scarcely more than a polite lip service to what the race has discovered to be changeless and humanly necessary.

By no means all of us are complacent in this fashion. There is a growing number of critics, though still only a minority of Americans belong to it, which sees not only that all is far from well in these United States but that what is wrong is more than incidental or accidental. This minority is as well aware as anyone can be of American virtues and abilities. It knows that we are competent to make, cheaply and for the most part well, almost anything we wish to make; and that we are as a nation incredibly, though not inexhaustibly, wealthy. It knows, too, that Americans are hospitable, kindly, generous, though they are usually unwilling to involve themselves, in order to assist others, in sacrifice which means pain. The minority is sure that our way of life is better than that which prevails in totalitarian countries, if for no other reason than that criticism of that which is is tolerated in our land if anyone cares to go in for it, reluctantly tolerated but still tolerated.

But somehow or other more than a few of us begin to see that while wealth accumulates in these United States, man seems to decay. Corruption corrodes our political and industrial doings. In our private lives a pervading relativism, an absence of conviction about what is the good life, a willingness to seek the easy way rather than the way of integrity, blunts the proddings of conscience, takes the zest out of living, creates a general boredom. We are not a happy people; our alleged gaiety is not spontaneous. Our boredom results not only in a reluctant morality but in shockingly bad manners, which most of us do not even know are bad manners. We become increasingly truculent. Our way of life, while opulent and brash and superficially friendly, is less and less conducive to peace of mind and security of soul . . .

A culture is that complex of attitudes and resultant actions in which are embodied and revealed the prevailing aspirations and desires of that congeries of human beings in the midst of which one lives. It is exceedingly difficult for anyone to escape the pressure of public opinion. It is hard to free oneself from it even in matters of minor and incidental importance. In a democracy like ours it is, indeed, commonly considered unforgivable to wish so to escape. But there must be those who know freedom from the clamorous crowd if there is to be any considerable improvement in the complexion of the common life. To better American character there must be those who understand the prevailing American culture; those who have discovered what ends our citizens chiefly pursue and train their children to pursue, and what means of pursuing these ends are deemed respectable. If the ends seem inadequate or the means reprehensible when viewed and evaluated in the light of the agelong history of human behavior, the patriot must reject and attack them, no matter at what risk to himself. He must refuse to swim with the current for the sake of popularity or ease.

The shrewd examination and stout resistance required make demands which are almost invariably too great for the intelligence and fortitude of the Common Man. He needs to be led by those who are more than usually percipient and courageous. Social reformation never originates with majorities. Always there must be those who have the wit and the temerity to oppose the majorities—a difficult and dangerous procedure. The least useful of would-be patriots is he who, when he knows better, uncritically conforms to the mores and condones such conformity on the ground that is is "democratic" to run with the pack whithersoever the pack desires to run. There must be those who resist our culture, the present culture of the Common Man . . .

The culture that determines our way of life is a generalization of the definitions of proper and fruitful objectives that are held by the usual American and of his actions resultant therefrom. This generalization reflects us. It reveals what notions prevail in the United States about the nature of the good life and how to come at it . . . The country is all of a piece. This is why to many foreign visitors the United States seems to be, as one of them once put it, "a homogeneity, so united as to be monotonous."

Nor do cultures vary greatly in the United States according to occupational or class backgrounds: rural and urban and suburban, agricultural or technological. There is among us no peculiarly bourgeois culture; everyone is bourgeois. There is no proletarian culture as distinct from middle-class culture; the two have become indistinguishable. And there are only faint traces left of that culture which once characterized the older elite. Those who have a hankering for old-fashioned patrician pleasures find it easier to go in for them mostly alone, secret drinkers of that which flows from classic springs, with just enough of the real thing in the potation to make it smell and taste a little as of yore, but adulterated with crude spirits for the sake of a popular kick. This is not the place to deplore these changes or to praise them; our present business is to understand and describe.

The children in American schools stand every day with one hand on the heart and the other stretched out toward the flag and say that they are pledged to serve an America which is "one and indivisible." This is not an aspiration any more; the oath involves only a statement of simple fact. We have moralized, unified, equalized, standardized our country from the Atlantic to the Pacific, from Canada to Mexico. This may turn out to be a blessing or it may turn out to be a curse; but at any rate it makes American life much easier for the thoughtful to examine and evaluate than was the case at the turn of the century, easier too for the unthinking to accept that which is with an unchallenging complacency. America is a very large country but its cultural pattern is single, becomes more so every day.

The way of life in any culture is revealed not by what is emotionally said or written about it by the boastful or by the scolding, but through examination of certain indexes. Among the ones usually relied on by social scientists as most revealing are the press (with its modern variants, radio and television); books and magazines commonly read; advertising; sports and recreation; music; the pictorial arts; the theater, including again the movies, radio and television; divorce and the permanency of the home; good or bad manners, including general attitudes toward disorder and noise; education and its objectives; religion and the concern or lack of esteem in which it is held. If anyone examines such indexes dispassionately, objectively, he will speedily discover what is the American way of life in these mid-century years. He will come to understand what the pressures are which have most to do with making him and you and me and the neighbors and the children what we all are, the pressures from which there is no chance of easy escape for anyone who believes in the sovereign rightness of the multitude. To understand our culture no special shrewdness is required — only honest observation of the indexes.

Read the newspapers, for instance. There are not more than a dozen of them among the thousands of local journals which show independent character or integrity, or which indicate a reading public that it would pay one to trust with his wallet, his wife, or his good name. Observe what they regard as the news that is important, the news that deserves to be featured; how gossip and scandal and crime and sensation are played up. See, also, how like as buttons they are in the way they tell what is happening nationally or internationally, and why it is happening. Most of the extra-local news is collected and distributed by syndicated agencies, agencies which can color the material just about as their governors may desire, by virtue of which fact American opinion and action are manageable as truly as in any censor-controlled totalitarian state, perhaps more effectively than in such a state because the reader in this country thinks he is perusing independent journals while, with rare exceptions, he is not. His suspicion of being manipulated is thereby lulled.

One interesting and typical example may be worth recalling. When Russia was Hitler's ally in World War II, the American people were told by the papers, and believed, that the Russians were little short of fiends. Suddenly Russia changed sides. For reasons not too creditable either to her or to us, she became our ally. At a dinner in New York at that time, I sat next to a high-up officer of one of the great news-collecting agencies. "I suppose," I ventured, "now that the Muscovites are on our side, the American people will have to be indoctrinated so as to stop thinking of them as devils and begin to regard them as noble fellows." "Of course," he replied. "We know what our job is in respect to that. We of the press will bring about a complete and almost unanimous *volte face* in the belief of the Common Man about the Russians. We shall do it within three weeks." He was right about it. The papers, fed by the news agencies, did just that; and in less time than he said it would take we were cheering for Papa Stalin and the Politburo who were, we now felt sure, liberty-loving democrats and entirely trustworthy. What extraordinary power! As Lord Acton said, "Power corrupts and absolute power absolutely corrupts." The point here is merely to note that we are led about by the press, and with what ease.

Notice, too, how brazenly the press violates proper rights to privacy, even in cases of deep sorrow or pitiable weakness; how it encourages its readers to be Peter Prys and Peeping Toms. See especially how it vulgarizes the nobilities inherent in marriage, in birth, in death. Consider, too, how the news columns plainly imply that next to nobody makes or sells or plans or says or does things, except for money or applause. And do not forget the page or two or three or four of what are fondly called "comic strips," the fiction of the Common Man, whereby he and his wife and his children revel sometimes in vulgarity, more often in sentimentality, more often still in sheer inanity, endlessly drawn out. None of these degradations of journalism would be indulged in for a moment if it were not that most of our people are delighted with such stuff.

As for weekly and monthly publications, there are very few of them which a maturely self-respecting citizen, if he thought about it, would let into his house through the front door, or even the back door. Most of the few of them that are reasonably decent, including a few with honorable pasts, keep trembling on the verge of bankruptcy. The ones of these which manage to hold their own or better, have to attract circulation by mixing with material of worth and wit and wisdom a great deal of other material that is shoddy rubbish if not worse, adding sensationalism and scandal for the many to an ever-lessening provision of sanity for the few. Of one of the best of the lot — it has a prodigious circulation — it has been truly said, "In every issue there is learning and lubricity, piety and pornography, and all of it decorated with astoundingly good photographs."

No one should make the mistake of supposing that our periodicals and their visual extensions, the radio and television, are what they are because devil-inspired publishers and broadcasters set out to degrade us. The producers and circulators, as a matter of fact, are frequently ashamed of their product but excuse themselves by saying that publishing and broadcasting are no longer to be regarded as honorable professions. Each is to be looked at as a business. The things they put out are what they are because we, the customers, are the kind of people we are and will buy nothing more reputable, at least in large enough quantity to bring in to the owners a sure and considerable profit. They print and broadcast what will build up mass circulation and so secure advertising, from which alone comes any large return on their investments. Surely, they insist, no reasonable American can fault them for being so typically American. Is not selection and presentation of news and entertainment entitled to the benefit of such free enterprise as theirs? Would it not be foolish to disregard the public, which is made up, as Mr. Barnum once said, of "one born every minute"?

Read the papers, then, daily and weekly and monthly, and get a notion of the folks who buy them. It is these purchasers who in the aggregate are our country, our state, our city, our neighborhood. You may also get new light on what you yourself have become or are becoming.

When one looks at books, another cultural index, one may again find oneself upset in one's notion of the culture which molds us and our children, especially if one has been accustomed to believe this culture essentially healthy and only incidently ill.

It would be foolish to aver that there are not a good many worthwhile books being written, published, read, perhaps as many as at any time in our history; but the point is that the Common Man does not read them. He reads something quite different. In former days a liberally educated minority bought books and read them; the rest, if not enlightened by letters, were not corrupt in respect to them. They did not extol trash, and worse than trash, as reputable literature. Nowadays Demos, having learned to read, reveals an infantile taste by what he reads, the greater part of it rubbish and not a little of it garbage.

Poetry, criticism, the essay, are not to Demos' taste. Fiction is what he goes in for, and such fiction! The publishers know what Demos will buy in quantity. He and his wife seek distraction from the dullness of a daily, weekly, monthly, yearly routine that has largely depersonalized them, a diet from which the vitamins have been eliminated. What Demos and his Lady desire is escape from monotony. They are looking for stories that are essentially romantic, stories that will help them forget a probably comfortable but somehow stuffy round. They welcome almost any kind of romance.

It is not merely the sword-and-dagger variety that attracts them, or the boy-meets-girl type. Realism of the most violent and sordid kind is even more satisfyingly romantic to readers whose days are too devitalized for normal enjoyments! Even the blood-and-guts of battle is romantic to read about for those who have never had to endure it. War novels are not much read by veterans. If violence is one of the chief characteristics of a potential best-seller, another is such eroticism as will enable Demos and his Lady to get away from conventionally domestic sex and go in vicariously for a lewdness which they are ashamed, or afraid, or too emotionally tired to indulge in firsthand. They dearly love to read about sex in the raw. And if a manuscript comes along which is both brutal and lustful, it is doubly certain of a large sale.

The most popular novelist in America today, if one may judge by the number of copies sold, is a meretricious brute of a fellow, almost ludicrously savage in his substance and his style. He writes tales of a violence that is near to madness plus a degenerate sexuality. His best-selling production reaches its climax when a woman, physically beautiful and fascinatingly wicked, undresses herself, with an almost incredible particularity of lascivious description, in the presence of a libidinous and savage hero. When she is quite bare, the hero shoots her twice in the belly. As she dies, she cries, "How could you?" He replies, "It was easy." End of the book. Over 1,200,000 copies of this masterpiece have been purchased. The sale of all his books, essentially the same in plot with minor differences of decoration, has passed the 10,000,000 mark in four years. This pander is indeed an exceptionally low creature, but he is at the moment the Common Man's delight. He has lots of imitators. Many of the more suave novels of the book clubs are not much better than his. And it has some significance that with rare exception the cheap paper-bound novels which clutter up every drugstore and railway bookstall carry lurid and pornographic cover pictures, even when the books themselves are not as wholly disreputable as many of them are. Violence plus sexosity equals sales.

Our popular literature reveals that our fellow citizens desire to escape from life as it is lived among us into a dream world of brutality and carnality, desire it with a passionate intensity which makes them buy in large quantity fiction much of which is worse than disreputable. A few books even yet, few among the many that are printed, are designed to be read by literate and decent people; most of the product of press and bindery is escapist trash. This fact certainly has cultural significance, especially in a society where the Common Man determines life patterns to the extent that he does in America.

Look at another index. Americans are immensely concerned with amusement; but their desire is not so much to amuse themselves as to be amused by someone else. Take music, for instance. Despite a growth in musical appreciation in this century which has been more than considerable, though perhaps it has not been so great as is sometimes supposed, we do not make nearly as much music today as our grandparents did. Instead, we are content to sit back and listen to someone else make music for us. Perhaps we are too lazy to sing and play instruments. Perhaps we are overawed by professional expertness, unaware that much more enjoyment is gained by singing or playing oneself, even though one does it badly, than from hearing it done, however perfectly. Our musical experience is largely receptive, not creative.

The same is true of other arts. We do not, for example, make or decorate our homes or the objects of common use within them, not to the extent that our grandparents did, and got great joy from it. We buy what mass producers tell us is in the best taste. It may or may not be good; but it is not ours, no matter how much we pay for it. Neither in creating nor arranging things domestic do we find much self-expression. The drama, too, we relegate to professionals whose performances we pay to look at, not often in a theater (for we have killed the theater by extravagance and exploitation) but at the motion pictures or over the radio and television. We write or produce or act next to no plays ourselves; and most of us, and our children, would rather be caught dead than observed playing charades or reciting monologues. Even general conversation, which to be amusing always involves dramatic give and take, has become nearly a lost art.

This same misfortune has overtaken what used to be the greatest American amusement of them all, the art called athletics. We are not really a sporting people, not any more. We do not, most of us, play games; we watch them. Our idea of sport is to buy seats in a stadium and look at paid gladiators do combat while we applaud them or abuse them or wager on them. The scandals of late in what used to be, and still purports to be, amateur sport, have not been caused by wicked betting rings. There would be not betting rings, no bribery by them, if it were not for the fact that we have sunk from a sporting activity into a sporting passivity. We would rather bet on a winner than contend. As long as this remains true of us, as it was not of our fathers, athletes will be subsidized and games fixed.

Another index of culture is the degree to which profession of political principles is or is not matched by responsible action. In respect to this, the situation in America reveals a good deal. We say that we believe in the rightness of majority rule, with due protection of the rights of minorities, all this made effective by law duly enacted and enforced by elected representatives. As a matter of fact, however, a large part of our people is unwilling to participate in such government, even to the extent of casting ballots at election time. In the Presidential contest in 1948, for example, 48,836,579 voted; but that year there was a minimum of 94,704,000 eligible to vote. Half the electorate stayed away from the polls. Similar proportion prevails when lesser or more local officers than President are being chosen. In elections for membership in Congress, the percentage of nonparticipation sometimes runs to as high as 70 per cent.[1]

Our people apparently do not care to take the trouble to help govern themselves or to choose their governors. Or else, it may be, they feel incompetent to judge the issues at stake, never having learned at home or in school how to judge anything. Or else they are of the opinion that no party or politician is better or worse than his or its rivals, that all politicians are rascals and all party platforms dishonest. These impressions may or may not be justified. This is not the place to argue that out. The significant thing to note here is the evident popular opinion that "politics and politicians are rotten" and that the citizens generally can do nothing about it. Or else they may suppose that it does not much matter who holds office since the real governors, they feel sure, are the lobbies of pressure groups which tell the officeholders, from the President and Congress down to the most humble bailiff, what is to be done, and when, to whom and not to whom.

The evident discrepancy between political theory and political action must alarm those who believe in our kind of democracy. The cultural

[1] These figures are from an article by Arthur Krock in *The New York Times, Feb. 21, 1952.*

indication is twofold. First, it would seem that most of us have such small respect for the body politic that we do not feel it worth while to bother about who are entrusted with the making or enforcement of the laws. Secondly, it reveals that a majority of us, a constantly growing majority, is willing to talk one way and act another, in respect to a basic human activity like government, with a nonchalance that is not even cynical.

Another index not to be ignored is the degree to which residence is stable or otherwise. If families move about, there are soon too little of those mutual connections which come from neighborly interrelationships.

What is a civilized man? By derivation of the word, he is one who lives and thinks in a city. The Greek city, the medieval city, the American city as it was before industrialization brought about huge agglomerations of urban population, was a community, a constant group of families each of which, and each of whose members, had a stake in the common welfare and was not permitted to forget it. Such a city was large enough for reasonable self-expression but small enough for public influence on behavior. One had not merely to obey the statute law or go to jail, but also the customs, the unwritten law, or be sent to Coventry. For a city to function, its population has to be not too great, and stable from year to year, if possible from generation to generation.

The late W. N. Guthrie used to say there was no civilized man or woman in New York City who had not been civilized somewhere else, in a small town on the plains, in the ghetto in Warsaw, on a southern plantation, somewhere like that. New York, he maintained, could civilize nobody for, while in that megalopolis there is opportunity to express oneself all over the map, there is next to no neighborhood opinion to exercise correction. There are, in fact, no neighborhoods, only frequently migrating human units, anarchs, so lonely that they will gladly follow any demagogic quack who pretends to be friendly. This was exaggeration, but not greatly so. With us the *mores* are no longer determined by mutual consent among friends. They are built up mechanically and anonymously; and because they are what they are, they no longer help as of yore. We still more or less obey statute law; we pay little heed to unwritten customs of mutual dignity, or even of decency. This is now true not only in such monstrosities as New York or Chicago or Detroit or Los Angeles or Houston but in much smaller places. Thanks to the frequent migration of vast segments of our people, all our cities have ceased to civilize, have ceased to be communities.

In such a situation it is not unnatural that individuals should live more and more each for self, with less and less consideration for the comfort, even for the safety, of the people next door or the family over the way. One does not know their names. Why bother to learn? They will soon be moving, or one will move oneself. After years of this there remains in

America little regard for the rights of others to privacy or peace. Let the radio blast. Let the children yell. Throw the rubbish where you will. The sanctity of property, either communal or personal, becomes nobody's proper concern. In New York City, for example, children in 1951 caused wanton damage to school property—windows, fences, tile, furniture, equipment, works of art—which it cost the taxpayers over $500,000 to replace. [2] Such vandalism is matched, in proportion to population, in hundreds of other municipalities. As for private property other than one's own, litter it, maul and deface it, walk off with it, make it necessary for the owners to keep it under lock and key; while open lawns and flower beds have become a nostalgic memory for many who once lived in a civilized fashion.

No such degeneration could happen if we were not a restlessly migratory folk. This index reveals a fundamental weakness in our way of life, one which cannot be ignored.

It does not seem too necessary further to conduct a guided tour into American culture. The indexes are at hand for anyone to use. It is only necessary to insist that they must not be disregarded by him who would see what our way of life is actually like. Let us not make the mistake of supposing that American culture of today is the culture of America a hundred years ago or fifty or twenty or ten. Nor is it the culture of the few which matters. It is the culture of the many that is American culture. This is the age of the Common Man. We may admire him as the only true gentleman or reject him as a stupid bounder or, with greater justice, look on him as one whose economic emancipation has gone on faster than he has been able constructively to assimilate it. However we regard him, we must know him for what he is. This is where the indexes help. What the Common Man's culture is worth, is another question.

What opinion of all this is held today by the small but growing critical minority of whom we were speaking at the beginning of this chapter? That minority is fairly well persuaded that no culture such as the indexes reveal will produce the kind of men and women who can long keep our people happy or our country competent to survive in the world as it is coming to be.

The first thing that strikes this critical minority, as it looks at the whole cultural picture, is that ours is a nation of new-rich people, well washed, all dressed up, rather pathetically unsure just what it is washed and dressed up for; a nation convinced that a multitude of material goods, standardized, furiously and expensively advertised by appeals to greed and vanity, will in themselves make life worth the living. Because we are new-rich, we overvalue possessions. Almost any individual who makes a great deal of money very rapidly supposes that mere possession of wealth is evidence

---

[2] According to a report to the Board of Education by Charles J. Bensley, chairman of the Board's committee on buildings and sites.

of worth. He also is apt to imagine that with his means he can buy happiness. These mistakes usually seem folly to the old-rich, to one who was born to property, whose father and mother were bred with it. Such a one knows that merely because he or his friends have it, is no sign that they are worth it, but quite commonly the contrary. He has learned through experience that money is not in itself very valuable stuff. Happiness, which is what all men desire, cannot be purchased; it is an illusive something not for sale. The old-rich know these things well enough, but the new-rich rarely discover them until they too have grown accustomed to possessions. So it seems to be with our society. We go in, almost without question and in all classes, for the sordid nonsense of supposing that externalities possessed ennoble the owners, that a full fist invariably indicates a fine spirit.

The second conviction on which our culture is based seems to be this, that animal appetites are mighty and to be sacrificed unto if we would enjoy a satisfactory existence; and the chief of all the appetites is sex. Our stage, our music, our dancing, our books and magazines, our advertising, our dress, strike strenuously an exaggerated note of sex appeal. We have even devised a popular moral philosophy based upon the supposition that, if one refuses to indulge sexual appetites, he or she is in danger of the madhouse. No reputable psychiatrist gives such advice to his clients; but we go for our psychology not to him but to the editor of the tabloid newspaper. No one will deny that sex is important; but it is not so centrally important as most of us seem to suppose. Man is a sexual animal; but he is a great deal more than that.

Our culture, in the third place, seems based upon a conviction that to be comfortable is utterly indispensable if man is to fulfill his destiny. It occurs only to exceptional people that the whole cult of comfort is petty, ignoble, unworthy of human nature, absurd. All too few ask whether it can possibly be that, since our primeval ancestors crawled from the slime of the sea, first the animal world and then the human race have struggled on, at cost of travail and pain and tears and death, merely that modern man may sit down and be comfortable.

The fourth impulse back of our cultural endeavors and achievements seems to be a ridiculous notion that whether a man be good or bad, wise or foolish, matters less than that he should conform to pattern. The pattern to which we are expected to conform is that set by the overgrown and depersonalized megalopolis. . . .

And fifth, our crowd-mindedness renders us suggestible, manipulatable, easy meat for almost any propagandist who is willing to flatter, to encourage animality, to promise ease and opulence with a minimum of labor expended to get them, and freedom from responsibility.

"Well, what of it?" someone asks. "If the culture we have is the culture we like, then it is what we like. Where is the harm as long as we approve of ourselves, which we most certainly do? And are not the other nations envious of us for the very things your critical minority calls our defects?" A word or two about these questions may be in order.

Do other peoples envy us? The answer, as may be discovered by any open-minded traveler, is that they have no desire to become like us in anything except technological know-how. They usually regard us otherwise with condescension mixed with dread that somehow or other we may overthrow what they regard as a better way of life and degrade them to our cultural level. This is no exaggeration. Not only is it so in Western Europe; it is the mood in Russia, in most of Asia and the Near East, in Latin America from the Rio Grande to Cape Horn. They look on our concern for size, speed, new models every year, as more than a little childish. They consider our effulgent and stentorian advertising both wasteful and ridiculous. They know too much about our restlessness. They see how our very mass production is preventing the joys of craftsmanship. They laugh at our hysterical enthusiasm for sports in which we take no part. They deplore our indifference to ideas and our disrespect for continuity and tradition. They sense in us tremendous power without our having any clear notion of what we desire to do with that power. They are afraid of us more than they admire us. They love us not. Is it conducive to a proper happiness or to our safety, that we should be held in such general disesteem?

"Where is the harm," the other question puts it, "if what we are suits us?" The harm lies in this, that down the ages no people whose compelling culture has been based on greed for goods, on avidity for sensation, on search for enervating comforts, on conformity to a type set by sub-human urbanization, on a divorcement of the people from the soil, on eager response to the flatteries of propagandists, ever has managed to exist very long. Our wrong emphases are acids which dissolve the social cements. Unsureness about what life is for eventually brings about ineffectiveness in all departments of living, after a while even in technological proficiency. Then, to cure an alarming disorder, in rides the Man on Horseback with plausible oversimplifications.

If we are to rescue America from Americans, we shall have to raise up a new generation which will live less immaturely. This can happen only if Demos recovers from his present self-applauding jamboree, only if once more he comes to know the comparative values of human living as the race has learned them down the millennia. As we stand revealed by candid examination of the indexes, our culture is childish. If we go on as we are, we shall not produce the kind of citizens necessary for America's continued happiness or safety. We shall not bring forth "a type of man who sums up in his character a quality of understanding, of humility, of truth, of humor, of moral stature, of strength and resourcefulness of mind, of pregnant ideas, of universal sympathy and friendship and love." If we and our children must live out our days in the sort of culture that the indexes indicate, can anything be done by us and for us in the circumstances? If nothing can be done to arrest disintegration, then how can those of us live happily who know what it means to be effectively human?

European anti-Americanism

3

Jacques Barzun   **God's Country and Mine**

Jacques Martin Barzun, historian, educator, and author, was born in France in 1907. He came to the United States in 1919 and entered Columbia University a few years later, where he received his Ph.D. in 1932. He has written extensively, The Teacher in America *(1945),* Berlioz and the Romantic Century *(1950), and* The House of Intellect *(1959), being among his best-known works. He is presently Dean of the Graduate Faculties of Columbia University and, since 1960, has been Seth Low Professor of History. In the selection quoted here, he examines the reasons for European anti-Americanism. For related ideas, see Brogan, Barzini, Toynbee.*

The America to which I came, in ridiculous short pants and ignorant of baseball, a third of a century ago is to all appearances as remote and irrecoverable as the America that Dickens (or Columbus) discovered. For one thing, it was physically and morally much farther away from Europe than it has since become. Its connection with the Old World was haphazard, uncertain, and strangely new. America's young men had been caught by what they had seen "over there" in 1917 and made haste to return to it, convinced that their native country had nothing to offer them but the means of making the trip. Art and the arts of living lured them into becoming expatriates and turned the best of them into excellent social critics. Babbitt was born of their new vision, and he was no sooner created than he became the means of his own extinction—at least in aboriginal form. This capacity for growth showed our corporate vigor, even when it seemed ungainly. Thus did the Jazz Age follow that of the Muckrakers who followed the Robber Barons—three Americas in fifty years, and the speed of change all unchecked.

Then came the Great Depression and with it a new knowledge of society. But the unfortunate setting and coloring of that lesson kept it from being properly digested, an accident whose ill effects have not yet abated. Still, during that decade of unemployment and emergency measures, we did learn the important truth that production is not enough, that the consumer is a tender plant which is indispensable to the functioning of our system, and whose vitaminous effect disappears when his pockets are empty. If it is ever true to say of a nation that it comes of age, it was then. We were in the midst of an adult breath when a second world war broke upon us.

The rest is recent misery; but meanwhile, over the twenty years between Prohibition and Pearl Harbor, all the surfaces of life had changed: food, drink, clothing, hours of work, hobbies, manners, secret and overt inclinations. The world was now coming to us rather than the other way around. In spite of all isolationism, the cosmopolitan touch had become natural and right. Everyone flew to the four corners of the earth and pronounced without shame the names of his landing places. The six o'clock news (and the commercials) made us worldly. Simple hearty men spoke of vintage years and the homiest home body could toss a salad. In a word, by the time I had forgotten the disgrace of my short pants and had replaced ignorance with a genuine passion for baseball, the American young were all skiing and, for city attire, wearing those selfsame short pants.

Whatever these hints may speak of or symbolize, it is also true that, within the latter half of my thirty-year span, there has been in the United States more and more expression of disgust at the world and our time, more and more yearning either to repudiate or to change what is felt to be most characteristically American—hurry, bustle, business, standardization, material increase, mechanical ability, even scientific research and the appurtenances of industrial and urban life.

This is a tendency that should not be discounted or ignored, but one may question much of the talk about it. Some of the fury is mere imitation of that European anti-Americanism, which has so little to do with America and so much to do with Europe's understandable distress. Another, more serious source of anger is that habit of over-abstracting and over-generalizing which, in other realms, produces race riots and national wars. The antimodernists among us begin by assuming that all they resent is peculiarly of this time and place, the fault of machine industry. They then equate machinery with the United States and declare war, so to speak, on their own country. They talk of "values" and grieve over dehumanization without ever making a single comparative judgment —precisely like the Europeans whose excuse at least is that they do not know whereof they speak.

It had been arranged several times that I should meet Dr. Anton

Schlagobers, the famous psychiatrist from Vienna. We had so much in common—he loved travel, music, argument. "Conversation," he was reported as having often said, "is the pastime of the gods." But his American patients persistently kept him on the demigod plane of his profession, where the talking is mostly on one side. I met him at my friends' house only after he had two or three times excused himself at the last minute, telephoning apologies that could be heard from the hall where they crackled to the fireside where we sat.

When I finally laid eyes on him his appearance matched his voice and reputation. Though not very tall, he was broad of frame and feature, heavy-boned and solid-fleshed, his head leonine above—like an idealized Beethoven—with a powerful jaw below, which spoiled the symmetry but heightened the impression of power. He spoke grammatical English with a good accent that grew thick (I discovered) only when he became excited. His handclasp was firm and friendly. The hands, face and person, however, suggested the special grooming and soaping of the well-kept European, rather than the unnoticeable hygiene of the native.

Though obviously a great man in everybody's eyes including his own and those of his wispy little wife, he had fine, even deferential manners. He said he had heard much about me and was happy to see me at last. I retorted that I had surely heard much more about him and had moreover read several of his books.

"Ah!" said he, as if we should get this straight at once. "Which ones?" I named them.

"Remarkable!" he boomed—"you do not say 'Doctor, I have read your book, you know.' Can you then really be American citizen?"

The company laughed. My friends shot me meaning glances. The doctor was certainly at ease and I am sure that one can spend altogether too much time after hours working over the lifeless carcasses of the shy. The doctor was as friendly to others as to himself. But his sally called for an answer, so I said I was indeed a citizen of the republic.

"Republic? No. Democracy, plutocracy, empire, if you like, republic, no!" You could see him precipitating the pastime of the gods. "A republic it implies a culture, *one* culture. Here is no such thing—yet, and I doubt ever will be."

At this point our hostess intervened to point out that we have a great deal of culture. Did not the *Times* say there were over six hundred and fifty symphony orchestras in the United States? And haven't thousands of people gone mad about chamber music and painting on Sundays?

To be sure, as her husband was quick to say, all that music and painting is imitative, not creative. We borrow from Europe. At which Dr. Schlagobers said, "It is so."

It is, but I'm not sure the fact of borrowing matters very much. Except among isolated primitive tribes, all art is as much a mixture as the population — no pure strain anywhere. The ancient Greek borrowed from the Cretans and Egyptians, the Romans from the Greeks, the Middle Ages from the Romans, the Arabs, and the Byzantines. Art lives by fits and starts. In the Renaissance, Italy gave a new spurt based on the ruins of the antique. The French and English plagiarized the Italians and one another — and so it goes. Why shouldn't the Americans, who have been in touch with Western Europe from the beginning — who are mostly transplanted Europeans — enjoy their heritage? If the Philharmonic played only Navajo tunes or Negro spirituals, our critics would be the first to complain. To this it may be retorted that every European country has *added* something to that which it borrowed, and made it special to itself — but these thoughts remind me of the Doctor's words:

"Here nothing is special. All is mixed up, as you say, changing all the time and *rroshing* somewhere else. Culture is impossible because business gives no rest to people like you and me. Creatiff art is impossible because you never really think about the human life. All you think of is how to make money, how to invent a machine to do the slightest thing what can so easily be done by hand. You do not contemplate. You wouldn't know how. You want comfort, you fear pain and tragedy. Art is tragedy, the beautiful pearl is growing inside the shell of long suffering. When you get over here people interested in art, it has right away to make money. Why? Because they have not suffered, they have not learned, so they decide — no money, it's no good; they do something else. In theatre, publishing, art galleries, concerts, it is all the same. Often said, I know, but it is yet so: you are a materialistic people. Doubtlessly, you and some of your friends enjoy the art *business,* it is gay to work at and brings prestige, but in the strict sense, as a nation, you have no culture *because you have no loaf of aarrt !*"

I had to confess that there was no way of disproving the accusation — if indeed it is one. And I was about to raise the question whether any ancient or modern nation loved art in the wholesale way that seems to be called for, when the doctor broke in again. "Now please don't tell me I should remember America is a young country: don't say 'Give us time!' That is nonsense. Plenty of time since George Washington, and nobody can proof anything by the year four t'ousand. And another thing you shall not say is that in Europe we have no running bathtubs, for which Rembrandts are no substitute."

The argument was in fact hopeless because, in order to set it on its feet one would have had to be excessively personal. Not that the doctor hesitated to call us materialistic, money-mad, gadgeteers and so on, but these are now such common insults they can scarcely rank as *personal* abuse. The true counterattack would have been to call him a professional European. What I mean is this. When a man has left his boyhood behind him, he begins to grow sentimental about his school, especially if it is an old-fashioned boarding school. He may have been homesick there, snubbed, bored and beaten, but on looking back it seems a happy life, filled with all that one still wishes were true about one's present condition. Youth is simply the one available place in which to jam these desires without danger of being put to the test. Now Europeans who come to the United States find themselves in much the same position. They are in distress — language, customs, people are all new and strange. Adaptation is difficult, and often the wrench of leaving Europe was accompanied by horrors that make one despair of the human race. Once safe over here, the idealization begins in order to heal over the wound. It is natural to create an imaginary world in which all unfulfilled wishes can be safely stowed. The professional European calls it culture. The truth is, he dislikes America not because we lack original poets, but because his situation is in itself very hard.

But who has landed him in it? His beloved fellow-Europeans. Their great culture has apparently not taught them how to live together. You may say that recent years have been exceptional, but that is not true. The emigré is a recurrent fact. In so-called peaceful times, rare enough in European history, the educated classes have lived in a perpetual state of cabal, envy, and bitterness. That is why, in a sense, all good Americans, early or late, are renegade Europeans. One would think it might interest other Europeans to find out why for three hundred years there has been such wholesale desertion: certain conditions of European life obviously were intolerable. The details are no secret: nation against nation, church against church, class against class, and poverty for the greater number. Now the big difference, which is also the reason we are "materialistic" as it is called, is that by good luck this country gave the former Europeans the means to divide abundance instead of scarcity. Men here are no longer trying to get a share of a fixed number of loaves and fishes, they are working like demons to multiply the total — which explains in turn the alleged money-madness and zest for machinery.

The critics of America simply confuse the principle of a civilization with a trait of character they profess to despise. They pretend that among all the peoples who have ever lived, only the Americans love comfort and seek wealth. It is truly astonishing to hear "cultivated" Europeans ignore history so brazenly. What do they suppose all the trade wars, all the looting and plundering, all the enslaving and colonizing since Alexander the Great have been about? It is no answer to say that the elite, the really refined, sensitive people, who stay out of politics and trade and loathe war and persecution, have always been a race apart, justifying the rest. The delicate tastes of the European upper crust prove nothing, because the argument works both ways. If modern Americans are to be convicted of greed and self-indulgence because they own cars and radios, then what is the meaning of the castles, statues, private parks, and beautiful objects of art that we are supposed to admire in Europe? The same love of ease, surely, and a far greater love of ostentation. Greed is written on every piece. Half the contents of European museums are stolen goods, gathered up by military conquest. The other half has been paid for out of taxes which the common man would have spent on his own pleasures if he hadn't been kicked and coerced into paying for those of the robber barons who had the upper hand. In this country, which is called greedy and barbaric, at least none of our public treasures have been seized by armed force. In less than two generations the spoils of *our* robber barons have been voluntarily given up by them to the public—and their spoils they had paid for. It is true, of course, that in Europe, too, much that was the appanage of the few has now been made public—that is, after it was seized by the mob in revolt, made greedy at last by the example of their betters. Violence and pillage from beginning to end—hallmark of the super-civilized!

All this is but one aspect of Europe's history. One can argue that times of troubles bring about transformations of progress, and that we should not forget the model lives of the best people when all is settled and decent. We know that Dr. Schlagobers and our other European friends have never personally invaded foreign countries or exploited the heathen to pay for their cultivated pleasures. But art is not separable from society. An elite is not a flock of angels, it is a social class. Where did they get their money? They inherited it—good. But somebody had to do the dirty work at some time. Go as far back as Charlemagne, or farther, and you find a European elite just acquiring its wealth in one of three ways: the nobles by killing and seizing the land of the late owner; the upper bourgeoisie by trade judiciously mixed with plunder and swindling; the others by miserly accumulation from father to son, on the farm or in the back shop. Nothing unheard of in other climes, except perhaps the tropics.

In short, materialism, greed, the urge to survive and then to rise in the world, are nearly universal traits. And if that is so, then it is absurd and dishonest to maintain the modern (and malicious) proposition: "Materialism is a purely American trait." The reverse, if anything, is true: it was Balzac who said "At the beginning of every great fortune is a great crime . . ." and his stories are a mass of instances which make American greed look like weak-minded innocence. To this day, a European nobleman or shopkeeper will stoop to doing things for money which an American would starve rather than do. *Not* because the American is more moral, but because he has had enough all his life and hasn't got it by penny-pinching or deliberate, traditional ferocity.

Of course, racketeering and political corruption exist among us too, but those are precisely professions outside the pale, whose bearing on American life I shall deal with later on. Let me say here that their activities match the past plunder enjoyed by all the aristocracies of Europe, and let us return to the modern, decent middle class in any country and its attitude toward life and culture.

It was at this point, as I remember, that Mrs. Schlagobers startled us all by fairly shouting, in a voice trembling with emotion, "What do *you* understand of our life of Europe! In Vienn-hah, we live modestly, not like here where it cost so much for what?—for nothing but elevators and telephone and washing machine that breaks the clothes. Instead, we have tasteful home with lovely old furniture, books and books, and a few pictures. My husband has an easy doctor practice of regular hours, and a little, just a little money left over for the theater, the opera, and the hospitality. Because my husband is quite known and loves conversation, we have wonderful friends. It was the same by me as a young girl. My father was a doctor too and at the house came Schnitzler, Hofmannstahl, Max Reinhardt, Richard Strauss—all of them, and once—" here she paused as if about to pray, "once *der grosse* Sigmund Freud."

There was no denying the fervor, no disbelieving the sincerity of Mrs. Schlagobers' recollection. She was momentarily under a spell and it arose from a real magic. I have never lived in Vienna but I have no doubt it held for a certain intellectual class the same enchantment I have known in in my father's house in Paris of the old days. But one has to be absolutely clear about one thing: this cultured enjoyment has nothing to do with creativeness, with furthering culture. It is a consumption, not production, and consumption of storage goods. All the European artists I have ever heard invariably denounce this well-to-do bourgeoisie, this elite, for its bland neglect of *living* art. The "grosse Sigmund Freud" himself knew something of its hostility. The creative spirits are generally sons of the bourgeoisie; they know what their families think of the career of an artist, they know how everybody in the fashionable and official worlds conspires to suppress their "crazy new-fangled ideas." The more art changes the more the relation stays the same. Before the Impressionist painters were ridiculed and the symbolist poets sneered at, the Romantics had been attacked for thirty years; and before them the classics had suffered persecution. Bourgeois or noble patron, it makes no difference. Under Louis XIV Racine was driven from the stage, cabals forced Poussin into exile, organized rioting by Moliére's enemies compelled his widow to bribe them before she could bury his body under cover of darkness. Don't shrug your shoulders at the undisciplined French. Go to Vienna and see Gluck treated there as a servant. by Maria Theresa, just as Mozart was by the Archbishop of Salzburg. Beethoven had a miserable time in that lovely city. Shubert died there in poverty, unrecognized. Wolf and Bruckner were kept down by a clique. In our day Alban Berg's operas were wholly neglected, and Bartok pined rather longer in his corner over there than over here in the Bronx.

The moral is plain: the European elite has always done what is now reproved in us Americans. It lets genius reveal itself as best it may while entertaining itself with fads. It lives on its heritage of old art after this has aged in the wood. The only difference is, the United States imports the article from a distance and Europe has it nearby. This is why I am not impressed by the claim that Europeans have for culture a natural affinity which we lack. There is not so much to choose. We are neither more materialistic nor stupider about genius than any other people.

This leaves open the question Mrs. Schlagobers raised about cultured leisure, an old-world *douceur de vivre* which is certainly unknown here. Its merits are not to be undervalued; it is one of the amenities, and it is sometimes claimed for it that this admittedly self-regarding mode of life indirectly benefits the creative minds that the great world neglects. The hardships, it is said, the conflicts and rebuffs, stimulate genius to create, and the soft life of some appreciative little group, perhaps a single family, gives that genius the aid and comfort he needs.

To this I reply that I do not believe in the supposed need to put artists on a diet of bread and water in order to get masterpieces out of them. I have yet to find any warrant for trusting the prescription. Consequently, the sentimental picture of the world-beaten artist periodically nursed back to strength by a household of sensitive Samaritans leaves me cold. I want rather to examine the social basis of this artistic elegance which is undoubtedly a European institution. It is bought at a price, and the price is the endless toil, the disappointed hopes, the ignorance, the moral and physical ugliness and brooding resentments of four fifths of the population.

This is where the American conception of civilization is diametrically opposed to the European. Almost any American of the background and with the tastes under discussion will gladly, angrily shoot any *douceur de vivre* down the drain when he comes to see the poor little undersized and overworked slaveys on whose backs the whole system rests: they get up at six and sweat till ten or eleven at night to keep everybody fed and happy. Then they retire to some hole in the wall or under the gable roof, and if you ask the cultivated dragon that runs the house how much time off she gives the girls, you are stared at for your pains or obsequiously assured that they are regularly let off for early mass on Sunday. Once in two or three weeks, you will see one of them working at double speed while the other has an afternoon off with a beau. Everybody above stairs thinks the arrangement perfect. It was laid down in the laws of the Medes and Persians.

Mrs. Schlagobers obviously had something to say to this, and she was very simple and straightforward about it: "We had three girls, all the time, fresh from the country. I looked after them like a mother. Each girl could have only one young man, which I talked to first, so there would be no trouble; and from me the girls learned all about housekeeping. I was very strict about that."

Just so. One need not doubt the lady's kind intentions or good faith. An American only feels that the system, understandable in its day, is now outmoded. He is shocked, for instance, at the idea of controlling these girls' choice of sweethearts, and for a pittance making friendless farm girls scrub floors in that desperate do-or-die fashion of a century ago. The mistress also expected them to wear her cast-off dresses, to eat second-grade food bought especially for their second-grade stomachs, and to stand snappishness and rebukes while they themselves must always behave like ladies-in-waiting to a princess. At the end of eight or ten years of unrelieved drudgery they might marry their dispirited beaux, which is to say, transfer their mop and pail to another, narrower, and noisier set of rooms, where they would bring into the world more of their kind to keep the cycle going.

The European answer to this is obvious and quite logical: why weep over the fate of plain, stupid girls and their plain, stupid men? How can one possibly match their lives and their sorrows with the conscious lives of people who for generations have sharpened their senses on beautiful things and trained themselves to reflect on the human condition? The American way, miscalled civilization, is simply to multiply man's actual littleness at the expense of his potential greatness. Which is why America is not a great country but only a big one—full of little people.

Nothing indeed could mark more clearly the parting of the ways, nor reveal to the comparing mind the fallacies of the modern European or pro-European view; the assumption, namely, that life is made for art, and not art for life; that the many are born to minister to the wants of the few; that beauty and philosophy can be kept in glass cases indefinitely without spoiling. For this last proposition is what all the delicate fingering of old masterpieces amounts to. It would make a European shudder or burst out laughing if you told him that one of our great artistic achievements in the United States has been to make pretty clothes cheap enough for all young women to buy; this being one aspect of our concern for good design in the products of industry. He would see in this only a weak-minded philanthropy or love of mediocrity, not recognizing the fact that the true and original artistic impulse is to embellish and refresh our lives by decorating the means of life. Man carves his wooden spoon, paints the roof of his cave, hangs beads around the neck of his mate. And he should keep doing it. It's only when the means are scarce or misapplied—as in Europe—that beauty is locked away in private safes and

private houses, and dirt and drabness are out in the open. The streets
are splendid but most creatures look dowdy and dejected. The last time
I was in Paris I remember coming across a magazine article entitled *"La
femme francaise est elegante."* All I had do was go downstairs and look
at my concierge to disprove it. By *The* Frenchwoman, the author meant
a couple of thousand out of twenty million. But go to any village in this
country and you will see hardly any difference between the farm girls and
the tidy numbers swinging their hips on Fifth Avenue.

The significance of the comparison is that art, culture, and beauty in
an industrial democracy are rightly applied to the common means of existence and belong first and foremost to those who make that existence possible. Our modern esthetic sense, unlike that of the past, is offended by
human ugliness and degradation. As for our living philosophy, it is not
the metaphysics of sorrow and tragedy but the ethics of equality. We are
as indignant at the arbitrary choice which dooms certain individuals to
servitude as any *precieux* may be at a misstep in logic or a *faux pas* in
society; this incidentally being the very same moral principle on which Dr.
Schlagobers and his friends acted in coming to this country. They resented
and resisted the arbitrary choice of the master race — the *Herrenvolk* — to
use them as raw material for their designs.

The only way a man can reasonably complain of injustice is to accept
equality of treatment as the common rule. Otherwise it's dog eat dog,
with the advantage going in the long run to the largest and hungriest
pack. It must have crossed many a doctor's mind, when some poor wretch
comes to him full of vice and disease, a burden on society, that if he
blotted out this useless life — for whatever motive — his own would be just
as much forfeit as if he had killed the Prime Minister or a leading scientist. Now if the mere continued breathing of another man is so important,
how much more important his moral and physical well-being before he
becomes a derelict.

To many Europeans this would seem bald Puritanism, and by its associations with America the word would sound like a conclusive argument:
"We talk about culture, you talk about social organization." I can hear
the echo of Dr. Schlagobers', voice: "Where Puritans are, iss no art!"
But it has been shown that genuine art has always had to take care of
itself. It cannot be provided for, and those who try to do so actually
provide against it. In a really free market of ideas, art will take care of
itself. The Puritan background has given us Hawthorne, Melville, Emerson, Henry James — not one monotonous note but several, sufficiently rich
in overtones. But even had it given us a whole octave, this would not
change the antiquated cliches about American culture, minted as they are
out of invincible ignorance.

Most of the time we do not perceive our own clearest characteristics.

We think of ourselves, vaguely, as English in our cultural descent, not only forgetting the Continental ingredients in our mixture, but failing to see that our popular culture is mainly German and our highbrow culture mainly French. The English heritage was absorbed and transformed long ago, and has vanished from our manners, habits, and tastes. Think of cricket's relation to baseball — or look for a word about it on a later page. . . .

Critics from abroad who come to visit acknowledge our cultural concern, and the existence of museums and orchestras where they thought there were only Indians. But they complain of what I may seem to have admitted by the phrase "commercially circulated." Our art is subjected to trade-like judgments. It has to break even or out it goes. The foundations put money into things they feel sure are wanted, as if art were a commodity like another. Nothing seems spontaneous and intimate, like Europe's little reviews and shoestring theaters.

Well, we have to do things in our own way, even when what we handle is borrowed — that is the first requisite of an independent culture. And there is an excellent reason why art costs so much in the United States, the same reason which makes the cost of living high: we pay the man power in art just as high as that which goes into making an icebox or installing a telephone. The printers of books, the stagehands, the driver who takes a truckload of old masters from New York to Chicago, are people of substance. If you ask them they will tell you they belong to the middle class.

Their reply is hardly an exaggeration, even from a European point of view: not long ago the window cleaner came to my apartment, and though I know him by sight I had never really talked with him. This time, as he climbed back in on his way to the next flat, he nodded toward an early Braque that hangs on my wall. "It holds up very well," says he, squinting at the date. "Have you studied art?" I asked. "No. I used to do the windows at the Art Students' League. You could see how everyone with the same model in front of them would draw something different — all right, then, why not this type of thing? It's full of pep, anyhow." And as he slung his pail over his shoulder, he added, "My furniture's a good deal like yours — Swedish modern from Macy's." I do not say every window cleaner has an eye for Braques. I report a fact.

There is no need, of course, to make the cultural future of the United States depend on observant window cleaners. It would be too easy to turn the incident around and make it point to our lack of intellectual discipline, our premature sophistication — not to speak of the free and easy ways of the workman in the house. These are plausible talking points. What is more worthy of note is that the new generations in France, Britain, Italy, and Germany show much the same characteristics. One's older friends abroad tell one that "since socialism" (they mean industrial democracy), all their cherished "values" have gone to the dogs. Children in school no longer learn anything, the use of the mother tongue has fallen into barbarism, every post is filled by cocky ignoramuses. What is it they see? They see the underside of society coming up. It is the plain, stupid housemaids of prewar times with their boy friends, who now talk to the rest as equals. They were kept illiterate and now the masters complain that they cannot spell. But if the notion of the long aging that is needed to make an elite has any truth in it, why expect the masses to ripen overnight?

Democracy has its drawbacks, no doubt, and it is wise to concede in order to rectify them. But it is also important to look below the surface and not judge exclusively by the presence or absence of familiar signs. My window cleaner would cut no figure at the Sorbonne or in Bloomsbury, but surely he is a born critic. Faced with something well past the Impressionists, he put his finger on two fundamental principles—that the painter's eye is a creative organ, and that good cubist work has energy. How many professors of art can put as much truth in as few words?

Again, I do not propose my favorite workman for an honorary degree. But there is perhaps one more generality to be got out of contemplating our culture in contrast with the European—or perhaps I should say our behavior on the plane where general and highbrow culture meet, and where, even though we would not meet window cleaners, we would meet a fair range of our fellow citizens. Their callings and their conversation would remind us that like the Germans' our minds had been deeply marked by industry, making efficiency our ideal in all things and organization our forte. This, we should not forget, is a form of mental and spiritual power. The airlift that saved Berlin was a feat of intelligence and self-control, not merely of strength; and for every nondescript city across our land we can show an ordered pattern of parkways and bridges that is breathtaking with a new kind of beauty. But—this is the capital point—there is no goosestep about our discipline. We do not work through frozen hierarchies. Our organization (we call it teamwork) has no use for the glassy eye. In short, our standard of personality is on the whole much more mature than that of any European country.

By standard of personality I mean the expectation as regards public behavior to which every type of individual unconsciously tries to conform. Take the case of an official who tells the press something about himself or his work in a general announcement. That image of the modern American is, I submit, the image of a mature man. In the first place, he does not boast about himself. Every accomplished Continental does. The European would be thought insignificant if he did not blow his own trumpet fortissimo amid the other brass. Second, the American prefers—other things being equal—to admit the facts. Just remember when the head of our Air Force proclaimed our technical inferiority to the Russians, and try to imagine the same thing happening in reverse. The daily paper provides dozens of similar examples—for instance the man in charge of sifting reports about flying saucers telling us that "if they are the guided missiles of another power, they're way ahead of us." These examples work both ways—telling and receiving. What is facing the truth if not a mature discipline? And if our people can stand it, then they're no longer infants who have to be shielded by grownups' lies.

In the third place, the American likes to hear what the rest of the crowd think. I know there are limits to this and just now our good habits are being badly strained. But in general, the man running the committee will give everybody his chance to speak. Often a majority vote will be too close to seem good even to the majority and the proposal is dropped. This happens in business, in clubs, on boards of hospitals, and in town governments, even when a certain amount of passion has been aroused. It is far from invariable but it is more common than uncommon, and it should be noted as mature.

Fourth, one may ask in what 'other culture individual reliability has been raised to the level of a common virtue, a matter of course. From the soda clerk and the gasman to the banker and the doctor, people do as they promise. "They deliver the goods." This is probably idiotic in the eyes of an Oriental sage, but it has its advantageous side. Not long ago, a very worthy enterprise operating abroad needed to have a long document translated into Italian, in Italy, and quickly. For speed and convenience the document was divided into ten parts, each being given to a highly recommended person. A week later, four of the ten translators had not only failed to do the work, they had lost the manuscript. *Dolce* no doubt, a sweet life; in the end it is nothing but a form of sponging on the community.

Fifth and last, we may cite the national dislike of pose. It is true we develop irritating poses abroad where we are under fire, but at home we are pretty much allowed to be as we are, too much so at times, for casualness may not sufficiently conceal individual defects. Still, our educated average often achieves the ideal expressed by the courtier of Louis XIV's time, who wrote in disgust: "The real gentleman would be he who never prided himself on anything." The best sort of college-bred, well-traveled American approximates to this. To watch him, you would never know what he was, had done, thought of himself, or wanted to seem in your eyes. He is not necessarily a great brain. You may fall asleep in his company, but you are not being prodded and picked over and marked down or basely flattered—all under cover of *politesse*—as you are by the various more or less childish types nurtured in Europe.

I concede at the outset that the best aristrocratic manners are the finest in the world. But they are and have always been extremely rare. The usual middle class habits in every European country are something quite different. You can read national history in each affectation—the barking and stiff click-clack of German high society; the frozen faces and tight embarrassed throats of an English dinner party; the oratorical preening and fencing-master style of a French one; the stolid steady disapproval of everybody except the Almighty, at Geneva; the twitter of improbable lies and miniature drama in the affable Italians; the buttering agreement and perpetual seducer-tactics of the Irish; the shut-in conceit and crusader's contempt in your Spanish host—none of it is any longer functional if it ever was, and it is a bore. Why should not the human face in the twentieth century be open and flexibly expressive, the voice easy and the gestures gentle, to greet every manifestation of life? Why the prepared mask, the limbs and tones of a puppet show?

This last question I must have asked aloud at some point in my inconclusive debate with Dr. Schlagobers, for I remember his leaning forward and saying: "There, *I* can tell *you* something. The pose, the rigidity, the stiff mask—they all tell of fears. You are right to describe certain European manners as signs of neurotic attitudes. But you badly overlook your own—your American neuroses. I do not see in my office the open faces, the gentle voice and easy gestures. I see tortured people who carry the shoulders—so. They speak in harsh tones or sometimes a whisper. They tell me this life is impossible to be borne. They take drugs and alcohol to shut it away. And one pattern repeats: the strong sensitive mother, the insensitive money-making father, and the boy a homosexual. I do not want to turn conversation into clinic, but I must notice you say not a word about the forces at work in your efficient, ethical, high-wage America to destroy the man-of-the-future you have described."

He finished quietly and there was a sudden pause. He had put so concisely what we could all recognize from our own experience that he entirely deserved to have the last word. He had found out—or so it seemed—where our weak spot really lay and had enumerated symptoms that were not to be cured by recourse to art galleries.

But is it *our* weak spot in particular, or is it, so to speak, an occupational disease of industrial man, bound to recur wherever machine production thrives and people multiply? Besides, what is the ghoul or monster that we dread and hide from? Where in the American scene does it lurk? Is it within us, and if so does it correspond to anything outside? The doctor's closest answers would have to do with particular individuals and their circumstances. His general answers were, in my opinion, false —imaginary tales from the Vienna woods—and I have tried to show that this is so. Yet there must be cultural answers as well as psychiatric to the real problem he posed.

4

Paul Goodman   Patriotism

*Paul Goodman, teacher and writer, was born in New York City in 1911.
He graduated with top honors from high school and in 1927 went to the
City College of New York. After graduation, he supported himself during
the depression by writing. He also attended classes in philosophy at Columbia University and received his Ph.D. in 1954. His thesis was published
as* The Structure of Literature. *He recently became the occupant of a new
chair at San Francisco State College which is supported by a student tax.
He has been called an American utopian, a visionary, and a radical, among
other things. Among his books are* Communitas, *written with his brother,
and several works of fiction of which* The Empire City *is particularly noteworthy. The book from which the following selection is taken has been
described as an attempt to explain "the more sensitive of American youth
to itself." For related ideas, see Hayden,* Newsweek, *Toynbee, Gabriel.*

1

In 1783 Washington sent a circular letter to the States, describing the
situation of the new nation as he saw it. "We have equal occasion to
felicitate ourselves," he said, "on the lot which Providence has assigned
to us, whether we view it in a natural, a political, or moral point of light."
He pointed to the natural resources of the new nation, its independence
and freedom, the Age of Reason during which it had come of age, an
age of "the free cultivation of letters, the unbounded extension of commerce, the progressive refinement of manners, the growing liberality of
sentiment, and above all the pure and benign light of Revelation . . . If
these citizens," he concluded, "should not be completely free and happy,
the fault will be certainly their own. Such is our situation and such are
our prospects."

It is hard to read these sentences without agitation and tears, for they
are simply true and simply patriotic.

In the next generations, almost to our own times, patriotic rhetoric did

From *Growing Up Absurd,* pp. 96–109, by Paul Goodman. © Copyright 1960 by Paul
Goodman. Reprinted by permission of Random House, Inc.

not cease to sound, more pompously and falsely, but never without a core of truth. There was always something special in the American destiny to be proud of. In 1825 it was the broad democracy. In 1850 it was the magnificent spread and settlement from coast to coast. In 1875, the material progress, the cable and the Pacific railroad, the building of modern industrialism. In 1900, America was the melting pot, the asylum of the poor and the oppressed.

In our century, the patriotic rhetoric began to be unbelievable — not by accident, for foreign wars (1898 and 1917) are incompatible with reasonable rhetoric. In recent decades there has been almost a surcease of such speech. Even references to the American Way, free enterprise, high production, and the economy of abundance have finally died out, because they call up the idea of tail fins and TV commercials. Highbrow journalists mention the American Way with scorn.

Our case is astounding. For the first time in recorded history, the mention of country, community, place has lost its power to animate. Nobody but a scoundrel even tries it. Our rejection of false patriotism is, of course, itself a badge of honor. But the positive loss is tragic and I cannot resign myself to it. A man has only one life and if during it he has no great environment, no community, he has been irreparably robbed of a human right. This loss is damaging especially in growing up, for it deprives outgoing growth, which begins with weaning from Mother and walking out of the house, of the chance of entering upon a great and honorable scene to develop in.

Culture is, first of all, city and patriotic culture. I shall try to show that patriotism is the culture of childhood and adolescence. Without this first culture, we come with a fatal emptiness to the humane culture of science, art, humanity and God; and this emptiness results in the best people *not* turning back, like Plato's philosopher who has emerged from the cave, to serve their country. Many of the best Americans have a strong philanthropic and local-community zeal, yet it would seem odd for somebody nowadays to put himself to a big and hard task just to serve his country, to make her better, and be proud of that. Young people aspire mightily to appearances on television and other kinds of notoriety, but I doubt that many now think of being honored by a statue in the park and winning "immortal" fame, the fame of big culture.

Let me make the same point by analyzing a remarkable proposition of Otto Jespersen, the grammarian. He shows that, contrary to expectation, a child does not learn his mother tongue at home from his mother and immediate family, he does not pick up their accent. The accent, vocabulary, syntax, and style that form his speech are learned from his first peer groups, outside the home. Jespersen does not explain it, but the psychology seems evident. Speech occurs at the stage of the developing

of the "I," it is a forming of the image of the self, it is a self-appoint-
ment to one's ideal and putting on its uniform. Changes occur as we
appoint ourselves to one peer group after another. At a certain stage a
lad appoints himself or commits himself to a band of friends and puts on
its jargon, jacket, tattoo, and masculine ring on the fourth finger of the
left hand. If he is insecure and disturbed, this conformity is a cowering
protection and the band is a delinquent gang, but in every case it is also,
we see by the blazon, an achievement. And one way in which the Governor of New York does not take the juveniles seriously, when he speaks
of giving them a sense of belonging, is that he does not offer an ideal
that promises equal manliness. He has none to offer.

It is tragic when there is no great adult peer group to meet growth.
Consider the case of an artist, my own case. To have simple and sounding
language, rather than merely the lovely colloquialism of Sherwood Anderson or William Carlos Williams, it is necessary to believe in the great national culture of one's people. Our popular culture does not warrant the
belief, even to make the sacrifice that Virgil made when he gave up his
best vision because strife-torn Rome needed a national poet. True, an
artist can then jump to the international and universal, for mankind and
God do not let him down (mankind is the fellow on one's own block),
but this is at the loss of pomp and glitter, of the glancing present.
Without a patriotic peer group, it is impossible to have the brilliance of
Handel, the material grandeur of Venice. With us the style of the big
bright sensation belongs to cheap musical dramas on Broadway.

2

The area of patriotism is intermediate between childhood and adult-
hood. We must delimit it carefully or we play into the hands of fools
and rogues who have done our country plenty of damage.

To what can we correctly attach the adjective "American"? There is
no "American" animal, sexual, or primary family life. The idea of American child-rearing or American medicine is idiotic, and the thought of an
"American family" is abominable. At the further extreme, there is no
"American" university, "American" science, religion, or peace. In only
an equivocal sense is there an "American" art: the subject matter may be
American, but the art is international and the aim is universal.

In between, however, there is an American landscape, an American primary and secondary education, an American classlessness, an American
Constitution, an Anglo-American language, and an American kind of enterprising. That is, just where a child ventures from home and grows up
through adolescence, the great environment becomes his scene, and this

is American, a characteristic geography and history, place and community. It is just in growing up, which is the subject of this book, that a patriotic opportunity is essential. It is just this opportunity that, for ingenuous youth, is corrupted. And so it is hard to grow up.

Let us be quite clear what this American landscape and community is. I quote from a recent issue of *Life:*

> (Teen-agers) own 10 million phonographs, over a million TV sets, 13 million cameras. Counting only what is spent to satisfy their special teen-age demands, the youngsters and their parents will shell out about $10 billion this year, a billion more than the total sales of GM. Until recently businessmen have largely ignored the teen-age market. But now they are spending millions on advertising and razzle-dazzle promotional stunts (*right*). If parents have any idea of organized revolt, it is already too late. Teen age spending is so important that such action would send quivers through the entire national economy.

This is a description of the landscape, and the prose of *Life* is part of the landscape.

3

Equal to our businessmen, our government and public spokesmen have a knack for debasing the noble and making the excellent trivial. The current disease is to make Cold War capital out of everything, no matter what. We cannot dedicate a building of Frank Lloyd Wright's in New York without our Ambassador to the United Nations pointing out that such an architect could not have flourished in Russia. This is tasteless; the matter becomes serious when our freedoms are involved.

Not long ago there was a great to-do about the Russian censorship of Pasternak's *Dr. Zhivago.* The editorials and the rhetoric of organized friends of culture kept repeating freedom of speech, freedom of culture. (You would think that we did not have our own means of censoring, by commercial selection and by swamping.) But the outcry about Pasternak was not sincere, it was propaganda in the Cold War. In the same year, for instance, the Archbishop of Dublin effectually banned the spring theater festival because of plays of O'Casey and Joyce. (He refused to say the festival Mass if those plays were to be given. The director then canceled the plays. But the actors manfully struck and would not play at all, and this resulted in an important loss of tourist revenue. Such admirable behavior is inconceivable in my country.) On this theme, the *New York Times* ran no editorials, no, nor the New York *Herald Tribune.* For we are not at cold war with the Catholic hierarchy. (I wrote a letter to the *Times* asking that this and *Zhivago* be coupled for mention, but no one was interested.) But such behavior is patriotically disastrous; it teaches that our spokesmen are not earnest; they pick and choose when to stand up for freedom of thought. How then can a boy be proud? (But to be sure, we have little such freedom, compared with the British, for our *mass* media are not, like theirs, open to fundamental controversy. It is not surprising, therefore, that for English Angry Young Men an important topic is their outraged patriotism, whereas our Beats do not care about that.)

4

Consider the behavior of our professors and universities during the Dies, McCarthy and Feinberg Law investigations. It is hard to say which set the worse example to the students during those hearings: the Communist professors fearful for their jobs, or the colleges that—with magnificent exceptions, like Harvard—supinely received the investigators. A monumental blunder was being made—which did us desperate damage among thoughtful Europeans—and our professors shivered in their boots and our "radicals" hid like roaches. The important thing is not which group betrays the ideal in any particular case, but that young people become cynical about political action and resigned about the possibility of making a change. Following a party line, Communist teachers, e.g., at New York's City College, denied their membership. This was a disastrous betrayal of the students. Not that it is wrong to avoid insolent force with fraud, but that young students can grow only by politically affirming themselves. With the young, honor is more important than tactics or even than prudence. Leaders of youth must be knightly—a grisly identity, but there it is.

We have now passed through a decade in which the students in our colleges showed a political apathy probably unexampled in student history. Several causes have conspired to it. First, simple shell shock: the war and the atom bomb aroused such deep anxiety that the only defense against it was conventionality. (I remember lecturing on Kafka in 1948 to a hall of collegians consisting largely of veterans on the G.I. bill, and they frantically protested that Kafka was psychotic and should be paid no attention, he had no relation to reality—they who had lived through some of the Trial and were even then roaming under the Castle!)

Secondly, the students have been seduced by business firms, which tempt and reward them for conformity; but as W. H. Whyte, Jr. points out, they are eager to conform even before they are paid. Correspondingly, in its appeal to lower-class boys, the Army has found it wise to accept the stirring slogan, "Retire at 37." If you question a boy draftee who has re-enlisted, he will explain that it is a "good deal." That is, the

Army has become the IBM of the poor boy.

But finally, is there any doubt that an important cause of the present political apathy of the young is the dishonorable radical leadership that they had in the Thirties and Forties? They now believe that *all* political thinking is a sell—just as those bright Catholic lads who stop believing the superstitions of scholasticism now believe that all philosophy is an intricate fraud, including the truths of scholasticism.

This hipster skepticism is pervasive. It is partly, of course, resignation that a revolution has failed and the way is too thorny; but students are usually more resilient. I think that a more important factor is disgust that the radicals were not bona fide; the students were had. But also, I fear, it is cynical superiority, an identification with either the fraudulent or the powerful.

I referred above to the similarity between some of the Communists and young Organization Men today, in their lust for control apart from any objective good and, more deeply, in their use of an organized power-system in order to make the ingenuous and worthy not exist. In the Thirties it came about that Communists had high status in Hollywood and somewhat in publishing, so the two kinds of organized systems worked in the same offices—nor do I doubt that many of the refinements of present-day organization life were learned during this cohabitation. But it has remained for our own decade to enjoy the brutal comedy of Mc-Carthy and the FBI investigating the Communists in Hollywood, so we had on one stage the three most cynical tribes in the country.

But let us go back to more simple ignobility.

5

Certainly the most thrilling and romantic happening of these years is the adventure in space, surpassing in promise the voyages of the fifteenth and sixteenth centuries. This adventure makes life worth the trouble again. When the Russians beat us out, we are miffed but we can be proud that these exploits have been performed by men and man is great; Copernicus was a Pole, Galileo an Italian, Kepler a German, Newton an Englishman—and the rockets were Chinese; and we hope that we shall win the next round, for it belongs to America to achieve first in this kind of enterprise. The experiments are expensive, but it seems mean-spirited to question the appropriations and few have done so. So far, grand. But now we have corrupted even the exploration of space into the Cold War. Against an agreement of the International Geophysical Year, we, like the Russians, withheld the wave length of a satellite for strategic reasons. (I was ashamed and again I wrote dutifully to the *New York Times,* but they again had no space for such an odd way of viewing the news.)

Next, we carried out a secret nuclear experiment in the ionosphere, and this one was kept secret not from the Russians for military reasons, but from the American people, because of possible objections to the fall out. The *Times* kept the secret till the Russians were about to publish it, explaining (March 19, 1959), that "it had learned of the plans for Project Argus last summer, some weeks before it took place. Nevertheless, scientists associated with the government said they feared that prior announcement of the experiment might lead to protests that would force its cancellation." A. J. Muste, an editor of *Liberation* magazine, asked them for an apology for this unexampled betrayal of journalistic responsibility, and got the astounding reply:

> It seems to me that you are suggesting that the *Times* enter the propaganda field and, in effect, set its judgment above that of military men and scientists as to what can be published . . . After all, the *Times* is a responsible newspaper. (!!) (Robert Garst, Assistant Managing Editor. In *Liberation,* May, 1959.)

But what is the effect on our people when we are told that our chief newspaper does not print the news? Constitutionally, for instance, *how in a democracy do they then deserve their mailing privileges, to circulate their official press releases and advertisements for department stores?* (The purpose of second-class mail is to circulate information.) When Muste wrote a letter for publication about the *Times'* handling of the story, the *Times* found no space for that letter.

But to my mind, even more important is the effect of cutting people off from the adventure of science, no matter what the risks. What an illiberal and dishonorable policy to pursue! Our government cannot see that noble things must not be made base, romance must not be turned into disillusion, or what will become of the young people? Take another example. This glorious enterprise of space! And now we have chosen seven astronauts for special training. But the nemesis of the organized system haunts us. All prove to be white Protestant, in their early or middle thirties, married, with small children, and coming from small towns — in brief, models of salesmen or junior executives for International Business Machines. And these seven have now made a solemn pact, reported in the press, that whichever one goes aloft will split evenly with the others his take from syndicated stories and TV appearances. Concerning them, Dr. George Ruff, the Air Force psychiatrist who tested them, has explained, "Knowing the qualities that made them this way, and working hard at applying those qualities in your daily life, can help you (too) to come closer to achieving what they have become: comfortable, mature, and well-integrated individuals. It's a worth-while goal."

Of course, by this writing (June 1960), it is commonly accepted that our new Midas satellite has the *function* of espionage. But it has remained for a proper scientist to hit the bottom: the professor who has advised us *not* to reply to any signals we might receive from outer space, because the astral beings are likely to be technically more advanced than we and they will come down and eat us up. This projection of the Cold War into the starry vault was favorably reported by the science editor of the *Herald Tribune.*

6

In the time of Washington, the public men — Adams, Jefferson, Madison, Marshall, Henry, Franklin, Hamilton, Jay — were a fair sampling of the good spirits in the country, humane, literate, brave, not self-seeking. (There is a remarkable letter of Jefferson's to David Rittenhouse, urging him to waste no more time in mere politics, for the world needed him more in his capacity as a scientist.) By and large, it could not be said of our presidents and governors at present, the symbols of the country, that they are a fair sampling of the best of us. It would not be difficult to make a list of a hundred, or two hundred, who are superior to them in every relevant way, in whom a boy could feel pride and trust.

On course this is not a new trouble among us. Just as the European writers of the eighteenth century idolized our statesmen as if they were demigods, so in the nineteenth they spoke of their inferiority. This is the consequence of another missed revolution, the democratic revolution. A man of sense obviously cannot waste his life learning to sue to an ignorant electorate and coming up through political ranks in which disinterestedness and pure convictions are not the most handy virtues. Yet the fault is not with democracy, but that we have failed to have enough of it. For instance, if our emphasis had been on perfecting the town meeting and the neighborhood commune, there would not be ignorant electors and they would choose great officers. If people had the opportunity to initiate community actions, they would be political; they would know that finally the way to accomplish something great is to get together with the like-minded and directly do it.

But the men in power do not think politically either. For instance, this year we have had the usual spectacle of politicians going about the country looking for nominators for the Presidency, presumably (why else?) because they have important new programs to offer. But as soon as it becomes clear that the county leaders of the party do not want them, they retire from the race and rally to elect whomever. What becomes of the programs? Since this is what political responsibility means to a politician, why should the electorate respect politics, and how could an honest boy be inspired to enter on such a career?

In a recent essay, the historian Henry Steele Commager asks how it is possible that we have an absolute dearth of statesmen at present in America (he cannot think of one). Characteristically, we have an immense amount of formal training in flourishing institutes for public administration at Harvard, Princeton, Syracuse, Tufts, etc., as if we could get the thing by learning the role. Commager sensibly concludes that that training does not begin early enough and it lacks the content of actual experience. The environment does not encourage public service, it does not esteem public goods. Few fathers give much thought to the distant generations of posterity, and children do not take fire in reading about the great men of history and thinking "Why not I?" as a plausible purpose. And finally, says Commager, the narrow chauvinism and energetic hostility to subversive ideas that are now the test of our politicians are precisely disastrous to patriotism, for that must be spacious, disinterested, and broadbased, otherwise it is intolerable foolishness. Let me quote a fine passage:

> The men who won our independence and laid the foundations of the American nation were devoted patriots but they were, too, men of the world. They were children of the enlightenment. Reason taught them that all men were brothers, that purely national distinctions were artificial, that there existed a great community of arts and letters and philosophy and science cutting across and transcending mere national boundaries . . . The nationalism of the eighteenth century did not rest on a narrow base but on a broad one. It did not find nourishment in fear and suspicion but in faith and confidence. Perhaps one reason for the decline in statesmanship is that we have hemmed our potential statesmen in, we have denied them tolerant and spacious ideas.

As it is, what must be the effect on a boy when he comes to realize that the public spokesman up there is not even speaking his own words, but repeating, like a performer, something written for him by a staff from Madison Avenue? The boy must learn to shout, "Shame! make your own speech at least!"

Our present President (Mr. Eisenhower) is an unusually uncultivated man. It is said that he has invited no real writer, no artist, no philosopher to the White House. Presumably he has no intellectual friends; that is his privilege. But recently he invited the chief of the Russian government to a banquet and musicale. And the formal music of that musicale was provided by a Fred Waring band playing "Oh, What a Beautiful Morning" and such other numbers. This is disgraceful.

W. W. Rostow   The Classic American Style   **5**

Walt Whitman Rostow, economist and presidential adviser, was born in 1916 in New York City. He graduated from Yale University in 1936 and received his Ph.D. from the same institution in 1939. He also holds a Master's degree from Balliol College, Oxford. He has served on a number of faculties, including Columbia University, Oxford University, Cambridge University and is currently Professor of Economics at the Massachusetts Institute of Technology. He has also held a number of public posts, including those of consultant to the Eisenhower administration, Counselor and Chairman of the U.S. Department of State, and member of the Policy Planning Council. His books include The American Diplomatic Record *(1947),* The Prospects for Communist China *(1953),* The Stages of Economic Growth *(1960). In the following selection, Rostow discusses three of the components that make up the American style: American ideals, materialism, and the drive for success. For related ideas, see Fuchs, Brogan, Kouwenhoven, Larrabee.*

The American Household. The classic American style is simply one way of coping with the inescapable dilemmas which are, universally, the substance of organized human life. Among the dilemmas which Americans, like others, have had to face are these: a consciousness of both good and evil in themselves and others, a compulsion to pursue individual advantage and a need to share the values and destiny of a larger community, an awareness of the uniqueness of particular circumstance and a compulsion to generalize, and an inborn instinct for order and continuity in social organization and the requirement of change and innovation in order to survive.

In finding the balances and compromises necessary to live with these dilemmas, men do not generally work out consistent institutions, values, or patterns of action. Neither individuals nor societies appear to be intrinsically well-integrated units. They somehow rock along, when they are viable, in patterns of apparently irrational balance.

In consequence, nations often appear to behave paradoxically when judged by arbitrary norms of consistency. In the case of the United States, we often appear simultaneously as among the most idealistic and the most materialistic of peoples. We are given simultaneously to extreme empiricism in dealing with reality and to applying peculiarly spacious abstractions to particular circumstances. We pride ourselves on efficient administration, while our most effective performances have been *ad hoc,* convulsive responses to acute crises. We elevate the individual uniquely in our social life and values and in our politics as well, but we maintain bureaucratic structures which weigh heavily on him, a political system peculiarly suspicious of personal power, and a set of social conventions which exact a high degree of conformity. The performance of other nations could be similarly evoked in terms of paradox. It is the content rather than the fact of paradox in the American style which concerns us here.

A national style—like the performance of a unique human personality— is likely to be the product of a variety of different elements. W. H. Auden once described T. S. Eliot not as a man but as a household: a high church archdeacon, a wise and passionate old peasant grandmother, and a young boy given to slightly malicious practical jokes, all living somehow together. The performance of nations is like that of individuals in that it combines discrete, fortuitous elements of heredity and environment, interacting, effectively coming to terms with problems (or failing to do so) in a recurrent fashion, building up over time relatively stable patterns of performance.

To understand the content of American style we must, therefore, establish the nature of the American household. Out of what basic elements did a distinctive American style emerge? Essentially, the classic American style emerged from the interaction of three powerful and persistent elements in the nation's experience: a nationalism and sense of community achieved by explicit commitment to particular ideal concepts of social and political organization, a day-to-day life challenged and dominated by the extraordinarily rich material potentials of the American scene, and a sequence of national life whose continuity and success appeared progressively to validate the initial commitments in the nation's culture and values, permitting innovation to take the form of a sequence of relatively minor, piecemeal adaptations of a stable basic structure.

It is to an examination of each of these three basic components of the classic national style that we now turn.

The Unifying Function of American Ideals. Many great nations have linked their nationality to a sense of mission which transcended their borders: in different ways and at different times the Chinese, Russians, Germans, British, French, and Spanish. The various concepts of national mission have generally been associated with pride in race, culture, cumulative national achievement, effective power, and religion. For limited periods the nationalism of several powers has been associated with a set of abstract ideas about how societies should be organized; for example, that of France and Russia in their postrevolutionary phases. American nationalism is special — in degree at least — because for almost two centuries, both its domestic and external manifestations, it has been strongly colored by the ideal principles on which American independence was asserted and toward which American society was subsequently committed to aspire.

In certain of the colonies the coming to America itself was associated with religious mission; down to the present, American nationalism has been suffused with a sense of higher sanction for the particular forms of social individualism, political democracy, and private enterprise which we have evolved. As Reinhold Niebuhr has pointed out, the Calvinist and deist traditions converged in this matter, permitting Americans to derive this higher sanction from either divine or natural law. Our social rituals conventionally open with a prayer followed by the salute to the flag — and we have elevated the Plymouth colony, with its special sense of pilgrimage — to a place in our folklore quite disproportionate to its objective role in the making of New England and, ultimately, the nation. In the minds of Americans — and throughout the world — the concept of the American nation retains a dimension of ideological experiment and of ideological leadership.

The "liberty and justice for all" toward which we were committed to aspire took on a special importance and power within the American continental community. These ideal national goals have been the essential device for unifying a society otherwise fragmented by acute individualism, regionalism, and race. We have lacked the cement of hierarchical political and social institutions, a long history, a common race, or even a common religion. But we fashioned national unity out of a mixture of seventeenth-century Protestant values, the dreams of the eighteenth-century Enlightenment, and then, as time moved on, the cumulative experiences and myths we built upon them.

The commitments to govern by methods which left maximum individual freedom and to organize social life on the principle of equality of opportunity have not only given content to American nationhood but, perhaps more important, they have served at all levels as the essential solvent, the source of compromise, the common meeting place in a society otherwise dedicated to the proposition that its affairs should be conducted by vigorous conflict and competition among individual, group, and regional interests. The vagueness of conventional articulation of the national ideals has, in itself, served the important function of permitting a maximum sense of association with the national ethos by groups whose more immediate interests and cultures widely diverged. Historically, our values, like our political institutions, have been federalized; and, in the midst of the diversity of the continent, the narrow but exalted area of national concensus mattered greatly. From the addresses of the President to the after-dinner speech of the most narrowly focused special interest group, the articulation of the society's common values and an evocation of the drama of successful American growth within their orbit play a role which in older societies is covered by the rituals of ancient legitimized tradition.

The role of shared values and of participation in the special adventure of America has thus been more than a substitute for a conventional patriotism. It has played a local and intimate role as well. Americans, living with the heavy weight placed on the individual by Protestant theology, in a society denied (like most other Protestant societies) the cushioning effects of a mediaeval heritage, have had to fashion alternative ways of mitigating the burdens of isolation and personally answerable responsibility. There is some truth in D. H. Lawrence's designation of American democracy as a negative creed: "Henceforth be masterless." Some truth but not the whole truth, for men are lonely and need connections beyond themselves. American individualism has meant, in a sense, merely that we have created a structure of masters different from the clans and the hierarchies, the clearly defined social rituals, the comforting familiar traditions of the Old World. Among our masters are a narrower but perhaps more intense family; a tendency overtly to conform to the will and manners of the political and social majority; a written Constitution elevated to a peculiar sanctity; a nationalism associated with an ambiguous but, in the end, meaningful idealism; a marvellously complex array of voluntary associations, built on the tradition of cooperation and compromise among like-minded equals, a variant of the English concept of liberty. And, as de Tocqueville perceived, the heroic image of the nation's adventure, and an identification with it, was a peculiarly important instrument for unifying a society of detached individuals:

> I readily admit that the Americans have no poets; I cannot allow that they have no poetic ideas. In Europe people talk a great deal of the wilds of America, but the Americans themselves never think about them; they are insensible to the wonders of inanimate nature and they may be said not to perceive the mighty forests that surround them till they fall beneath the hatchet. Their eyes are fixed upon another sight: the American people views its own march across these wilds, draining swamps, turning the course of rivers, peopling solitudes, and subduing nature. This magnificent image of themselves does not meet the gaze of the Americans at intervals only; it may be said to haunt every one of them in his least as well as his most important actions and to be always flitting before his mind.

Virtually all cultures create ideals of behavior to which the individual cannot fully or regularly conform. There is nothing unique about the commitment of the American to values which he must, to a degree, violate in order to live in the world as it is. In most societies, however, the political and social life of the community—and its diplomacy—are not so directly tied to explicit moral purposes. Despite the early defeat of theocracy in New England and the lack of an established national church, there remains a sense in which we have continued to identify church and state. This identification of nationhood with a commitment to strive for good purposes accounts for the "moral overstrain" which, Gunnar Myrdal noted, remains a peculiarly powerful engine within American society. It had led a less friendly foreign observer to conclude:

> Americanism is not merely a myth that clever propaganda stuffs into people's heads but something every American continually reinvents in his gropings. It is at one and the same time a great external reality rising up at the entrance to the port of New York across from the Statue of Liberty and the daily product of anxious liberties.

The Operator's Way with Ideas. Counterpoised against the society's active commitment to great ideal goals was the character of American life in the classic period: a life of hard, absorbing, material pursuits, executed on the basis of individual initiative, conducted to individual advantage.

The nation has been extremely rich in land and other natural resources in relation to its population. It was enormous in scale relative to means of communication over the nation's formative period. It presented for more than two and one-half centuries the challenge and possibility of an open frontier; and, for a full three centuries, the American environment made economically attractive to many a virtually unobstructed flow of immigration. In this setting individual effort and competence yielded high returns in economic welfare, the attainment and expansion of which drew off the bulk of the society's talent and energies.

The attraction of economic life was, however, negative as well as positive. In the classic century—and notably after the Civil War—the society's internal structure and relations to the outside world were such that positions in neither church nor state represented roles of great national prestige and authority; let alone affluence. Men came to seek in the adventure of the American economy—in the test of the market—not only material advantage but also the sense of power, achievement, and status elsewhere granted by a less monolithic, more heterogeneous scale of values.

The mobility of American life, the lack of stable connection with family and place, heightened the attraction and psychological importance of individual achievement. The divorce of the individual from a sense of direct connection with a stable, structured community was further increased by the flow of immigrants. The problems and pace of adjustment varied, of course, with each wave and source of immigration and social class of immigrant as well as with the region and community within which the immigrant settled. Despite great variation, however, between the hungry forties andWorld War I each wave of immigration faced a pattern of adjustment to the prevalent values and culture of the nation which was, by and large, accomplished by generational stages. In this process of adjustment the demonstration by the individual of effective performance in economic and political markets played a substantial role. The man who could solve palpably urgent material problems, organize and operate profitably a productive enterprise, deal effectively with the day-to-day compromises and accommodations of local social and political life thus rose in status; his operational cast of mind came to dominate the American scene, a cast of mind biased toward the assessment by individuals of concrete, particular problems, empirical in method, pragmatic in solutions.

But men have a need and instinct to generalize their experience, to organize, somehow, the chaos around them; and when Americans, busy with limited practical chores, building a new continental society, reached out for larger abstractions they tended to balloon out concepts derived from personal, practical experience. They generalized what they intimately knew. De Tocqueville described vividly how it came about that a nation of individualist empiricists were powerfully drawn to a particular use of highly abstract concepts:

> The Americans are much more addicted to the use of general ideas than the English and entertain a much greater relish for them . . . He who inhabits a democratic country sees around him on every hand men differing but little from one another; he cannot turn his mind to any one portion of mankind without expanding and dilating his thought till it embraces the whole. All the truths that are applicable to himself appear to him equally and similarly applicable to each of his fellow citizens and fellow men. Having contracted the habit of generalizing his ideas in the study which engages him most and interests him most, he transfers the same habit to all his pursuits; and thus it is that the craving to discover general laws in everything, to include a great number of objects under the same formula, and to explain a mass of facts by a single cause becomes an ardent and sometimes an undiscerning passion in the human mind . . . When I repudiate the traditions of rank, professions, and birth, when I escape from the authority of example to seek out, by the single effort of my reason, the path to be followed, I am inclined to derive the motives of my opinions from human nature itself, and this leads me necessarily, and almost unconsciously, to adopt a great number of very general notions . . . Men who live in ages of equality have a great deal of curiosity and little leisure; their life is so practical, so confused, so excited, so active, that but little time remains to them for thought. Such men are prone to general ideas because they are thereby spared the trouble of studying particulars; they contain, if I may so speak, a great deal in a little compass, and give, in a little time, a great return. If, then, on a brief and inattentive investigation, they think they discern a common relation between certain objects, inquiry is not pushed any further; and without examining in detail how far these several objects agree or differ, they are hastily arranged under one formula, in order to pass to another subject.

The American mind, devoted to arduous practical tasks, came, then, also to be equipped with an arsenal of general concepts—often legitimate but partial insights—not rigorously related to each other or to the bodies of fact they were meant to illuminate.

On balance there was little in American life—its content and its values —that encouraged the care and contemplation required to array the intermediate structure of abstractions, test them for internal consistency, and make orderly patterns of thought. Regions, towns, and families did, it is true, exhibit something of the Buddenbrooks dynamics, that is, a third generation (symbolically or in fact) born to both money and social status turning to the life of the mind. But these enclaves of reflective leisure could not hold up for long against the vortex of American life. Even in the older, more stable sections of the East Coast the proportion of first-rate talent that could be drawn and held in intellectual pursuits—as against the claims of business and finance, railroads and the West, shipping, or the law—remained small, down to and beyond World War I.

The national style reinforced itself, moreover, by coming to suffuse the widening process of public education. The principle of free public education was fought through in the North during the pre-Civil War decades; and the new elementary schools reflected a bias toward practical, usable thought, as did the high schools which carried the educational revolution forward from about 1870. In a sense the gospel of education for explicitly practical purposes had been written into national law by the Morrill Act which, in itself, set in motion a self-reinforcing process in the land grant colleges. Toward the end of the classic period, the nation produced in Dewey a philosopher of education who challenged the *status quo;* his challenge was not to the gospel of teaching practical things but to how they were taught and to the cost of existing methods for the individual personality.

When American institutions of higher learning moved toward maturity at the close of the nineteenth century, the architects of the new graduate schools were instinctively drawn to German university models. The Germans—who had left an imprint on American education earlier in the century—placed a high premium on facts and their ordering by precise rules of evidence. Their concept of professional hard-working scholarship harmonized with the instincts of a nation of empiricists entering into an age of industrialism and specialization. The nineteenth-century Germans, when they came to generalize in the social sciences, were, like Americans, prone to broad concepts, only loosely linked to the bodies of fact they so painstakingly compiled. On the whole, Americans pulled up short of the cosmic level of German abstractions, mainly steering clear of universal systems; but a family resemblance remains. We have continued, in a substantial part of the nation's intellectual life, "to explain a mass of facts by a single cause."

American education and intellectual life generally have altered radically
in the past several decades. Nevertheless, the dominant, if changing, mode
of advanced education is a specialized empiricism whose fragmented results
are bound into unity, if at all, by vague high-order generalizations. In the
classic period American intellectual and scientific life produced many knowledgeable men; a number of creative insights; and, at its best, figures of
wisdom with great sensibility about the nature of the physical world or
about how human life is really conducted. But it yielded few general
theoretical structures of distinction.

In both its dimensions — a devotion to the ordering of fact in terms of
low-order abstraction and a certain vague disorder at high levels of abstraction — the classic American intellectual style has reflected the operator's
biases and fitted his needs. Committed to do the best he can in terms of
goals defined by the concrete task he has undertaken or the institutions of
which he is a part, the operator desires to know in detail his field of action but wishes to be as eclectic as he need be and as unhampered as
possible by considerations outside those implicit in his operations.

The classic American manner of dealing with ideas in relation to reality
is by no means unique, but it is distinctive. We are evidently a part of
the Western European intellectual and philosophical tradition. But cut
loose from the surviving mediaeval traditions and institutions of Western
Europe, devoted overwhelmingly to building a rich modern society out of
an empty continent, we developed an empiricism more acute and energetic than that of our contemporaries.

Continuity, Success, and the Ad Hoc *Formula.* How was the gap
bridged between a heightened reliance on idealism to define and maintain
a sense of nation and community and a heightened reliance on the vigorous interplay of individual, regional, and group interests to do the day's
work? How was the gap bridged between a concentration of effort on
particular chores, perceived in terms of low-order abstractions, and the
rich but somewhat disorderly kit bag of higher abstractions into which
Americans reached for their general organizing principles? The answer
appears to be that Americans built their style around the task of solving
problems. They were content to leave implicity the moral and philosophic
ambiguities which flowed from the method of compromise and experiment.
Relatively little attention in formal thought or articulation was given to
the common law formulae which emerged from these living processes because of two massive facts: the first is the extraordinary continuity of the
American experience over the classic period, a continuity which persists in
many domains down to the present; the second, that as a national society
the United States was a distinct success. Men are more inclined to examine with intellectual refinement a complex system of which they are a
part which is confronted with radically new problems or which is failing

than a going concern. And when, toward the close of the classic century, some Americans became more reflective and articulate about their society they tended to elevate "life, experience, process, growth, context, function" over "logic, abstraction, deduction, mathematics, and mechanics." Holmes' dictum embraced more of the national style than the law: "The life of the law has not been logic: it has been experience."

The continuity and success of the national experience had a number of distinct dimensions which converged to produce the result.

First, of course, was the frontier. From the earliest stages of the Massachusetts and Virginia colonies down to the twentieth century—for almost three centuries—the existence of an accessible and productive frontier gave a special reality to the individualistic values of the society, strongly coloring its institutions, from the family to politics, and its culture. The frontier was a long historical process, not a piece of real estate; and American economic, political, and social life consisted in good part of the interplay and balancing of interests between the frontier areas and the more stable communities and institutions that moved in behind the frontier. Certain political patterns (for example, the conflict of interest between soft money, indebted farmers, and hard-money urban property owners, between those who wanted the state to build "public improvements" and those who wanted to lower taxes) are continuous from one end of American history to the other; and Americans became expert at working with them in their many variants. More than that, the concept of the frontier, its existence somewhere to the West, imparted a continuing sense of promise, possibility, and adventure to those who lived their lives out in more ordered eastern settings.

Despite the expanding frontier, however, the task of maintaining unity was, in one sense, eased as time went on. The scale of the nation was roughly matched and then outmatched by the development of communications capable of binding the regions together and giving them unity. In terms of the central problem of achieving and maintaining nationhood among a group of regions with powerful distinctive interests and attitudes, the working techniques of federalism proved essentially viable with only incremental modification.

Similarly, the initial *tour de force* of generating effective (even barely effective) national action from a dispersed and locally oriented population—in the 1770s and 1780s—has been somehow maintained despite the increase and physical spread of the population, the impact of diverse immigrations, and the emergence or sharpening of class groupings as industrialization and urbanization proceeded. The attachment of American nationalism to certain overriding principles of social and political organization has served adequately as a rallying point for nationhood, surviving the brutal test of civil war. The structure of private social groupings has continued to ramify and to weave a highly individualistic and mobile population into a firm social fabric; these groupings have come to share a widening area of common values. Above all, the canny insights of the Founding Fathers yielded a constitutional structure which, when supplemented by the intermediation of a two-party system, a Supreme Court, and an Anglo-American system of law, has weathered the gross changes in the scale and character of American society.

The maintenance of national unity was eased, of course, by the degree of vertical mobility American society continued to offer. Although social mobility in an urban, industrial setting is a quite different phenomenon from social mobility in a setting where it consists mainly in the possibility of acquiring cheaply an agricultural homestead, Americans have made the transition from one to the other without ceasing to envisage as possible for themselves — and especially for their children — a marked rise in social and economic status on the basis of individual capabilities and performance. The nation's evolution has steadily confirmed and reconfirmed the central unifying concept of equality of opportunity in a sufficiently meaningful way to maintain loyalty to the nation's social system.

Both the adjustment to conflicting regional and group interests within our national society and the process of social mobility have been enormously aided by the sustained growth and high output per head which has marked the history of the modern American economy. This not only gave reality to the concept of progress but also permitted men to achieve compromises in which they shared the increments to communal wealth without the bitter, corrosive conflicts which come about when men feel they can rise only at the expense of someone else's decline. In one sense, it was precisely because the land to the west was not congenial to cotton culture and could no longer be divided evenly between slave and free states that the Civil War ensued: the South felt that the nation's extension to the West Coast could only be at the expense of decline or loss of its way of life. In that sense, the great exception reinforces the general rule.

Above all, the cast of American values and institutions and the tendency to adapt them by cumulative experiment rather than to change them radically has been progressively strengthened by the image of the gathering success of the American adventure, whether it was judged on economic grounds, on grounds of political workability, or in terms, even, of international status. The nation, founded in defiance of a major power, living for a time at bay in both a military and a political sense, came early in its history to feel that its initial concept of a transcendent ideological destiny was justified by the turn of events in the world outside. Until well into the twentieth century there were grounds for believing that the American pattern was, indeed, the wave of the future; and, although somewhat chastened by the experience of recent decades, Americans have by no means wholly lost a sense of mission, based on confidence and pride in the success of a unique moral, political, economic, and social experiment.

We can now sum up briefly. The moral problem posed for Americans has been solved by an incessant process of compromise and conflict and evolutionary adaption taking place within a continuous framework of institutions, hammered out of a colonial life and a revolution rooted in inherited British values. The philosophical problem posed for Americans has been solved by a dedication to the vigorous extension of economic, political, and social processes. With certain notable exceptions, the accidents of history and the American environment made it possible for these processes of extension to be conducted by incremental modification arrived at by widespread experiment after vigorous debate. The whole cacophony of American articulation about politics, social values, economics, and ethics has had a real importance in keeping alive the nation's unifying values; but more significant for how the nation actually worked have been the subtly balanced concepts left implicitly in the working processes of a society blessed, for most of its life, by the possibility of solving its essential problems in relative continuity with its past experience. American ideals have a living place within these working processes, but a place more compromised, less innocent than our conventional modes of articulation would allow.

But the intellectual content of a process is immensely complex. It involves many factors interacting over time. The normal forms of rigorous logical exposition can grip only elements within the process and are likely to give them a more rigid and static cast than, in fact, they have; the number of unknowns is likely to be greater than the number of equations that can usefully be formulated. Men successfully operate processes by accumulating experience, feel, judgment, by sensing recurrent patterns rather than isolating clean-cut logical connections of cause and effect. This is how good captains of sailing vessels have worked — good politicians, good businessmen. This has been the typical American style in operating and developing the nation's society.

Its success, however, is dependent on two conditions which are, to a degree, alternatives. First, the problems confronted must be, in their essence, relatively familiar and capable of solution by only moderately radical innovation on the basis of existing principles or institutions. Second, there must be sufficient time for the experimental exploration of possible solutions and the osmotic process of accepting change. The more time permitted, the greater the workability of a technique of problem solving by empirical experiment.

It is, therefore, in the less radical orders of innovation—in science, industry, and politics—that the nation has excelled. Or, put another way, the American style is least effective when it confronts issues which require radical innovation promptly.

The great vigor and relative success with which American society has thus far overcome crises should not conceal the fact that many of those crises represent failures in the workings of the society. But it is of the nature of crisis that action can no longer be postponed; and, in addition, crises transcend in their implications the immediate issues in contention and threaten more basic values and institutions. In the American case the basic values and institutions of the nation have, by and large, commanded the support of a substantial majority. The crisis thus becomes a concrete operational problem to whose immediate resolution a unified nation turns. And the need for action—in the American case, its success —often permits the underlying causes for the crisis to persist, unexamined and obscure.

In short, a gift for vigorous communal action in the face of crisis— invaluable as it is—should not be confused with a talent for prompt and radical innovation in the face of new circumstances. This is the essence of the danger which confronts contemporary America, notably in its military and political relations with the world where the pace of technological change and of revolutionary political transformation may give us neither the continuity of experience nor the time the classic American style inherently requires for success. Resolution of our current problems by the technique of crisis action may yield misdirected efforts or action undertaken too late to ensure the society's interests.

Seminal contributions

6

Arthur M. Schlesinger, Sr.   **Our Ten Contributions
                                                    to Civilization**

Arthur Meier Schlesinger, Sr., the eminent historian, was born in Ohio in 1888 and died in 1965. He received the Pulitzer Prize for The History of American Life. *He taught history for over fifty years, in Ohio, Iowa, and as Francis Lee Higginson Professor of History at Harvard. He was a prolific author. His other works include* The Rise of the City *(1933) and* The American as Reformer *(1950). In the following selection, as the title indicates, Professor Schlesinger lists ten important American contributions to civilization. For related ideas, see Gabriel, Rostow, Glazier and Moynihan.*

Since the United States has now become the leader of the free world, our allies are asking, and we ourselves should be asking, what this portends for the future of civilization. The key to the answer, I suggest, lies in what I venture to call America's seminal contributions of the past. In my view there have been at least ten.

The Right of Revolution

First and foremost stands the concept of the inherent and universal right of revolution proclaimed in the Declaration of Independence: the doctrine that "all men are created equal" possessing "unalienable rights" to "life, liberty, and the pursuit of happiness," with the corollary that governments derive "their just powers from the consent of the governed" and that therefore the people have the right to supplant a government "destructive of these ends" with one which they believe "most likely to effect their safety and happiness." True, the history of England provided precedents for the men of 1776, and the Age of Enlightenment supplied intellectual support; but the flaming pronouncement, followed by its vindication on the battlefield, made the doctrine ever afterward an irrepressible agency in "the course of human events."

Europe was the first to respond. In 1789 occurred the great French Revolution, the forerunner of two later ones of the French people during the nineteenth century; and neighboring countries were not slow to follow. A series of revolts, centering in 1830 and 1848, drove the Turks from Greece, overturned or strove to overturn illiberal governments through most of the rest of the Continent, and hastened political reforms in other lands to forestall popular upheavals.

These convulsions all had their internal causes, but in every instance the leaders derived inspiration from America's achievement of popular rule as well as from its freely expressed interest in their similar aspirations. Presidents, Congresses, and civic gatherings applauded the uprisings, and American volunteers actually fought in the Greek war of liberation. After Russia helped Austria to suppress the Hungarian rebellion, a United States warship late in 1851 brought the Magyar patriot Kossuth to this country, where he received the honors of an American hero. The citizens of Spring-

From *The Atlantic Monthly* (March 1959). Copyright © 1959, by The Atlantic Monthly Company, Boston, Mass. 02116. Reprinted with permission of The Atlantic Monthly Company and Mrs. Arthur M. Schlesinger, Sr. Pp. 65–69.

field, Illinois, for example, rallied to his cause in words which have a fresh and poignant significance for us today. Affirming "the right of any people . . . to throw off . . . their existing form of government, and to establish such other in its stead as they may choose," they condemned the "interference of Russia in the Hungarian struggle" as "illegal and unwarrantable" and asserted that "to have resisted Russia . . . would have been no violation of our own cherished principles . . . but, on the contrary, would be ever meritorious, in us, or any independent nation." Abraham Lincoln, then in private life, was one of the authors of the resolutions.

The doctrine of revolution, however, had still broader implications. The European eruptions in most instances sought merely to replace domestic regimes; the American revolt, to cast off a distant yoke. It was the first of the great colonial insurrections, an example all the more potent because Washington's ill-trained soldiers defeated the mightiest nation in the world. The Spanish dependencies to the south took heed and early in the nineteenth century won their freedom. Then, oddly enough, came a setback to the trend as a large part of Asia and Africa and many islands of the Pacific fell under the sway of Old World powers. And after a time even the United States, forgetful of its own once colonial status, followed suit.

But in the twentieth century the two world wars radically changed the situation, recalling the United States to its historic heritage, crippling the military strength of the European imperialist countries, and awakening subject peoples everywhere to their right of self-determination. America led the way by relinquishing its Caribbean protectorates and granting independence to the Philippines, and soon the Old World governments fell into line, some voluntarily to anticipate the inevitable, as in the case of England, and others because they were unable to quell native rebellions, as in the cases of France and Holland.

Although more than a century and a half has elapsed since America proclaimed the right of revolution, these events of our own day evidence its continuing vitality. Lest I be accused of claiming too much for a precedent so far in the past, consider the words of President Sukarno of Indonesia three and a half years ago in his address of welcome to the Bandung Conference. This Asian-African gathering, the first of its kind in history, brought together delegates from twenty-nine nations, most of them newly free. "The battle against colonialism," Sukarno declared,

> has been a long one, and do you know that today is a famous anniversary in that battle? On the eighteenth day of April, one thousand seven hundred and seventy-five, just one hundred and eighty years ago, Paul Revere rode at midnight through the New England countryside, warning of the approach of British troops and of the opening of the American War

of Independence, the first successful anticolonial war in history. About this midnight ride the poet Longfellow wrote:

> A cry of defiance and not of fear,
> A voice in the darkness, a knock at the door,
> And a word that shall echo for evermore. . . .

Yes [he concluded], it shall echo for evermore . . . until we can survey this our own world, and can say that colonialism is dead.

The Principle of Federalism

Because of the difficulties experienced under the Articles of Confederation, the Constitution of 1787 established a partnership of self-governing commonwealths with an overall elective government powerful enough to protect and promote their joint concerns and — what was no less important — with a provision for admitting later states on a plane of full equality. This was something new in history; Tocqueville called it "a great discovery in modern political science," for no other people had ever devised a federal structure over so large an area or with a central government chosen by popular vote or on such generous terms for future members. It offered mankind a key to the age-old problem of reconciling legitimate local interests with the general good.

Mexico, Argentina, and other Latin American countries adopted variants of the plan, and so did Germany and Austria-Hungary. Britain applied it to two of its largest colonies, Canada and Australia, and in the twentieth century recast most of its empire into a Commonwealth of Nations on the same basis. More dramatically, the principle caused men to conceive of some sort of federation of the world, first in the League of Nations and then in the United Nations, both sponsored by American Presidents; and in the not too distant future it promises to bring about a United States of Western Europe.

The Consent of the Governed

Neither the doctrine of revolution nor the principle of federalism necessarily ensured that the government so established would rest on the consent of the governed. This was an entirely different matter, as the history of Latin American dictatorships as well as that of other nations proves. But, as we have seen, it was a basic tenet of the founders of the United States and may well be regarded as America's third contribution to humanity.

The framers of the Constitution spurned European tradition by rejecting a monarchy, a nobility, or a hereditary legislative chamber, placing their trust in a government of the people, by the people, and for the people,

one which should rule by counting heads instead of breaking them. Starting with a somewhat limited number of voters but in better proportion
than in any other country, the suffrage was broadened generation by generation until it came to include all adults of both sexes; and at every
point America set the pace for the Old World. The underlying philosophy
was not that the common man is all-wise, but only that he can govern
himself better than anyone else can do it for him.

The Status of Women

Women played a man's part as well as a woman's in taming the wilderness, and until very recently, moreover, they were fewer in number than
the opposite sex and hence commanded a high scarcity value. From early
times foreign observers marveled at the unusual educational opportunities
open to them, their immunity from molestation when traveling alone, their
freedom to go out of the home to agitate for temperance, antislavery, and
other reforms. "From the captain of a western steamboat to the roughest
miner in California," wrote one visitor, "from north, south, east, and
west, we hear but one voice. Women are to be protected, respected, supported, and petted."

The organized feminist movement arose earlier in the United States than
in any other nation not because American women enjoyed so few privileges but because they had so many that they demanded more—in short,
all those exercised by their husbands and brothers, including that of suffrage. The famous women's rights convention at Seneca Falls, New York,
in 1848, the first in the history of the world, turned the Declaration of
Independence to account by proclaiming "all men and women are created
equal" with the same unalienable rights to "life, liberty, and the pursuit
of happiness." It took the women many years to achieve that goal, but
in time they succeeded, and every victory spurred their sisters in other
lands to similar endeavors.

The Melting Pot

A fifth contribution of the United States has been the fusing of many
different nationalities in a single society. America has been in the best
sense of the term a melting pot, every ingredient adding its particular
element of strength. The constant infusion of new blood has enriched
our cultural life, speeded our material growth, and produced some of our
ablest statesmen. Over 17 million immigrants arrived in the single period
from the Civil War to World War I—more than America's total population in 1840—and today English and Scottish blood, the principal strain

in colonial times, constitutes considerably less than half the whole.

Many other peoples, it is true, are also of mixed origin; but the American achievement stands alone in the scale, thoroughness, and rapidity of the process and, above all, in the fact that it has been the outcome not of forcible incorporation but of peaceful absorption. Significantly, the very nationalities which had habitually warred with one another in the Old World have lived together in harmony in the New. America has demonstrated for everyone with eyes to see that those things which unite peoples are greater than those which divide them, that war is not the inevitable fate of mankind.

Our most tragic failure has involved our Negro citizens, now a tenth of our number. Taken forcibly from Africa, trammeled in slavery for two and a half centuries, denied their constitutional rights after emancipation in the states where most of them lived, this ill-used race has been a standing reproach to our professions of democracy and has enabled Communist spokesmen as well as other foreign critics to impugn the very principle of human equality on which the republic was founded. Nevertheless, even these injured people have not been unwilling Americans, as the Irish before winning their freedom were unwilling Britons: they have only been unwilling to be halfway Americans or second-class citizens. Hence they have unhesitatingly rejected the blandishments of Soviet propaganda. Fortunately they can now at long last look forward to the final rectification of the wrongs they have so patiently endured.

Freedom of Worship

The recognition that the relations between man and his Creator are a private affair into which government must not intrude contravened the age-long European practice of uniting church and state and imposing harsh restrictions on dissenters. The American system was a legacy of colonial times, when the theological motive for settlement was intense and the multiplicity of denominations suggested the need for mutual forbearance. Rhode Island, Maryland, and Pennsylvania in the persons of Roger Williams, Lord Baltimore, and William Penn set the pattern to which the Bill of Rights of the federal Constitution gave nationwide sanction. Religion by choice was the natural counterpart of government by consent, and, contrary to Old World belief, the separation of church and state did not in fact weaken either but strengthened both.

The Public School

The principle of government by consent made it imperative that the people be literate and well informed if they were to vote intelligently. To ensure this essential condition, statesmen agreed that society must at its own initiative and expense supply the means of schooling. This, too, broke drastically with the Old World concept that education should be a privately financed undertaking for the upper classes, the rank and file supposedly having little need for any in what was deemed to be their permanently inferior station.

New England inaugurated the practice in colonial days; then, with the swift extension of the franchise during the first half of the nineteenth century, it was adopted throughout the North and later in the South. Free public education thus became the article of American faith it has continued to be ever since. From the United States the plan spread in modified form around the world. Japan, for example, in 1872 made it the cornerstone of its program of modernization. Probably America has conferred no greater boon on mankind, for popular education is the seedbed of virtually all other human aspirations.

Voluntary Giving

Foreigners have always criticized the American for his pursuit of the almighty dollar, but have seldom gone on to note that he has in unparalleled degree returned the fruits of his labors to society. If he has been hardheaded about making money, he has, so to speak, been softhearted about spending it. This constitutes the American version of the Old World concept of *noblesse oblige* carried to a point the Old World has never approached. Even long before Carnegie and Rockefeller amassed their colossal fortunes, men and women of modest means gave freely to schools, churches, foreign missions, colleges, hospitals, charities, and other projects for social betterment.

In the twentieth century this same concern has led men of wealth to set up some four thousand philanthropic foundations staffed with experts to administer the funds with maximum usefulness and for nearly every conceivable object of human benefit. Their programs, exceeding all earlier bounds, include the control of epidemic diseases and far-reaching researches in the natural and social sciences. Even so, the lion's share of the more than 6.5 billion dollars devoted to altruistic purposes last year still derived from other than foundation sources.

And, increasingly, Americans have extended their beneficence to foreign peoples. Over a century ago popular subscriptions helped relieve Irish suffering during the terrible potato famines of the 1840s and later aided with equal generosity the victims of natural catastrophes in other lands. And, besides the work of the Red Cross in peace and war, the great foundations have in our own day improved health, educational, and agricultural conditions in many countries. In the same tradition the private organization known as CARE has, since World War II, channeled gifts of food, clothing, medicine, and the like to the needy of Europe, Asia, Africa, and Latin America. Thanks to this ingrained trait of the national character, the government found it easy to mobilize our people behind the Marshall Plan, a costly tax-supported program for repairing the war-stricken economies of Western Europe. Though these official undertakings were in part designed to halt the spread of Communism, they arose from deeper springs of human compassion and have no parallel in history.

Technology

Mechanical ingenuity, or what today is called technological know-how, contrary to common belief is by no means a late development. From the mid-eighteenth century on, the people, confronted with a chronic shortage of labor and the problems arising from formidable distances and poor communications, devised means to overcome these handicaps as well as to ameliorate other conditions of life. The record is truly remarkable. Before the end of the nineteenth century Benjamin Franklin, Eli Whitney, and their successors produced such epochal inventions as the lightning rod, the cotton gin, the steamboat, the metal plow, the harvester, vulcanized rubber, the sewing machine, the telegraph, the telephone, and the electric light, among others. In still other instances they greatly improved on what had come to them from abroad.

The upshot was not only to transform American life but that of peoples everywhere. President Truman therefore was not occupying wholly new ground when in 1949 he proposed his Point Four Program to make "the benefits of our scientific advances and industrial progress available for the improvement and growth of underdeveloped areas" and thus "help them realize their aspirations for a better life." Under this program the United States has sent experts in industry, engineering, and agriculture to many lands; built roads and bridges in Iran, irrigation works in India, and fertilizer plants in Korea; and endeavored in countless other ways to remove the obstacles that have barred less enterprising countries from the advantages of modern civilization. Just as the government has made our philanthropic impulse a vital instrument of foreign policy, so also it has done with our technological skill.

Evolutionary Progress

The United States is often considered a young nation, but in fact it is next to the oldest continuous government in the world. The reason is that the spirit of its people has always been empirical and pragmatic, dedicated to equalitarian ends but willing to realize them by flexible means. In the European sense of the term, America's major political parties are not parties at all, because they do not divide over basic ideologies. Neither wishes to overturn or replace the existing political and economic order; they merely desire to alter it at slower or faster rates of speed.

One of our proudest achievements has been the creation of a system of controlled capitalism that yields the highest living standards on earth and has made possible a society as nearly classless as man has ever known. The profit system as it has developed in America is a multiprofit system, sharing its benefits with all segments of society: capital, labor, and the consuming masses. Yet even this was not due to a preconceived blueprint; it too was the result of trial and error. Unprincipled businessmen had first to be brought to heel by government restraints and the growing power of organized labor before they came to learn that they must serve the general good in pursuing their selfish interests. Now labor is feeling the restraint.

Even our creed of democracy is no fixed and immutable dogma. Thus the statesmen of the early republic, though they were stalwart champions of private enterprise, chose to make the post office a government monopoly and to confide the schools to public ownership. Since then, by fits and starts, and most recently under the New Deal, the United States has taken on many of the characteristics of a welfare state. This has occurred, however, not under the banner of socialism or of any other "ism," but simply because the Americans hold with Lincoln that "the legitimate object of government is to do for a community of people whatever they need to have done but cannot do at all, or cannot do so well for themselves, in their separate and individual capacities."

Viewed as a whole, the contributions of America to civilization will be seen to have been for the most part in the nature of methods or processes. They have aimed to release men from political and religious disabilities, from ignorance and poverty, from backbreaking toil. They have struck at the fetters which from time immemorial the Old World had fastened on human beings. They have opened the doors of opportunity for the many while still assuring them to the few, in the belief that everyone should have an equal chance to be as unequal as he can without denying the same right to others. In brief, they have sought to substitute fluidity for rigid class distinctions as the vital principle of social well-being. And the consequence has been a general leveling of society upward instead of downward.

But what of the future? I recall what a thoughtful Hollander said to me a few years after World War II. Observing that Europe's age of greatness was now over and that Americans must henceforth take the lead in the advancement of civilization, he wondered whether they would be equal to the task. Plainly he had grave doubts, for like most foreigners he thought of us as having been only beneficiaries of the bounty of the Old World without making any creative returns in kind. But for an American historian the answer is clear. The true measure of our past contributions lies in the very fact that they have become so woven into the life of mankind that my Dutch friend was unaware of them. If we can only preserve our free institutions and our faith in the untrammeled human spirit, we shall triumphantly meet the challenge now before us.

**An intrinsically attractive type
of human possibility**

D. W. Brogan   **The Character of American Life**   7

Sir Denis W. Brogan, one of Britain's most astute observers of America, was born in 1900 in Glasgow, Scotland. He studied at the University of Glasgow, at Oxford's Balliol College and received his Master's degree in American history from Harvard. He is Professor of Political Science at the University of Cambridge and was knighted in the summer of 1963. His works include Politics and Law in the United States *(1941),* The English People *(1943), and* The American Character *(1944). In the following selection, Brogan deals with a variety of topics, including equality and the role of business. Also, Brogan rejects the concepts of the "other-directed" man and the "organization" man. Interestingly, this foreign observer finds more diversity in American culture than many Americans do. For related ideas, see Riesman, Whyte, Wheelis, Rostow, Mills, Goodman, Barzun.*

I am only too conscious of the boldness, the absurdity, of undertaking to say anything of interest or even of minimal good sense on so vast a topic as the character of American life. Despite the boldness of my title, I am more timid or more sensible than may appear and what I propose is to attempt something bold enough in itself and yet more practicable than the vast adventure which my title might suggest.

I shall begin by saying that there are vast areas of American life that I

From *America in the Modern World* by D. W. Brogan. New Brunswick, N.J.: Rutgers University Press, 1960. Reprinted by permission of the publisher. Pp. 44–63.

shall ignore. Most of what may be called political economy I shall slip
away from. I have no doubt that the economic problems of the farmer
are deeply important and reveal something of the character of American
life, but I shall do no more than bow at the problem, be silent on the
solution, and deal with the farmer only as part of the rapidly changing
panorama of American society. There is the role of American women; I
shall not ignore it entirely, but again there are many problems concerned
with her status, her social and economic role that I shall ignore, both
from timidity and from wisdom. For example, I shall not develop my belief that the American woman is to some extent a victim of a confidence
trick played by the American man—who is much smarter than the American woman realizes and gives to her more the appearance than the reality
of power and equality. The vast fields covered by "education" and "culture" I shall deal with separately and, without apology, ignore here.

I shall try to say something positive, but I shall try to pick on *some*
salient marks of American society, of American life, both for their intrinsic
interest and for their relevance to my basic theme—the competitive strength
of the United States in the dangerous world in which it now has to live.
That is to say, I shall make some parallels with European society, stressing
resemblances as well as differences. And I shall try to weigh some features
of American life, if not quite like an observer from outer space at least
with the comparative objectivity of a foreigner.

Comparative objectivity, for it would be idle to pretend that I come here
as a stranger or a neutral. If I may be permitted some autobiography, I
first came to the United States nearly thirty-four years ago when I had
just left Oxford, having created some scandal there by insisting on going
to America to study the scarcely respectable subject of American history.
I have visited America nearly every year since; I even managed to make
three visits during the war, and I have sometimes made more than one
visit in a year. Altogether I have spent six or seven years in this country
and its study has been my chief academic and literary activity since I first
came here, an innocent pilgrim, in the golden day of Calvin Coolidge. I
come not really as a neutral but as a most friendly observer who has
tried hard to understand this country and to pass on what knowledge he
has acquired to his often moderately receptive countrymen. Whatever I
do, however hard I try to be the stern impartial critic, friendliness and
optimism will keep creeping in.

Catholics talk of the "marks" of the Church and I should like to begin
by describing some of the marks of American society as I see them. First
I shall follow in the footsteps of my great predecessor, Alexis de Tocqueville, and stress the mark of equality. No one not blinded by prejudice, no
one knowing Britain or France or Germany, can fail to be struck by the
fact that "equality" is as much a distinguishing mark of American society

as it was one hundred thirty years ago when Tocqueville made his famous journey.

True, there are apparent differences. There are far more rich people today than there were then; there are many more millions of Americans who can be classified as part of "le peuple," as Tocqueville's countrymen put it then and now. Economic inequality is more visible now than it was then. Then, if we believe Tocqueville, the rich rather concealed their wealth and if they enjoyed it they enjoyed it in secret. They played it down if they wished to enter politics and ostentatious display of democratic tastes was called for in candidates for public office. It would be wrong today to deny that candidates profess an enthusiasm that may be genuine for hot dogs and blintzes, for baseball and basketball. But few doubted in 1958 that Governor Harriman or Nelson Rockefeller normally lived on rather more sophisticated diet than what may be called electoral nutriment or that, if they had democratic tastes, they also had tastes whose gratification required very large incomes. There is no cheap, democratic way of collecting French Impressionists, no really democratic way of playing polo; and it is notorious that ex-Governor Harriman and Governor Rockefeller are more than comfortably off and that other governors, many senators, and even a few lesser public figures are at least comfortably off. It may not help them politically (I refuse to speculate) but it does not visibly hurt them. The American voter has got used to economic inequality and no longer resents it in itself. Nor does he resent even the most outrageous display of conspicuous consumption by what is called, I believe, "cafe society," except possibly when he is paying his modest income tax and wondering what it is like to have a really fat expense account. The popular idols of the screen, the stage, and TV are expected to show appreciation of their good fortune by garish display, and even in contemplating the Texas oil millionaire who can't have a swimming pool because every time he builds one he strikes oil the American is inclined to say "nice work if you can get it" rather than "Workers of the world, unite."

My examples of an American attitude have not been chosen quite at random or to provoke easy laughter. Behind them lies an American attitude that Tocqueville did not stress, although I find it hard to believe that it was not visible in his time and it is certainly very visible and worth noting in our time. The United States is a country in which simple jealousy plays a comparatively innocuous and unimportant role in political and social life. Note I do not say in private life. I have read too many powerful novels, too many reports of murder trials when all went black and there on the floor was a dead husband or wife, not to know that Americans are subject to the human if ignoble emotion of jealousy just like other people. But if Americans can endure or even accept with ease a great deal of economic and social inequality in public life, in economic life, in sport and diversion, it is in great part because of the absence of jealousy in the American attitude.

No one who has moved around in England, France or Germany can doubt that in all these countries jealous, resentful envy is an important source of political animus and of national disunion and weakness. Why is America different?

I shall advance a thesis that is not very novel and not very profound, but has, I think, the advantage of making this important difference appear not simply as an inexplicable difference or even as a proof of American stupidity and gullibility. (If the American common man knew his business as a common man he would be jealous. So many a European intellectual argues—though perhaps not quite in those words.)

The American political and economic environment has been from the beginning unkind to pretensions that did not have some apparent relation to achievement either in the present or in the recent and what may be called the "usable" past. It is a commonplace of American historiography that all attempts to export feudalism failed. The European entrepreneur who wanted to turn his assets into a political and social superiority that he could leave to his family was making a mistake if he took his capital to British North America. For various reasons that I can do no more than allude to it proved impossible to set up a hereditary landowning or office-owning class to which admission would be slow, irregular, and not important enough in numbers to flood the existing class structure in each generation to a degree that would destroy its exclusiveness.

I hasten to say that I am not under the illusion that there are no social fences in America, no social barriers that are hard to pass, no cult of exclusiveness. Indeed it could be said that some American social groups are more exclusive than their European counterparts, less willing to admit the promoting power of money. I have lived in Boston and visited Philadelphia!

But even in their great days, the Back Bay and the Main Line were not accepted as their English or French and, still more, German equivalents were, as part of the nature of things. They were picturesque anomalies with, I suspect, more power to bruise than to hurt seriously and less power to give pleasure and comfort than the aspiring climbers hoped. What was and is the use of being admitted to an exclusive society if the vast majority of those excluded don't really care or, what is worse, don't really know that they are being excluded?

The very emphasis on barriers, on clubs, on fraternities, on exclusive schools and pools reveals a social order in which equality is constantly intruding, in which it takes a lot of money and energy and, I should suggest, a high degree of humorlessness, to get men and women to take the trouble to exclude and to include on any grounds but those of social fitness and utility and personal attraction. An English student from Oxford or Cambridge introduced to the full rigors of the secret society system at Yale is astounded and amused or horrified, according to temperament and political bias. But if he is a good observer and remembers Oxford or Cambridge when he is at Yale he will, I think, be forced to conclude that Yale, for all the mystery of Bones, is more democratic than either Oxford or Cambridge, where the barriers are less visible, less stressed but far more difficult to surmount and far more wounding to fail to surmount. I have deliberately chosen an academic example, partly because I know both Oxford and Cambridge well and have seen something of Yale, but partly because it is in the American school system, in its widest sense, that equality loses.

Elsewhere I shall suggest that this is not always a good thing, but it is sufficient for the moment to note that economic inequality in America has, in the main, only economic consequences. As Scott Fitzgerald put it in his celebrated dialogue with Hemingway, "The rich are not like us." "Yes, they have more money," said Hemingway. I would be the last to deny that having more money is important; but having less money is even more important, for the poor suffer from their poverty more than the rich gain from their wealth. Yet in America merely having more money pays less in extra dividends, less in bought servility, less in reverence or its opposite, envious rancor, than it does in any other country known to me.

Because it is assumed (often wrongly) that wealth represents past or present useful service to the economy or, what the average man appreciates quite as much, the democracy of more luck — more luck in striking an oil well, more luck in answering in the dear dead days the $64,000 question — the American takes inequalities in his stride. He may be a victim of an illusion. He probably exaggerates, if not for himself, then for his children, their chances of promotion in the economic and social scale. He may neglect the power of the power elite in a naive way. He may think that his political rights give him in the mass some control over the power elite and that money and the control of the economy are not everything (in my opinion he is right in so thinking), but here we are concerned not with his intelligence, his power of judgment *sub specie orbis*. A man who feels happy is happy; a man who is contented, by and large, has in that attitude a source of happiness that is not to be neglected or despised. In the pursuit of happiness the race may be to the swift and the handicapping not quite just, but it is an asset for a country that the race is believed to be so open that nearly everybody wants to run in it.

This attractiveness of the race accounts for the good temper with which, in general, its results are accepted as beneficial, which is a great social asset. If the contentment of the American were a passive contentment, if it were contentment not with the general system but with his particular place in it, as has often been the meaning of contentment in torpid, tradition-ridden societies, then much could be said for stirring up discontent, divine or simply human. But I think it can hardly be denied that one source of American wealth has been the belief in the rewards of economic virtue and the adequate correspondence of that belief with the facts.

Turning for a moment to the outside world, it must be stressed that the role of this competitive spirit, this American theory of the economic game, is not fully understood anywhere else and over a great part of the world is not understood at all. Contemplating the American economic miracle, the European and still more the Asian or the African is not as a rule willing to allow for the role of the businessman or to accept the fact that to get his particular type of social usefulness he must be willing to ignore formal economic equality or the pretense of it, must be willing to accept in their role as entrepreneurs some very rough diamonds and perhaps some persons who are not even semiprecious stones. The European, the Asian, the African, in a descending order of comprehension, finds it hard to believe that the highest virtues and the highest talents can possibly be observed in a man who devotes the greater part of his life to the accumulation of wealth.

But one will rightly protest, the American businessman as a type does not devote himself to the accumulation of wealth as such; he devotes himself to the production of wealth and his share in it, handsome as it may be, is only a legitimate price for what he gives society in his pursuit of the satisfactions of the business life. This I believe to be true. But at the risk of seeming to lay down general laws that cannot be proved I shall assert that this acceptance of the business life as one worthy of calling out all the powers of a really able man, giving him the satisfactions of a really worthy lifework, may not be solely American but it is peculiarly American. And it is one of the reasons why America is so wealthy and so comparatively free from the crippling social barriers and social resentments of Europe.

Maurice Zinkin has argued that what India needs is more good businessmen and more respect for good businessmen. I believe this is true also of Britain and even of that businessman's paradise, Western Germany. To be epigrammatic at the risk of seeming foolish I should say that outside the United States more respect for business achievement is needed and inside the United States one should, without losing one's natural respect for the businessman for what he does well, be more willing to accept the possibility that there are things well worth doing that businessmen cannot do and that cannot be done in a "businesslike way."

Given the American experience, where most successful social enterprises have been run by businessmen for businessmen (and for the economy in general as well), it is natural that this experience should be extended to the outside world. But, in the first place, it is too simple a view of American history to see the growth of the American economy as taking place without political directions, without the state's playing more than a minor or a positively nefarious role. The American businessman owes both the existence of his opportunities and the character of his opportunities to the success of the United States as a body politic. The existence of the Union was necessary in order to create the American market and so was its maintenance. Thus Madison and Hamilton, Lincoln and Grant—none of them, not even Hamilton, a business type—are among the most potent makers of the American market and so of the American economy in which the American businessman has flourished.

I shall dogmatically assert that a Lincoln is not only a more interesting but a much more important figure than a Ford or a Rockefeller. Someone would have invented the equivalent of the Model T or the Standard Oil Company. But Lincolns are scarcer and in 1861 the United States could not have afforded to wait until the turn of the wheel brought up an equivalent of Lincoln and put him into the White House. This is the first important modification of the exalted picture I have honestly painted of the role and the utility of the American businessman. He has played so useful a role and his role has been so handsomely rewarded in cash and credit that he has naturally been tempted to exalt himself even above his merits, which are great, and by implication to denigrate other groups whose essential services to the American experiment have been as great but not so well rewarded as those of the businessman.

The businessman has as a rule taken an ironical view of the politician. He has seen him as a parasite, as a tool, sometimes as a demagogic nuisance who has to be fought or bought off or suffered not in silence but in noisy wrath. He has contrasted the things that business does (and usually does well) with the things the political organizations have done—at every level, city, county, state, nation—and has stressed the things that these political units have done badly—and there are many of them. He has tended to forget that not all businesses have been well run; the bankruptcy courts show that.

The history of American railroads is not an argument for leaving all to the businessman and if some of the energetic men who made great fortunes out of the railroads were national benefactors some were morally on the level of Jesse James and charged a high price for their services, a high price in money and a higher price in damage to the social and political fabric. I am aware that things have changed, that the days of the robber barons are over or almost over (it is harder to be a robber baron than it used to be; there are more policemen of various kinds). But even if we believe all that business tells us about itself—and I don't believe quite all of it—we have to remember that in many parts of the world the robber

barons are still with us and are not, even in the kindest and most generous eyes, as much builders as were some of the most rapacious of the leaders and makers and exploiters of the American economy of the second
half of the nineteenth century.

The American businessman, looking abroad and conscious of the services he renders (and charges quite highly for), is liable to ignore important
facts about the outside world, facts that alter the picture he paints for himself and imposes on the American government, facts that demand a toleration of "unbusinesslike" methods that shocks the doctrinaires of "free enterprise." If the United States is going to have an economic foreign policy
it will have to deal with societies in which there is no business class or a
disastrously rapacious and incompetent business class and in which the only
substitute for the absent competent businessman is the state. And the
state may be the only competent manager of large-scale enterprise that the
country in question either has or can hope to have in the not-unlimited
time of competition with the rival Soviet system. This is, I think, the case
in India and will continue to be the case in the critical years in which the
fate of India—and more than the fate of India—will be decided.

Thus the exaltation of the businessman in the United States, the belief
that the standards of the American business economy are easily exported
and that there is something sinful in not admitting this fact, is a great
handicap to the government of the United States in its economic foreign
policy. It may be necessary to strengthen "socialist" economies, to accept
irritating political controls, to tolerate what are, objectively, absurdly wasteful ways of doing things simply because the world happens to be like that
and most foreign societies have no choice: they have no more right to have
an effective business class than they have to have an equivalent of Niagara
Falls or of the Grand Canyon.

It is only partly a paradox to suggest that the American businessman
(who sets the tone of a great deal of American life though perhaps not
quite so much as he thinks and as his predecessors did) is too modest. He
underestimates his own uniqueness. And when painful experience teaches
him that the business methods of other societies are very different from
and very inferior to his he is less prone to go up to the altar of the temple and thank God that he is not as other men than to think up ways of
converting the inferior European or Asian or African model into a 100 per
cent imitation of the 100 per cent American businessman.

This generous ambition is a foolish one. Though the American businessman is less conscious than he should be of his unique character, he is
more conscious than he should be of his unique role in making the American way of life that business has so deeply and, on the whole, so benefi-
cially marked. For the American economy is only a part of the American
way of life; the American businessman is only one of the makers of the

American economy. I have already alluded to the role of the politician in making and preserving the Union. But I would rank as equally important the role of the politician in producing the illusion (which has, I hold, often been the reality) of a nonbusiness power that could protect the average man both in his interests and in his sentiments. The democratic way of life, American version, has been largely a matter of making—not final, not profound, not revolutionary—adjustments in the way in which the American economy was run, adjustments that for a great part of its formative period, made the necessary harshness of that economy tolerable and did not destroy the faith of the average man in the American way. For there is apparently no way in which an economy can make the take-off, to use Professor W. W. Rostow's admirable metaphor, that does not involve suffering, injustice, flagrantly unequal ways of paying the costs, and the destruction of old and comforting habits.

The histories of Britain and the United States, of the Soviet Union and Communist China alike tell this story. That the story as told in the United States has been one of a continuing faith in the American process is due, as much as to any other group, to the much-maligned politicians who, high as was their price, delivered the goods, the climate of opinion, of generosity, of admiration for achievement in which the American businessman has flourished. And to return to my first theme, the American businessman has been the chief but not the sole maker of the American economic way of life and deserves half the praise he gives himself; and this is, I suspect, about the amount of praise that the American non-businessman gives him in his friendly but rather skeptical fashion.

I have already dealt, though necessarily briefly, with the mechanics of the American political system and their relevance to the contemporary world of political competition. Now, dealing with the marks of American society, it is necessary to say something of the mark that the American politician represents. Earlier I spoke of the special service, the fundamental service that the politician has rendered in creating and preserving the Union and in creating the climate of opinion in which the businessman has been able to work with such success. I now want to describe briefly not only the achievement of the politician but his methods, the peculiar contribution he makes to the American way of doing things and the revelation of the character of American society that this political way provides.

I have alluded to the low ideological content of American party politics and have indicated my doubts as to whether the United States would gain by adopting rigorously doctrinaire systems of party differentiation and organization. Here I shall take it for granted that a political system which organizes democratic choice of persons and, very loosely, controls pressures from one group or another, serves a useful purpose and preserves a higher degree of human values than does the rival and in many ways efficacious system that we call communism. For communism, we must remember, is a *political* solution to the economic problem of the forced-draft progress of a backward agrarian society into the modern technological society. It is the political omnipotence of the Russian Communist party that accounts for Sputnik, as well as for the now-visible economic progress to the threshold of abundance that marks the Soviet Union.

The problem in a sense is the same everywhere. How is one to provide the necessary political authority without which the jump over to the more abundant life, to Professor Galbraith's affluent society, cannot be made? Within wide political controls, often intermittent in action, the American method has been to leave the specifically economic problems to a specifically economic class and to leave the organization of consent to this delegation of power and the tempering of its results to a specifically political class. The two classes, naturally, are never in a state of complete harmony or mutually supporting cooperation. There is almost always an imbalance and one can, I think, see two such imbalances in recent American history: in favor of politics under Presidents Roosevelt and Truman; in favor of business under President Eisenhower. Neither imbalance was necessarily wrong, at the time it occurred, and I ostentatiously refrain from asserting that either was necessarily right.

But, given this distribution of functions and this imbalance, what has been the peculiarly American character, the American mark of the American politician? It has not been true all the time that the American politician was not a doctrinaire. Jefferson was one of the most skilled, perhaps the most skilled, of American politicians but he was by temperament a doctrinaire. There was a basic unshakable bias in Lincoln, a bias in favor of human as against legal or property rights, a conviction that some institutions, however respectable by age, however plausible their claims as practical solutions, were wrong. But, like Jefferson, Lincoln was what is called a "practical politician." He worked, and knew he could only work, in the terms given by the American situation. Also, Lincoln was more self-critical than Jefferson and carefully distinguished between his public and his private duties and feelings. Neither was prepared to let the best be the enemy of the good. And in this sense of realities, in this readiness to separate the ideal from the immediately attainable, these two great Americans were representative and serviceable American politicians. They bear the American mark.

At the other end of the scale we have the moral equivalents of the "robber barons" — the city and state bosses. These, in their scientifically purest form, emptied politics of any.trace of ideology that might have been found in it. Their allegiance to one party rather than the other — Democratic in New York, Republican in Philadelphia — was purely formal, purely traditional, and there is no known instance of their sacrificing their own interests and that of their organizations to the remote principles and needs of the national parties. Yet these odious figures played a useful, though expensive, part in the adjustment to the often painful and novel necessities of the American way of life of the millions of immigrants who provided the necessary labor force on whose blood, sweat, and tears the American economy was erected. The bosses may not notably have diminished the blood and sweat, but they did diminish the tears. They made the new society intelligible, tolerable, and gave it a human aspect, including in that aspect the very human attribute of erratic and all the more welcome favor.

That the bosses overcharged for their services is not to be doubted. They were brothers under the skin of the magnates who also overcharged but, like them, did in fact give much in return. And as in the parallel case of the business magnates, the greatest cost was not the cost in dollars, it was the cost in faith in the honest purpose of government, in the rational basis of society. If the average American still finds it difficult to take the purposes and practices of government seriously, or to understand European faith in the potentialities of government, that is part of the price paid for the rule of the bosses and for their utility (which I do not deny was real). And since there are a vast number of things that should be done, even in the United States, and that can be done only by state action, the price is still being paid. If this leads to the postponement of necessary action in the public sector, it may in the world we must live in have a very high price indeed.

But between the great national figures and the mere bosses there lay and still lies a useful and necessary class — the politicians, who are more than mere manipulators of consent though less than statesmen of long and adequately profound views. Because they are not doctrinaire, they are taken more seriously than if they set forth a system of coherent or allegedly coherent doctrines in the European fashion. That the American does not take intellectual coherence seriously enough is a proposition I shall advance in another context. But here I am concerned with a particular fact about American life, a mark of American life. That mark is the readiness of Americans to do things, to try experiments even though total consistency would debar them from trying the experiments, since they are often inconsistent with what is alleged to be the basic and unbreakable principle of American life.

For if principles will not break they will bend, and how adroit the American politician is in bending them! How many Americans appreciate enough the astonishing ingenuity of the primary system? When the late Senator Borah laid it down that, even if a candidate advocated the nationalization of the means of production, distribution and exchange, if he had won in a Republican primary he was a Republican, he turned with great boldness the flank of the unideological party system and made it possible for all doctrines to be advocated without any basic doctrines being called in question — or observed. Needless to say, there is an ugly side to this flexibility.

"You can have fascism in the United States. Only you must call it anti-fascism." This alleged saying of the late Huey Long has about it an ominous ring of plausibility. Coming from a continent which has pursued consistency to the edge of suicide regarding a rival society that has not yet found a way of escaping from crippling and dangerous dogma, where it is still necessary in fact to find a harmony between the needs of the world of Sputnik and the H-bomb and the systematic intuitions of a man (Karl Marx) who died before the invention of the internal-combustion engine or of an economically effective dynamo, it is hard not to prefer the American way.

If there has been anything to worry about in the state of the American public mind in the past few years, it has been a tendency to react along doctrinaire lines, to be blinded by phrases, by slogans, by the erection of the slogans into systems of political action. Lincoln, Jefferson, Boss Tweed, and Senator Borah would have, in different ways, protested against this bad and new habit, and in our rapidly changing world to react to the doctrines and actions of the adversary merely on a plan of negation and contradiction laid down in advance is to be profoundly anti-American. But I firmly believe that the pragmatic genius of the American people will come to the rescue. So will the boredom of the American people with an attitude that does not pay off quickly and that calls for a degree of doctrinal rigidity which comes hard to the people who have taken the simple political structure of 1789 and have made of it a "more perfect union" than any Hamilton dreamed of.

Now to conclude. I have had to put on one side one of the most visible marks of the American genius, the proliferation of private organizations that strikes even a visitor from England with surprise and strikes a Frenchman or a German with far more surprise. These societies, service clubs, churches, organizations for all conceivable and some barely credible projects have been since Tocqueville's time a mark of American society. And they have, usually in a more respectable way, done much the same kind of service as the political machines. (I say usually, because a body like the Ku Klux Klan is very American. Even the Mafia has taken on an American covering, and what could be less ideological than the higher direction of the Teamsters?)

The societies, secular as well as religious, have mediated between the vast, formal, often apparently inhuman claims of the "American way of life" and the harassed, intimidated, bewildered private citizen. They have also provided a channel for the zeal and energy of countless men and women whom the mere politics of the regular parties repelled or bored.

To keep so much zeal from going sour is no small contribution to the commonwealth! And in the endless combinations and permutations of American societal life, the American is made to feel and act as a social and not as a merely economic or political animal. His total role in life has been enriched, even by intrinsically foolish activities.

Even the busybody is better than the type that the Greeks called "the idiot," the citizen who had no interest in the well-being of the commonwealth. To be a member of a society is as much the mark of the American as any I can think of. I can only note the fact and promise to deal with one or two aspects of it at another time.

But as I have expounded my, on the whole, optimistic view of the marks of American society I have been conscious of some natural skepticism: "Hasn't he read Riesman?" "Hasn't he read *The Organization Man?*" "Doesn't he know that the young today eschew the life of action and its risks and seek, in the womb of Big Business or Big Government, the security that they crave? What is the use of stressing the virtues and even the vices of traditional American polity when it is being changed visibly and at high speed under one's eyes?"

I have read both Mr. Riesman and Mr. Whyte; I have observed some of these phenomena for myself. I think that American society and, notably, American education require a great deal of rethinking in theory and in practice. I am aware that the high degree of mutual toleration that marks the class structure of contemporary America is, for some, simply a proof that the American people can be bought off by a share in the more abundant material life, that this toleration may not survive a serious falling off in economic well-being and that, as has been asserted, it is paid for very highly by the universal acceptance of a gadget-and-gimmick civilization. Socrates thought the unexamined life not worth living but the unexamined life is the American life of the current American ideal—if it can be dignified by such a noble name.

So runs the argument of the devil's advocate. I do not deny its plausibility or its important element of truth. But the "organization man" is not the only type of American nor even the only type of American businessman and he is not, as commonly pretended, the whole man of the organization chart. The organization ideal takes less out of a man and uses up less of the whole man than did the simple ferocious life of the businessman in pursuit of "the bitch goddess, Success" a generation ago. And the results of this loss of the full measure of devotion are, on the whole, good.

The United States is now affluent enough, if not to afford all that Professor Galbraith wants, at least to afford far more laziness and consequent opportunity for reflection than any past American generation has known. There may be a falling off in economic drive and productivity, but the competition to which I constantly recur is not only in material well-being but in real or alleged goods of the spirit, of what we loosely call culture. "Things are in the saddle, and ride mankind" was written a century ago. Was Emerson describing his age or prophesying ours? I think he has done both, and one cure for some current pessimism is to look back at the plausible descriptions and predictions of doom that previous generations have listened to, with half an ear cocked and half a complete dose of faith in the prophets. I have no belief that American productive capacity and genius is in for any serious decline. My fears are of the direction that may be given to that capacity and genius.

If American society preserves, in necessarily modified forms, the marks that I have sought to identify, it will survive its ordeal. I think it can do now without bosses. Business will never again have and never again should have its old immunity from criticism and control. The national government will never be "cut down to size" in face of the political power of the Soviet Union and Communist China. The day (I am ready to say, alas!) is to the strong, the united, the politically dominated. But American society has immense historical as well as physical resources. If it can assess those assets correctly and take corrective action it will hold its own in the battle that is a battle for mankind's hopes as well as its fears.

If America can hold her own can she fail, in a not-limitlessly remote future, to win? For the "new man the American" represents not only a unique historical experience but an intrinsically attractive type of human possibility. If you (and we in Western Europe are included in that "you") can survive the immediate and terrible crisis that faces all of us, we shall find much working for us in men's minds and hearts. If we and you deserve leadership, it will be offered to us. And one of the ways that we can deserve it is for each of the countries of the Western alliance to hold to that which is good in its own traditions. If Americans do that, intelligently, the battle is more than half won and a great part of that half is, to be sure, in our own hearts, that we believe in and trust our way of dealing with the human situation. So far we have no need to fear comparison or competition.

Eric Larrabee   The Self-Conscious Society   **8**

*Eric Larrabee was born in Melrose, Massachusetts, on March 6, 1922,
and was educated at Harvard, from which he received his Bachelor's degree
in 1943.* He has been an editor of a number of magazines, including
Harper's *and* American Heritage *and is currently editor of* Horizon. *He
has also written* American Panorama *(1957) and* American Perspectives
(1961). He is a regular contributor to Harper's Magazine. *In his discussion
here of European and American culture Larrabee suggests that the European
expresses his contempt for us by admiring the wrong things, and he concludes that America has produced a culture. For related ideas, see Bell,
Barzun, Kouwenhoven.*

Americans are perennially fascinated by themselves. Perhaps this is a
bad sign. If you were to judge us by Whitehead's axiom, that "a culture is in its finest flower before it begins to analyze itself," then we have
never had a flowering, for Americans were self-conscious from the start.
What is this new man? asked Hector St. Jean de Crevecoeur, and the
new men have ever since been eagerly offering to tell him.

We originated in an act of self-consciousness. We had not "always"
been here, and a nation had to be declared into existence. "The land was
ours," as Robert Frost says it, "before we were the land's." The consequences of being what we were, of being this people, on these shores,
had to be worked out. Frost conceives of us responding "to the land
vaguely realizing westward," which is a partial way of putting what Turner called the Frontier Hypothesis—that our character was shaped in the
experiences of subduing a continent—but one could as well say that we
built in the wilderness what Europe had caused us to desire.

Americans are self-conscious because, among other things, they wonder
about whether they exist. Is there really any such animal as the American,
or are we simply a subspecies of European transplanted to another hemisphere? Our forefathers scorned this derivative role. They liked to think
of themselves as standing on the threshold of a new age. In his book,
The American Adam, R. W. B. Lewis has shown how much it meant to

From *The Self-Conscious Society* by Eric Larrabee (Garden City, N.Y.: Doubleday &
Company, Inc., 1960), pp. 11-23. Reprinted by permission of the author.

the young republic to imagine life and history as just beginning. "American glory begins at the dawn," said Noah Webster, and in a short story of Hawthorne's there is a great bonfire on the midwestern prairie in which the world's "outworn trumpery" is destroyed. "Our national birth . . ." said the *Democratic Review,* "separates us from the past and connects us with the future only."

We came from Europe, but we are different. On this axis has turned a dialogue in which generations of Americans have been involved, despite themselves, and often involved as though for the very first time. By dismissing the past we became what Lewis calls a "one-generation culture," with the sons rediscovering afresh the same questions that had preoccupied their fathers. "We regularly return," Lewis writes, "decade after decade and with the same pain and amazement, to all the old conflicts. . . . We consume our powers in hoisting ourselves back to the plane of understanding reached a century ago and at intervals since."

A hundred years pass and we are still tugging at the same apron strings. It seems almost as though time had stood still since that August day in 1837 when Emerson got up before the Phi Beta Kappa society at Harvard and announced that our day of dependence, "our long apprenticeship to the learning of other lands," was drawing to a close. It is one of the central Emersonian ideas; he regularly returns to it. "We have listened too long to the courtly muses of Europe," he was to be saying later in the same speech. Emerson is American self-consciousness personified; he made it a permanent condition. One would still be hard put to tell how we think differently from Europeans without continually echoing Emerson—his sense of the immediate present, of the importance of the commonplace, of the infinity within the individual.

Can we never, he once asked, "can we never extract this tapeworm of Europe from the brain of our countrymen?" Apparently not, for we are still struggling to liberate what he called "the American scholar"—and what we would call educated Americans—from the dominance of European ideas. Our higher education is still, for better or worse, Europe-oriented. It has to be. What else is there to study? We still have no better way of learning and exercising the disciplines of art, literature, and history than on the Western European past, no other sciences than those of quantitative measurement which Europeans developed, no other place to visualize ourselves historically but at the end of Western Man's long adventure. In their sense we cannot innovate, we can only continue and amplify. "You must remember," a French government official told me once in Dakar, "that even the most cultivated American is not cultured in our sense of the word."

Nor is he in ours, but I did not tell him that. He would not have understood if I had. For it is one of the conditions of the transatlantic dialogue that communication goes only one way; the Americans do not talk back. We care about things they do not care about; we are engaged in experimenting with a mass society which they regard either with amusement or abhorrence. So we do not take great trouble to explain ourselves. We understand them better than they understand us, if only because we have for so long used them as models, measuring ourselves against the only standards available, and deploring the fact that our governmental machinery is not British, our music is not German, and our drug stores are not French cafes. We are endlessly polite to European visitors, especially the ones who detest us as wholeheartedly as, let us say, Mrs. Trollope ("I do not like them," she said of us. "I do not like their principles. I do not like their manners. I do not like their opinions.") If they do not understand us, however, it is because they do not know there is anything here to be understood.

The London *Times* Literary Supplement on "The American Imagination," which is near-embarrassing in its praise for our accomplishments, is in part remarkable for being such a rare and recent example of sympathetic treatment. As one of its contributors is led to remark, "up to now the Englishman has not seen American literature as a sufficiently distinctive thing for him to devote himself to it as a separate area of study." American professors who have gone abroad to teach have frequently commented on related but less engaging attitudes. Stanley Williams, who went to Sweden on an exchange from Yale, has recorded the "contempt for our country which in some measure every teacher of American literature in Europe still encounters," while Perry Miller, who went to Holland from Harvard, speaks of "the deep and ubiquitous anti-Americanism that the visitor gradually senses behind the most charming cordiality and hospitality."

The European has another gambit in this game, which is to "admire" America for the wrong things. He too regards our culture — to the extent that culture consists of art, learning, and civilized behavior generally — as an imitation of his own, and therefore without value or interest. What strikes his eye are the aspects unfamiliar to him, such as tall buildings, teen-age singers, and too many automobiles — *ergo,* America is the country of tall buildings, teen-age singers, and too many automobiles. He has, as Professor Miller says, "no conception of America which permits it to figure as a champion of culture." When Professor Williams lectured at Uppsala on American literature to an audience of thirty, his wife lectured in an adjacent hall on the American kitchen to an audience of three hundred.

This kind of argument, from the European point of view, has the merit of being impossible for them to lose or for us to win. Whatever is "cultured" is theirs, whatever is not is ours. Some years ago, for example,

D. H. Lawrence, in an essay called "Men Must Work and Women as Well," excoriated us for failing to invent a machine which could wash dishes. Lawrence's point was that the modern world, which he vaguely identified with science and Henry Ford, led people to expect freedom from drudgery without actually being able so to free them. There will always be dirty work, Lawrence said. His was the authentic voice of feudalism; he not only wanted servants to stay in their place but to love it. ("In the past, cooks really enjoyed cooking and housemaids enjoyed scrubbing.") Now that we have provided the washing machine, I am sure that Lawrence—were he around—would be the first to damn it as an example of our soul-less, gadget-ridden materialism.

One reason the European intellectual feels this way is that he sees in America what Europe, but for the grace of history, might be. Matthew Arnold—who divided society into Barbarians, Philistines, and the True Populace—saw America as just like Europe but "with the Barbarians quite left out. This leaves the Philistines," he added, "as the great bulk of the nation . . . so it is notorious that the people of the United States issue from this class, and reproduce its tendencies. . . ." We have enlarged the middle class to include the whole society, and made a middle class out of what in Europe would be a lower middle class, a petty bourgeoisie. We have given European vulgarity a chance to express itself. "The ugliness of American decoration," writes Mary McCarthy, "American entertainment, American literature—is not this . . . a manifestation of all the backwardness, deprivation, and want that arrived here in boatloads from Europe? . . . The European traveler, viewing with distaste a movie palace, or a motorola, is only looking into the terrible concavity of his continent of hunger inverted startlingly into the convex."

Eric Hoffer implies something similar when he speaks of this country as being built by "hordes of undesirables"—the useless and defeated—who came here from the Old World. "History contrived an earth-shaking joke," he writes, "when it lifted by the nape of the neck lowly peasants, shopkeepers, laborers, paupers, jailbirds, and drunks from the midst of Europe, dumped them on a vast, virgin continent and said: 'Go to it; it is yours!'" They were, as Santayana characterized them, "voluntary exiles . . . the wilder instincts or dissatisfaction tempted them beyond the horizon." And Thornton Wilder describes them as a "selection of a selection," adding that they all had one thing in common: "Their sense of identity did not derive from their relation to their environment. . . . They did not need to be supported, framed, consoled, by the known, the habitual, the loved. . . ." They were the self-conscious, the self-selected.

From being the pagan paradise of Chateaubriand's Noble Savage, America in the mind of Europe has therefore drifted into becoming a new barbarism—a place where all their own tawdriness manifests itself, a playground of the forbidden, a teasing stimulant for jaded appetites. This imaginary America is a necessary backdrop to such thoroughly European works as, for instance, Weill and Brecht's *Rise and Fall of the City of Mahogonny* (1930), with its nightmare landscape located somewhere between Florida and the Gold Rush, and populated by the dregs of the Weimar Republic. The American novelists who have since then appealed to a postwar French taste are those who satisfy a similar craving for both vitality and decay, the sense of incongruously brutal and energetic disintegration. After Andre Gide was discovered in North Africa by the British Eighth Army in May, 1943, he announced that he had been reading with great pleasure one of the most sparely written but pointlessly murderous of American detective stories, Dashiell Hammett's *Red Harvest* —"A remarkable achievement," he called it, "the last word in atrocity, cynicism, and horror."

One could as easily counterpoise the two continents to one another on other scales, depending on the degree of calculation and mendacity on either side. I do not mean to suggest that we also have not found it convenient to cultivate our own myths about Europe, and to belabor what Melvin Lasky, then the American editor of a German-language magazine published under the Occupation, called the "old, tortured formulae"— "The Jeffersonian version: America is young, vigorous, progressive; Europe is old, tired, decadent. The Jamesian version: America is raw, innocent, susceptible; Europe is dark, engaging, profound. The Rooseveltian version: America is practical, experimental, promising; Europe is helpless, reactionary, tragic."

These are the stereotypes in which every "cultivated" American is to some extent involved, since the higher learning in America has had to take account of them—if only to throw them off. At worst, the result has been a screen of fixed ideas between the educated and the day-to-day world around him—the "popular culture" that has only recently become a proper subject of serious attention. Even at their best, the stereotypes of Europe and America have given a kind of hothouse immortality to our sense of unfulfilled mission. We are still trying to explain ourselves, especially to ourselves. We are still insisting that the differences have not yet been quite correctly defined, and we are still invigorated by every real or imaginary bond to Europe that we break. We are young again every time we think how unlike Europe we are.

The obstacles that education puts between us and our native culture vary, of course, from generation to generation. The domain of ideas is no more free than any other from fashionable enthusiasms or sudden, unexplained declines; and in our own time these oscillations have been deep and rapid. They hit different people, moreover, at different times, for in a multilayered and widely spread society what to some may be a new and

amusing view of America will seem old hat to others, and the irreverence
of the advanced may look like sacrilege to the backward. When the editors of *Partisan Review* came to conduct a symposium in 1952 called
"Our Country and Our Culture," they were reminded by at least one
contributor that such a title would have been inconceivable for the *PR*
of two decades earlier; it would have been considered sentimental and
chauvinistic, while the idea of trying to adapt oneself to the present-day
environment — suggested by the symposium prospectus — would have been
regarded, and not only by *PR* readers, as outrageous.

Less than ten years ago I would have described the atmosphere of colleges and universities — in fact, I may as well admit that I did so describe
it — as "pervasively antipathetic" to most of what interests me about America. Needless to say, it is now nothing of the kind. What was then a
minority view has since become a fad, and before long — shameful thought!
— will perhaps turn into an orthodoxy as blind and inflexible as the one
the minority then thought it was attacking. My generation, children of
parents who had been liberated by the skepticism of the 1920s, grew up
in thorough familiarity with the idea that contemporary America was a
suitable object for ridicule and satire. But these approaches seemed to
have no bearing on the home country that was revealed to our startled
gaze when the smoke of World War II cleared away; and I can well
remember the exhilaration of reading, in *Harper's Magazine* for October
1946, a remark of the Denver poet-businessman Thomas Hornsby Ferril
to the effect that America, "having won world leadership by default, has
a renaissance by the tail and doesn't know it."

In retrospect, one might possibly argue that we do indeed have a renaissance by the tail, but it is certainly no longer true that no one knows
it. Self-disparagement has for some time now ceased to be a dominant
theme. With the turn of the mid-century came a stream of books in which
the national virtues were celebrated, and the appearance of the *Partisan
Review* symposium not long afterward represented, in a manner of speaking, the surrender of the last citadel of fastidious literary despair. These
were years of organized communal soul-searching. It became respectable,
if not conventional, for academics to join with businessmen in meditative
discussions, for corporations to subsidize art, and for highbrows to vie
with middlebrows in their curiosity about lowbrow culture. It was a
great period for giving conferences, which might be called the Group
Therapy Method of trying to find out who we are — of trying, as Margaret Mead put it at the Corning Conference in 1951, "to make self-consciousness bearable to Americans."

But a renaissance? Many of the statistics are, of course, impressive.
In 1952 *Science* magazine published an article called "The American Explosion," by Fenton B. Turck, in which numbers of them were assembled.

Turck combined on one graph fifty-three of the possible indexes of national vitality in such a way as to show that the broken line, rising intermittently from 1890 to 1940, takes a sharp bend upward in the ensuing decade. Increases begin to come, not by addition, but by multiplication; the progression goes geometric—a greater increase in the use of electricity than in the entire time since electric power became available, a greater increase in the output of petroleum than in all the years since oil was discovered, more Bibles sold than in the previous forty years, and so on, *ad nauseum.* Turck also produced one piece of data which threatens to outlive us all: in 1951 Americans spent more money on classical music concerts than on baseball games—a fact that has constantly reappeared ever since, like an incantation, whenever anyone was determined to demonstrate our cultural maturity.

But a renaissance?

There are historical precedents for such things. First come the innovators of less than first-rate ability who try out new techniques; France had to have its Hardy before it got Corneille and Racine, England had to have Kyd's *Hamlet* before it could have Shakespeare's. (Our 'twenties and 'thirties were similarly tentative and half-baked.) Then, after victory in war—the Armada? V-J Day?—there is a great surge of national energy and the floodgates open. But is this it? The conditions have been fulfilled and the stage is set. We look about ourselves and wait. Where are the actors? Admittedly, we are not going to know it instantaneously when our indigenous geniuses arrive; they will not come bearing packages neatly labeled "masterpiece." Indeed we will be lucky if we even guess the medium in which the major talents of the time will turn out to have expressed themselves—the traditional forms like novels and poetry? or something private and unknown, like a diary? or something unprecedented, like a movie or a jazz recording? We shall not know until too late.

Yet we are far enough into this high point of the human experience to know that it is not quite what we had in mind. We are ill at ease in Zion. After fifteen years of unexampled prosperity we are as nervous about it as when we began, and cyclic changes now come so rapidly that we are still worrying about one extreme when its opposite overtakes us. Voices were still being raised to decry conformity among the youth when the Beatniks came along, taking the sermons about gray flannel suits to heart, and creating a whole new area of potential anxiety by changing the uniform to blue-jeans and beards. I know it is conventional to attribute the general air of American malaise to the Cold War, or the Bomb, or the "rapid pace of daily life," or something, but I am quite convinced that these amount to nothing alongside the unusual nature of our self-consciousness—this curious state of being aware of every breath and gesture, but uncertain what they all add up to.

"It is difficult to be an American," as Thornton Wilder said, in his
Charles Eliot Norton lectures at Harvard in 1952, "because there is as
yet no code, grammar, decalogue by which to orient oneself. Americans
are still engaged in inventing what it is to be an American. That is at
once an exhilarating and a painful occupation. All about us we see the
lives that have been shattered by it—not the least those lives that have
tried to resolve the problem by the European patterns."

There is, however, one unexpected advantage in being an invented people, in lacking the roots to the land and to history that makes a "nation"
in the normal sense of the word. This is our implicit internationalism.
Having been colonials—and in this respect South America is on a par
with North—we have been able to borrow in all directions, with equan-
imity, from the entire patrimony of the earth. Since we had to go so
often to Europe "for our cultural equipment," wrote the Mexican essayist Alfonso Reyes, we "in this way have become accustomed to handle
ideas of foreign origin as though they were our own." We do not think
of our difficulties and their solution as parochial, but assume that what
works for us will work elsewhere. "The American makes no distinction,"
as Sartre puts it, "between American reason and ordinary reason. . . . The
peculiarity of the American . . . is the fact that he regards his thought as
universal." He has, in Thornton Wilder's phrase, "the first planetary
mind." . . .

The writer wishes he could protect himself against the charge of being
too optimistic, since it will quickly appear to the reader that I regard
many conventional worries as groundless, and take pleasure in many of
the aspects of mass culture, so-called, which numerous critics have defined
as poisonous and contemptible. Perhaps I can only excuse myself by saying that I fear for my country, and judge it harshly, but on a different
set of standards. I take it that our experiment with the twentieth century
—with the marriage of industrialism and democracy, or whatever you
want to call it—is being carried on by proxy for the rest of mankind;
and I care less whether we achieve one more "high" civilization than that
the experiment be carried through to the end, come what may.

"It is the destiny of America," as the English writer Wyndham Lewis
said it for us, "not to be just another 'great nation,' but to be the great,
big, promiscuous grave into which tumble, and there disintegrate, all that
was previously race, class, or nationhood." This is no virtue of ours; we
happened into it three hundred years ago—all starry-eyed with innocence,
greed, and aspiration—when we stumbled onto the richest continent that
divine bounty had provided. We are what we are; our only justification
will be to have been something more. What is required is not only of our
society but of the individuals in it; for the way forward will need new
men and women, and first they must exist. "A radical transformation

might well begin here on this broad continent"—the words are, surprisingly enough, Henry Miller's—"for this is the crucible, the fiery furnace in which the soul of man is being tried to the utmost. If Europe is playing a losing game, we are playing a still more perilous one. We are nearer the end, further gone in every respect."

And if we lose, we lose for all.

"Process" is the American quality

John A. Kouwenhoven   **What's "American" about America?**   **9**

John Atlee Kouwenhoven, teacher and writer, was born in Yonkers, New York, in 1909. He graduated from Wesleyan University and received his Master's degree (1933) and Ph.D. (1948) from Columbia University. He is presently professor of English at Barnard College. His works include Adventures of America, 1857–1900 *(1938),* Columbia Historical Portrait of New York *(1953),* Made in America *(1948). In the following essay, Professor Kouwenhoven attempts to determine the American quality by examining twelve American "artifacts," ranging from the Manhattan skyline, through jazz, to chewing gum in order to find a common element. For related ideas, see Parkes, Rostow, Nairn, Larrabee, Fitch.*

The discovery of America has never been a more popular pastime than it is today. Scarcely a week goes by without someone's publishing a new book of travels in the bright continent. Magazines here and abroad provide a steady flow of articles by journalists, historians, sociologists, and philosophers who want to explain the United States to themselves, or to itself, or to others.

The discoverers of America have, of course, been describing their experiences ever since Captain John Smith wrote his first book about America almost three hundred and fifty years ago. But as Smith himself noted, not everyone "who hath bin at Virginia, understandeth or knows what

From *The Beer Can by the Highway* by John A. Kouwenhoven. Copyright © 1961 by John A. Kouwenhoven. Reprinted by permission of Doubleday & Company, Inc. Quotations from *Pudd'nhead Wilson*, pp. 208–211, by Mark Twain, are reprinted by permission of Harper & Row, Publishers.

Virginia is." Indeed, just a few years ago the Carnegie Corporation, which supports a number of college programs in American Studies, entitled its quarterly report "Who Knows America?" and went on to imply that nobody does, not even "our lawmakers, journalists, civic leaders, diplomats, teachers, and others."

There is, of course, the possibility that some of the writers who have explored, vicariously or in person, this country's past and present may have come to understand or know what America really is. But how is the lay inquirer to judge which accounts to trust? Especially since most of the explorers seem to have found not one but two or more antipodal and irreconcilable Americas. The Americans, we are convincingly told, are the most materialistic of peoples, and, on the other hand, they are the most idealistic; the most revolutionary, and, conversely, the most conservative; the most rampantly individualistic, and, simultaneously, the most gregarious and herdlike; the most irreverent toward their elders, and, contrariwise, the most abject worshipers of "Mom." They have an unbridled admiration of everything big, from bulldozers to bosoms; and they are in love with everything diminutive, from the "small hotel" in the song to the "little woman" in the kitchen.

Maybe, as Henry James thought when he wrote *The American Scene,* it is simply that the country is "too large for any human convenience," too diverse in geography and in blood strains to make sense as any sort of unit. Whatever the reason, the conflicting evidence turns up wherever you look, and the observer has to content himself with some sort of pluralistic conception. The philosopher Santayana's way out was to say that the American mind was split in half, one half symbolized by the skyscraper, the other by neat reproductions of Colonial mansions (with surreptitious modern conveniences). "The American will," he concluded, "inhabits the skyscraper; the American intellect inherits the Colonial mansion." Mark Twain also defined the split in architectural terms, but more succinctly: American houses, he said had Queen Anne fronts and Mary Ann behinds.

And yet, for all the contrarieties, there remains something which I think we all feel to be distinctively American, some quality or characteristic underlying the polarities which — as Henry James himself went on to say — makes the American way of doing things differ more from any other nation's way than the ways of any two other Western nations differ from each other.

I am aware of the risks in generalizing. And yet it would be silly, I am convinced, to assert that there are not certain things which are more American than others. Take the New York City skyline, for example — that ragged man-made Sierra at the eastern edge of the continent. Clearly, in the minds of immigrants and returning travelers, in the iconography of the admen who use it as a backdrop for the bourbon and airplane luggage they are selling, in the eyes of poets and of military strategists, it is one of the prime American symbols.

Let me start, then, with the Manhattan skyline and list a few things which occur to me as distinctively American. Then, when we have the list, let us see what, if anything, these things have in common. Here are a dozen items to consider:

The Manhattan skyline	Mark Twain's writing
The gridiron town plan	Whitman's *Leaves of Grass*
The skyscraper	Comic strips
The Model-T Ford	Soap operas
Jazz	Assembly-line production
The Constitution	Chewing gum

Here we have a round dozen artifacts which are, it seems to me, recognizably American, not likely to have been produced elsewhere. Granted that some of us take more pleasure in some of them than in others—that many people prefer soap opera to *Leaves of Grass* while others think Mark Twain's storytelling is less offensive than chewing gum—all twelve items are, I believe, widely held to be indigenous to our culture. The fact that many people in other lands like them too, and that some of them are nearly as acceptable overseas as they are here at home, does not in any way detract from their obviously American character. It merely serves to remind us that to be American does not mean to be inhuman—a fact which, in certain moods of self-criticism, we are inclined to forget.

What, then, is the "American" quality which these dozen items share? And what can that quality tell us about the character of our culture, about the nature of our civilization?

Skylines and Skyscrapers

Those engaged in discovering America often begin by discovering the Manhattan skyline, and here as well as elsewhere they discover apparently irreconcilable opposites. They notice at once that it doesn't make any sense, in human or aesthetic terms. It is the product of insane politics, greed, competitive ostentation, megalomania, the worship of false gods. Its by-products, in turn, are traffic jams, bad ventilation, noise, and all the other ills that metropolitan flesh is heir to. And the net result is, illogically enough, one of the most exaltedly beautiful things man has ever made.

Perhaps this paradoxical result will be less bewildering if we look for a moment at the formal and structural principles involved in the skyline. It may be helpful to consider the skyline as we might consider a lyric poem, or a novel, if we were trying to analyze its aesthetic quality.

Looked at in this way, it is clear that the total effect which we call "the Manhattan skyline" is made up of almost innumerable buildings, each in competition (for height, or glamour, or efficiency, or respectability) with all of the others. Each goes its own way, as it were, in a carnival of rugged architectural individualism. And yet—as witness the universal feeling of exaltation and aspiration which the skyline as a whole evokes— out of this irrational, unplanned, and often infuriating chaos, an unforeseen unity has evolved. No building ever built in New York was placed where it was, or shaped as it was, because it would contribute to the aesthetic effect of the skyline—lifting it here, giving it mass there, or lending a needed emphasis. Each was built, all those now under construction are being built, with no thought for their subordination to any over-all effect.

What, then, makes possible the fluid and ever-changing unity which does, in fact, exist? Quite simply, there are two things, both simple in themselves, which do the job. If they were not simple, they would not work; but they are, and they do.

One is the gridiron pattern of the city's streets—the same basic pattern which accounts for Denver, Houston, Little Rock, Birmingham, and almost any American town you can name, and the same pattern which, in the form of square townships, sections, and quarter sections, was imposed by the Ordinance of 1785 on an almost continental scale as what Wolfgang Langewiesche has called "a diagram of the idea of the Social Contract," a blueprint for a future society in which men would live each in his own domain, free and equal, each man's domain clearly divided from his neighbor's.

Whatever its shortcomings when compared with the "discontinuous patterns" of modern planned communities, this artificial geometric grid— imposed upon the land without regard to contours or any preconceived pattern of social zoning—had at least the quality of rational simplicity. The section lines, along which roads and fences run due north-south and due east-west, and which are so clearly visible from a plane over most of the U.S.A., make most of the nation exactly what an airplane pilot wants country to be: graph paper. As Langewiesche, the pilot, has said: "You can time your [plane's] shadow with a stop-watch across two lines, and get your exact speed. You can head the airplane down a section line and check your compass. But you hardly need a compass. You simply draw your course on the map and see what angle it makes. Then you cross the sections at the same angle. You can't miss. If you want to go exactly west, you get on a fence and follow it." And this simple gridiron pattern, mimicked in the city's streets, horizontally controls the spacing and arrangement of the isolated rectangular shafts which go to make up the skyline.

The other thing which holds the skyline's diversity together is the structural principle of the skyscraper. When we think of individual buildings, we tend to think of details of texture, color, and form, or surface ornamentation or the lack of it. But as elements in Manhattan's skyline, these things are of little consequence. What matters there is the vertical thrust, the motion upward; and that is the product of cage, or skeleton, construction in steel—a system of construction which is, in effect, merely a three-dimensional variant of the gridiron street plan, extending vertically instead of horizontally.

The aesthetics of cage, or skeleton, construction have never been fully analyzed, nor am I equipped to analzye them. But as a lay observer, I am struck by fundamental differences between the effect created by height in the RCA building at Rockefeller Center, for example, and the effect created by height. in Chartres cathedral or in Giotto's companile. In both the latter (as in all the great architecture of the past) proportion and symmetry, the relation of height to width, are constituent to the effect. One can say of a Gothic cathedral, this tower is too high; of a Romanesque dome, this is top-heavy. But there is nothing inherent in cage construction to invite such judgments. A true skyscraper like the RCA building could be eighteen or twenty stories taller, or ten or a dozen stories shorter, without changing its essential aesthetic effect. Once steel cage construction has passed a certain height, the effect of transactive upward motion has been established; from there on, the point at which you cut it off is arbitrary and makes no difference.

Those who are familiar with the history of the skyscraper will remember how slowly this fact was realized. Even Louis Sullivan—greatest of the early skyscraper architects—thought in terms of having to close off and climax the upward motion of the tall building with an "attic" or cornice which should be, in its outward expression, "specific and conclusive." His lesser contemporaries worked for years on the blind assumption that the proportion and symmetry of masonry architecture must be preserved in the new technique. If with the steel cage one could go higher than with load-bearing masonry walls, the old aesthetic effects could be counterfeited by dressing the facade as if one or more buildings had been piled on top of another—each retaining the illusion of being complete in itself. You can still see such buildings in New York: the first five stories perhaps a Greco-Roman temple, the next ten a neuter warehouse, and the final five or six an Aztec pyramid. That Aztec pyramid is simply a cheap and thoughtless equivalent of the more subtle Sullivan cornice. Both structures attempt to close and climax the upward thrust, to provide an effect similar to that of the *Katharsis* of Greek tragedy.

But the logic of the cage construction requires no such climax. It has less to do with the inner logic of masonry forms than with that of the old

Globe-Wernicke sectional bookcases, whose interchangeable units (with glass-flap fronts) anticipated by fifty years the modular unit systems of so-called modern furniture. Those bookcases were advertised in the nineties as "always complete but never finished" — a phrase which could with equal propriety have been applied to the Model-T Ford. Many of us remember with affection that admirably simple mechanism, forever susceptible to added gadgets or improved parts, each of which was interchangeable with what you already had.

Here, then, are the two things which serve to tie together the otherwise irrelevant components of the Manhattan skyline: the gridiron ground plan and the three-dimensional vertical grid of steel cage construction. And both of these are closely related to one another. Both are composed of simple and infinitely repeatable units.

The Structure of Jazz

It was the French architect, Le Corbusier, who described New York's skyline as "hot jazz in stone and steel." At first glance this may sound as if it were merely a slick updating of Schelling's "Architecture . . . is frozen music," but it is more than that if one thinks in terms of the structural principles we have been discussing and the structural principles of jazz.

Let me begin by making clear that I am using the term jazz in its broadest significant application. There are circumstances in which it is important to define the term with considerable precision, as when you are involved in discussion with a disciple of one of the many cults, orthodox or progressive, which devote themselves to some particular subspecies of jazz. But in our present context we need to focus upon what all the subspecies (Dixieland, Swing, Bop, or Progressive Jazz) have in common; in other words, we must neglect the by no means uninteresting qualities differentiating one from another, since it is what they have in common which can tell us most about the civilization which produced them.

There is no definition of jazz, academic or otherwise, which does not acknowledge that its essential ingredient is a particular kind of rhythm. Improvisation is also frequently mentioned as an essential; but even if it were true that jazz always involves improvisation, that would not distinguish it from a good deal of Western European music of the past. It is the distinctive rhythm which differentiates all types of jazz from all other music and which gives to all of its types a basic family resemblance.

It is not easy to define that distinctive rhythm. Winthrop Sargeant has described it as the product of two superimposed devices: syncopation and polyrythm, both of which have the effect of constantly upsetting rhymical expectations. Andre Hodeir, in his analytical study, *Jazz: Its Evolution and*

Essence, speaks of "an alternation of syncopations and notes played on the beat," which "gives rise to a kind of expectation that is one of jazz's sublest effects."

As you can readily hear, if you listen to any jazz performance (whether of the Louis Armstrong, Benny Goodman, or Dave Brubeck variety), the rhythmical effect depends upon there being a clearly defined basic rhythmic pattern to enforce the expectations which are to be upset. That basic pattern is the 4/4 or 2/4 beat underlying all jazz. Hence the importance of the percussive instruments in jazz: the drums, the guitar or banjo, the bull fiddle, the piano. Hence too the insistent thump, thump, thump, thump which is so boring when you only half-hear jazz—either because you are too far away, across the lake or in the next room, or simply because you will not listen attentively. But hence also the delight, the subtle effects good jazz provides as the melodic phrases evade, anticipate, and return to, and then again evade the steady basic four-beat pulse which persists, implicitly or explicitly, throughout the performance.

In other words, the structure of a jazz performance is, like that of the New York skyline, a tension of cross-purposes. In jazz at its characteristic best, each player seems to be—and has the sense of being—on his own. Each goes his own way, inventing rhythmic and melodic patterns which, superficially, seem to have as little relevance to one another as the United Nations building does to the Empire State. And yet the outcome is a dazzlingly precise creative unity.

In jazz that unity of effect is, of course, the result of the very thing each of the players is flouting: namely, the basic 4/4 beat—that simple rhythmic gridiron of identical and infinitely extendible units which holds the performance together. As Louis Armstrong once wrote, you would expect that if every man in a band "had his own way and could play as he wanted, all you would get would be a lot of jumbled-up, crazy noise." But, as he goes on to say, that does not happen, because the players know "by ear and sheer musical instinct" just when to leave the underlying pattern and when to get back on it.

What it adds up to, as I have argued elsewhere, is that jazz is the first art form to give full expression to Emerson's ideal of a union which is perfect only "when all the uniters are isolated." That Emerson's ideal is deeply rooted in our national experience need not be argued. Frederick Jackson Turner quotes a letter written by a frontier settler to friends back East, which in simple, unself-conscious words expressed the same reconciling of opposites. "It is a universal rule here," the frontiersman wrote, "to help one another, each one keeping an eye single to his own business."

One need only remember that the Constitution itself, by providing for a federation of separate units, became the infinitely extendible framework for the process of reconciling liberty and unity over vast areas and conflicting interests. Its seven brief articles, providing for checks and balances between interests, classes, and branches of the government, establish, in effect, the underlying beat which gives momentum and direction to a political process Richard Hofstadter has called "a harmonious system of mutual frustration" — a description that fits a jazz performance as well as it fits our politics.

The aesthetic effects of jazz, as Winthrop Sargeant long ago suggested, have as little to do with symmetry and proportion as have those of a skyscraper. Like the skyscraper, the total jazz performance does not build to an organically required climax; it can simply cease. The "piece" which the musicians are playing may, and often does, have a rudimentary Aristotelian pattern of beginning, middle, and end; but the jazz performance need not. In traditional Western European music, themes are developed. In jazz they are toyed with and dismantled. There is no inherent reason why the jazz performance should not continue for another 12 or 16 or 24 or 32 measures (for these are the rhythmic cages in jazz corresponding to the cages of a steel skeleton in architecture). As in the skyscraper, the aesthetic effect is one of motion, in this case horizontal rather than vertical.

Jazz rhythms create what can only be called momentum. When the rhythm of one voice (say the trumpet, off on a rhythmic and melodic excursion) lags behind the underlying beat, its four-beat measure carries over beyond the end of the underlying beat's measure into the succeeding one, which has already begun. Conversely, when the trumpet anticipates the beat, it starts a new measure before the steady underlying beat has ended one. And the result is an exhilarating forward motion which the jazz trumpeter Wingy Manone once described as "feeling an increase in tempo though you're still playing at the same tempo." Hence the importance in jazz of timing, and hence the delight and amusement of the so-called "break," in which the basic 4/4 beat ceases and a soloist goes off on a flight of fancy which nevertheless comes back surprisingly and unerringly to encounter the beat precisely where it would have been if it had kept going.

Once the momentum is established, it can continue until — after an interval dictated by some such external factor as the conventional length of phonograph records or the endurance of dancers — it stops. ("No stopping," as the signs on the thruways and parkways have it, "except for repairs.") And as if to guard against any Aristotelian misconceptions about an end, it is likely to stop on an unresolved chord, so that harmonically, as well as rhythmically, everything is left up in the air. Even the various coda-like devices employed by jazz performers at dances, such as the corny old "without a shirt" phrase of blessed memory, are often harmonically unresolved. They are merely conventional ways of saying "we quit," not, like Beethoven's insistent codas, ways of saying, "There now; that ties off all the loose ends; I'm going to stop; now; done; finished; concluded; signed, sealed, delivered."

We think of jazz as a twentieth-century phenomenon, and it is true that it did not emerge as a national music until after the First World War. But there are close (and unexplored) analogies between jazz and other forms of popular arts which have deep roots in our national life. One is the nineteenth-century minstrel show. Constance Rourke gives a vivid description of it in her classic work on *American Humor:*

> Endmen and interlocutors spun out their talk with an air of improvisation. . . . In the dancing a strong individualism appeared, and the single dancer might perform his feats on a peck measure, and dancers might be matched against each other with high careerings which belonged to each one alone; but these excursions were caught within the broad effect. Beneath them all ran the deep insurgence of the Negro choruses . . . and the choral dancing of the walk-around made a resonant primitive groundwork.

Here we have several analogies with the structure of jazz—especially the improvisatory manner and the individual flights of fancy and fantasy held together by a rhythmic groundwork (the 4/4 beat of the walk-around). And there are other ways in which jazz is related to the minstrel show. The minstrel characters—Jim Crow, Zip Coon, Dan Tucker—were blackface creations, and many jazz musicians, both white and Negro, perpetuate the atmosphere of burnt-cork masquerade.

Related to these analogies are those between the form of jazz and the form of the humorous monologue, the dominant form in the tradition of American humor, from Seba Smith's Mayor Jack Downing to Mark Twain and Mr. Dooley and on down to the TV and night-club entertainers of our own time. In these humorous monologues the apparent "subject" is of as little importance as is the tune from which a jazz performance takes off. It is the "talking around" the subject without hitting it, the digressing and ramifying, which matters.

Twain and Whitman

Since Mark Twain is the acknowledged master of the humorous monologue in our literature, let us look at an example of his work. His writing was, of course, very largely the product of oral influences. He was a born storyteller, and he always insisted that the oral form of the humorous story was high art. Its essential tool (or weapon), he said, is the pause—which is to say, timing. "If the pause is too long the impressive point is passed," he wrote, "and the audience have had time to divine that a surprise is intended—and then you can't surprise them, of course." In other words, he saw the pause as a device for upsetting expectations, like the jazz "break."

Mark, as you know, was by no means a formal perfectionist. In fact he took delight in being irreverent about literary form. Take, for example,

his account of the way *Pudd'nhead Wilson* came into being. It started
out to be a story called "Those Extraordinary Twins," about a youthful
freak consisting, he said, of "a combination consisting of two heads and
four arms joined to a single body and a single pair of legs—and I thought
I would write an extravagantly fantastic little story with this freak of nature for hero—or heroes—a silly young Miss [named Rowena] for heroine,
and two old ladies and two boys for the minor parts."

But as he got writing the tale, it kept spreading along and other people
began intruding themselves—among them Pudd'nhead, and a woman named
Roxana, and a young fellow named Tom Driscoll, who before the book
was half finished had taken things almost entirely into their own hands
and were "working the whole tale as a private venture of their own."

From this point, I want to quote Mark directly, because in the process
of making fun of fiction's formal conventions he employs a technique which
is the verbal equivalent of the jazz "break"—a technique of which he
was a master.

> When the book was finished and I came to look round to see what had
> become of the team I had originally started out with—Aunt Patsy Cooper,
> Aunt Betsy Hale, the two boys, and Rowena the light-weight heroine—
> they were nowhere to be seen; they had disappeared from the story some
> time or other. I hunted about and found them—found them stranded,
> idle, forgotten, and permanently useless. It was very awkward. It was
> awkward all around, but more particularly in the case of Rowena, because
> there was a love match on, between her and one of the twins that con-
> stituted the freak, and I had worked it up to a blistering heat and thrown
> in a quite dramatic love quarrel, [now watch Mark take off like a jazz
> trumpeter flying off on his own in a fantastic break] wherein Rowena
> scathingly denounced her betrothed for getting drunk, and scoffed at his
> explanation of how it had happened, and wouldn't listen to it, and had
> driven him from her in the usual "forever" way; and now here she sat
> crying and brokenhearted; for she had found that he had spoken only the
> truth; that it was not he, but the other half of the freak that had drunk
> the liquor that made him drunk; that her half was a prohibitionist and
> had never drunk a drop in his life, and although tight as a brick three
> days in the week, was wholly innocent of blame; and indeed, when sober,
> was constantly doing all he could to reform his brother, the other half,
> who never got any satisfaction out of drinking, anyway, because liquor
> never affected him. (Now he's going to get back on the basic beat again.)
> Yes, here she was, stranded with that deep injustice of hers torturing her
> poor torn heart.

Mark didn't know what to do with her. He couldn't just leave her there,
of course, after making such a to-do over her; he'd have to account to
the reader for her somehow. So he finally decided that all he could do
was "give her the grand bounce." It grieved him, because he'd come to
like her after a fashion, "notwithstanding she was such an ass and said

such stupid, irritating things and was so nauseatingly sentimental"; but it had to be done. So he started Chapter Seventeen with: "Rowena went out in the back yard after supper to see the fireworks and fell down the well and got drowned."

> It seemed abrupt (Mark went on), but I thought maybe the reader wouldn't notice it, because I changed the subject right away to something else. Anyway it loosened up Rowena from where she was stuck and got her out of the way, and that was the main thing. It seemed a prompt good way of weeding out people that had got stalled, and a plenty good enough way for those others; so I hunted up the two boys and said "they went out back one night to stone the cat and fell down the well and got drowned." Next I searched around and found old Aunt Patsy Cooper and Aunt Betsy Hale where they were aground, and said "they went out back one night to visit the sick and fell down the well and got drowned." I was going to drown some of the others, but I gave up the idea, partly because I believed that if I kept that up it would arouse attention . . . and partly because it was not a large well and would not hold any more anyway.

That was a long excursion—but it makes the point: that Mark didn't have much reverence for conventional story structure. Even his greatest book, which is perhaps also the greatest book written on this continent— *Huckleberry Finn*—is troublesome. One can scarcely find a criticism of the book which does not object, for instance, to the final episodes, in which Tom rejoins Huck and they go through that burlesque business of "freeing" the old Negro Jim—who is, it turns out, already free. But, as T. S. Eliot was, I think, the first to observe, the real structure of *Huck Finn* has nothing to do with the traditional form of the novel—with exposition, climax, and resolution. Its structure is like that of the great river itself— without beginning and without end. Its structural units, or "cages," are the episodes of which it is composed. Its momentum is that of the tension between the river's steady flow and the eccentric superimposed rhythms of Huck's flights from, and near recapture by, the restricting forces of routine and convention.

It is not a novel of escape; if it were, it would be Jim's novel, not Huck's. Huck is free at the start, and still free at the end. Looked at in this way, it is clear that *Huckleberry Finn* has as little need of a "conclusion" as has a skyscraper or a jazz performance. Questions of proportion and symmetry are as irrelevant to its structure as they are to the total effect of the New York skyline.

There is not room here for more than brief reference to the other "literary" items on our list: Whitman's *Leaves of Grass,* comic strips, and soap opera. Perhaps it is enough to remind you that *Leaves of Grass* has discomfited many a critic by its lack of symmetry and proportion, and that Whitman himself insisted: "I round and finish little, if anything; and could not, consistently with my scheme." As for the words of true poems, Whitman said in the "Song of the Answerer"—

> They bring none to his or her terminus or to be content and full,
> Whom they take they take into space to behold the birth of stars, to learn one of the meanings,
> To launch off with absolute faith, to sweep through the ceaseless rings and never be quiet again.

Although this is not the place for a detailed analysis of Whitman's verse techniques, it is worth noting in passing how the rhythm of these lines reinforces their logical meaning. The basic rhythmical unit, throughout, is a three-beat phrase of which there are two in the first line (accents falling on *none, his,* and *term . . . be, tent,* and *full*), three in the second (*take, take,* and *space . . . hold, birth, stars : . . learn, one, mean*), and three in the third (*launch, ab, faith . . . sweep, cease, rings . . . nev. qui, gain*).

Superimposed upon the basic three-beat measure there is a flexible, non-metrical rhythm of colloquial phrasing. That rhythm is controlled in part by the visual effect of the arrangement in long lines, to each of which the reader tends to give equal duration, and in part by the punctuation within the lines. For example, the comma pause after the second three-beat measure in line two (after *stars)* tends, since the first line consisted of two such measures, to establish an expectation of rest which is upset by the line's continuing for another measure. Then, in the final line, the placement of the comma pause reverses the pattern, requiring a rest after the first measure and doubling up the remaining two.

It is the tension between the flexible, superimposed rhythm of the rhetorical patterns and the basic three-beat measure of the underlying framework which unites with the imagery and the logical meaning of the words to give the passage its restless, sweeping movement. It is this tension and other analogous aspects of the structure of *Leaves of Grass* which give to the book that "vista" Whitman himself claimed for it.

If I may apply to it T. S. Eliot's idea about *Huckleberry Finn,* the structure of the *Leaves* is open at the end. Its key poem may well be the "Song of the Open Road," as D. H. Lawrence believed. "Toward no goal," Lawrence wrote. "Always the open road. Having no direction even . . . This was Whitman. And the true rhythm of the American continent speaking out in him."

As for the comics and soap opera, they too—on their own frequently humdrum level—have devised structures which provide for no ultimate climax, which come to no end demanded by symmetry or proportion. In them both there is a shift in interest away from the "How does it come out?" of traditional storytelling to "How are things going?" In a typical installment of Harold Gray's *Little Orphan Annie,* the final panel shows Annie walking purposefully down a path with her dog, Sandy, saying:

"But if we're goin', why horse around? It's a fine night for walkin' . . . C'mon, Sandy . . . Let's go . . . " (It doesn't even end with a period, or a full stop, but with the conventional three dots or suspension points, to indicate incompletion.) So too, in the soap operas, *Portia Faces Life,* in one form or another, day after day, over and over again. And the operative word is the verb "faces." It is the process of facing that matters.

America is Process

Here, I think, we are approaching the central quality which all the diverse items on our list have in common. That quality I would define as a concern with process rather than product—or, to re-use Mark Twain's words, a concern with the manner of handling experience or materials rather than with the experience or materials themselves. Emerson, a century ago, was fascinated by the way "becoming somewhat else is the perpetual game of nature." The universe, he said, "exists only in transit," and man is great "not in his goals but in his transitions."

This preoccupation with process is, of course, basic to modern science. "Matter" itself is no longer to be thought of as something fixed, but fluid and ever-changing. The modern sciences, as Veblen observed forty years ago, cluster about the "notion of process," the notion of "a sequence, or complex, of consecutive change." Similarly, modern economic theory has abandoned the "static equilibrium" analysis of the neo-classic economists, and in philosophy John Dewey's instrumentalism abandoned the classic philosophical interest in final causes for a scientific interest in the "mechanism of occurrences"—that is, process.

It is obvious, I think, that the American system of industrial mass production reflects this same focus of interest in its concern with production rather than products. And it is the mass-production system, *not* machinery, which has been America's contribution to industry.

In that system there is an emphasis different from that characteristic of handicraft production or even of machine manufacture. In both of these there was an almost total disregard of the means of production. The aristocratic ideal inevitably relegated interest in the means exclusively to anonymous peasants and slaves; what mattered to those who controlled and administered production was, quite simply, the finished product. In a mass-production system, on the other hand, it is the process of production itself which becomes the center of interest, rather than the product.

If we are aware of this fact, we usually regard it as a misfortune. We hear a lot, for instance, of the notion that our system "dehumanizes" the worker, turning him into a machine and depriving him of the satisfactions of finishing anything, since he performs only some repetitive operation. It is true that the unit of work in mass production is not a product but an operation. But the development of the system, in contrast with Charlie Chaplin's wonderful but wild fantasy of the assembly line, has shown the intermediacy of the stage in which the worker is doomed to frustrating boredom. Merely repetitive work, in the logic of mass production, can and must be done by machine. It is unskilled work which is doomed by it, not the worker. More and more skilled workers are needed to design products, analyze jobs, cut patterns, attend complicated machines, and coordinate the processes which comprise the productive system.

The skills required for these jobs are different, of course, from those required to make handmade boots or to carve stone ornament, but they are not in themselves less interesting or less human. Operating a crane in a steel mill, or a turret lathe, is an infinitely more varied and stimulating job than shaping boots day after day by hand. A recent study of a group of workers on an automobile assembly line makes it clear that many of the men object, for a variety of reasons, to those monotonous, repetitive jobs which (as we have already noted) should be — but in many cases are not yet — done by machine; but those who *like* such jobs like them because they enjoy the process. As one of them said: "Repeating the same thing you can catch up and keep ahead of yourself . . . you can get in the swing of it." The report of members of a team of British workers who visited twenty American steel foundries in 1949 includes this description of the technique of "snatching" a steel casting with a magnet, maneuvered by a gantry crane running on overhead rails:

> In its operation, the crane approaches a pile of castings at high speed with the magnet hanging fairly near floor level. The crane comes to a stop somewhere short of the castings, while the magnet swings forward over the pile, is dropped on to it, current switched on, and the hoist begun, at the same moment as the crane starts on its return journey. (And then, in words which might equally be applied to a jazz musician, the report adds:) The whole operation requires timing of a high order, and the impression gained is that the crane drivers derive a good deal of satisfaction from the swinging rhythm of the process.

This fascination with process has possessed Americans ever since Oliver Evans in 1785 created the first wholly automatic factory: a flour mill in Delaware in which mechanical conveyors — belt conveyors, bucket conveyors, screw conveyors — are interlinked with machines in a continuous process of production. But even if there were no other visible sign of the national preoccupation with process, it would be enough to point out that it was an American who invented chewing gum (in 1869) and that it is the Americans who have spread it — in all senses of the verb — throughout the world. A non-consumable confection, its sole appeal is the process of chewing it.

The apprehensions which many people feel about a civilization absorbed with process—about its mobility and wastefulness as well as about the "de-humanizing" effects of its jobs—derive, I suppose, from old habit and the persistence of values and tastes which were indigenous to a very different social and economic system. Whitman pointed out in *Democratic Vistas* ninety years ago that America was a stranger in her own house, that many of our social institutions, like our theories of literature and art, had been taken over almost without change from a culture which was not, as ours is, the product of political democracy and the machine. Those institutions and theories, and the values implicit in them, are still around, though some (like collegiate gothic, of both the architectural and intellectual variety) are less widely admired than formerly.

Change, or the process of consecutive occurrences, is, we tend to feel, a bewildering and confusing and lonely thing. All of us, in some moods, feel the "preference for the stable over the precarious and uncompleted" which, as John Dewey recognized, tempts philosophers to posit their absolutes. We talk fondly of the need for roots—as if man were a vegetable, not an animal with legs whose distinction it is that he can move and "get on with it." We would do well to make ourselves more familiar with the idea that the process of development is universal, that it is "the form and order of nature." As Lancelot Law Whyte has said, in *The Next Development in Man:*

> Man shares the special form of the universal formative process which is common to all organisms, and herein lies the root of his unity with the rest of organic nature. While life is maintained, the component processes in man never attain the relative isolation and static perfection of inorganic processes . . . The individual may seek, or believe that he seeks, independence, permanence, or perfection, but that is only through his failure to recognize and accept his actual situation.

As an "organic system" man cannot, of course, expect to achieve stability or permanent harmony, though he can create (and in the great arts of the past, has created) the illusion of them. What he can achieve is a continuing development in response to his environment. The factor which gives vitality to all the component processes in the individual and in society is "not permanence but development."

To say this is not to deny the past. It is simply to recognize that for a variety of reasons people living in America have, on the whole, been better able to relish process than those who have lived under the imposing shadow of the arts and institutions which western man created in his tragic search for permanence and perfection—for a "closed system." They find it easy to understand what that very American philosopher William James meant when he told his sister that his house in Chocorua, New Hampshire, was "the most delightful house you ever saw; it has fourteen doors, all opening outwards." They are used to living in grid-patterned cities and towns whose streets, as Jean-Paul Sartre observed, are not, like those of European cities, "closed at both ends." As Sartre says in his essay on New York, the long straight streets and avenues of a gridiron city do not permit the buildings to "cluster like sheep" and protect one against the sense of space. "They are not sober little walks closed in between houses, but national highways. The moment you set foot on one of them, you understand that it has to go on to Boston or Chicago."

So, too, the past of those who live in the United States, like their future, is open-ended. It does not, like the past of most other people, extend downward into the soil out of which their immediate community or neighborhood has grown. It extends laterally backward across the plains, the mountains, or the sea to somewhere else, just as their future may at any moment lead them down the open road, the endless-vistaed street.

Our history is the process of motion into and out of cities; of westering and the counter-process of return; of motion up and down the social ladder — a long, complex, and sometimes terrifyingly rapid sequence of consecutive change. And it is this sequence, and the attitudes and habits and forms which it has bred, to which the term "America" really refers.

"America" is not a synonym for the United States. It is not an artifact. It is not a fixed and immutable ideal toward which citizens of this nation strive. It has not order or proportion, but neither is it chaos except as that is chaotic whose components no single mind can comprehend or control. America is process. And in so far as Americans have been "American" — as distinguished from being (as most of us, in at least some of our activities, have been) mere carriers of transplanted cultural traditions — the concern with process has been reflected in the work of their heads and hearts and hands.

Old ideas and assumptions have been found wanting

10

John G. Sproat   **Recent Trends in American Social Thought**

John G. Sproat, born in 1921 in Los Angeles, studied English and History at San Jose State College. He received his Master's degree (1952) and Ph.D. (1959) from the University of California at Berkeley. During the 1961-1962 academic year, he was Fulbright Lecturer at the University of Hamburg, where the following selection was written. He is currently professor of history at Lake Forest College, Illinois. In this selection, originally an informal conversation for a German audience, Professor Sproat discussed the changing concepts of success and achievement, the American spiritual revival, and the idea of progress in American society. For related ideas, see Schlesinger, Sr.; Herberg; Fuchs; Cox; Toynbee; McConnell.

During the past 10 or 15 years, a good many intellectuals in the United States have been conducting what might be called an "agonizing reappraisal" of American social thought and its basic assumptions. A staggering number of books and magazine articles has bombarded the reading public with critiques of American life, inquiries into the nature of the American experience, and supposedly definitive interpretations of the American temper, past and present. There is, for example, Max Lerner's massive effort to interpret all of American civilization in terms of his own liberal point of view. There is Daniel Boorstin's *The Americans,* an effort to interpret American civilization in terms of the colonial experience. There is C. Wright Mills's highly provocative but vulnerable *The Power Elite,* which asserts that America is ruled by a readily-identifiable "power elite," composed of a relatively few men at the top. There is *Life* magazine's search, among members of the "power elite," for new statements of America's purposes and the American Mission. Louis Hartz, in his *The Liberal Tradition in America,* argues that the truly unique feature of American civilization is the lack of a feudal past, the lack of an aristocratic heritage. David Potter, on the other hand, suggests in *People of Plenty* that the American experience can be understood best in terms of the abundance with which Americans have been blessed throughout their history.

Few of these works have been lacking in distinction and all have contributed something of value to the historian, who must evaluate the past, and to the social scientist, who must wrestle with the problems of the present. There are, of course, many more such works, for I have named only a few.

What has prompted these scholars to call into question the assumptions of the past and by clear implication to seek new ideologies? Doubtless the rapidity of changes in technology and science, plus an awareness that the future requires clear thinking, have persuaded many people that now is a time for reassessment. But there is more to be said in answer to the question. Obviously, in the minds of many Americans, the old ideologies and assumptions have been found wanting in relevance and utility in the modern age. Something has gone wrong with the view of the world that

"Recent Trends in American Social Thought" by John G. Sproat is reprinted from *Spirit of a Free Society: Essays in Honor of Senator James William Fulbright on the Occasion of the Tenth Anniversary of the German Fulbright Program* (Heidelberg: Quelle and Meyer, Publishers, 1962), pp. 104–121, by permission of the author and publisher.

Americans had at the turn of the century and even in the early 1930's. Something has indeed gone wrong. The three decades between 1930 and 1960 have an intensity peculiar in history — an almost cataclysmic intensity that would be enough to weaken the most deeply-rooted of man's beliefs about himself and his fellow men. One calamity has followed another, one change has overlapped the other: world-wide depression and sharp class struggle; war on a scale hitherto unknown to man; the bureaucratized murder of millions in concentration camps; the development of weapons with destructive potentialities that stagger the imagination; the aggressive advance of totalitarianism, first as Fascism and then under the benevolent guise of Communism. Little wonder that for many members of the generation most affected by these dismal happenings it has become all but impossible to hold on to ideologies that once seemed so congenial. As for the assumptions that underlay the old ideologies, events have swept away many of these, too.

A basic assumption in American thought, for example, has been the idea of progress, stemming from the Enlightenment view of man as a perfectible being. During the past 30 years man has shown himself to be anything but perfectible, and the whole idea of progress has been at least partially discredited in both formal and public philosophy in America. For toward what goal is man to progress given the recent evidence that he prefers to regress? Or examine the idea that man is master of his destiny — an idea which underlies much of the American belief in individualism. If the economic collapse of the 1930's and the ensuing barbaric war were not enough to persuade man that some vengeful force, cosmic or otherwise, had a power that he could not even contemplate, surely the ominous threat of nuclear annihilation has disabused him of vain ideas. Ideology has become a nasty word for some people, while for others it is a word to be profoundly distrusted. Yet because man does not, after all, live by bread alone, he is compelled to replace ideas which have failed him or which seem to lack relevance with some other views about the nature of man, society, and the universe. Thus the disillusionment of the postwar years gives way, these days, not so much to optimism and hope as to the search for an ideological way out of present dilemmas. . . .

Most of what I have said applies as much to European intellectual activity in recent years as to American. But there is one unique feature of the American effort that, so far as I know, Europeans have not had to contend with. And that is the fact that American social thought has always been too hopelessly fragmented to admit of easy generalization or synthesis. Social philosophers have found it all but impossible to apply a single, formal ideological standard to the whole of the American experience. That experience has been too varied, too dynamic, too mutable, and perhaps too disordered and full of evident contradictions. Only the

Puritans, early in the history of Massachusetts Bay Colony, were able to offer a philosophy which could claim to encompass the beliefs of the community as a whole . . . . By the end of the 17th century it had lost much of its original meaning. Nothing that came later ever matched that earliest Puritan success — not Transcendentalism, not Social Darwinism, not Reform Darwinism, not even pragmatism and instrumentalism which offered explanations so congenial to what could be observed in American life. Each attempt to categorize the American experience in terms of a single ideology or set of assumptions was almost immediately confuted by other, equally valid interpretations.

And yet, American thinkers have never given up the quest for a single synthesis. In the end, they almost invariably emerge from their ruminations bearing such phrases as "the American Democratic Faith" or "the Democratic Way of Life" to describe the gist of their findings. Beset by their colleagues to be more precise about what they mean, they can only resort to describing — and, occasionally, to analyzing — a set of conditions and assumptions which, they argue, comprise the whole. Seldom can they elaborate on the synthesis itself.

Past experience has shown, I think, that this is the only meaningful approach one can take, if one would seek a satisfactory consideration of American social thought. Fragmented into 15 or more ingredients or basic assumptions, American ideology leaves to the intelligent observer the task of evolving a synthesis of the whole. Needless to say, any two observers seldom reach precisely the same conclusions.

I should like to examine, therefore, some of the basic assumptions of American social thought as I see them and to discuss how they have fared in this unsettled era of ours. To complete the pattern which I have been describing, I shall even attempt, at the end, to synthesize the components into a whole; but I warn you that the synthesis will be a very simple and, I think, very obvious one. Note, too, that when we examine these assumptions we are, in a real sense, dissecting the American national character, and perhaps this will serve us well in our attempt to delineate the Image of America today.

Often the statement is heard that Americans are a hard-working people, whose goal in life is success in the accumulation of material things. In that statement we encounter several basic assumptions of American ideology, as, for example, the assumption that Americans are convinced of the desirability of success and achievement. It is an assumption rooted deeply in the American past, when the high priests of Puritanism extolled the virtue of doing one's best so as to please God. It stems, too, from the actual experiences of the early Americans on the frontier in an overwhelmingly worldly environment. From the beginning, in the give and take existence on the frontier and in pioneer rural areas, men engaged in competition to see who could do best at a given task. The individual who achieved the most success in the quickest time often became the most respected member of the community. During the late 19th and early 20th centuries, however, the idea of success developed into a "cult of success," in which doing one's best came to mean simply accumulating as much money as possible and then displaying one's affluence as ostentatiously as possible. These were the years when Social Darwinism became the ideology of the American businessman and his apologists. Led by William Graham Sumner, a distinguished economist and sociologist at Yale University, a group of scholars and publicists seized on Herbert Spencer's effort to apply Darwin's biological theories to human society and found in it an easy rationale for the more predatory activities of the great American capitalists and entrepreneurs. Social Darwinism glorified the struggle of man against man in life, a struggle in which only the fittest survived. Thus the individual who achieved the most success in the quickest time now became not only the most respected member of the community, but the fittest member of society as well. If pressed for an explanation of the unethical, indeed unhumanitarian, aspects of their attitude, businessmen of the time could come up only with something along the lines of Commodore Vanderbilt's frank "The Public be damned!" approach, or perhaps with old John D. Rockefeller's heartfelt insistence that "God gave me my money!"

All the assumptions behind Social Darwinism received a near fatal shock in 1929, when the Great Depression settled over the country and struck at successful men, as well as at those who had not made it to the top. That experience caused many Americans to re-evaluate their concepts of success; but it should be noted that the re-evaluation did not deviate significantly from the essentially materialistic approach of the past. Success now came to be interpreted not so much in terms of money itself, which had been the case in the past, but in terms of job security or economic security. A generation of Americans grew up believing that success in one's work was to be measured in terms of how much unemployment compensation one received, what kind of retirement plan lay at the end of one's life work, what kind of group health insurance coverage a job offered, and so forth. Young people seemed to have no other goal in life but to go from school or college into a job that promised security, and they seemed consciously to shun any activity in which the element of risk or adventure played a part. No longer was John D. Rockefeller, the man who had created a great oil empire out of nothing, the ideal of the younger generation. Something called security, perhaps something called "welfarism", seemed to be replacing the older image in the minds of college students. Naturally, all this caused much shaking of heads among members of the older generation, who thought that America's morale was being weakened and that the structure of American society was in danger.

It is hardly surprising, therefore, that social thought in recent years has been concerned with the effects of this changing attitude toward the concept of success and achievement. Increasingly, Americans are asking themselves whether success is an end desirable in itself—whether there might not be higher goals in life than simply the top of the economic ladder. One of the strangest phenomena of modern America, it seems to me, is the middle-aged man, successful by any of the past standards, who is tormented by the suspicion that he is a failure. He turns everywhere in his restlessness seeking some sort of relief. Unable to find it in his business, he seeks it in activities outside his normal routine—in community activities, in work with his local schools, and in decidedly frivolous areas as well. Social psychologists are hard put to explain this man and the troubles lying behind his torment. Some say that the mass society has robbed him of his individuality and left him alone amidst a "Lonely Crowd." If so, it is at least encouraging to note that he is aware of something wrong in his life. Perhaps his torment today may cause him in the future to discover new and worthier standards of success. But if you asked me—or him—what those standards should be, the answers would be vague indeed.

An assumption closely related to the idea of success is that Americans are a people preoccupied with material comforts. Again, the truth of the assumption is rooted in past experience. After all, a pioneer people must be interested in material things. Concerned with the basic task of making a living, working hard to accumulate enough material things to make life bearable, they have little time for reflection or other philosophic activities. Moreover, early Puritanism glorified the acquisition of material things, albeit the injunction to be moderate in all things was intended to apply here as well as in matters of the spirit. Puritanism was as much a secular philosophy as a religion; but with the early breakdown of the structure of Puritanism, the secular, materialist aspects began to dominate the religious. No great harm resulted from this attitude in the early years of the republic, and it can be argued that Benjamin Franklin's *Poor Richard* expressed a rather good balance between the American desire to accumulate material things and the view that accumulation should never be an end unto itself.

But, again, later in the 19th century, in the period after the Civil War known as the Gilded Age, the American view toward material things developed into a concept which we might call the "divine right of property." Although some of the great entrepreneurs devoted themselves to the production of wealth in these years, a good many lesser men seemed concerned only with the accumulation of wealth. Moralists and social thinkers alike found much to deplore in this intensely materialistic society, but the only remedy most of them could offer was the regeneration of businessmen through time-tested religious means. These were not enough, and the concern of American thinkers about American materialism has persisted to the present day. Theodore Roosevelt, of course, had a somewhat different remedy to offer. Moral regeneration, he insisted, could be effected if one lived the "strenuous life." Activity would prevent America from "going soft." Roosevelt practiced what he preached, taking diplomats, cabinet members, and Supreme Court justices out on long, arduous hikes through Washington's hilly parks. Indeed, it was not an uncommon sight in those days to see the President striding briskly along a wooded path trailing behind him a bedraggled string of statesmen, politicians, and newsmen — all but Mr. Roosevelt panting and probably fearing that their hearts would give out at any moment. This was the "strenuous life," and Theodore Roosevelt thought that by putting activity almost on a spiritual plane he might persuade Americans to take their minds off material things.

Materialism still poses a social and moral problem for a good many Americans. What does one do with all the material things one accumulates? How many television sets can one own? How many automobiles can one family put to good use? Is it really necessary for a family to have not only a refrigerator but a deep freezer as well? Critics offer few alternatives to the present condition, save to insist that Americans must rise above materialism or that they must return to the old values of the past. Seldom do they specify just what it is that lies "above" materialism, and always they are confronted with the historical fact that the old values invariably glorified, in one form or another, the accumulation of material things. Even *Life* magazine's ambitious survey of great Americans has turned up very little in the way of a solution to this dilemma, except perhaps an appeal for spiritual revival.

But America has been experiencing something very close to a spiritual revival in recent years. One of the most interesting occurrences in recent American history is the religious revival led by the Reverend Dr. Billy Graham. Doubtless, you are familiar with Dr. Graham, for he has been inflicted on almost the entire world. Now Billy Graham, an able and conscientious minister of the Gospel, has nevertheless lent himself to the commercialization of religion in America — and, perhaps, in the rest of the world as well. Obviously, he has responded to a need in the United States, otherwise there would not be so many people flocking to his meetings, making professions of conversion and of spiritual remorse. The trouble is that these people neither stay converted nor very convincingly demonstrate that they are truly remorseful. It is all a rather superficial religious extravaganza, and I doubt very much that it serves the cause of heartfelt religious belief very well. Indeed, my own opinion is that this type of commercialized revivalism capitalizes on and exploits the very real anxiety that exists in the hearts of many Americans today.

There may well be a real need for spiritual revival in America. Certainly it is true that Americans have lost much of their old-time religious belief, or, at least, that the beliefs have been seriously weakened in modern times. But the ministers and the social critics must come up with something more than a simple demand for new emphasis upon old spiritual values. If material things are placed at the disposal of people and can be shown to lessen life's little drudgeries, then obviously people are going to want these material things. Moralists who deplore the altogether natural tendency of people to make life somewhat easier, and who offer little more than a clucking of tongues and a call to the "old-time religion" are really wasting everyone's time.

Another assumption in my earlier statement about Americans is that they are a hard-working people. Once again, past experience determined what the national character should be. In colonial days, a man either had to "make it" or fall by the wayside, and the only way to "make it" was to work hard. Americans in the past also played hard.

Indeed, they went about everything with an intensity, which reflected both the hardships of life and the demands imposed by the idea of success. It might be noted, however, that not all men in early America worked hard or succeeded at very much of anything. Large areas in the Carolinas, for example, were from the very beginning slum areas, and they have remained such to the present day. But by and large, hard work has been both the lot and the choice of the average American, and it is a characteristic that has been celebrated in fiction and essays throughout our history. Benjamin Franklin's *Poor Richard* combined hard work with a common sense approach to life, thereby establishing an ideal to which most Americans have always aspired. But with the rise of the "rags to riches" myth in the late 19th century, hard work assumed almost religious aspects. Horatio Alger, in his stories for young people, convinced a good many Americans that any boy could rise to the top of the economic and social ladder simply by practicing the traditional virtues of thrift, honesty, enterprise, and, most important, industry. Americans were tremendously attracted to this gospel of "rags to riches," and I do not doubt for a moment that a good many people still firmly believe in it. After all, American history contains just enough cases of people who *have* gone from rags to riches to make the idea a plausible one, and a few Americans, usually Texas oil men, still seem to prove the idea's validity.

Of course, the speculative boom of the late 1920's and the ensuing depression disabused most people of the view that hard work, alone, is enough to insure success in the world. Instead of working hard, indeed, too many people in the 1920's sought the quickest and easiest way of accumulating wealth — indiscriminate speculation on the stock market. Then during the 1930's the Federal government stepped in with recovery and reform measures, the effect of which was to lift from the shoulders of the average citizen the burden of independent economic survival. Whether a man works hard or not, he knows now that he is no longer entirely at the mercy of economic forces beyond his control. Doubtless, the advent of the democratic welfare state in America has contributed to a lessening of faith in the doctrine of hard work. Far more influential, however, has been the rise of the affluent society, in which, as a matter of pure fact, the individual simply does not have to work as hard as in bygone days in order to reach a comfortable level of living.

All this disturbs some American social thinkers and moralists, who charge that, as a nation, we are becoming lazy, that we think increasingly in terms of getting something for nothing. John Steinbeck, the American author, for example, argues that the slogan of the average American today seems to be: "A guy has to make a buck," and he has explored — and deplored — this attitude extensively in his most recent novel, *The Winter of Our Discontent*. But while the attitude is deplored, neither Steinbeck nor the other critics can provide an alternative attitude — save a plea for a renewed emphasis on the dignity of work. It remains to be seen whether anyone, in this age of seemingly permanent affluence, can be persuaded to work as hard as, say, 19th century Americans. Incidentally, when President Kennedy calls upon the American people for sacrifices, he is really asking them to work harder. The word sacrifice, as I have learned in conversations with you here at this conference, means something quite different to you than it does to us. To Americans it is not at all a dangerous word, but rather a term dealing with harder work and a greater sense of determination in what one does in life — a less haphazard attitude toward life in general than has been the case, according to President Kennedy, in the recent past.

One very basic assumption in American social thought is belief in the inevitability and desirability of progress. As I noted earlier, the belief has its roots in the Enlightenment and it found in America, from the beginning, a permanent, congenial home. No conservative opposition arose there to challenge it. No Edmund Burke stood up to question the assumption that progress itself might be questionable. Throughout the history of American thought, one finds renewed affirmations of both the desirability and the inevitability of progress — in Franklin, in Jefferson, in Madison, in Emerson, in James, in Dewey. Indeed, the belief is the very cornerstone of whatever is systematic in American social thought. Perhaps the belief was most widespread just after the turn of the century, in the years known as the Progressive Era of American politics. Progressives never doubted for a moment that man was a perfectible being, and they believed that, given adequate political instruments, man would work consistently to perfect his society. This was the great period of reform in modern American life, and the Progressives did some very important things with their weapon of political action. During those years Herbert Croly wrote his important book *The Promise of American Life,* in which the idea of progress was reaffirmed, but reaffirmed in terms of a collective approach to social problems rather than the old reliance upon the individual alone. Theodore Roosevelt was only the most influential of the politicians who took up Croly's ideas and began to interweave the idea of progress with the idea of the welfare state. Franklin D. Roosevelt's New Deal carried on this reaffirmation and restatement.

Yet, if the Progressive politicans and thinkers were able to instill new, vigorous life into the idea of progress, the practical experiences of Americans during the past 30 or 40 years have served to bring about a degree of disenchantment with the concept. Even before the Progressive Era was over, it became clear that the tools with which man was to create a more perfect society were weak, imperfect tools. The idea that man, by reforming his political machinery, could make a more perfect society proved illusory. Once they got into office, for example, some reformers turned into crooks. But above all, I think, disenchantment stemmed from the American people's misreading of Woodrow Wilson's idealism. Actually, the whole world misread Wilson—and most people still misread him. Perhaps Wilson himself should be blamed for the misreading, for he put his highly concrete views of man and the world in strongly moralistic terms. At any rate, the collapse of Wilsonian idealism at the end of the First World War accelerated general disenchantment with the idea of progress.

Today, the great task of liberal social thought in the United States is to recapture the old faith in progress; for liberalism itself is dead if liberals lose their belief in the inevitability of progress. Arthur M. Schlesinger, Jr., Adlai E. Stevenson, John Kenneth Galbraith, and John F. Kennedy, together with many other thinkers and writers, thus are engaged in a new search for means of recapturing faith in progress for the cause of liberalism in America. They have been restating the old convictions, but in new terms. Where is America to progress, they ask. To a better life, they answer—by which they mean a fuller realization of the American promise in all its aspects, material, spiritual, and moral. Americans must achieve the goal of equality for all citizens, and they must, above all, work constantly for world peace. With the achievement of general economic security, indeed, equality and peace have become the "great crusades" in modern America, the causes which most attract youth and the imaginative. "Sit-ins," "freedom rides," the Peace Corps—all of these activities demonstrate convincingly that the idea of progress still has validity to a good many, mainly young, Americans.

Frankly, I cannot imagine an American society in which the idea of progress lacked vitality. Yet, the idea has always been attacked by ultra-conservative elements in the body politic—elements which, by and large, have been outside the main stream of American thought. Most American conservatives are really only cautious liberals, and few in the past have been totally out of sympathy with the liberal tradition and the idea of progress. But one recalls John C. Calhoun and his futile effort to save the Old South, or the classical economists of the late 19th century led by William Graham Sumner, with their fixed, rigid economic "laws" and view of society. In our own time, there has been an ambitious effort to create, literally, a Burkean tradition in American thought—a tradition of European conservatism, that is. It is, of course, an exercise of intellectual futility, for few if any of the conditions favorable to true conservatism exist in the United States. Burkean conservatism, for example, rests on assumptions that are alien to the American experience. The attempt itself, however, is a rather healthy development, for it has stimulated young college people, especially, to think anew about the assumptions in American social thought. Because there has been a much-heralded "conservative revival" on the campus, there is also occuring a "liberal revival." I have no doubt but that the latter revival will long outlast the former, for the so-called New Conservatism is little more than a reiteration of the old 19th century doctrine of "the divine right of property."

For example, the stronghold of the young conservatives, the Neo-Burkeans, is an organization known as the Intercollegiate Society of Individualists (no member of the ISI has yet explained how you can have a society of individualists). The preamble to this organization's constitution is a high-sounding statement, full of beautifully expressed phrases—as that "foremost among the transcendent values is the individual's use of his God-given free will, whence derives his right to be free from the restrictions of arbitrary force." All well and good, and a statement most Americans can agree with. But a little farther on in this constitution, one learns that "when government interferes with the work of the market economy, it tends to reduce the moral and physical strength of the nation; that when it takes from one man to bestow on another, it diminishes the incentive of the first, the integrity of the second, and the moral autonomy of both." Which is to say that members of the ISI believe that the income tax, social security, free milk for school children, and so forth, are all immoral. You see, American conservatism can go nowhere save in the direction of further glorifying the divine right of property, which, in America, is money. All the rest is nonsense, frequently fatuous nonsense, as, for example, when these self-styled conservatives attempt to pass themselves off as moralists. At the height of the McCarthy period in the 1950's, a leading spokesman for the "new Conservatives" gave us a peek at the political morality of his movement when he observed, in apparent seriousness, that "McCarthyism is a movement around which men of good will and stern morality may close ranks"!

No, the liberal tradition *is* the American tradition, and no amount of intellectual juggling of historical fact can make it otherwise. Fundamental to the liberal tradition is the idea of progress, which liberals must revitalize if they are to keep America essentially what it has been in the past. Thus the work of contemporary liberal thinkers is something to study closely, in order to determine their success in recapturing or reaffirming the basic American faith.

Another ingredient in American social thought is humanitarianism. Perhaps this is the ingredient best known to the rest of the world. America has a strong, deeply-rooted tradition of reform that has always been essentially humanitarian in its approach to social and economic problems. Examples of this approach are legion, from the attempt during the colonial period to do away with imprisonment for debt, through the crusade to abolish slavery, to the current struggle to achieve first class citizenship for Negroes. Humanitarianism, like the idea of progress, is an essential part of American liberalism, but it also leavens responsible American conservatism, making the latter, as I have said, really only a more cautious liberalism.

At times in the past, the humanitarian outlook has provided Americans with a rationale for actions that raise doubts. For example, a good many people in the United States harbor feelings of guilt about the fact that we dropped the atomic bomb at Hiroshima. But most of them have rationalized their guilt by arguing that, in the long run, lives were saved by our action. Then there is the overly-zealous humanitarianism about which Graham Greene wrote in his book *The Quiet American*—a humanitarianism which is, for some Americans, an end in itself and which can become an essentially destructive force. I think that young Americans, in particular, are today very much aware of the dangers in this attitude, and I am much encouraged to note that volunteers for the Peace Corps seem to be taking a hard-headed, common sense view of the humanitarian role they are assuming. They are aware, in short, that American humanitarianism can make enemies as well as friends.

Two very basic assumptions lying behind all American social thought and seemingly in conflict with each other are, first, that Americans are a highly individualistic people, and, second, that they are also inveterate "joiners." Individualism as a national trait, or course, is common to all peoples who experienced the Reformation and the Enlightenment. It reached a high state of development in America because both movements found such congenial homes there and because physical conditions in the New World isolated men from one another and forced the individual to rely upon his own talents. The same isolation, plus the fact that man is by nature a gregarious animal, drove early Americans to seek the company of others and to join with them in collective enterprises at every possible opportunity.

These two strains in American thought have been in continuous, often strange, conflict throughout American history. Individualism has been championed by every collective interest that wished to further its own ends. Collectivism has been championed by reformers who insist that a collective approach to the problems of an industrial society is the only means of preserving individualism. The conflict, thus, is not only one of direct clash, but of rather chaotic intermingling as well.

Today, the tradition of individualism in America is in a state of crisis. For the growth of the mass society, an inevitable result of industrialization, has to an appreciable extent submerged the individual and rendered him a tool of mass advertising, mass entertainment, mass indoctrination. To many, it seems that the individual ultimately will be swallowed up by the mass, and virtually every commentator on recent trends in American social thought has called attention to this problem. Yet few have proposed viable solutions. Indeed, about the only strong check against the loss of individualism in American society seems to be the force of tradition—the tradition of individualism, which Americans have always revered and which they are loathe to abandon in any way today. Every attempt in the past to deny the individual his integrity or position has been strongly resisted, and so it is today. Yet time and events wear down resistance, and each year another little bit of individualism is gone, seemingly forever. The tyranny of the majority has always plagued the United States—or, at least, the threat of that tyranny has always concerned Americans and foreign observers. Tocqueville noted the threat more than a century ago. Calhoun laboriously tried to work out a system wherein minority opinion (albeit minority opinion of his own choosing) would be respected in American politics.

Today the loss of individualism is to be seen in politics, where there no longer seems to be a place for the maverick—the eccentric individual who stirs up things and keeps the politicians in power alert to their responsibilities. With two major parties in complete control of the political machinery, where can true dissent appear? Where can the man with really different ideas find a platform and an audience? The problem is made worse by the Cold War, which has placed a premium on political conformity and which has even led to a denial of certain basic rights in America. Any American can think as he pleases; but he must be cautious about what he says in public, regarding certain aspects of foreign policy and domestic security. The problem is a relative one, for Americans still enjoy as much free speech as any peoples in the world; but the trend is a dangerous one. It is also a universal trend, for individualism is being swallowed up by the mass in most parts of the world today and there seems little that one can do about it save reassert, continuously, the need to respect the dignity of the individual.

Patriotism, or love of America, has always been a part of social thought in the United States — and this ingredient, too, has undergone change in recent years. No longer do Fourth of July celebrations reflect an exciting, rather naive, completely open kind of patriotism. Today Americans take their patriotism pretty much for granted, feeling that open displays of loyalty are really not very necessary. Attempts to instill a more outspoken attitude, unfortunately, have been marked in recent years by the excessive and essentially false kind of "super-Americanism" that we associate with the late Senator McCarthy. In the 1960's there appears to be an awareness that patriotism must be sincerely felt; but most people know, too, that, in time of extreme tension, it can get out of control and result, as it did in the 1950's, in a whittling away at the Bill of Rights. Still, there are people who believe that one's loyalty to one's country must be advertised in neon signs, and these people profit from the tensions of the Cold War.

Finally, the democratic tradition itself forms an essential assumption in all American social thought. Does the tradition still have meaning in America? If we examine briefly the three elements in the democratic tradition, we can see that it has lost none of its appeal to the American people. First is the element of equality. Today the equalitarian principle shows more vitality in the United States than it has since the days of the abolitionist crusade before the Civil War. It is most evident among the Negro people, especially among young Negro people; but it is enjoying a great revival among whites, as well. I do not doubt for a minute but that most white Americans deep down have some feeling of satisfaction that the Negro today is doing for himself that which the white man has failed to do for him for so many years. Second, there is the conviction among Americans that their nation remains the "land of the free," the stronghold of man's inalienable rights. As I have noted, the Cold War poses a threat to this conviction and had resulted in attacks upon the Bill of Rights. But, on balance, the record of the American people in recent years is a good one. Momentary lapses into hysteria by some elements of the population have been countered by the good sense of the courts, of Congress, of the press, and of the public in general. Indeed, in one sense, recent attacks on the "rights of man" have served the useful purpose of alerting the people to the ever-present danger of their losing those rights in moments of fear and crisis.

Third, the democratic tradition in America still remains firmly grounded on a base of moral principle. Much has been said in recent years of the "moral crisis" in the United States. The fact is that moral crises appear periodically in every society, and not least in such an open society as the American people enjoy. No era in American history has been without its "moral crisis" — and usually critics have said too much and written too carelessly about these crises. For moralistic critics have a tendency to speak and write in very superficial terms, emphasizing the external and transient aspects of what they call immoralities. Too many moralists to-day, for example, ignore or gloss over the essential immorality of our age, which is the lawlessness in international affairs that sets an example leading to a breakdown of law, order, and morality in almost every aspect of human activity. If there is a "moral crisis" today, it is a world-wide crisis, not one confined exclusively to the United States. Minor scandals in government, cheating in university examinations, television quiz scandals, and the rest, are, in the larger scheme of things, really unimportant occurrences. They provide work for the everyday reformer and certainly should be dealt with by society. But the breakdown of law and order generally in the world breeds a contempt for moral principles that can do more to undermine free, democratic societies, than all other weapons of international Communism put together.

That Americans remain essentially moralistic in their world outlook is, I think, obvious. Indeed, they may too often take what George Kennan has called a moralistic, legalistic approach to world problems — an approach seen in the Open Door Policy, in the Spanish-American War, in American relations with Japan during the 1920's and 1930's, in World War II diplomacy, in relation to the Chinese Revolution, and, most recently, in the Cuban Fiasco. But I would emphasize that in foreign affairs the United States is still a young nation that has much to learn, and that already there are encouraging signs that it is learning well the lessons taught by past experiences. On the other hand, Americans will continue to think of foreign policy in moralistic terms, for they view themselves as a moralistic people — and this will lead to new mistakes in the future.

Yet, is not morality in foreign affairs a desirable attribute for a nation? If there are universal standards of right and wrong — standards agreed upon by men and nations convened in such an organization as the United Nations — surely Americans are not to be condemned for attempting to adhere to standards of right. The difficulty, of course, has always been in designating just what is moral and what is immoral; but I suggest that, in recent years, the area of choice has been appreciably narrowed for all of us.

In a very informal manner, I have discussed with you some of the basic assumptions of traditional social thought in America and I have tried to note the state of those assumptions today. To me, the only meaningful synthesis of all this is a simple one: that the American ideal is still a society of free men, acting responsibly to realize the fullest possible development of the individual. You will note that in that short phrase are to be found traces of all of the assumptions I have been talking about. The ideal has not always commanded the respect of all Americans; neither has it ever been ignored by most Americans. I suggest that the editors of *Life* magazine, in seeking a new statement of purpose for Americans, need look no further than to this simple ideal. I suggest that American foreign policy needs no other selling point, no other grandiose expression of purpose than this simple ideal. I am aware that man does not live by bread alone. I am also aware that, without bread, man does not live. But I think that, given bread, given opportunities for self-development, given economic stability, all men will in due time begin the pursuit of this ideal, even though they may express it in their own terms.

I admit that my views are rather traditionally and characteristically American, born out of a faith that man *was* born free and that his goal in life must always be to retain his freedom. But I think, too, that the ideal has universal appeal and is by no means the exclusive property of Americans. That it today is a part of the American Image is, I believe, simply the splendid good fortune of the American people.

**Anti-revolutionary,
conservative America**

Arnold Toynbee   America and the World Revolution

11

Arnold Toynbee is an eminent British historian and student of international affairs. His greatest work, A Study of History *(1934-1961), traces in twelve volumes, a pattern of growth, maturity, and decay in twenty-one different civilizations. Toynbee believes that a society thrives best when responding to a challenge, and that its most important task is to create a religion. He places his hope in the future formation of a spiritually oriented world society.*

The selection that follows is from a series of lectures delivered by Toynbee at the University of Pennsylvania in 1961. Toynbee's purpose is to explain what he terms America's abandoning of her original mission. In a way, Toynbee reflects Hannah Arendt's thesis that the French revolution is the significant international revolution. For related ideas, see Gabriel, Sproat, Parkes, Barzun.

From *America and the World Revolution* by Arnold J. Toynbee. © 1962 by Arnold J. Toynbee. Reprinted by permission of Oxford University Press, Inc. Pp. 16-26.

Today America is no longer the inspirer and leader of the World Revolution, and I have an impression that she is embarrassed and annoyed when she is reminded that this was her original mission. No one else laid this mission upon America. She chose it for herself, and for one hundred and forty-two years, reckoning from the year 1775, she pursued this revolutionary mission with an enthusiasm which has proved deservedly infectious. By contrast, America is today the leader of a world-wide anti-revolutionary movement in defence of vested interests. She now stands for what Rome stood for. Rome consistently supported the rich against the poor in all foreign communities that fell under her sway; and, since the poor, so far, have always and everywhere been far more numerous than the rich, Rome's policy made for inequality, for injustice, and for the least happiness of the greatest number. America's decision to adopt Rome's role has been deliberate, if I have gauged it right. It has been deliberate, yet, in the spirit that animates this recent American movement in reverse, I miss the enthusiasm and the confidence that made the old revolutionary America irresistible. Lafayette pays a high psychological price when he transforms himself into Metternich. Playing Metternich is not a happy role. It is not a hero's role, and not a winner's, and the player knows it. But, in those early nineteenth-century years when the real Metternich was fighting his losing battle to shore up the rickety edifice of restored 'legitimacy', who in the World would have guessed that America, of all countries, would one day cast herself for Metternich's dreary part?

What has happened? The simplest account of it is, I suppose, that America has joined the minority. In 1775 she was in the ranks of the majority, and this is one reason why the American Revolution has evoked a world-wide response. For the non-American majority of the majority, the American revolutionary appeal has been as attractive as it was for eighteenth-century America herself. Eighteenth-century America was still appreciably poorer than the richest of the eighteenth-century West European countries: Britain, Holland, the Austrian Netherlands, France. No doubt America was, even then, already considerably richer than Asia or Africa; yet, even measured by this standard, her wealth at that time was not enormous. What has happened? While the sound of the shot fired beside the bridge at Concord has been three times circling the globe, and has each time been inciting all people outside America to redouble their revolutionary efforts, America herself has been engaged on another job than the one that she finished on her own soil in 1783. She has been winning the West and has been mastering the technique of industrial productivity. In consequence, she has become rich beyond all precedent. And, when the American sputnik's third round raised the temperature of the World Revolution to a height that was also unprecedented, America felt herself impelled to defend the wealth that she had now gained against the mounting revolutionary forces that she herself had first called into existence.

What was the date at which America boxed the compass in steering her political course? As I see it, this date is pin-pointed by three events: the reaction in the United States to the second Russian revolution of 1917 and the two United States immigration restriction acts of 1921 and 1924.

The American reaction to the Bolshevik revolution in Russia was not, of course, peculiar to the American people. It was the same as the reaction of the rich people in all countries. Only, in the United States, it was a nation-wide reaction, because, in the United States, the well-to-do section of the population had become, by that time, a large majority, not the small minority that the rich have been and still are in most other parts of the World so far.

Rich people, not only in the United States but everywhere, have, I think, taken Communism in a very personal way. They have seen in Communism a threat to their pocket-books. So Communism, even when it has raised its head in some far-away country, has not felt to the rich like a foreign affair; the threat has seemed close and immediate, like the threat from gangsters in the streets of one's home town. I think this explains the fact — and I am sure this is the fact — that Russian Communist aggression has got under the skins of the well-to-do in the Western World, while German nationalist aggression has not angered them to the same degree. This relative complacency towards German aggressiveness, as contrasted with the violence of the reaction to Russian aggressiveness, has made an impression on me because, I confess, it makes me bristle. I have noticed it among the rich minority in my own country, and I have noticed it still more among a wider circle of people in the United States. It is a rather startling piece of self-exposure. It is startling because, among the various dangers with which we have been threatened in our time, the danger to our personal property is not the one that we ought really to take most tragically. As a matter of fact, the well-to-do Western middle class would have been fleeced economically by the Germans, as thoroughly as this could be done by any Communists, if Germany had happened to win either the first or the second world war — and Germany came within an ace of winning each of these wars in turn. But the tragic loss that would have been inflicted on the Western World by a German victory would have been the loss of our political and our spiritual liberty. In two fearful wars that have been brought upon us by Germany within the span of a single life-time, we have saved our liberty at an immense loss in infinitely precious human lives. We have had no war with Russia in our life-time, and the Western and the Communist camp are not doomed to go to war with each other, though at present the common threat of self-annihilation in an atomic third world war hangs over us all.

Of course someone might reply to what I have just been saying by admitting the whole of my indictment of Germany but pointing out, at the same time, that Russia, too, threatens our political and spiritual freedom, besides threatening just our pockets. This is true. Yet, if I had to make the terrible choice between being conquered by a nationalist Germany and being conquered by a Communist Russia, I myself would opt for Russian Communism as against German nationalism. I would opt for it as being the less odious of the two regimes to live under. Nationalism, German or other, has no aim beyond the narrow-hearted aim of pursuing one's own national self-interest at the expense of the rest of the human race. By contrast, Communism has in it an element of universalism. It does stand in principle for winning social justice for that great majority of mankind that has hitherto received less than its fair share of the benefits of civilization. I know very well that, in politics, principle is never more than partially translated into practice; I know that the generous-minded vein in Communism is marred by the violent and intolerant-minded vein in it. I also recognize that Communism in both Russia and China has been partly harnessed to a Russian and a Chinese nationalism that is no more estimable than German nationalism or any other nationalism is. Yet, when all this has been said, I still find myself feeling that the reaction of rich individuals and rich nations in the West to Communism since 1917 has been an 'acid test', to use President Wilson's memorable words. Anyway, it is, I think, indisputable that the reaction in the United States to Communism in and since the year 1917 has been a symptom of a reversal of America's political course. It is a sign, I think, that the American people is now feeling and acting as a champion of an affluent minority's vested interests, in dramatic contrast to America's historic role as the revolutionary leader of the depressed majority of mankind.

The United States immigration restriction acts of 1921 and 1924 are, I believe, pointers to the same change in the American people's attitude during and immediately after the First World War. Naturally I realize the urgent practical considerations that moved the Administration and the Congress to enact this legislation. The First World War had just brought to light a disturbing feature in this country's domestic life: I mean, the persistence of the hyphen. An appreciable number of United States citizens, and of immigrants who were on their way to becoming citizens, had proved still to have divided loyalties. The American melting-pot had not yet purged out of their hearts the last residue of their hereditary attachment to their countries of origin on the European side of the Atlantic. There was evidently a long road still to travel before the process of assimilation would be completed, and this race between assimilation and immigration might never be won for Americanism unless the annual intake of immigrants were drastically reduced. Moreover, the pre-war immigrants were under criticism not only for still being pulled two ways by divided loyalties; they were also under suspicion of perhaps not being representative samples of the best European human material. The introduction of an annual quota would enable the United States Bureau of Immigration to sift the candidates for admission and to select those who promised to make the best future American citizens, and the policy of restriction was thus recommended by a eugenic motive as well as by a political one.

These considerations, by themselves, would have made some measure of restriction and selection desirable after the First World War anyway. But the main motive for the enactment of the acts of 1921 and 1924 was, I believe, a different one. Europe had just been ravaged by a war of unprecedented magnitude and severity. European belligerent governments had stopped their subjects from emigrating in order to conserve their supplies of cannon-fodder. And, now that the war was over, it was feared in the United States that the flow of immigration would start again, and this time in an unprecedented volume. A flood of penniless Europeans might pour into the United States in quest of fortunes in the New World to compensate for ruin in the Old World, and this probable rush of millions of European paupers to win a share in America's prosperity was felt to be a menace to the economic interests of the existing inhabitants of the United States, who had a monopoly of America's wealth at present.

If I am right in this diagnosis of the main motive for the United States immigration restriction acts of 1921 and 1924, the American people went on the defensive at this time against the impact of European immigration for the same reason that made America react so strongly against Communism. Both these reactions were those of a rich man who is concerned to defend his private property against the importunity of a mass of poorer people who are surging all round him and are loudly demanding a share in the rich man's wealth.

What would have been the effects on America's economic life if immigration into the United States had been left, down to this day, as free as it was during the century ending in 1921? Presumably the present population of the United States would have been much larger than it actually is, but it does not necessarily follow that the average income per head would have been lower. Experience tells us that a country's total annual product is not a fixed amount. It may be increased by various factors. One of these stimuli to production may be a steep rise in the volume of population through a reinforcement of the natural increase by immigration. For example, the massive and unrestricted immigration into West Germany from East Germany since the end of the Second World War has been one, at least, of the causes of West Germany's unexpected and surprising post-war economic prosperity. On this analogy it is conceivable that the economic effects of the United States immigration acts of 1921 and 1924 was contrary to the legislators' intentions and expectations. While conserving the previous income per head of the existing population of the United States, the immigration restriction acts may have prevented the income per head from rising so fast and so high as it might have done if immigration had been left unrestricted. A continuance of unrestricted immigration might also perhaps have saved the United States from the great depression of the nineteen-thirties. These are hypothetical questions which even an economist might find it hard to answer, and I am not an economist. But I would suggest to you that, whatever the economic consequences of those immigration restriction acts may have been, these economic consequences have not been the most important. The political and psychological consequences have, I should say, counted for more, and these non-economic consequences have, I should also say, been unfortunate for America as well as for Europe.

So long as immigration into the United States from Europe was unrestricted, America's ever open door kept America in touch with the common lot of the human race. The human race, as a whole, was poor, as it still is; and America was then still a poor man's country. She was a poor man's country in the stimulating sense of being the country that was the poor man's hope. She was the country, of all countries, in which a poor immigrant could look forward to improving his economic position by his own efforts. America did not, of course, even then, offer this opportunity to immigrants from the whole of the Old World. The opportunity was always restricted to immigrants from one small corner of the Old World, namely Europe. All the same, so long as America still offered herself as even just the European poor man's hope, she retained her footing as part of the majority of the human race. In so far as she has closed her doors since 1921, she has cut herself off from the majority. This self-insulation is the inevitable penalty of finding that one has become rich and then taking steps to protect one's new-found well-being. The impulse to protect wealth, if one has it, is one of the natural human impulses. It is not particularly sinful, but it automatically brings a penalty with it that is out of proportion to its sinfulness. This penalty is isolation. It is a fearful thing to be isolated from the majority of one's fellow-creatures, and this will continue to be the social and moral price of wealth so long as poverty continues to be the normal condition of the World's ordinary men and women.

I will close this first lecture in the present series by trying to drive this point home in a piece of fantasy. Let us imagine a transmigration of souls in reverse. Let us slip our own generation's souls into the bodies of the generation of 1775, and then set the reel of history unwinding with this change in its make-up. The result that we shall obtain by this sleight of hand will be startlingly different from the actual course of events in 1775 and thereafter. The Declaration of Independence will now be made, not in Philadelphia, but at Westminster. King George III will raise his standard, not at the Court of St. James's, but at Independence Hall (of course that building will not bear its historic revolutionary name; it will be called 'Royal Hall' or 'Legitimacy Hall' or some other respectable conservative name of the kind). The other George, George Washington, will take command of his royal namesake's army. There will be no Continental Congress here in Philadelphia for George Washington to serve. The revolutionary parliament will be on the other side of the ocean. It will be at Westminster. And the revolutionary leader will not be a George, but a Charles, namely Charles James Fox. The bridge beside which the embattled farmers will fire their shot will not be the bridge at Concord. The flood that it spans will be the Thames. The shot will be heard round the World, but it will be an Old-World shot, not a New-World one.

This nonsense that I have just been talking will have had its use if it has illustrated my thesis. I am maintaining that, since 1917, America has reversed her role in the World. She has become the arch-conservative power instead of the arch-revolutionary one. Stranger still, she has made a present of her glorious discarded role to the country which was the arch-conservative power in the nineteenth century, the country which, since 1946, has been regarded by America as being America's Enemy Number One. America has presented her historic revolutionary role to Russia. . . .

Every society creates ideal images

Ralph H. Gabriel   **Traditional Values in**   **12**
                                        American Life

Ralph Henry Gabriel, one of America's eminent historians, was born in Reading, New York, in 1890. He studied at Yale, receiving his Ph.D. there in 1919. He has served on numerous faculties, including Yale, American University, School of International Service, and the War Department School of Military Government. He was a member of the U.S. delegation to the UNESCO Paris Conference in 1958. His extensive writings include Toilers of Land and Sea *(1926),* The Course of American Democratic Thought *(1956). The selection quoted here, taken from a pamphlet prepared for the U.S. National Commission for UNESCO while he was a*

*member, offers a comprehensive list of the underlying principles of Ameri-
can life. For related ideas, see Parkes; Schlesinger, Sr; Larrabee; Brogan;
Fuchs.*

American Values in Politics

Out of the heritage from England, the experience with government in
the colonies, the struggle for independence, the weakness of the Confederation, the creation of the Federal Republic, and the experience of more
than a century and a half of independence, including four years of civil
war (1861 – 1865), have come American values in the area of politics:

1. The concept of the state as a utilitarian device created to provide
for the common defense and to further the general welfare.
2. Freedom and responsibility of the individual adult citizen to have a
voice in the government under which he lives, as exemplified in the right
and responsibility to vote.
3. Freedom of access to knowledge of all kinds save only when dis-
closure of particular information would endanger the whole community.
This access is achieved through a system of public education, the practice
of academic freedom, and the existence of a free press.
4. Freedom to express orally or in writing opinions honestly held concerning economic, religious, political, or social matters. In the case of
political opinions, this freedom is limited by the requirements that actions
to carry opinions into effect must conform to the procedures for changing
the policies or structure of the state as set forth in the Constitution of
the United States. A further general limitation is that expression of opinion
must not be so inciting as to create a clear and present danger of panic
or disorder.
5. The protection of the free citizen against unreasonable invasions of
privacy by officers of government.
6. The right of free citizens to assemble peaceably.
7. The supremacy of civil authority over the military in conformity
with the principle that the civil authority is the decision-making power and
the military is the instrument, when needed, to carry decisions into effect.
8. The concept of the American Federation as a "permanent union of
permanent states," firmly established after the Civil War, maintained by
judicial enforcement of the Constitution and forbidding nullification or secession on the part of the states.

From *Traditional Values in American Life* by Ralph H. Gabriel. Reprinted by permission
of Harcourt, Brace & World, Inc.

Law in American Values

1. The concept of a "government of law and not of men." In the United States this means the supremacy of law administered by the regular courts over the officers and agencies of government.

2. The concept of law as a living growth, changing with the evolution of society.

3. The right of every person to be free to move about and to choose his occupation, unless convicted of crime and subject only to the general law, thus forbidding slavery or involuntary servitude.

4. The right of every person to be informed specifically of any charges made by the state against him, to speedy and public trial, to compulsory process for obtaining witnesses, and to legal counsel assuring him equal protection of the laws.

5. The right of a person to refuse to testify against himself. This right prevents the forced and often false confession that is a most revolting aspect of totalitarian tyranny.

6. The right to a trial by a jury of peers when the United States government brings the charges. In some states a defendant has the option to choose trial by a judge.

7. The protection of persons from being "twice put in jeopardy of life or limb" for the same offense or, if convicted, from "cruel or unusual punishments."

8. The denial to government of the power to punish a person through the instrumentality of an *ex post facto* law, that is, a law formulated to make an act an offense after the act had taken place.

Religion in American Values

1. The idea that the state is not coterminous with society but that religious institutions exist of their own right in society independent of the state—the separation of church and state.

2. The freedom to believe and to propagate one's faith as the conscience of the individual person directs, or freedom to refrain from worship. This freedom of worship does not extend to practices that debase the community.

3. The idea of the church as a free association of believers who assume responsibility for its support.

4. The widespread but not universal emphasis on some form of theism as a frame for explaining the meaning of human life.

5. The idea, widely but not universally held, that ethical standards spring from religion.

6. The idea that the furthering of the brotherhood of man under the fatherhood of God calls for the outreach of the churches to the far corners of the world on errands of mercy, to assist social evolution toward a better life, and to further mutually helpful cooperation among all peoples.

7. A sense of charity, stemming in part from the humanistic tradition and in part from that of Judeo-Christianity, coupled with the idea that the performance of acts that contribute to the well-being of individual persons and of society are in themselves religious activities of merit. Some of the religious beliefs and practices are closer to the understandings and teachings of social psychology than they are to traditional spiritual doctrines. Historically, religion in America has created educational and humanitarian institutions, and the practice continues.

8. The idea that the state must respect the convictions of the conscientious objector to refrain from participation in the bloody violence of war, but that the state may require of the conscientious objector in time of emergency special service of a nonviolent nature.

Education in American Values

1. The idea that effective self-government requires that a significant proportion of the electorate have sufficient education to be able to inform themselves of issues and to consider them rationally.

2. The idea that equality of educational opportunity for all citizens is the just and desirable foundation for a democratic society.

3. The idea that the state has an obligation not only to provide educational opportunities from kindergarten through the university, but to require children to attend school until their early teens.

4. The idea that the state should not have a monopoly of education and that independent, privately supported schools, colleges, and universities bring to the educational system a diversity and variety that further the general welfare.

5. The idea that education, particularly advanced education, by training specialists to work in a society which emphasizes specialization, increases the opportunities of the individual person to find for himself a useful place in the community and to achieve an income commensurate with his abilities.

6. The idea that from the elementary grades to the bachelor's degree, the school exists for the training of the student as a social being as well as for the cultural enrichment of the individual and the training of the mind.

7. At the level of the university, the idea that general education should precede or pace side by side with the training of the specialist to the end

that the specially trained person have breadth of view and flexibility of mind along with a particular competence.

8. The idea of academic freedom which asserts that teachers in higher education should be free to search for and to teach the truth as they see it without compulsion from the state, the church, the business community, or the administrative authorities of the institution and to this end should enjoy security of tenure.

9. The idea that education should be a lifelong process and that opportunities for post-school training should be available to adults as far as practicable.

Social Values

1. The dignity and importance of the individual person. The individual person is, himself, a unique center of power and value. He does not exist for the state. The state, in fact, is no more than an organized community of persons. The state has no being or meaning apart from these persons. The state is an instrument to further the welfare of the persons who compose it. When the state enslaves the persons who compose it, these persons lose that power and dignity which derives ultimately from their humanity.

2. Freedom of thought and action of the individual person. If a person is to have dignity and if his life is to have significance, he must have a large measure of freedom. Nature, of course, sets limitations to that freedom. The prime social limitation lies in the fact that the individual person must manage his behavior so as not to impair the freedom of his fellows.

3. Freedom, and so far as possible equal opportunity, of the individual person to make of his life what he can in accordance with his abilities. The corollary of this concept—the expectation of a status in society that derives from his qualities and achievements.

4. Regard for the group and for group activity as a means to the ends of developing individual personality and of enlarging the possibilities for effective action that has importance for the individual person, resulting in the formation of voluntary associations in extraordinary number and for a wide range of interests.

5. Regard for the family as the basic social institution. Within the family, emphasis on the separate individualities of husband, wife, and children, and the enjoyment by women of equal legal and political rights. Protection in law and custom of the privacy and mutual loyalty of its members—one spouse may not be compelled to testify in court against the other. The concept that loyalty of its members to the family is a virtue at least equal to loyalty to the state—a conviction evidenced by the complete absence in the United States of efforts by the state to use chil-

dren or adult members of a family as informers to the state against other members.

6. Regard for work leading to recognizable accomplishment — professional preferment, the accumulation of property — as a normal aspect of the good life. The value expressed in the fact that having a job gives in itself a kind of social status. The tendency to look down upon an idle man unless the idleness is due to infirmity or age. This value expresses the activism in American civilization.

7. Concern for the physical and mental health of the community. This value emerged in the latter half of the 19th century when scientific advances enlarged the ability of the doctor to cure disease and made preventive medicine possible. Other scientific advances brought into being rational methods for dealing with mental disorders. This value reached its full expression in public health organizations, regulations, and activities.

8. Regard for voluntary public service by private individuals. This value had its first significant expression in the humanitarian movement of the first half of the 19th century. In that period the tradition of humanism of the Enlightenment united with an urge to individual and social betterment in evangelical Protestantism to produce a number of societies and movements to attack social evils and to ameliorate the plight of suffering or oppressed persons. The humanitarian emphasis of the time reached its culmination in the antislavery crusade. The humanitarian movement continued after the Civil War in attempts to deal with the insecurities of a rapidly developing industrialism and with the vice and suffering of the slums of the cities growing swiftly in size as a flood of immigrants came from abroad. A rough division of function took place between governmental and private efforts to deal with the problem of individual and social maladjustments. Now, in the middle of the 20th century, municipalities and states provide relief and the arrangements that go under the name of social security. Private agencies work in the field of character-building, rehabilitation of individuals and families, and special training for the handicapped. Beginning in the latter half of the 19th century, men of wealth in the United States created a number of foundations, which had large endowments administered in the public interest by professional staffs. The Rockefeller Foundation, the Ford Foundation, and others carry on worldwide activities.

Regard for voluntary public service implies two things. It suggests, on the one hand, the habit that has been developed among citizens of the United States, from the wage earner to the man of wealth, to make regular voluntary contributions of money to institutions and causes which further the general welfare. It implies, on the other hand, willingness on the part of private persons to serve without compensation in the management and promotion of such institutions and causes. The ideal of voluntary public service by private individuals ranks high in the hierarchy of American values.

9. Acceptance of change as a normal aspect of social life and regard for the social sciences as instruments for gaining an understanding of society and for the formulation of improvements. The social sciences are primarily a 20th-century development in the United States. By the mid-20th century, through the knowledge social scientists had acquired and the applications of that knowledge to specific social problems, an important impact on American civilization had been made. In a society in which rapid industrial evolution causes swift and important social changes, the social sciences represent efforts to provide rational solutions to complex and urgent problems.

Science in American Values

1. Regard for rationality—the critical approach to the phenomena of nature and of society, coupled with the effort to reduce these phenomena to ever more consistent, orderly, and generalized forms of understanding.

2. The conviction that man must dare to unlock the secrets of nature to the extent that his abilities permit.

3. The conviction that man must accept and not shirk the moral responsibility for the use of whatever new power increased knowledge brings to him.

4. The understanding that the method of science, combining precise reasoning with accurate observation and controlled experiment, can achieve new knowledge when and only when it conforms to an ethical code, a code that might almost be described as the laws of creative thought. These laws are stated in 5,6, and 7 below.

5. The scholar who seeks new knowledge must have freedom to explore, to reason on the basis of discovered fact, and to express his conclusions.

6. In communicating what he has found, the scholar must be faithful to the truth he has discovered; he must describe honestly what he has observed or found by calculation.

7. The scholar must approach the solution of problems with objectivity, a willingness to accept evidence and to reject disproved hypotheses, no matter what the consequences.

8. Regard for the application of scientific knowledge through technology to the affairs of life. Among the values relating to science, regard for technology was primary among Americans until after World War II. The scientific achievements in the 1950's, however, brought home to the citizens of the United States the fact that perhaps even national survival depends on pushing out the boundaries of knowledge on all fronts. The huge sums that the federal government has made available for basic research give evidence that Americans have achieved a new perspective.

Values in American Economy

1. Work on the part of the individual person has been valued since the theology of the 17th-century Puritans sanctified it. A job, no matter how humble, gives honorable status to an individual and is the normal way of life.

2. Economic well-being of the individual person is valued not only as the cornerstone of a sound economy but as the essential foundation for a full and rounded individual life. Economic well-being frequently is defined in very simple terms in a material sense. Poverty, as in certain religious orders, is not an important value.

3. The sanctity of contract and respect for property are valued as the foundation for orderly and dependable economic relations.

4. Production of goods is valued as a prerequisite to economic well-being. The drive toward more efficient and increasing production is one of the most important in the American economy.

5. Private enterprise is valued because it gives opportunity for the creative potentialities of the entrepreneur or of corporate management, because it gives the entrepreneur the largest measure of freedom in working out the destinies of the particular concern, and because the opportunities of sharing in the profits resulting from successful management provides a stimulus for individual effort.

6. The profit system is valued because only where there are profits can private enterprise long continue. The profit system is modified or limited by government entry into the economy through laws dealing with manufacturing and price competition, such as those dealing with monopolies, unfair methods of competition, and rate fixing for public utilities; laws dealing with the quality of products sold; laws governing the conditions of work in mines, factories, and service undertakings; tax laws that appropriate for the general use a considerable percentage of the profits of private industry; and government operation of certain enterprises to prevent abuses by private monopoly or near monopoly.

7. The economic well-being of the community (from the local community to the Nation) is valued for the same reason that the economic well-being of individual persons is valued and for the following other reasons: The economy can function successfully only so long as the mass of the people enjoy a considerable measure of economic well-being; production depends upon consumption; the economy can operate properly only when the consuming public can purchase the fruits of production; wage policies by private enterprise are conditioned by the need for economic well-being of the community because the ability to consume for most of the population derives from wages and salaries. This same need conditions governmental policies having to do with credit and in particular with the distribution of the national wealth through taxes on profits and through

graduated income and estate taxes. The graduated income tax has made the concentration of a great percentage of the national income in the hands of a few persons impossible. A prime motive of the income tax is to maintain the economic well-being of the community.

8. Social security for the individual person is valued. It takes the form of insurance plans under the auspices of the state. It applies to the unemployed, to the industrially insured, and to the aged. Private and cooperative social security is valued for two reasons. It preserves to a degree the economic well-being of the individual, with all of the implications of that goal. It helps to maintain the purchasing power of the mass of the people and so serves the goal of the economic well-being of the community.

9. The principle of assistance by the state to certain economic groups is valued because it furthers the economic prosperity of the community. The state provides price supports for some agricultural commodities so that the farmers may continue to function normally as producers and as consumers. The state sets a minimum wage rate so that wage earners may continue to function as consumers. These are the economic reasons. Behind these are the reasons of humanity expressed in the goal (before considered) of the economic well-being of the individual person.

10. In spite of the fact that the policy of price supports by the government for agricultural products prevents competition among producing farmers from bringing down prices below certain levels, Americans value the principle and practice of competition in the production and distribution of goods and services. This approval is specifically expressed in laws forbidding monopoly, save in certain fields such as the telephone. Americans fear that monopoly power in private hands may lead to exploitation of the community. The states and the federal government have created agencies for the regulation of monopolies that are inherently desirable.

11. In the production of goods, rationalization and mechanization are valued. Mass production of goods, such as automobiles or refrigerators, brings down the price of the individual unit to a point where it can be purchased by the mass of the people. The result is the furthering of the economic well-being of the individual person and of the community.

12. The principle of collective bargaining is valued because it enables the worker to negotiate with the employer on more nearly equal terms and, as a result, have a voice in the formulation of policies of vital importance to his life as a workman.

13. Opportunity for the individual employee to rise in the managerial hierarchy of an enterprise through promotions based on efficiency is valued for two reasons: It provides for the mobilization of the maximum ability in the management of the enterprise; and it expresses the larger American ideal of giving the individual person the opportunity to make of his life what he can.

14. Americans value government in the roles not only of maintaining order and administering justice, but also in those aiding stable economic growth and preventing excessive economic inequalities.

The Arts in American Life

1. Regard for the creation and presentation of music, reflected in the multiplication of composers, the growth of musical organizations, and the vast importance of recorded music.

2. Regard for the collection of and making available to the public in museums painting, sculpture, and the crafts, both classical and contemporary.

3. Regard for the quality of design in the artifacts of everyday life.

4. Regard for creative literature as an instrument for the fuller and deeper understanding of life.

5. Regard for the drama and the dance as presented in stage, film, and TV as instruments for enriching human life.

6. Regard for tradition and for innovation in painting, sculpture, and the crafts and for popular and mature participation in these arts.

7. Regard for tradition and innovation, together with the principles of form and function, in the architecture of a nation building to meet the needs of an increasing population and a swiftly evolving civilization.

8. Regard for criticism by scholars and specialists in the various arts to encourage discrimination by the public in appraising performance and recognizing excellence.

Values in International Relations

1. The principle that changes in the relations between nation-states be accomplished by peaceful means alone—the rejection of violence as an instrument of policy.

2. The principle of national sovereignty under international law. Because Americans value this principle for their own country, they regard as axiomatic the right of other nations, small or large, to security of their territory and the determination of their own form of government and economy and of their own foreign and domestic policy. This concept is a projection into the area of international relations and an extension to nations of that basic value in American thought; namely, the free and responsible individual person.

3. The value of collective security within an organization of nation-states has been increasingly recognized in the 20th century, superseding the older isolationism. As the individual person is a unit in a society and is conditioned by that society, the independent nation is a unit in a society

of nation-states and must accept those limitations on independence of action which derive from that fact. These limitations have become increasingly important as improvement in transportation and communication have crowded the nations close together. A corollary to the value of collective security is the understanding that no nation can enjoy prosperity in isolation, that, in general, prosperity in neighboring nations reinforces prosperity at home. Out of this understanding has come in the United States the value that emphasizes the well-being of the community of nations through arrangements for mutual aid. These have included bilateral arrangements between the Republic and another power, but the United States has increasingly participated in the multilateral arrangements through the United Nations, UNESCO, the World Bank, and other international organizations.

4. The observance of international law and international commitments formally undertaken. The honoring of treaties is a basic responsibility of a free nation. It is the prerequisite of orderly relations among nations and of any significant world organization of nation-states.

5. The use of international adjudication to settle legal disputes. American Presidents have urged formal commitments to this effect since 1896, and the Senate has often agreed to submit specific disputes to adjudication.

6. The concept that free nations should practice neighborliness and that the stronger and more advanced among them should respond to requests for help, particularly from peoples struggling to escape from inherited poverty.

7. The concept that government should encourage and support cultural exchange among peoples, on the ground that increased understanding among diverse civilizations and mutual appreciation of their art and their values further the cause of fellowship among men of good will, and so of peace.

13

Lyndon B. Johnson

The Great Society

*Speaking at the University of Michigan in Ann Arbor on May 22, 1964,
President Lyndon B. Johnson developed in broad outline a vision of the
future shape of American civilization, a vision which has been called "The
Great Society."*

*However one feels about President Johnson, the fact is that the concept
of the Great Society and its implementation has become a central political
issue of our time. This speech is important for at least three reasons. First,
like the other readings in this book, it provides an insightful critique of
present-day American civilization. Second, it reveals an awareness of the
actions and ideas which have shaped America in the past, and at the same
time it implicitly hints at the causes for the radical transformations which
have taken place in American society since World War II. Finally, and
most important, Johnson's speech reveals an awareness of the potential that
exists for shaping the American present and future, and it explicitly sets
forth a bold pattern for change in a number of important areas. For related ideas, see Galbraith, Carson, Nairn.*

. . . I have come today from the turmoil of your Capital to the tran-
quility of your campus to speak about the future of your country.

The purpose of protecting the life of our Nation and preserving the
liberty of our citizens is to pursue the happiness of our people. Our success in that pursuit is the test of our success as a Nation.

For a century we labored to settle and to subdue a continent. For half
a century we called upon unbounded invention and untiring industry to
create an order of plenty for all of our people.

The challenge of the next half century is whether we have the wisdom
to use the wealth to enrich and elevate our national life, and to advance
the quality of our American civilization.

Your imagination, your initiative, and your indignation will determine
whether we build a society where progress is the servant of our needs, or
a society where old values and new visions are buried under unbridled
growth. For in your time we have the opportunity to move not only to-

Public Papers of the President: Lyndon B. Johnson, 1963–64, Vol. I (Washington, U.S.
Government Printing Office, 1965), pp. 704–707.

ward the rich society and the powerful society, but upward to the Great Society.

The Great Society rests on abundance and liberty for all. It demands an end to poverty and racial injustice, to which we are totally committed in our time. But that is just the beginning.

The Great Society is a place where every child can find knowledge to enrich his mind and to enlarge his talents. It is a place where leisure is a welcome chance to build and reflect, not a feared cause of boredom and restlessness. It is a place where the city of man serves not only the needs of the body and the demands of commerce but the desire for beauty and the hunger for community.

It is a place where man can renew contact with nature. It is a place which honors creation for its own sake and for what it adds to the understanding of the race. It is a place where men are more concerned with the quality of their goals than the quantity of their goods.

But most of all, the Great Society is not a safe harbor, a resting place, a final objective, a finished work. It is a challenge constantly renewed, beckoning us toward a destiny where the meaning of our lives matches the marvelous products of our labor.

So I want to talk to you today about three places where we begin to build the Great Society—in our cities, in our countryside, and in our classrooms.

Many of you will live to see the day, perhaps 50 years from now, when there will be 400 million Americans—four-fifths of them in urban areas. In the remainder of this century urban population will double, city land will double, and we will have to build homes, highways, and facilities equal to all those built since this country was first settled. So in the next 40 years we must rebuild the entire urban United States.

Aristotle said: "Men come together in cities in order to live, but they remain together in order to live the good life." It is harder and harder to live the good life in American cities today.

The catalog of ills is long: there is the decay of the centers and the despoiling of the suburbs. There is not enough housing for our people or transportation for our traffic. Open land is vanishing and old landmarks are violated.

Worst of all, expansion is eroding the precious and time honored values of community with neighbors and communion with nature. The loss of these values breeds loneliness and boredom and indifference.

Our society will never be great until our cities are great. Today the frontier of imagination and innovation is inside those cities and not beyond their borders.

New experiments are already going on. It will be the task of your generation to make the American city a place where future generations will come, not only to live but to live the good life.

I understand that if I stayed here tonight I would see that Michigan students are really doing their best to live the good life.

This is the place where the Peace Corps was started. It is inspiring to to see how all of you, while you are in this country, are trying so hard to live at the level of the people.

A second place where we begin to build the Great Society is in our countryside. We have always prided ourselves on being not only America the strong and America the free, but America the beautiful. Today that beauty is in danger. The water we drink, the food we eat, the very air we breathe, are threatened with pollution. Our parks are overcrowded, our seashores overburdened. Green fields and dense forests are disappearing.

A few years ago we were greatly concerned about the "Ugly American." Today we must act to prevent an ugly America.

For once the battle is lost, once our natural splendor is destroyed, it can never be recaptured. And once man can no longer walk with beauty or wonder at nature his spirit will wither and his sustenance be wasted.

A third place to build the Great Society is in the classrooms of America. There your children's lives will be shaped. Our society will not be great until every young mind is set free to scan the farthest reaches of thought and imagination. We are still far from that goal.

Today, 8 million adult Americans, more than the entire population of Michigan, have not finished 5 years of school. Nearly 20 million have not finished 8 years of school. Nearly 54 million—more than one-quarter of all America—have not even finished high school.

Each year more than 100,000 high school graduates, with proved ability, do not enter college because they cannot afford it. And if we cannot educate today's youth, what will we do in 1970 when elementary school enrollment will be 5 million greater than 1960? And high school enrollment will rise by 5 million. College enrollment will increase by more than 3 million.

In many places, classrooms are overcrowded and curricula are outdated. Most of our qualified teachers are underpaid, and many of our paid teachers are unqualified. So we must give every child a place to sit and a teacher to learn from. Poverty must not be a bar to learning, and learning must offer an escape from poverty.

But more classrooms and more teachers are not enough. We must seek an educational system which grows in excellence as it grows in size. This means better training for our teachers. It means preparing youth to enjoy their hours of labor. It means exploring new techniques of teaching, to find new ways to stimulate the love of learning and the capacity for creation.

These are three of the central issues of the Great Society. While our Government has many programs directed at those issues, I do not pretend that we have the full answer to those problems.

But I do promise this: We are going to assemble the best thought and the broadest knowledge from all over the world to find those answers for America. I intend to establish working groups to prepare a series of White House conferences and meetings—on the cities, on natural beauty, on the quality of education, and on other emerging challenges. And from these meetings and from this inspiration and from these studies we will begin to set our course toward the Great Society.

The solution to these problems does not rest on a massive program in Washington, nor can it rely solely on the strained resources of local authority. They require us to create new concepts of cooperation, a creative federalism, between the National Capital and the leaders of local communities.

Woodrow Wilson once wrote: "Every man sent out from his university should be a man of his Nation as well as a man of his time."

Within your lifetime powerful forces, already loosed, will take us toward a way of life beyond the realm of our experience, almost beyond the bounds of our imagination.

For better or for worse, your generation has been appointed by history to deal with those problems and to lead America toward a new age. You have the chance never before afforded to any people in any age. You can help build a society where the demands of morality, and the needs of the spirit, can be realized in the life of the Nation.

So, will you join in the battle to give every citizen the full equality which God enjoins and the law requires, whatever his belief, or race, or the color of his skin?

Will you join in the battle to give every citizen an escape from the crushing weight of poverty?

Will you join in the battle to make it possible for all nations to live in enduring peace—as neighbors and not as mortal enemies?

Will you join in the battle to build the Great Society, to prove that our material progress is only the foundation on which we will build a richer life of mind and spirit?

There are those timid souls who say this battle cannot be won; that we are condemned to a soulless wealth. I do not agree. We have the power to shape the civilization that we want. But we need your will, your labor, your hearts, if we are to build that kind of society.

Those who came to this land sought to build more than just a new country. They sought a new world. So I have come here today to your campus to say that you can make their vision our reality. So let us from this moment begin our work so that in the future men will look back and say: It was then, after a long and weary way, that man turned the exploits of his genius to the full enrichment of his life.

14

Lord Taylor

Deep Analysis of
the American Mind

*Lord Taylor, a psychiatrist and Member of Parliament, is currently Presi-
dent and Vice-Chancellor of the Memorial University of Newfoundland. In
the following selection, he diagnoses the American mind. In a communication to the editors, Lord Taylor suggests about the article: "Its title should
not include the word 'deep.' It is not a deep analysis. Indeed it can only
claim to be an analysis of the American mind using the word in its ordinary English sense and not in its Freudian sense." For related ideas, see
Whyte, Wheelis, Sleikeu.*

The wealth of critical writing on the mind of America by the Americans
themselves might suggest a nation of introspective psychopaths. Nothing
could be further from the truth. To the impartial observer the Americans
seem to enjoy themselves as much as any people on earth, and more than
most. But they are the victims of insatiable curiosity. They like knowing
what makes things tick, including themselves.

In this analysis, there are two themes. The first is that by using simple
descriptive psychiatric techniques, it is possible to draw up a useful profile
of any community. Examination of the common types of mental illness
shows that each is more than an exaggeration of one facet of normal personality. By estimating the predominant facets in enough individuals, a
valid picture of national character emerges.

The second theme is that, while the basic personality is largely determined genetically, the physical and social environment modifies the basic
personality in ways which are easy enough to understand, provided one
looks for the right things and asks the right questions.

America is a continent of immense physical and human diversity. Yet
despite this, it has achieved a remarkable degree of cultural and psychiatric uniformity; in this are blended certain clear-cut European patterns,
altered and often improved by a powerful and extensive environment.

For centuries, the people of Western Europe have lived in tightly packed
nations, each developing certain characteristic virtues and vices, partly

From *The New York Times Magazine,* February 23, 1964. © 1964 by The New York
Times Company. Reprinted by permission of The New York Times Company and the
author.

through common historic experience and partly through inborn patterns of behavior. From these diverse nations came the people of America, often strong in personality, determined to make a new life, and above all determined to enjoy a freedom denied to them in their native lands.

It was natural enough that all should regard themselves as fundamentally equal, with equal inherent values, rights and opportunities. Since many were escaping from tyranny — a tyranny of social category, economic barriers and religious conformity, all reinforced by governmental action, it is not surprising that the Americans do not love the machinery of government. So they have deliberately created a system of government which will permit each of them to do what he likes to a degree unknown elsewhere in the world. The result has been the greatest display of human energy in the history of mankind.

At once three outstanding characteristics of the American mind are apparent — equalitarianism, love of freedom, and bounding energy. But the most deep-seated, I am sure, is energy. Put into simple psychiatric terms, the American people show a greater measure of vigorously directed "hypomania" than any other nation.

Hypomania

Hypomania is an admirable human characteristic when it comes to getting things done. Its flowering in America is partly a response to opportunity, a result of nature's abundance in food and raw materials. But it is even more a product of the inborn drive of those who displayed the initial energy to escape from the Old World and pioneer in the New. These people were the best of the "have-nots," whose only capital was within them, who were determined to pull themselves and their children up by their own bootstraps. If they lacked the culture of the "haves" who stayed behind, they were ready to prove by their own efforts that in the long run they were just as good, if not better. Today in most fields of human endeavor, they are doing just that. Secondary features of hypomania are optimism, and a free and easy approach to one's fellow men. To the Americans, all things are possible, provided you try to see what you can do. It is no accident that William James's pragmatism should have become the national philosophy and hospitality the national hobby.

Hypomania is also characterized by apparently easy swings of attitude and behavior. The hypomanic is often strong in his expression of views yet seldom inflexible. He is ready to see another point of view, and indeed to give it a trial. Hence, the amazingly rapid swings in American public attitudes and the readiness to explore and exploit fully novelties in machinery or ideas.

Fortunately, the hypomanic swings of the American personality leave the fundamental beliefs of Americans strangely untouched. They cling to their love of freedom and their belief in personal equality and the value of individual achievement with tenacity—simply because in the long run they are pragmatically justified. They work, so they are O.K.

Depression

But with hypomania there is another side to the coin. At first sight, it is less obviously desirable, though it is possible that it is no more than a biological necessity, a natural recovery period after the energy output of prolonged hypomania. Whether or not this is true, it is certainly a fact that, from time to time, hypomanics become depressed. And the depressed American, like the sick doctor, is a sorry sight. Hence the volatility of the American stock market. When America manages to fire off a generalized economic depression, it is quite a phenomenon. In hypomanics, depression is in some measure infectious; but insofar as it is infectious, it can be countered by environmental adjustment. Hence the importance of political and economic measures to counter either excessive inflation or deflation.

In its milder degrees, emotional depression leads to a decline in striving, particularly in marginal activities. In the broad picture of American politics, the most usual result is a tendency to return to isolationism. But thanks to the practical pragmatic reaction to the threat of atomic missile war, its effects are far less marked today than in the nineteen-twenties and thirties.

Hysteria

The hypomanic personality is often linked with some of the manifestations of hysteria. Hysteria may be defined briefly as the unconscious production of physical or mental symptoms to achieve a supposed material or emotional gain. The hysterical personality, in which symptoms most commonly occur, is characterized by emotional display as a means of self-gratification, often as an alternative to hard work or hard thought.

Most of us are, on occasion, capable of behaving hysterically, and a tincture of hysteria adds a spice to life; but more than a tincture is a burden to the flesh.

In a sense, hysteria is the hypomanic's method of escape from a too difficult reality. In its milder forms, American hysteria is harmless and often delightful. The innocent dressing up, the display and the excessive rapture over genuine achievement are colorful treats to the staid English onlooker. In another direction, hypochondria of the American businessman is harmless enough to society, though perhaps not so harmless to the sufferer himself.

The tincture of hysteria also shows itself in an excessive enjoyment of self-examination and self-criticism, sometimes linked with an excessive sensitivity to criticism by others.

Occasionally, the hysterical component in the American personality gets out of hand. When it does so, it is usually a localized phenomenon. The nearest approach to mass hysteria was the social disease of McCarthyism. Yet even when this epidemic was at its height there remained a great number of quietly sensible Americans who treated the phenomenon with the contempt it deserved and provided a backbone of objective common sense which ultimately brought the nation back to sanity.

To the outsider, the attitude of the articulate white American to the racial problem seems to include hysterical sentimentality and hysterical anxiety and yet fundamental decency and respect for the individual. Hysterical sentimentality is as embarrassing to the subject to which it is directed as it is ineffectual in solving the underlying problem. Hysterical anxiety is, in minor key, akin to the feelings whipped up by Hitler about the Jews. This is sometimes spoken of as paranoia; it was, in fact, nothing of the kind.

The essence of paranoia is the tortuous systematization of an elaborate pattern of delusions. Hysteria may have a paranoid twist to it, but it is far more superficial and less carefully thought out. Hysterical anxiety all too easily erupts into hysterical and unreasoning hatred.

One of the bad things about hysteria is its infectiousness. Once a situation becomes hysterically charged, both sides are likely to react hysterically. Negroes are neither less nor more hysterical than the rest of the human race, but when caught up in a hysteria-producing situation, they will give as much as they get.

So both sides have to handle this matter calmly. The problem of racial integration will need more than courage and goodwill to solve it, valuable though they are. It will need hard intellectual thinking and painful economic action. But I have no doubt that the pragmatic genius and good sense of the American people is equal to the challenge here presented.

Obsessional Features

Energy without thoroughness is seldom effective. A substantial part of the American success story is due to the Teutonic and Scandinavian personality feature of attention to detail. Despite a certain civic untidiness, the Americans are a meticulous and obsessional people. Time and again, when one examines American textbooks, encyclopedias, guidebooks and children's books, one is reminded not of British but of German works.

American academic teaching and scholarship are thorough and comprehensive to an almost painful degree.

It is the same in industry, engineering and commerce. The obsessional personality likes to have everything explained and docketed. Visit any American business office and the cross-filing makes one dizzy. In an American bookshop, every conceivable subject is covered, from the behavior of bats to Greek philosophy. In every civil servant's office stands a *prie-dieu* on which rests Webster's International Dictionary. In the midst of this vast quantity of instruction and enlightenment, a touch of humor is starting to appear. But to the average European it is still just a trifle dull.

In scientific research, the obsessional approach pays dividends but only at the price of much unproductive labor. Every channel must be carefully explored before the main river can be identified. In Britain, we tend to take intellectual and scientific short cuts, and often our methods yield as much as (but no more than) American techniques, but for considerably less labor.

The obsessional personality facet carries with it one major disadvantage. Excessive systematization reduces the capacity to adjust to the unexpected. Often, the American takes longer to get going on a new track than he would if he were more slapdash. Thus, in dealing with new cultures, the American appears to take longer to adapt and find his feet than his Anglo-Saxon cousin. That he does eventually is due less to an intuitive appreciation of the other person's point of view than to a thorough study of all aspects of the problem presented. In the long run, thoroughness pays off, but the length of the run is often surprising.

However, this, like all generalizations about the Americans, remains a partial truth only. Americans who grow up outside the great cities seem to retain more flexibility, and are often no mean adaptors to new cultures. It may be that they have not had their innate understanding of other people ironed out by the massive impact of instruction on every conceivable subject. Mr. Harry Truman, looking out from Independence, Mo., without benefit of college instruction, can see more of the game than any Ph.D.'s in social psychology.

Schizoid Features

The schizoid personality is self-sufficient, nongregarious and given to deep speculation about the meaning of things. It is among the schizoids that we find most great artists and writers, poets and painters. And, despite their remarkable achievements, it is here that the Americans still have a long way to go. We English live so close to one another that we deliberately build physical, social and emotional barriers between our houses, but in a figurative way, most Americans are still on the frontier, where every traveler is a friend or at least a companion. So the barriers are down, the telephone extends to every room, and every man's garden is also his neighbor's.

It may be that the schizoid personality is a slow product of long-continuing civilization, that it can only come when men have ceased to give top ratings to material prosperity and practical success. Most Americans value people for their achievement. Dollars are still a convenient yardstick, yet not quite as much as they were. The great scientist, on a relatively small salary, now commands equal esteem with the successful industrialist. But few Americans would rate contentment with one's lot as an essential human condition.

Of course, the creative schizoid personality burns with an inner discontent. But it is seldom a discontent with material achievement. There must be few artists who could not have made more doing something else. They do what they do because they want to do it, regardless of the attitudes of those around them. And in so doing, they see much which remains hidden to their more practically occupied neighbors. It seems to me no accident that, up to now, few new philosophies or ways of thought have had their origins in America.

France is the apotheosis of the schizoid nation. And this perhaps explains why most Americans find the French so difficult to understand.

For the Frenchman, the pleasures of the family, the table, the bedchamber, the town and the countryside (provided they are in France), the joys of solitude and company, of wit and paradox, are to be savored and enjoyed beyond material prosperity, while proper sense of the value of money is nevertheless maintained. Motivation is not material success but satisfaction with the task in hand. The French are at the same time more realistic and more complicated than the Americans.

Despite the Americans' love of personal liberty, their emotional climate resembles that of Russia in one respect. Both nations are intolerant of nonconformity and are in consequence inimical to the development of the schizoid personality. It is at first sight strange that a society built by libertarians from the Old World should be so intolerant of intellectual exploration in its own midst. American universities are models of technical and scientific efficiency. Yet they still largely lack the gorgeous contempt for established thought-processes which is apt to break out in Britain.

Yet even here things are changing. The quiet American, the mildly depressed schizoid, whom we in Britain so much admire, is starting to emerge as a familiar variant on the American scene. He shows his hand in much of America's humor, with its readiness to laugh at the most sacred traditions of traditional America.

Paranoia

If France is the apotheosis of the schizoid nation, Russia is the apotheosis of the paranoid. Paranoia implies an unjustifiable suspicion of one's fellows, linked with an excessive intellectual tortuosity. On both these counts, the Americans stand acquitted.

To those used to the convolutions of European thinking, the direct and straightforward minds of the Americans are a delight. Indeed, from the point of view of their own advantage, this straightforwardness is often misunderstood or exploited by more tortuous peoples.

It may be objected that the American attitude to Communism is as much paranoid as the Communist attitude to American capitalism. I do not think this is so. The Americans like their country, they like the way they live, and indeed it is hard to see why they should not. For America is a splendid and magnificent place, where most ordinary people enjoy greater plenty, opportunity and freedom than anywhere else on earth. (It is only the extraordinary people who suffer for their nonconformity, and even for them the suffering is seldom severe.)

To Americans, Communism offers nothing but poverty and the servitude from which they or their forebears came to America to escape. Though they may sometimes overreact hysterically, their determination to perserve the American way of life seems to me entirely free from paranoia and no more than a realistic appreciation of the facts of life. It is this same realism which ultimately makes coexistence a practical possibility.

Their attitude to the Chinese is more complex, yet again it springs from simplicity plus practical experience rather than paranoia. Until China went Communist, for over a century it was a favored country in American eyes. Then in a short span of years all was changed. The favorite child had revolted and aligned itself with the enemy. Father was hurt beyond measure. An oversimplification of a complex people had failed to pay off. It will be some years yet before the Americans will be prepared to look again objectively at the mainland of China.

The directness of the American mind shows itself also in the American attitude to religion, to value for money and to snobbery.

The Americans are at bottom a deeply moral people, earnest in their desire to act out the golden rule within a sound business context. The creed of John D. Rockefeller Jr., inscribed on a tablet at the foot of the Channel Gardens in Rockefeller Center, tells one much about this facet of the American character. The text of the creed proclaims, among other things, a belief "in the supreme worth of the individual" and that "the rendering of useful service is the common duty of mankind."

To most Englishmen, trained not to give expression to their deeper feelings and indeed seldom even to formulate them, such a creed explicitly stated is corny, exhibitionistic and in bad taste. To most Americans, Mr.

Rockefeller simply put into precise words the basis of their fundamental system of values.

At times, the American's religion becomes no more than a desirable community activity. But beneath this there is a real and genuine feeling for the Bible, the church and the Christian ethic. I attended, with the local doctors, the First Presbyterian Church in a small town in Oklahoma on Soil Stewardship Sunday. The sermon, on "The Parable of the Sower," was a mixture of good theology and sound advice on soil conservation. The general level of preaching in America is both scholarly and practical, to a degree very rare in England. It is only in the bizarre evangelical fringe that emotionalism becomes an important component.

To get and to give value for money is another part of the basic American ethical code. Of course, there are many exceptions, many who seek to exploit their fellows. But to most Americans, trade, commerce and industry are ethical and moral occupations. This is why medicine can be conducted on a commercial basis without destroying the integrity of the individual doctor. This is why, if one thinks one has failed to get value for money, a lawsuit is looked upon as a sound ethical procedure.

Snobbery, save in New England, seems definitely an un-American activity. Snobbery implies a social hierarchy, with exaggerated respect for and servility toward those above and contempt for those below. To be sure, there are snobs in America and, in large business organizations there are plenty who kowtow to their superiors. But, comparatively, these instances are rare. The principle is to judge each person on his achievement and performance, regardless of his origin or connections.

Good performance in any job is a matter for general satisfaction. The waiters and waitresses in any American restaurant are fellow human beings, not insulated automatons. The truck driver or road laborer can be, and indeed often is, one's own son doing a holiday job between college terms. The alleged dollar snobbery is, in my experience, no more than the use of money as a means of measuring achievement and performance, based on the belief that money is normally well and properly earned, and that human worth, like everything else, can be expressed in mathematical terms if only one finds the right units.

To me, at any rate, the simple nontortuous American approach to the basic essentials of life is immensely attractive. Sometimes it oversimplifies. But it also simplifies much that we in Britain unnecessarily overcomplicate. It helps one to get on with the job. It is one of the factors which make America the vigorous, kindly and happy society it is.

Quest for Excellence

Having won the battle for abundance, the Americans are now concerned to move forward into new fields. I have been told by some Americans that the most important book of the last decade is "Excellence" by John W. Gardner, president of the Carnegie Corporation. Its subtitle sums up a current American dilemma, "Can we be equal and excellent, too?"

The Americans are now setting out, with characteristic directness and simplicity, to cultivate every available human talent they can find. This quest for quality and excellence is leading them on to an educational expansion without parallel in human history. It will undoubtedly produce many strains and much heart-searching and unhappiness. But the theory behind it, that "the man who does a slovenly job—whether he is a janitor or a judge, a surgeon or a technician—lowers the tone of society," reconciles the two aspects of American philosophy: that all men are equal and that all are to be judged by their achievement.

So the new prototype is becoming the quiet American whose apparent modesty rests on the firm foundation of his belief that his pattern of society is not only good but right. Strangely enough, he has much in common with his Anglo-Saxon cousin across the Atlantic. I suspect that our two societies have never been closer since the old Colonial days. In the growth of cross-fertilization in business and industry, in politics, science and education, there is much we can both gain, with a fine spin-off of benefit for the rest of the world.

**The interactions of science and
society are stronger**

15

Steven Dedijer   **One View of the Other USA**

Steven Dedijer, born in Yugoslavia, was once head of Marshall Tito's Atomic Energy Institute. He quit Yugoslavian Communism in 1957 and left the country in 1961. He is now a Swedish citizen and a Sociologist at the Sociological Institute of Lund University. The following speech was delivered in Stockholm on June 13, 1965, before the Royal Swedish Academy of Engineering Sciences. It is a discussion of the interaction of science and society. Dedijer is one of the few to describe a phenomenon which is usually

"Remarks at the June 13 meeting of the Research Policy Seminar of the Royal Swedish Academy of Engineering Sciences, Stockholm" (*Dagans Nyheter,* August 31, 1965). English translation provided by the author.

obscured by what we know as "cultural lag." For related ideas, see Henry;
Schlesinger, Sr.; Brooks; Kouwenhoven.

Because of Vietnam and San Domingo, two kinds of people are angry
with the United States: its friends and its enemies. Looking through the
Eastern and Western newspapers and periodicals after a visit to the USA,
I have the impression that this anger is overshadowing for both of them
the other USA, which I just saw: an awe inspiring social system imploding
with change. Digesting this three-months visit—and I have spent at different times altogether seventeen years in the United States—I again concluded that to experience, so to say, through one's eyes and ears what
social change is one must go the USA. There, more than anywhere else
I have been, one is pounded by evidence that everything within the USA,
not only its technology and landscape, but its ideas, values, goals, habits,
institutions and patterns of social behaviour are changing rapidly. The
United States is a social system that can't stand still, where innovation
is a way of life. To the question "what is the direction of this change?"
some pragmatic Americans (as so many of them are), bewildered midst
this apparently random change, still like to tell foreign visitors with helpless pride: "The USA is moving in all directions at once." Here, I want
to challenge such a view, for my impression was different.

I spent this visit just like the one in 1963 studying at the Department of
the History of Science of Yale University what I consider the most sensitive field in every country for detecting and identifying social change: the
field of interaction of science—basic and applied, natural and social—and
society. Every kind of "capitalist" and every kind of "communist" including those from "the third world" proclaim that today, more than
anything else, science creates social change and that it is beginning to tell
us and should tell us how to cope with it: how to identify and rationalize
the current and to predict and project with the hope to control at least
some of the future changes of society. Because more research of the most
modern kind is done and more of its results are used in the United States
than in any other country of the world, the interactions of science and
society there are stronger and the resulting social changes are more rapid
and intense than anywhere else I have been. These interactions in the
United States are easier to follow than elsewhere, for it produces more
public information on what science and society are doing to each other
than any other three or four countries of the world taken together.

To advance my view of the direction of the USA social change, I shall
present two kinds of social problems the USA is increasingly concerned
with as the result of this strong current interaction of research and society.
These are, first, problems which other developed countries have not yet
begun to feel or discuss intensely, and second, social problems which other

countries have been dealing with for years, whereas because of its own social, economic, ideological conditions the USA is just beginning to face squarely now. Both kinds of problems are in my opinion best reflected in the debates going on in what I call research policy workshops. These are dozens of seminars, conferences, symposia, and hearings being held all over the USA on various problems having to do with science and society, organized by numerous government agencies, academic, business, research and other institutions with participants from all of them.

The debate on how to determine as rationally as possible the priorities in a country's research work, familiar to everyone interested or engaged in research policy, is right now extremely sharp and wide-spread in the United States, raising fundamental issues in the nation's life. This debate is sharpened through the realization that the USA spends a relatively high percentage of its Gross National Product, higher than any other country in the world, on military research and on space research. Starting from the assumption that a major war is not imminent an increasing section of the informed public in the USA, especially those engaged in research policy, is debating should the USA give a higher priority to research leading to the improvement of the material and social standard of living, to create a more stable and pleasant environment in the USA from a social esthetic, psychological and material point of view for all the geographic sections and all the strata of its population? This debate on research policy criteria is turning first of all into a debate on the basic values and goals of USA society, on the methods to achieve them and the required social and institutional changes.

This debate is both a cause and an effect of the changing idea of social progress in the USA. Most Americans categorically deny that there is any such thing as a national USA ideology. Yet for example, nowhere in the world has the idea of progress been so strongly embedded for so long in the social beliefs and values of its leading elite and so wide-spread among the population as in the United States. From its inception, throughout its history, the idea of progress has dominated the thought and the soul of the United States and has always won out in decisive moments when challenged by the opposite tendency, which occasionally gained prominence in its political life through the "know-nothings" and slaveocrats in 19th century, the "America Firsters" in the nineteen thirties and the Goldwaterites of our day. In the past the idea of progress in the USA was generally identified with the increase of material well-being and technological innovation to be achieved through self-centered, individual enterprise with a minimum of social constraints and responsibilities. A man's worth in the United States is still measured in folk parlance in dollars he has or earns or number of people he employs or has power over. Yet, today, the business leaders themselves are more and more active in fostering the idea that the material progress must be broadened into the concept of social progress for all sectors and strata of USA society. The idea that life should be individually creative for broad sections of population midst improving esthetic, social, psychological surroundings is fighting its way slowly to dominance over the former valuations of "good life" based on material influence and affluence and individual initiative at the expense of society. The creators of new knowledge, of innovation, constitute today a higher percentage of population in the USA than in any other country and represent the fastest growing section of its labour force. Their evaluation of the importance of the work done to discover knowledge and create innovation are exerting an increasing social pressure in all directions and through all the strata of USA society. This only renders more complicated and more pressing the debate on "should we be learning about stars before or after we eliminate the slums," or "how many schools, hospitals, roads, operas and PhD's could we produce with the resources used to put a man on the moon."

The changes in social values are also shown in the tendency of all participants in research policy debates—including business—to consider the problems of interaction of science and society from the point of view of the present state of "the whole USA social system" and its desired future state. Many people, including the champions of "private" enterprise are beginning to look with new eyes on the broad USA scene. Among the immense riches and creative potential of the overall social system they are now also seeing its unseemly aspects: poverty, ugliness, ignorance, psychologically unpleasant atmosphere, extreme insecurity and enormous social strains.

The identification of all these long-range social problems of the "whole social system" is, among other, fostering increased activities in all kinds of social planning at all levels of key social institutions. Although practically every government department and agency in the USA has active planning divisions often staffed or counseled by social scientists, it is not government but business that does most planning. I made this surprising conclusion while examining the relation of research planning to economic planning on the micro-level. It is my guess that a systematic comparative study of planning activities of enterprises in various countries would show that those in the USA do more and better planning by far and have more experience in it than the enterprises in the communist countries. As if in derision of Marx, the profit motive has spurred the USA business firms, large and small, to engage during the past generation in increasingly accurate planning of sales, investments, productivity, new products, processes and capacities. The macro-economic planning in the USA has not, as yet, reached the stage of setting production targets. In recent years, however, a certain rate of growth of the Gross National Product has been set as desirable, and the government through the control of demand by financial measures is attempting to stir the economy in the direction desired. The macro-planning of the overall USA economy has now reached the stage of building models simulating various sectors of the system. One example of this is the 60 branch model of USA industry developed in the Commerce department by means of the input-output technique. With this model one may study the policy implications for the whole USA industry of the change in the production of one single raw-material, semi-finished good or a process in a given industry.

As regards research, nowhere in the world are so many plans for its development right now being produced as in the USA. The National Academy of Sciences during the past two years has published a series of long range plans of research programs, manpower, equipment, institutions and investments for such branches of basic research as the high energy physics, ground based astronomy, oceanography and is about to publish those for physics, chemistry, while preparing the plan for social sciences. A number of institutions and individuals have produced long range plans for research manpower in basic and applied sciences, including the first analytical "science of science" models based on quantitative data to guide the development of research manpower policies and programs. The coordination and dovetailing of all these plans into an overall national research plan for the USA may prove to be the next logical step. This, most probably will have to wait for the issue of the current debate on civilian technological research. This is now being discussed, first, in terms of the "whole system," as the civilian technology of importance for the solution of national problems, for the improvement of the general environment, including problems of urbanization, transport, communication, preservation and development of natural resources, etc. It is also being considered at the micro-level, as the problem of stimulation of innovation in private enterprises, a problem which until recently, was considered taboo both by the Congress and the executive branch. Yet, this last aspect is being more and more discussed in research policy workshops. Economic, social, political limitations to the stimulation and development of civilian technology at the firm level are being identified and institutional and policy changes required are being carefully searched for by representatives of government, science, universities and business.

The changing social values, the trend to look at the "whole social system," the planning activities and the rapid development of the newest branches of basic and applied research with strong social implications and impacts has given rise to a prolific development of "futurology" in the United States. A world-wide survey of literature shows that nowhere so many studies, predictions, forecasts are being made on various aspects of science and society up to the year 2000 and beyond as in the

United States. One interesting focus of debate has to do with a central problem of the future of research. At present about 3 percent of the USA labour force is engaged in research, development and engineering. The question whether this percentage is reaching a saturation limit or whether in the near future 10 percent or 20 percent of the labour force will engage in this kind of work is a subject of discussion involving geneticists, psychologists, educators, philosophers, sociologists, and those engaged directly in the study and practical research policy activities.

This accelerating interaction of science and society is giving rise to an increasing social demand for the development of social science. Social scientists—including historians and philosophers—are more and more to be found not only in every research policy workshop—but also in the planning and executive divisions of government agencies. This rising demand for social science will, no doubt, give rise to systematic efforts based on national levels plans for its development and utilization. One consequence of all this on the social sciences in the United States will be to direct them from preponderantly micro-social studies, made in tight single discipline compartments and projects, toward interdisciplinary macro studies of the major social problems leading to an increasing understanding of the whole social system and the problems of its stable change.

Debates and discussions on science and society, on plans and predictions, on values and goals of the USA society are words and wishes. Can these words and wishes on what the USA social system "ought to be" become policies transformed into social reality? Is the USA society evolving and is it possible for it to evolve into a more rationalized and stable social system under the impact of modern science—basic and applied, social and natural? There are many who strongly doubt it, and there are those, some Marxist social scientists first of all, who deny categorically that this is possible. As far back as 1930, they say by way of example, President Hoover sponsored a study on "Recent Social Trends in the USA," calling for action on the whole US social system so that "agriculture, labour, industry, education, religion and science may develop a higher degree of coordination in the next phase of national growth" and advocating macro-economic planning, which at that time, the report said, still only "represents a social need rather than a social capacity." These social scientists claim that the inherent "social laws" operating independently of the will of men in USA society prevented all past and will prevent all future attempts to turn these social needs into social reality. It is my impression at first hand based on considerable quantitative data on all these problems that the USA during the past generation has been evolving, by changing all "laws of capitalism," exactly in a direction Marxist social scientists claim that it could not go. The "New Deal" of Roosevelt, the half-started "New Frontier" of Kennedy and the "Great Society" of Johnson are not simply "vote-getting gimmicks," but seem to be all a part of an increasing conscious effort—now being made with new insights and greater pressures from the interactions of science and society—attempting to rationalize, as it is at present humanly possible, the US society into a stably evolving, creative and innovative social system based on an enlarged complex of social values.

**The giant corporation
has transformed America**

16

John Brooks   The Great Leap

John Brooks was born in New York City and grew up in Trenton, New Jersey. He was educated at the Kent School in Connecticut and at Princeton University, where he graduated in 1942, and served with the Air Force in Europe. He specializes in articles about business and financial happenings, and his writings frequently appear in The New Yorker. *His novel* The Big Wheel, *a best-seller, was published in 1949. He is also the author of* The Fate of the Edsel and Other Business Adventures. *The following selection deals with the role of the corporation in the development of American affluence. His book* The Great Leap *is primarily concerned with the quantitative differences between the America of pre-World War II and that of the present-day. For related ideas, see Berle, Galbraith, Brogan, Henry, Communist Party, U.S.A.*

The growth of the giant corporations into supergiants, and the transformation of their character that accompanied it, seem to me to be the single economic change that has had the farthest-reaching effects over the past quarter-century. If it isn't the key to the whole transformation of American life—and I don't think it can be called that—it is, at any rate, a sort of master key capable of opening many rooms in our national house. "Since the end of the Second World War, the corporate form has emerged as the characteristic institution of American society," Andrew Hacker of Cornell wrote recently. True enough, and happily enough, it has not become the all-powerful and all-embracing institution on which everyone's livelihood depends. Even now, the one hundred largest corporations provide only about six million jobs, or less than one-tenth of the national total, and even the five hundred largest provide no more than ten million jobs. Economically, and probably culturally as well, small business, from the corner cigar store to the hi-fi or electronic-component firm set up in a loft by two or three brainy young Ph.D.s, is still close to the heart of our national life. But how many small businesses have huge corporations as their most important customers, or live by supplying goods or services to the employees of huge corporations, or otherwise depend upon them! To put it in terms of sheer economic power, about half of the productive assets of American manufacturing are held by about 150 corporations, and it has been estimated that about two-thirds of such assets, agriculture excluded, are held by not more than five hundred.

Consider, as an index, the fantastic growth of the national economy that was set off by, and in large measure accounted for by, the growth of big corporations. In 1964 we had disposable personal income—after taxes—of some $435 billion; for 1939 the figure was about $76 billion. Per capita, man, woman, and child, the figure rose from under $600 to well over $2,000. (It is interesting to note that national-income statistics themselves were comparatively new in the 1930s. The very machinery by which national economic growth is now measured was a recent invention.) Just the *interest* on our public debt is now about equal to the *total national budget* of the late 1930s. What all this means in terms of wages is that in June, 1963, the national average weekly earnings of factory workers for the first time ever passed the $100 mark—which in the 1930s had become almost the established figure denoting affluence. What it means in terms of easy living is that by 1964 more than 80 percent of American families owned at least one automobile, as against less than 60 percent in 1939; that sales of household appliances, many of which did not yet exist in 1939, were at near-record levels, and sales of all kinds of clothing were the highest ever; while services, ranging from motel rooms to laundromats and diaper services, were operating at levels undreamed of even a decade earlier. As a European diplomat said in 1964, "The American economy has become so big that it is beyond the imagination to comprehend. But now on top of size you are getting rapid growth as well. It is a situation of fundamental power unequaled in the history of the world."

Consider in detail one or two parts of the vast anatomy of that power. The directors of a corporation, let us say, decide to spend a million dollars—or ten million, or a hundred million, or a billion—on plant expansion. Is this simply a business gamble, a play on the free-enterprise roulette wheel, of interest chiefly to the gambler and the croupier? Indeed not. Such a decision, as Hacker points out, may well determine the quality of life for a substantial segment of society. Men and materials will move across continents; old communities will decay and new ones will prosper; tastes and habits will alter; new skills will be demanded, and the education of a nation will adjust itself accordingly; even government will fall into line, providing public services that corporate developments make necessary.

So it has been the past decade and more; the advent of a plant of IBM or General Electric or Corning Glass to some sleepy hamlet has time and again transformed it into a bustling small city, with new people and a new social structure and new ideas about life. If anyone doubts the economic muscle of the individual corporate investment decision, let him contemplate the fact that in 1964 General Motors alone spent about one billion on new construction. Yet even that fantastic figure is dwarfed by the $3.9 billion spent in 1965 by the largest company in the world, American Telephone and Telegraph.

It is startling to realize the number of ways in which the big companies have served as the magnets around which our national life has come to arrange itself in directed patterns. Urbanization, the flight from the farm and the hamlet to the city and the suburb, has been one of the most marked national trends in recent years. Corporations produced the equipment and the fertilizer that made the farm hand superfluous; corporations offered him the job that brought him to the city. Suburbia itself is the corporation's creation: the corporation needs a city to serve it, and the corporation employee needs a place to live. (Lately, some corporations have taken to setting up offices and even small factories *in* the suburbs, thereby changing them into cities.)

It is the giant corporation, far more than any single force, that has transformed America over the past quarter-century from a country in which several fairly distinct social and economic classes were still easily discernible, and usually acknowledged by their respective members, into a country in which a single group, the middle class, includes a majority of the whole population and seems to be heading toward becoming more or less universal. (I intend to take up the social consequences of this change in later chapters.) The giant corporation, in alliance with the most efficacious advertising medium ever invented, the television screen, has done more than anything else to establish our present habits of consumption and thus to a great extent set the style and pattern of our lives. And it has changed our relations with the rest of the world. Between 1940 and 1961 U.S. assets and investments abroad went from $12 billion to $80 billion. The increase, apart from its effect on the economies of other countries, and on that of our own, meant that hundreds of thousands more Americans were traveling to and living in foreign parts, not as tourists to be smirked at and fleeced, but as employees with the responsibility of earning a living—that is to say, not as objects but as people. Sometimes such Americans have been liked, and sometimes they have been hated; in all cases, they have become better known.

Finally, the giant corporation, almost inadvertently, has tended to become a force against race discrimination at home. Its impartial and practical devotion to the idea of profit; the fact that its scope is national, with tentacles reaching into all parts of the country; and the fact that the federal government, by virtue of so often being among its biggest customers, is in a position to put direct economic pressure on it—all these factors have combined to make the typical national corporation's Southern plants become in many cases the quiet, and sometimes reluctant, leaders of local integration of races. The Southern-born and Southern-bred manager of the Atlanta branch of a national firm expressed the matter well in 1964. "We've already about put an end to what was left of the Old South," he said. "Doing business in national companies and competitive markets, the requirements of manufacturing technology, and, in a funny way, the impersonality of the big corporation that a lot of people conplain about—they all spelled the end of the old way. I haven't had a mint julep in years."

How did the corporation explosion come about? Like so many postwar developments, it was set in motion by the war itself. With a war to be won and industrial production on an unprecedented scale needed to turn out weapons, it was no time for denunciations of bigness or sentimentality about handicrafts; the national heroes of wartime in the field of economics were not the idealistic New Dealers but the tough production bosses like William Knudsen and Donald Nelson. Gross national product more than doubled between 1940 and 1945, while the cost of government and government enterprises was more than quadrupling. But what would happen to the economy when the war ended, removing the need for war production and thus taking the props from under the artificial boom? Industrial managers and academic economists were, for once, in agreement: both groups expected a collapse. Nothing of the kind took place. The wartime props were summarily removed, all right—from the wartime peak of almost $100 billion in 1944 and 1945, government expenditures dropped off to only $33 billion in 1948—but so great was the public's appetite for automobiles and other items of consumer goods of which it had been deprived all through the war that the total output of the economy dropped hardly at all.

The appetite had to become sated eventually, of course, and there was some hard going for a couple of years—especially in 1948, which has been called the one real peacetime year in postwar history, when the federal budget reached its low point; but even then families were expanding at an unprecedented rate, wages were rising rapidly, demand for housing and all kinds of household equipment was at a high level, and the economy was holding its own. Then in 1950 came the Korean War, and the prop of high military spending was back, and, though no one could know it at the time, the modern era in American economic life was inaugurated. Military spending was to be a continuing major factor. By the time the Korean War ended in 1953, the Cold War was a well-established fact; soon technological developments like the thermonuclear bomb and rocketry made the waging of the Cold War incomparably more complex and more expensive, and in the early 1960s roughly half of the government's annual income was being spent on defense. Meanwhile, beginning with the end of the Korean War, the nation went on a consumer-goods-buying binge such as had never been seen before, and besides, as the population grew by leaps and bounds, the number of customers swelled proportionately. Thanks to the presence of two voracious customers — the government and the ordinary citizen — the corporations were sitting pretty.

It would be a mistake, though, to suggest that the big companies were merely beneficiaries of an expanding economy, and that postwar growth was just something nice that happened to them. On the contrary, they can take a good deal of the credit themselves. Even in the early postwar years, when economic pessimism was so prevalent, they were betting on their own and the country's future in a big way. Immediately before the war, American corporations were reinvesting about 40 percent of their profits after taxes in expansion of one sort or another; during the 1946-48 period the figure was up sharply to 62 percent. Thus when the fat years came in the middle 1950s, the corporations were in a position to exploit prosperity, and in so doing to increase it — something that they would have had a great deal of difficulty in doing if they had spent the late 1940s cautiously hoarding their profits in cash or passing them along to stockholders as dividends.

In part, this corporate foresightedness was undoubtedly adventitious, an incidental product of government tax policy; income-tax rates had soared so high during the war, and remained so high in the postwar period, that many stockholders in the higher brackets didn't particularly want big dividends on which they would have to pay top rates, and preferred to see profits on their money reinvested so that they could eventually take capital gains, on which they would be taxed at much lower rates. But undoubtedly there was a deeper reason, too. The old, innate, often naive optimism of the American businessman, which went all the way back to the early nineteenth century, and which had suffered such a punishing series of setbacks during the depression that by 1939 it was practically eroded away, had now come back strong. The war was over, thought the men who made the corporate decisions; the country was growing again; the future was a shining promise; to hell with the pessimists! On this occasion, whether or not for the right reasons, the optimists were right.

And there was more to it than that. The whole climate of the postwar

United States favored the further growth of big business. The reformist spirit of the Thirties had faded — or at least, most of its main tenets had seeped into the national mainstream, so that they no longer could be called reform. There was little public enthusiasm for antitrust activities; when the government's long-drawn-out antitrust cases against AT&T and the leading Wall Street investment bankers in the early 1950s were lost, most of those who cared one way or the other approved the decisions. Tired of both reform and war, the country seemed to want above everything both the consumer products and the comparatively secure jobs that only huge corporations could provide in profusion. The old hostility between big business and government from New Deal days became more or less perfunctory during President Harry S. Truman's Administration, and changed to warm friendship with the advent to the White House of Dwight D. Eisenhower. It was a time when Americans wanted their leaders, institutions and men alike, to be bland, benign, fatherly — and big.

But which is the key word — "benign" or "big"? Where there is power, there is a need for responsibility; a professor at the Harvard Business School told me recently that the main thing he tries to impress on his students is that power has a moral dimension. If the American economy has recently developed a store of power unequaled in world history, and if that power resides chiefly in huge corporations, the question immediately arises: How well is the power being used? The answer, I am convinced, is that it is being used less well than it should be and a good deal less badly than it might be. Certainly it is being used in different, and generally far, far better, ways than anyone — New Deal economist or company executive — could have predicted in 1939. And no wonder, because, as the contrasting annual reports of 1939 and 1964 suggest, the change in corporations has been as much in kind as in size.

For one thing, in the process of increasing in quantity the corporate power has been diffused. It has become so great as to be almost invisible.

Everyone knew who wielded the power in the traditional American family-controlled corporation, which, though already losing ground, was still probably the characteristic American corporation at the end of the 1930s. The controlling family wielded it, and no bones made. In *Middletown in Transition* the Lynds describe how in Middletown in the Thirties the "X" family, through their corporation and its power, ran the town: not only could they choose the factory pay scale ($15 to $17 a week) and keep unions out; they could also choose the city's mayor, deprive a liberal minister of his pulpit, control the morning newspaper, and baronially shift the select residential area from one place to another according to whim. Everyone in Middletown. knew who wielded the poker; the "X" family did. If not everyone knew who wielded the power in the Ford Motor Company, at least the choice was a narrow one; it might be old Henry Ford, the founder, or it might be his son Edsel—there was no question of its being any third party. But family capitalism was near the end of the road. Various postwar factors, probably the chief of which were the tax structure and the need for new capital for expansion, forced one company after another to "go public" by selling its shares on the open market, until in the late Fifties Daniel Bell could write that in two decades the Lynds' picture of the "X" family "has become a picture of the past rather than of contemporary society." Ford itself, one of the last holdouts among the giants, went public in 1956 by distributing over ten million shares to more than a quarter of a million investors for a sum in the neighborhood of $650 million, in what still stands as the most spectacular stock distribution on record.

Where did the power go? Theoretically, to the new owners, the stockholders; but in practice they are usually utterly unable to exercise it because there are so many of them. The degeneration of the stockholder from a real force in management to a mere receiver of dividends or putter-in-the-wastebasket of proxy statements has been commented on again and again over the past decade. It has been pointed out that there is a disturbing parallel between the "elections" held at corporate annual meetings and the political elections in Russia, since in each case the officially sponsored slate invariably gets at least 99 percent of the votes cast. As A. A. Berle writes, "When corporations were still small, the stockholder powerfully influenced the director, but today they are so far apart that the stockholder can hardly communicate with management even by megaphone. We go through the ancient forms . . . but everyone knows that a stockholders' meeting is a kind of ancient, meaningless ritual."

The directors who represent the stockholders more immediately control the power; but many boards of directors are made up largely of men from "outside" the company, without intimate knowledge of its myriad complicated affairs, who are compelled by sheer lack of acquaintance with detail to act as rubber stamps for the decisions of the day-to-day operating officers. Thus the power is apt to fall to that new breed, the trained, high-salaried professional managers who are often not substantial owners. Yet by the nature of their training and the dynamics of their situation, these men are inclined to make cautious, safe-and-sound "consensus" decisions that will not stir up the sleeping giants who might unseat them, the directors and stockholders.

Furthermore, so complex are the affairs of the supergiant corporations that even the professional managers, skilled and dedicated as they may be, cannot always know what is going on within their commands. A case very much in point is the electrical-industry conspiracy of the late Fifties—the biggest business scandal of the post-war years—in which executives of the leading manufacturers contrived, by an elaborate system involving secret

telephone calls, hotel-room meetings, and codes, to defeat the free market
by illegally fixing prices on billions of dollars' worth of equipment. When
the conspiracy was uncovered, the guilty executives of General Electric,
the biggest company involved, said they believed that in conspiring they
had been acting on orders from their superiors. On the other hand, Ralph
J. Cordiner, General Electric's chief executive officer, said that he had not
even known about the conspiracy, far less ordered it. Many people under-
standably refused to believe that Cordiner was telling the truth. Yet the
fact remains that it is entirely possible, in view of the confusion and misunderstanding that attends the bureaucratic operations of a supergiant corporation, that Cordiner *was* telling the truth. In that case, his men had
been acting on orders that had originated — nowhere! By way of further
contrast, imagine a family capitalist like old Henry Ford, or Mr. X of
Middletown, excusing himself by pleading that he had not known what
was going on in his command. It would have been unthinkable! But Cordiner could do it, to the satisfaction of his board of directors and a good
portion of the business community, for a simple reason: they thought it
perfectly natural that neither Cordiner nor anyone else had the power to
oversee General Electric.

Headless as they sometimes seem to have become in the process of growing unthinkably big, the corporations have assumed the status almost of
national states. And in many respects, ironically enough, the particular
states they tend to resemble are socialized rather than free-enterprise ones.
What is General Motors, an American economic analyst asked recently,
but a vast planned economy, similar in many respects to the Polish economy, which happens to be not a great deal larger? The top officers of
American Telephone and Telegraph are not being pretentious when they
speak of their regular Monday morning gatherings in the company's board
room in lower Manhattan as "cabinet meetings." Possessing economic
power greater than most of the nations of the world, and political influence less great but still far from negligible, AT&T is quite worthy of
having a cabinet.

In the past quarter-century the biggest corporations have gone a long
way toward converting themselves into welfare states. The whole array of
"fringe benefits" — medical plans, group insurance plans, pension trusts,
and so on — have come to provide many corporate employees with something approaching cradle-to-grave security, and have attained such importance in the eyes of employees that they now often take precedence over
wages and salaries in union negotiations and as inducements to executive
talent. (The staggering sum of around $100 billion was owned by private
pension funds of all types in 1965, as against $4 billion in 1940 and $15
billion as recently as 1955. By the nature of these trusts, the figure is increasing inexorably, year by year, and at least one such trust, that of

Sears, Roebuck & Company's employees, now owns a controlling interest in the company. Thus, Sears, Roebuck has, in effect, socialized itself, and the list of companies in which the same thing happens is bound to grow rapidly as time goes on.)

At the same time, companies have shown the extent to which they have come to regard themselves as polities, with constituents to be wooed and even served rather than with mere employees to be compensated for work, by setting up all kinds of social facilities. They send their employees back to college, or set up entirely new colleges. IBM has its country clubs, Richfield Oil has its model homes, Reynolds Tobacco has its chaplains, RCA has its company neckties not in lieu of wages or to forestall labor troubles but to give employees a sense of belonging—to make them feel that the company is their community rather than merely their meal ticket. As Andrew Hacker has written, "The national government, as socialists throughout the world have discovered, is too large and unwieldy to provide satisfaction [of people's need for a sense of community]; and local governments are too weak and ineffectual to cater to such deep-seated needs." Small wonder that du Pont and Eastman Kodak are far from being the only companies that have available for employee consultation their own staffs of psychiatrists.

And along with their growing sense of responsibility for conditions and needs within their own organizations, the corporations, by and large, have come to look upon themselves as citizens with duties toward their local communities. In a very important respect, this is something entirely new since 1939. The old family capitalist could, and of course often did, make large charitable contributions *as an individual.* But he was legally prevented from contributing a penny of his company's money for such purposes unless he owned every share of the company's stock himself; otherwise, if he tried it, he was subject to suit by stockholders for misappropriating company funds. Since the end of the war, states have passed laws permitting corporations to make contributions to charity—and deduct them from federal tax—just like people. As a result, now it is an unenlightened great corporation indeed that does not have its own foundation through which it channels contributions for all kinds of good works, and one of the favorite good works is the enrichment of the local communities in which the company maintains facilities. Such a company, on setting up a new plant in a small town, might first undertake to help out the local hospitals; before long, it might be enlarging the library, bringing speakers and concerts to the local auditorium, setting up a symphony orchestra, establishing a community college, and engaging in a whole collection of other locally beneficial and uplifting activities.

What the community gains from all this is obvious; but it also incurs loss in the form of a certain enslavement, largely psychological rather than economic, to the corporation that is its benefactor. The company town survives in the America of the Sixties, but it is different from the traditional American barony in at least two ways. In the first place, the company, in intent and in effect, is now incomparably more beneficent. In the second place, because of the diffusion of corporate power that I have discussed, the baron himself is now invisible because he simply doesn't exist. He is a committee, or, more likely a collection of committees.

Not the least of the ways in which corporations in recent years have contributed to the life around them has been by making themselves physically a lot less forbidding. The "dark Satanic mill" of the nineteenth century, red-brick, four-square, and threatening with its rows of windows like accusing eyes, still stands slowly crumbling beside the river in many a New England or Midwestern town, but at some time since 1939 it has probably been abandoned as an operating plant. The heavy-industry factory with its rows of smokestacks belching soot still flourishes, of course, but for administrative offices and for factories in the lighter industries that have come into more and more prominence with recent technological change, modern architecture and landscaping have come to be all the rage. The buildings are low and glassy, brightened with cheerful (or, perhaps, garish) patches of color; their large green lawns are often used to display not just the familiar company sign with its trade-mark but sometimes a few pieces of abstract sculpture as well. Unfortunately, these new temples of industry, with their bland, antiseptic quality, sometimes convey a coldness and a sameness of a sort different only in style from that of the old-fashioned brick kind. And the mounting problem of air and water pollution caused by industry attests to the fact that its sense of responsibility to the community still has a long way to go . . .

But even in these times of supergiantism and invisible power a giant corporation is still the people who work for it, and especially the people who make the decisions in it. Hacker is not alone in believing that these men are "new breeds . . . whose behavior can no longer be accounted for by conventional rules of conduct." In a brilliant and influential book first published in 1956, *The Organization Man,* William H. Whyte, Jr. argued that the main characteristic of the new businessman operating in a large organization is his abandonment of the "Protestant ethic" — the old belief in hard work and thrift as prime virtues, and of the drawing of moral guidance from interior "character" as shaped by traditional authority — and his adoption of a new "social ethic," whereby one draws authority from one's contemporaries and one's surroundings, assiduously avoids moral confrontations in the belief that they would be evidence of social maladjustment, and concentrates on "getting along" in both senses of that phrase. But Whyte was focusing his attention on the younger executives who in the 1950s were occupying the lower-middle and middle ranks of corporate management. What these men will be like as time passes and they, or a few of them, assume the more powerful top ranks of management and become the moving forces in corporate life is beyond the scope of Whyte's study. As to present top and near-top management, I'm convinced that while the change here over the past generation is fully as great as the one Whyte describes, it is of a more complicated and somewhat different sort.

The business leader of the late 1930s swore by the Protestant ethic, all right. Henry Bamford Parkes has summed up the big businessmen of the great era of expansion following the Civil War by saying that "they could preach laissez-faire as vigorously as Adam Smith . . . and could denounce the growth of government as bitterly as Thomas Jefferson." Three-quarters of a socially eventful century later, the bosses of the Thirties still clung largely to those beliefs; Sewell Avery, the tough, fiercely independent, cash-hoarding, depression-fearing chief of Montgomery Ward, was prototypical of the time. Like most of his peers in the business elite, Avery had grown up in well-to-do circumstances and been given a first-class education that had provided him with a fully satisfactory set of practical and moral underpinnings for his conservative policies. Like most big business-men of the time, he does not seem to have suffered much doubt about the rightness of his decisions. He *knew* he was right.

Now much of that is changed; the characteristic business manager of the 1960s is more optimistic, more venturesome with capital funds, more group-minded and therefore less venturesome with personal policies, more social-minded, less conservative in politics, less sure of himself in all things. For one thing, he begins as a somewhat different sort of fellow — that is, he is apt to have had a different background. "Recruitment of business leaders from the bottom is taking place now and seems to be increasing," writes the sociologist W. Lloyd Warner. "Mobility to the top is not decreasing; in fact, for at least the last quarter century, it has been increasing." In other words, the famous Horatio Alger legend of rags-to-riches has become more, rather than less, factual than it was in Alger's time. The difference is that, what with ballooning national affluence, the "rags" have become more figurative than literal (and what with the incessant complaining of executives about how taxes prevent them from building up a large estate out of their high salaries, the riches may have become somewhat figurative, too).

The characteristic big-business leader of today is the child of good-citizen, lower-middle-class parents who were ambitious for him and scraped together their pennies to give him a fairly good education; he is seldom the product of real poverty, equally seldom of inherited wealth. Moreover, he has had more formal education than his predecessor in the earlier America. (Almost 60 percent of the big-business leaders of 1952 were college graduates, as against only a little more than 30 percent in 1928; and only a tiny fraction in 1952 had never finished high school, as against more than 25 percent in 1928.) On the other hand, he is less likely than formerly to be a graduate of one of the old Ivy League colleges of the Northeast. These famous institutions have long supplied the backbone cadre in the professions and in finance, and they continue to do so; but their graduates, many of whom still were content with or even enthusiastic about big business as a career as recently as 1939, are now inclined to shy away from the prospect of taking their chances in the "rat race" of a vast organization interested primarily in results and less so in educational or social backgrounds—except, of course, when they enter business by way of specialized graduate training at some leading kingmaking institution like the Harvard Business School, and thus come into the corporation already marked for leadership.

Far more often, the big-business boss of today is a graduate of some smaller and less celebrated college. And he is far less likely than formerly to be an Anglo-Saxon Protestant whose forebears have been in this country for many generations. The melting pot has done its work, as far as business leadership is concerned. One of the striking and little-noticed phenomena of contemporary life is the gulf—in social life, ways of thinking, communication, and personal contact of any sort aside from occasional meetings in some board of directors room—between the leaders of big business on the one hand and the people sometimes called the Establishment, who come from old families, went to Ivy League colleges, and wield much of the power in finance, philanthropy, and government, on the other. The notion that there is a single, homogeneous power elite in the United States is as wrong as it could be.

Conspicuously, the new business leader is embarrassed rather than smug or exultant about the extent of his power, as evidenced by his unwillingness to admit, perhaps even to himself, that it really exists. "As is well known," W. H. Ferry has written, "this country did not seek its role as world leader, but stumbled into it. By similar chance and circumstance, the corporation stumbled into the leadership of American society." One might well carry the argument a step further and say that the big businessmen stumbled—or would have you believe he stumbled—into his position as the leader of the leader. John Kenneth Galbraith has put the matter with his characteristic acid wit. For one thing, he says, the big businessman finds it convenient to deny his exercise of economic power so that he can logically justify his unwillingness to accept federal regulation. Furthermore, says Galbraith, he finds a deeper reason for avoiding the appearance of power in the American cultural grain:

> The privilege of controlling the actions or of affecting the income and property of others is something that no one of us can profess to seek or admit to possessing. No American ever runs for office because of an avowed desire to govern. He seeks to serve . . . . The same scrupulous avoidance of the terminology of power characterizes American business.

Was a Commodore Vanderbilt, a Henry Clay Frick, or even a Sewell Avery reluctant to affirm that he exercised power? Emphatically not. He had no trouble believing that he was competent to exercise it, that his exercise of it was wiser than would be that of somebody else—even, in certain cases, that he was born to exercise it. Contrast, then, the attitude of Roger M. Blough, whose stand on pricing in the steel industry in 1962 set off the greatest confrontation between government and business in recent history, and who as chairman of U.S. Steel is probably among the half-dozen most powerful businessmen in the country. At a conference in Corning, New York, in 1961, Charles Wyzanski, a Boston judge who happened to be sitting across the table from Mr. Blough, was emphasizing how the diffusion of power in modern corporations waters down the power of individuals. Not without a mischievous intent to provoke, Judge Wyzanski remarked that "Mr. Blough has far less power than his predecessors in the United States Steel Corporation. He can't do half the things. He is a constitutional monarch with the diffused power of the Queen [of England]." As Mr. Blough well knew, the Queen has virtually no substantive power at all, while Mr. Blough, in spite of all diffusion, has a great deal and does not hesitate to exercise it on occasion. Everyone turned to Mr. Blough, expecting him to enter at least a mild demurrer to this downgrading of his function. Not at all; instead, Mr. Blough objected to the word "monarch" as making him sound too omnipotent!

Undoubtedly the biggest single change in the big businessman has taken place within his mind. In 1939 his creed was clear enough: competition and the free-price system—Adam Smith's "invisible hand"—insure that business' pursuit of self-interest will serve the public interest. By and large, he still believes that creed, at least in theory, but in practice he does not always live by it. And for good reason; with the influence of government what it is today and with government being far and away business' biggest customer, business can ill afford to give government the back of its hand as Adam Smith would have wished. As *Business Week* put it in 1964: "Cut defense spending, the businessman says, but not my contract and not in my region. Increase international trade, but don't touch my tariff. Down with government subsidies—but not mine." *Business Week* went so far as to suggest a parallel between the two faces of modern business and the two characters of Dr. Jekyll and Mr. Hyde—tactfully omitting to say which face of business it considered to be Jekyll and which Hyde.

And beyond the matter of his own and his company's interest, the big businessman no longer finds enough justification in the unvarnished Adam Smith philosophy to satisfy him personally. He may allow, and even encourage, his spokesmen like the National Association of Manufacturers and the U.S. Chamber of Commerce to parrot it over and over again, but he fails to practice it. Under the Smith system a business that did something not in the interest of profit was not merely eccentric; it was actually subversive of a beneficent system. Now, as we have seen, businesses do things not in the interest of profit all the time. The writer George Lichtheim has suggested that the way to sell capitalism to the people in backward countries is by calling it socialism; perhaps it is not too much to say that United States business now, upon occasion, sells socialism to the American people by calling it capitalism. . . .

What have we done to our land? Basically, I think, to the extent that we have despoiled it we have done so by trusting too much to laissez-faire economics, which had their beginnings in Europe and were never intended to be applied without restraint to a mass society spread across a vast continent. Not that we have not been conscious of the problem of conservation since Theodore Roosevelt's time, and not that we were unconscious of it at the end of the 1930s. Indeed, the New Deal with its Civilian Conservation Corps and its many reclamation projects was in one sense a high point in the annals of conservation. Boulder Dam was finished in 1936, Shasta begun in 1938; in 1939 four major dams were completed and twelve others, including Grand Coulee, were under construction. Other determined government efforts were being directed toward the conservation of mineral resources, petroleum, and natural gas; so great was the interest in conservation that in 1938 there had been an unsuccessful legislative attempt to change the Department of the Interior into a Department of Conservation.

But there is an important distinction to be made here: conservation in the 1930s was very largely an economic rather than an aesthetic matter. It was directed toward dams that would bring people electric power, agricultural programs that would prevent the impoverishment of farmers through dust storms, mineral and timber-saving programs that would keep us from depleting our national resources — but seldom toward keeping the landscape beautiful or providing better facilities for recreation. (It is interesting to note that the building of dams and power plants in naturally unspoiled places is thought of now as the exact opposite of conservation. A plan of the Army Corps of Engineers to build two power-producing dams on the Upper Missouri River was denounced by the New York Times in March, 1965, as "an act of vandalism" and "a desecration"; the following month, a speaker at a Wilderness Conference in San Francisco happily predicted the eventual tearing down of all our hydroelectric dams except perhaps for Hoover, which would be preserved as an historic monument. In a quarter-century the meaning of conservation to most people has been precisely reversed.) National parks were then being looked on quizzically. In California the view was growing that the creation of more parks there would conflict with the state's economic welfare. A resolution was actually introduced in Congress in June, 1939, proposing the abolition of Grand Teton National Park. At the end of the longest and by far the most disastrous depression in our history, we clearly did not feel that we could afford the luxury of worrying about beauty.

And, in any case, at the end of the Thirties the great forces that work toward the destruction of beauty—industrialization and urbanization—were temporarily pretty much at bay. Our farm population had remained nearly constant for many years, and, indeed, it was slightly higher at the end of the 1930s than it had been at the end of the 1920s (although nothing like so much higher as the urban population was). As industrial jobs became more and more scarce during the depression and labor-management strife more and more destructive, a back-to-the-land movement of significant proportions—surely the last such movement in the nation's history—developed. "The estimate in 1935 that there were almost two million Americans in the countryside who had not been there five years earlier may have exaggerated the extent to which that represented an actual return to rural living," Oscar Handlin has written, "but the trend was nevertheless significant. Largely these were fugitives from the depression, people who had sought their fortunes in the cities and failed, and who now returned to family homesteads; for although these were already 'fished-out ponds,' the security they offered, poor as it was, was preferable to the unlimited risks of life in the towns." A practical guide to how to conduct a small farm, *Five Acres and Independence,* originally published in 1935, had run through five editions by 1940, and by the end of the war it had sold half a million copies. Malcolm Cowley in *Exile's Return* tells about how hundreds of writers in the Thirties left the cities and settled in old farmhouses without central heat or plumbing—not out of any desire to be close to the land, but simply out of a desire to avoid the necessity of doing hack work in order to pay city bills.

Others, though, were returning to the land primarily for spiritual and ideological rather than practical reasons; disillusioned with the contemporary scene, they were making nostalgic excursions into the simpler, sweeter American past. Such a one was Charles Allen Smart, Harvard '26, who left a city job to take over a small farm that he had inherited in southern Ohio, and who described his experiences in a popular and charming book entitled *R.F.D.,* published in 1938. Smart and his wife brought quite a good many of their city attitudes and artifacts to the farm with them—they put reproductions of Toulouse-Lautrec, Laurencin, and Chirico in their WPA-built privy—but he was genuinely and quite movingly rhapsodic about the farm life:

> The harvesting of wheat . . . is like sowing seed, or the births of the animals, or the making of wine. Flesh and blood, bread and wine, seeds and death . . . no thank you, gentlemen, you can keep your offices and trains, your files and accounts, your wing collars and umbrellas. . . . Farming is immeasurably more sympathetic to thought than is business, for ex-

ample, and it is more stimulating and vitalizing to it than is teaching in a school.

How little the Americans of 1939 saw the shape of the urban problems ahead is dramatically shown by the World's Fair Futurama. Here was a frank attempt to envision perfection in the human use of land and its resources. Among the chief elements that made up the vision were bigger and more efficient highways designed to convey more automobiles into cities faster (with little said about parking facilities); disruption of existing urban areas by the intrusion of these highways; and the rigid compartmentalization of cities into residential, commercial, and industrial areas. Even allowing for the fact that the Futurama was presented on behalf of an automobile manufacturer, it appears now as a remarkable essay in reversed values. As I have noted before, many of its prophecies of Heaven have become facts; the only trouble is that now that they are here they look more like the lineaments of Hell.

What the nation considered its "conservation" problem in 1939 — the problem of making the most of natural resources, and thus raising standards of living — has been triumphantly solved; now it is exclusively the problem of those remote places that we call underdeveloped (or, more delicately, "less developed") countries. It is significant to note that David Lilienthal, who became famous in the Thirties as one of the heads of the pioneer resource-development project, the TVA, now heads a firm that specializes in similar projects for foreign countries. And one effect of the solution was to help cause a shift in the center of gravity of national life from the farm to the city and its suburbs, with an accompanying change, almost amounting to a reversal, in the national style of living.

Many things contributed to the shift. On the one hand, the growth of industry, accompanied as it was by the rising power of labor unions, made for millions of appetizing high-pay jobs in urban areas, where industry was concentrated. On the other hand, the products of industry — new machines, fertilizers, and pesticides that have become the marvels of the agricultural world — tended to reduce the amount of human labor necessary to farming and thus do the farm hand out of his job, and also to convert successful farming from a small, individualistic enterprise into a vast, impersonal business. What could the small farmer do? Despite government subsidies, he had to sell out to a big combine, go to the city, and take an industrial job.

Specifically: we now produce 60 percent more food than we did in 1940 from about the same number of acres of farmland. In 1940 we had a little more than six million farms of which 2.2 million consisted of less than fifty acres, and 100,000 of a thousand acres or more; in 1959 the national total of farms was down to 3.7 million, of which just over one million consisted of less than fifty acres and 136,000 of more than a thousand acres; and the Department of Agriculture says that a corn farmer now *must* have at least a thousand acres or his costs will make it impossible for him to meet competitive prices. Meanwhile—and here is the key figure from a social standpoint—the number of man-hours of labor required to do the country's farm work decreased from more than twenty million in 1940 to under nine million in 1963.

The annual decline in the farm population has been almost, but not quite, in a straight line. In 1939 we had about 31 million farmers, or not quite a quarter of the whole population; in 1963 we had 13.7 million, or 7.1 percent. After falling off sharply during the war, the total turned upward slightly in the first postwar years, 1946 and 1947, proving that a few ex-GIs could be returned to the farm at least temporarily. There has been a net loss in every year since then except for 1955, and in some years during the 1950's the net loss amounted to almost a million farmers. Between 1950 and 1962, one out of every five farmers became a former farmer.

It is true enough that the process of urbanization in American life had been going on for decades, even generations—hadn't William Jennings Bryan himself, in his famous "Cross of Gold" speech, warned the country, "Destroy our farms, and the grass will grow in the streets of every city in the country"?—but only in the years after the Second World War has the flight from the farm become a rout. And something, unquestionably, has been lost in the process—something very old and very American, not just peasant shrewdness but a straightforwardness, steadfastness, and simplicity of heart that usually more than counterbalanced the lack of intellect or formal education that went with it. . . .

The seventeen million farmers who have left the land in the past quarter-century are urbanites now, and must be considered in an urban context; but for those who stayed, life has changed, too. The nature of the change is nicely documented in two books on a more or less typical farming community in the Ozark foothills of Missouri—*Plainville, U.S.A,* by James West, describing the community as it was in 1939, and *Plainville Fifteen Years Later,* by Art Gallaher, Jr., describing it in 1954.

West in 1939 found Plainville a small, relatively isolated community where farming methods were technologically backward, and where farming was not just a living but a way of life. Although there was a rising discontent, based apparently on exposure to national mass communications media, with the traditional local social structure, nevertheless that structure remained firmly in place. Essentially, it consisted of a two-class system based not so much on wealth as on such other matters as whether one lived in the hills (that was lower-class) or on the prairie (upper-class). And nonmonetary values extended, West found, into the conduct of work;

harvesting, threshing, butchering, and sawing wood were often group or even community activities, and a farmer would "lend a boy" to his neighbor for a day or two when the neighbor needed extra help, expecting nothing in return other than similar consideration when *he* had a problem. Plainville had some of the aspects of a kind of primitive socialism — never, needless to say, called by that name. "The roots of her tradition," West wrote, "are still in the frontier."

Three crucial things had happened to Plainville by the time Gallaher studied it in 1954. A highway going through it had been completed in 1940; television had come to it, as it had to almost every other place in the nation, soon after 1950; and the technical revolution in farming methods had been progressively affecting it over the whole period. As a result of these things, Gallaher wrote, "Plainvillers are increasingly drawn into the mainstream of modern urban America"; in particular, they had become less cooperative, more individualistic, more technology-minded, and, above all, far more devoted to the almighty dollar: "The major desire of Plainvillers is (now) more money." The population of the town had dropped 12 percent between the census of 1940 and that of 1950. The number of farms in the county had dropped 37 percent in the years between the end of the war and 1954, and the size of the average farm had increased from 151 acres to 217 acres. Meanwhile, Plainvillers had become far richer — the average gross annual sales of the local merchants went from $5,300 in 1939 to $27,600 in 1949 — and this, combined with their increasing exposure to national ideas as to styles and standards of living, had changed their aspirations; living conditions that had been thought satisfactory in 1939 were now thought substandard as the new ranch house with its jalousie windows and its antenna replaced the old homestead with its backyard outhouse. Largely gone was the two-class system based on traditional ideas, replaced by a new hierarchy based frankly on affluence; gone was the habit of offering and expecting mutual help on work.

And along with all this went a basic reversal in attitude: the old nostalgia for the past and indifference to technology had been replaced by a sense of superiority to the past and an almost religious devotion to technological change as the potential solution to all problems. Plainville, Gallaher found, now looked instinctively for authority not to its own past but to the rest of the country — above all, to the rich cities with their skyscrapers and washing machines and shiny new automobiles. Not only had the method of the farm been industrialized; in the process, it seemed, the mind of the farmer had been industrialized and urbanized too, and in that sense even those who stayed on the farms did not remain farmers at heart.

17

Elmo Roper

How Culturally Active
Are Americans?

*Elmo Roper is one of America's foremost public opinion analysts and mar-
ket researchers. In the following selection, he reports the result of a survey
indicating a very low level of cultural activity among Americans. It would
seem that the so-called cultural effloresence, which includes the paperback
revolution, the establishment of symphony orchestras, and the building of
culture palaces across the nation, involves a relatively small number of
people. The old hope that abundance and leisure would lead to the cultivation of the individual has not yet been realized. For related ideas, see
Larrabee, Bell, Parkes, Goodrich.*

In an era when culture is being promoted with all the enthusiasm once
reserved for breakfast cereal and we are being reminded daily that ignorance is obsolete, how "cultural" are Americans? Where does learning
rank in our range of interest?

The answers to some questions recently asked of a cross-section of adult
Americans shed some light on our intellectual and cultural involvement.
To begin with, respondents were offered a list of subjects and asked to
name those in which they had "a good deal of interest." The results appear below:

Religion	49%	Home decoration	35%
Sports	47	History	22
Music	46	Science	20
Politics and government	40	Literature	19
International affairs	37	Art	13
Cooking	36	No opinion	7

Clearly, the egghead still has a long way to go before he replaces the
baseball player as a national hero. Religion, sports, and music command
the broadest appeal and top the list of interests. Politics and international
affairs, interests that for various people have varying degrees of intellectual content, barely edge out the frankly down-to-earth concerns of home

From *Saturday Review* (May 14, 1966). Reprinted by permission of *Saturday Review*
and the author.

and kitchen. And at the very bottom lie the clearly intellectual and cultural subjects (with the exception of music, which may or may not reflect as deep a cultural interest), each mentioned by less than a quarter of the people interviewed: history by 22 per cent, science by 20 per cent, literature 19 per cent, with art trailing off at 13 per cent.

The next question inquired how often people read books that they felt would "advance their knowledge or education in some way." Twenty-two per cent replied "frequently," 29 per cent said they did so "occasionally," and 46 per cent said "rarely" or "never." Another question found that 35 per cent had less than twenty-five books in the home, and another 35 per cent between twenty-five and 100, with only 27 per cent owning more than 100 books (3 per cent didn't know). Other questions also were asked about newspaper and magazine reading, and educational achievement.

Who, then, are the culturally and intellectually involved? Needless to say, the various indices do not all work in the same direction. While the heavy book *readers* are apt to be found among the young (20-34), the heaviest book *ownership* comes at a later age (35-55). Interest in international affairs goes up with age; interest in science is higher with youth. Among the intellectually involved, traditional sex differences in interests are very much in evidence, with women leaning toward such subjects as art and literature, men toward science and politics.

But perhaps the most interesting difference is that women, particularly college-educated women, have *more* interests than men. On the list of interests, seven items were singled out as subjects of a "good deal of interest" by 50 per cent or more of college women. Among college men, only three items elicited that degree of interest. Also, the low point of intellectual interest for college women is science, which nevertheless is called interesting by 24 per cent. The cultural "low" of college men is art, which at 18 per cent is comparable with their interest in the female realm of home decorating (16 per cent) and cooking (10 per cent).

To get a rough measure of the general level of cultural and intellectual activity in the population, a scale was developed on which each respondent was given a score. Respondents were given one point each for such activities as regular reading of two or more newspapers or "fairly regular" reading of any leading news magazines with intellectual content such as *Harper's,* the *New Yorker,* or *Saturday Review:* one point each for expressing a "good deal of interest" in politics and government, international affairs, art, history, science or literature; five points each for "frequent" reading of books to advance knowledge or having more than 100 books in the home; two points for attending college; five points for graduating; and five points for taking academic, business or professional courses since graduating from college—with a maximum possible score of thirty-five points.

Using this measure of what might be loosely described as the "level of

cultural activity," respondents fell into four main groups. Fifty-one per
cent received scores from zero to three, and might be described as the
"culturally inert." Another 26 percent received scores of from four to
nine, and might therefore be considered "fairly inactive" culturally. Thir-
teen per cent received scores of from ten to fifteen, and might be described
as "fairly active." Only 10 per cent received scores over fifteen (out of a
possible thirty-five), thereby gaining the description of "culturally active" —
the term is relative!

What is the relationship between cultural activity and formal education?
If you're culturally active, does it mean you've been to college? And if
you've been to college, are you thereby culturally active?

The answer to the first question is, by and large, yes. Only 1 per cent
of grade school people and only 4 per cent of the high school educated
fell into the culturally active category, whereas 26 per cent of those who
had had some college and 62 per cent of people with college degrees received culturally active scores (abetted, of course, by the credit given for
college in their scores).

But the answer to the second question is another thing. Before everyone
who's been to college starts resting on his cultural laurels, thinking of the
great gap that separates him from the lowly people who make up the rest
of the population, let him take a look at the ranking of interests by those
with college backgrounds:

Has a good deal of interest in:

International affairs	60%	Literature	39%
Politics and government	59	History	37
Music	56	Science	36
Sports	53	Home decoration	36
Religion	49	Cooking	31
	Art 26%		

Political and international events replace religion, sports and music as
the prime interests of the college educated. But pure cultural and intellectual interests still cluster, along with cooking and home decor, at the bottom of the list. Asked how often they read edifying books, 44 per cent
of college educated people answered "frequently" — which means that a
majority read to learn infrequently after they leave the academic groves.
Asked about book ownership (an easier test than book reading, and the
books could be about anything, nearly one quarter (23 per cent) of the
college educated had less than fifty books in their homes, and just slightly
over half (56 per cent) owned more than 100 books.

All in all, it must be said that intellectual and cultural activity is still
distinctly a minority taste. A college education is no guarantee of developed
cultural or intellectual interests, although it certainly makes such interests

more probable. In our national rush to get more and more people to college, it should perhaps be kept in mind that half the people who have gotten there show only minor intellectual after-effects. Regarding the other half who can be described as culturally and intellectually involved, the most important question is one that can not be answered by a survey. It is the depth and quality of that involvement.

Some years ago I wrote, "There is an urgent need—in fact a national survival need—for invigorating intellectual life, for upgrading the general regard for intellectual excellence. The United States must experience an intellectual renaissance or it will experience defeat. The time cannot be far off—if indeed it is not already here—when the *strength* of a nation, measured in terms of any kind of world competition, will depend less on the number of its bombs than on the number of its learned men."

The statement is equally valid today. Unquestionably, there have been changes in recent years in our attitude toward the intellectual life. But the changes have not gone far enough. There is no upsurge of intellectual interest in the young—except in the field of science. And too many people who consider themselves educated have really just gone through the motions. The question that should most concern our educators is not how far they can spread learning but how deep it goes.

part two

**Particulars,
Specifics,
and Potshots**

Karl Shapiro   Of Love and Death in
                                        the Garrison State I Sing

Of love and death in the Garrison State I sing. From uniformed populations
rises the High Art, *Oedipus King,* the No, the ballerina bleeding in her
slippers. At the Officers Club adultery is rationed (their children are not
allowed to play with guns. This helps whet their appetite). The ladies are
discussing the chemical control of behavior by radio waves: that will solve
the problem of neighbors. Symposia on causes of desertion draw record-
breaking crowds. The handsomer pacifists are invited to the most sought-
after cocktail parties. The women try their hand at them in the rumpus
room; some progress reported. Waves of asceticism sweep the automobile
industry. The mere sight of a Sam Browne belt, which used to inspire contempt, brings tears to the eyes of highschool boys. All flabby citizens are
automatically put under surveillance. Chess problems supersede crap in the
non-coms barracks. The sacred number is Two: two parties, two powers
sworn to mutual death, two poles of everything from ethics to magnetics.
It's a balanced society.

Today the order goes out: all distant places are to be abolished: beachcombers
are shot like looters. Established poets are forced to wear beards and blue-
jeans; they are treated kindly in bohemian zoos; mysterious stipends drift
their way. They can trade soap for peyote at specified libraries. Children's
prizes are given for essays on the pleasures of crisis. Historians are awarded
all the key posts in the foreign office. Sculptors who use old shrapnel are
made the heads of schools of design. Highways move underground like
veins of ore. The Anti-Sky Association (volunteer contributions only) meets
naked at high noon and prays for color-blindness.

"Color is a biological luxury."

                                              II

How are the neighbors astounded and shocked when the handsome Army flyer
kills with his shotgun on a well-mown street his wife, his great Dane and
his two little children. The newspapers seize on the word *berserk,* not looking it up. The neighbors contribute to his exemplary character, calm, polite,
affable, well-spoken, in love with his sports-car of foreign make. The one
paragraph on his drinking habits tells nothing at all. It passes from the

news like weather. It's Cold Wartime. And though it's front page, it's only of local interest.

As we used to say in the Army: ratings open.

III

It is the garbage boy who has killed eleven in as many hours and he is loose with his shotguns somewhere close. The garbage boy with his pretty consort of fourteen years, his Juliet. She at least will escape the electric chair. Our quiet town is internationally famous overnight. Quiet town with its excellent schools and so many churches. Reporters fly in from the cultural centers, famous photographers detailed to be in on the kill. The police have ordered the closing of schools. Fathers come home to pack children in cars, houses are locked, guns taken down. Neighbors are shouldering rifles everywhere. It's a war against one. Who would have thought so many people were armed?

The newspapers scream like demented women: red-headed bandy-legged garbage boy. The newspapers jeer like schoolboys in a yard: four-eyed red-headed band-legged garbage boy. More bodies are found, other atrocities (not even fit for the ears of newspapers). The mad afternoon progresses in all directions. Is he here, in my neighborhood? Anyone can be next. The world is his enemy and killing is easy, too easy. The body is soft to the slugs and the fine buckshot. There's nothing to it. Perhaps there should be more, more pleasure in it. He fails at a rape — the weather is too cold. In secret testimony says — "I couldn't bring it to a point." Then the whole panic rots apart, almost too soon. They've got the killer, across the Wyoming line, by accident more or less. And they all drive back to the city of the killings, a small triumphal procession.

18

William Lloyd Warner

The Ideology of Democracy
in a Class System

William Lloyd Warner, anthropologist and sociologist, was born in California in 1898 and graduated from the University of California in 1925. He has taught in a variety of institutions and has done field work in Australia. He is currently University Professor at Michigan State University. Among his works are The Yankee City *(1963) and* Social Class in America *(1949). In the following selection, Warner lists what he calls the basic social logics of status and class in America. For related ideas, see Mills, Whyte, Brogan, Gabriel, and Fuchs.*

Five generations have lived on the banks of The River since Will Taylor and his people founded the City of the Common Man and the other Jonesvilles of the midland prairie. All that has happened and is happening in Jonesville has happened to America. We said earlier that this community "reflects and symbolizes the significant principles on which the American social system rests. Borrowing from the Gospel of John," we went on to say, "Jonesville is in all Americans, and all Americans are in Jonesville, for he that dwelleth in America dwelleth in Jonesville and Jonesville in Him." Easily the most important fact about this community is that its beliefs and values are founded on basic contradictions, and its social logics, the basic precepts on which action is founded, are a series of paradoxes.

Some of our basic social logics, many of them contradictory, are enumerated below:

(1) All men are equal.

(2) Some men are superior in status, others inferior.

The two propositions are restated in the social logics of

(3) "All men are equal, but some of us are more equal than others"; Sometimes expressed in another form, more subtle and less easy to see at a glance, "all of us are equal because all of us have an equal opportunity to achieve," or, more pessimistically, "from shirtsleeves to shirtsleeves."

(4) All men are equal in the sight of God, but within His church and among His people power and position are too often present.

These four statements apply to every aspect of the society. There are many other basic propositions contained within them which are their corollaries and help buttress their power:

(5) All occupations are to be respected, for all are necessary for the common life, but they have varying degrees of prestige and power and are ranked accordingly.

(6) The values inherent within occupational ranking place the skilled jobs above those with less skill and reward them accordingly.

(7) These same occupational values rank jobs demanding more schooling above those requiring less.

(8) Clean jobs outrank dirty ones; white-collar men, those who labor.

(9) Jobs may be organized into interconnected hierarchies (factories, etc.) where the success or failure of a man may be measured by his movement up or down the hierarchy.

Our social logics about money, as revealed in behavior, reflect some of the fundamentals of our value system. Some of the more important ones are:

(10) The greater amount of money a family or individual possesses, the higher the economic ranking; however,

(11) While the possession of larger and smaller amounts of money is a factor in social class, the mere possession of money is insufficient for achieving social status, for the successful use of money for class purposes demands its translation into socially approved behavior which expresses prestige in the values of the superior classes. Therefore,

(12) It is better to spend one's money on good works, philanthropy, higher education, and the works of God, or objects of conspicuous display, and achieve contact and perhaps identification with the great and highly placed than to hoard it and live in the lowly position of the miser or in the respected but subordinate position of the common man.

(13) Those who accumulate money but hoard or invest it and refuse to translate their money symbols into social and status symbols accumulate economic power which is recognized, but they never achieve top social status, no matter how large their accumulated wealth, for such status depends on their recognition by others and acceptance by those at the top.

(14) Any kind of money is important and necessary for maintaining social advantage, but the income from investments is better than other sources, for the coupon-clipper who has made his money is superior to him who still earns profits or fees.

(15) Unearned income is better than earned wealth, for income from investment, although highly evaluated, is not ranked as high as inherited symbols of money. In other words, to have a silver spoon in one's mouth

at birth is better than being a self-made man. Successful social mobility in the American mind is a magnificent performance but is never as good as being born to the group of those who already belong.

(16) Profits and fees as forms of income are better than salaries, but salaries *as forms* of getting money are better than wages.

(17) Wages, while low, are earned money and as such are better than public or private aid; for the recipient of unilateral "gifts" is always subordinate and in an inferior position. Truly in America when one is poor it is better to give than to receive.

(18) Recipients of "public welfare aid," the lowest *form* of income, are ranked accordingly and penalized by social sanction.

No doubt the reader has noticed that the writer has emphasized a sharp distinction between the *form* of getting money and the amount. We all know the amount of money that a man has is of great importance, but everyone knows that the small salary that supports a clerk's family is superior to what might be the larger combined income of a family whose form of income is public relief. Each realm, the form and the amount, has its own hierarchy of values; each realm of value interpenetrates the other in practice, yet each too is at the same time separate. Occupation, and source and amount of income have their own rankings, and their values are reflected in social-class position. Other value systems are ranked and contribute their share to the status a man or his family enjoys or suffers in Jonesville. Certain other propositions about the social logics of status need to be added.

(19) A family's house, its furniture, and other such equipment express and help symbolize its social-class position. Inferior families live in inferior houses, superior families in superior houses. For example, well-cared for, large houses which express the values of the elect are superior; the poorly cared for small houses are likely to be those of the inferior classes.

(20) The dwelling areas of Jonesville are socially graded. Those who live in inferior areas are likely to be inferior; those who live in superior areas are likely to be superior.

(21) Learning too is graded and ranked. Those who have been exposed to the higher grades of learning are superior; those stopping further down are inferior. But

(22) It is whom you know not what you know that is important.

(23) The way each of the above prestige-giving factors operates in the life of an individual in his community depends on how the other members of the community evaluate them and incorporate them into his social reputation and membership in the status-giving institutions of Jonesville.

(24) It is possible for individuals to move up or down in this social-class hierarchy.

(25) The principal methods of upward mobility are accumulation of

money and its transformation into socially approved symbols, educational advancement, recognition of trained talent, marriage into a higher level, the use of beauty and sex, the acquisition of moral and ethical social codes of superior groups, the acquisition of secular rituals at superior levels, learning the social skills (speech, etc.) of those in the higher groups, and participation in cliques, associations, and churches that are frequented by the higher groups.

(26) Downward mobility is caused by loss of money, marriage at lower levels, loss of moral and ethical behavior, and participation in associations, cliques, churches, and other institutions below those you previously used.

Clearly these propositions just reviewed indicate that the equalitarian principle expressed in the precepts sacred to our democratic creed are in opposition to the hard facts that press upon the citizens of Jonesville when they experience the secular realities of social class. It is clear that the "truths" of either system, social hierarchy or democratic equality, are not true in themselves. Each is made known to us only by understanding what the other is and by ferreting out the way the two contradictory systems are interrelated. We cannot give our entire attention to one and not recognize the other, for the two constitute the realities of American democracy. The democracy of the American Dream is true only because of the social gradation on the ladder where successful men are permitted to realize their ambitions. The social-class system is true only because the precepts of the Dream provide the moral code which enforces the rules of social mobility by insisting that all able men who obey the rules of the game have "the right" to climb. To many it will seem paradoxical that the truth about American belief can only be found by relating two contradictory principles of human value and human action. Careful scrutiny of what is involved scientifically reduces this paradox to simple scientific propositions.

Complete equality does not exist in any society which is highly complex and differentiated into many occupations and positions. All the parts of a complex society are always evaluated and ranked. The operation of the family system throughout the generations helps to perpetuate this system of ranking and to select certain kinds of people for higher and lower social positions. No society with a large population can exist without a high division of labor to perform the tasks necessary for its survival; hence it is certain that no populous society can exist without one or more systems of rank.

If this last statement is true, the fundamental question for Americans to answer should be "Is the American insistence on equality nonsense and sentimental delusion and should honest men abandon such ideals and principles?" The answer is clearly no; for these equalitarian beliefs and values are of absolute importance to us. Without them our social-class system would become rigid and inflexible; there would be little or no movement between the classes.

The worth of the individual under such circumstances would be decided by the principles of fixed status rather than by the flexible rules permitting social mobility. Although our system is not entirely democratic and equalitarian, belief in a democratic ideology provides an ideal toward which we strive. The strength of the democratic ideal provides the counterbalancing, opposing force against the power of our social hierarchy which, although naturally and inherently a part of our complex culture, if unopposed would reduce American life to a fixed rank order and destroy our present system of open classes where the individual is defined as someone who has choice about what he does. This is a system whose principles say that no man or family shall remain in the status to which he was born.

Close behavorial conformity

19

David Riesman   **A Definition of Other-Direction**

David Riesman was born in 1909 in Philadelphia, Pennsylvania. He studied at Harvard and received his Law degree there in 1934. He started his career as a law clerk in the office of Justice Brandeis and eventually became a professor of law. He is currently a professor in the Department of Social Relations at Harvard. He has dealt with a number of contemporary concerns in his writings, which include Constraint and Variety in American Education *(1956) and* Abundance for What?, and Other Essays *(1964). In the selection that follows, Riesman defines the character of the "other-directed" person, who is found predominantly among the upper middle class of our larger cities. For related ideas, see Wheelis, Whyte, Brogan, Brooks.*

The type of character I shall describe as other-directed seems to be emerging in very recent years in the upper middle class of our larger cities:

From *The Lonely Crowd* by David Riesman (New Haven: Yale University Press, 1950), pp. 19–25. Reprinted by permission of the publisher.

more prominent in New York than in Boston, in Los Angeles than in Spokane, in Cincinnati than in Chillicothe. Yet in some respects this type is strikingly similar to *the* American, whom Tocqueville and other curious and astonished visitors from Europe, even before the Revolution, thought to be a new kind of man. Indeed, travelers' reports on America impress us with their unanimity. The American is said to be shallower, freer with his money, friendlier, more uncertain of himself and his values, more demanding of approval than the European. It all adds up to a pattern which, without stretching matters too far, resembles the kind of character that a number of social scientists have seen as developing in contemporary, highly industrialized, and bureaucratic America: Fromm's "marketer," Mills's "fixer," Arnold Green's "middle class male child." [1]

This raises several questions which, as I said earlier, I have not been able to answer. It is my impression that the middle-class American of today is decisively different from those Americans of Tocqueville's writings who strike us as so contemporary, and much of this book will be devoted to discussing these differences. [2] It is also my impression that the conditions I believe to be responsible for other-direction are affecting increasing numbers of people in the metropolitan centers of the advanced industrial countries. However, the available comparative studies of European "national character," broken down by social class, are not yet sufficiently inclusive to permit comparison. Given impetus by the late Ruth Benedict, Gorer, Kardiner, Kluckhohn, Margaret Mead, and others, such studies are now under way. Meanwhile, my analysis of the other-directed character is at once an analysis of the American and of contemporary man. Much of the time I find it hard or impossible to say where one ends and the other begins. Tentatively, I am inclined to think that the other-directed type does find itself most at home in America, due to certain constant

---

[1] See Erich Fromm, *Man for Himself;* C. Wright Mills, "The Competitive Personality," *Partisan Review,* XIII (1946), 433; Arnold Green, "The Middle Class Male Child and Neurosis," *American Sociological Review,* XI (1946), 31. See also the work of Jurgen Ruesch, Martin B. Loeb, and co-workers on the "infantile personality."

[2] I have tried to discover, by reading the eyewitness social observers of the early nineteenth century in America, whether Tocqueville "saw" America or "foresaw" it, to what extent he was influenced — as visiting firemen of today also are — by American snobs who take their image of Europe as the norm in describing their own countrymen. And to what extent, in establishing America's polarity from Europe, he tendentiously noticed those things that were different rather than those that were the same. From conversations with Phillips Bradley and Arthur Schlesinger, Jr., and from G. W. Pierson, *Tocqueville and Beaumont in America* (New York, Oxford University Press, 1938) I get the impression that all these qualifications must be put on Tocqueville's picture of America in the 1830's. On the general problem of whether there is an American character, and if so what are its sources, and how such questions might be investigated, I have profited from the work of Oscar Handlin and from suggestions made by him. Thomas and Znaniecki's *Polish Peasant* may be thought of as a pioneer effort, unfortunately too little followed up, to attack the problem in terms of the experience of a particular ethnic group.

elements in American society, such as its recruitment from Europe and its lack of any seriously feudal past. As against this, I am also inclined to put more weight on capitalism, industrialism, and urbanization—these being international tendencies—than on any character-forming peculiarities of the American scene.

Bearing these qualifications in mind, it seems appropriate to treat contemporary metropolitan America as our illustration of a society—so far, perhaps, the only illustration—in which other-direction is the dominant mode of insuring conformity. It would be premature, however, to say that it is already the dominant mode in America as a whole. But since the other-directed types are to be found among the young, in the larger cities, and among the upper income groups, we may assume that, unless present trends are reversed, the hegemony of other-direction lies not far off.

If we wanted to cast our social character types into social class molds, we could say that inner-direction is the typical character of the "old" middle class—the banker, the tradesman, the small entrepreneur, the technically oriented engineer, etc.—while other-direction is becoming the typical character of the "new" middle class—the bureaucrat, the salaried employee in business, etc. Many of the economic factors associated with the recent growth of the "new" middle class are well known. They have been discussed by James Burnham, Colin Clark, Peter Drucker, and others. There is a decline in the numbers and in the proportion of the working population engaged in production and extraction—agriculture, heavy industry, heavy transport—and an increase in the numbers and the proportion engaged in white-collar work and the service trades.

Furthermore, societies in the phase of incipient decline (societies, that is, in which we expect other-directed types to come to the fore) are not only highly urbanized but have a high level of capital equipment and technological skill built up during the period of transitional growth. People who are literate, educated, and provided with the necessities of life by machine industry and agriculture, turn increasingly to the "tertiary" economic realm. The service industries prosper among the people as a whole and no longer only in court circles. Education, leisure, services, these go together with an increased consumption of words and images from the mass media of communications in societies that have moved into the incipient decline stage via the route of industrialization. Hence, while societies in the phase of transitional growth begin the process of distributing words from urban centers, the flow becomes a torrent in the societies of incipient population decline. This process, while modulated by profound national and class differences, connected with differences in literacy and loquacity, takes place everywhere in the industrialized lands. Increasingly, relations with the outer world and with oneself are mediated by the flow of mass communication. For the other-directed types political events are

likewise experienced through a screen of words by which the events are
habitually atomized and personalized—or pseudopersonalized. For the
inner-directed person who remains still extant in this period the tendency
is rather to systematize and moralize this flow of words.

These developments lead, for large numbers of people, to changes in
paths to success and to the requirement of more "socialized" behavior
both for success and for marital and personal adaptation. Connected with
such changes are changes in the family and in child-rearing practices. In
the smaller families of urban life, and with the spread of "permissive"
child care to ever wider strata of the population, there is a relaxation of
older patterns of discipline. Under these newer patterns the peer-group
(the age- and class-graded group in a child's school and neighborhood)
becomes much more important to the child, while the parents make him
feel guilty not so much about violation of inner standards as about failure
to be popular or otherwise to manage his relations with these other children. Moreover, the pressures of the school and the peer-group are reinforced and continued—in a manner whose inner paradoxes I shall discuss
later—by the mass media: movies, radio, comics, and popular culture
media generally. Under these conditions types of character emerge that we
shall here term other-directed. *What is common to all other-directeds is that
their contemporaries are the source of direction for the individual—either
those known to him or those with whom he is indirectly acquainted, through
friends and through the mass media. This source is of course "internalized"
in the sense that dependence on it for guidance in life is implanted early.
The goals toward which the other-directed person strives shift with that
guidance: it is only the process of striving itself and the process of paying
close attention to the signals from others that remain unaltered throughout life.* This mode of keeping in touch with others permits a close behavioral conformity, not through drill in behavior itself, as in the tradition-
directed character, but rather through an exceptional sensitivity to the actions and wishes of others.

Of course, it matters very much who these "others" are: whether they
are the individual's immediate circle or a "higher" circle or the anonymous
voices of the mass media; whether the individual fears the hostility of
chance acquaintances or only of those who "count." But his need for approval and direction from others—and contemporary others rather than
ancestors—goes beyond the reasons that lead most people in any era to
care very much what others think of them. While all people want and
need to be liked by some of the people some of the time, it is only the
modern other-directed types who make this their chief source of direction
and chief area of sensitivity.

20

John W. Aldridge   After the Lost Generation

*John W. Aldridge, teacher and critic, was born in Sioux City, Iowa, in
1922. Since receiving his Bachelor's degree from the University of California at Berkeley in 1947, he has been a lecturer and teacher in a number
of universities. He was awarded the Bronze Star Medal with five battle
stars while serving with the United States Army in World War II. His critical writings include* In Search of Heresy *(1956), and a novel,* The Party at
Cranton *(1960). His latest critical work,* Time to Murder and Create,
*was published in 1966. He is a frequent contributor to numerous publica-
tions. In the selection here, Aldridge describes post-World-War-II writers
as "reporters," and compares them unfavorably with those writers who
appeared after World War I. See also Hassan; Schlesinger, Jr.; Larabee;
Sproat.*

. . . The best young writers of the second war and its aftermath, have
not had the advantage of either the perspective or the values of another
and more stable age. They have come to maturity at the end of the period
of transition and loss when the wreckage of the old order has been made
complete and the energy of rebellion has been dissipated. Perhaps the
most unfortunate aspect of their dilemma is that, although they have been
denied the energy, they have inherited the wreckage and are obliged to
face it nakedly and coldly without resources. There is no longer for them
the possibility of a literature of consciousness, such as Joyce, Woolf, and
the others evolved, nor of a literature that draws its power from disillusion, shock, and social change. The techniques of science that were exploited so brilliantly by the founders of the literature of consciousness are
not the bright new instruments they were when they were discovered. They
no longer promise to open fresh and unexplored fields to the novelist.
They would seem, rather, to offer only to lead him back over old ground
to the kind of material which Joyce and Woolf explored thoroughly and
for all time. Besides, since the new writers cannot possibly use those techniques with the same sense of defiant discovery, they would probably use
them badly and with a paralyzing realization of their triteness. For much

From *After the Lost Generation* by John W. Aldridge (New York: McGraw-Hill Book
Company, Inc., 1951) pp. 238–245. Reprinted by permission of the author.

the same reason they cannot follow in the paths of Lewis, Fitzgerald, Dos Passos, and Hemingway. The basic social changes brought about by the rise of modern America in the first three decades of the century have been largely completed. The social patterns have been set. The Babbitt class is no longer new; it has, in fact, been so thoroughly absorbed into American life that no standard exists by which it can be satirized. Fitzgerald's golden dream of Paradise died in the Depression; and even though there has been a pathetic attempt to revive it, we should be able to see by now that it does not belong to the America of today. The workers are winning their fight without the help of new Dos Passoses; besides, the cause of labor is an unfashionable, if not a downright dangerous, one for writers today. The problems which concerned the writers of the 1930's might just as well have never existed. Steinbeck's Okies have been absorbed into the California countryside; and no one cares to hear any more about the sweaty struggles of young Studs Lonigans. Because of this, the new writers are faced with the task of maintaining themselves as writers at a time when there are no strongly prevailing attitudes or issues to help give value to their work.

The result is that, whether they have sought to maintain themselves through the simple reporting of facts and events, the exploitation of such shock value as they can find in race problems or sexual maladjustment, or the creation of a private world of pure prose, these writers have been constantly handicapped by the emptiness of the characters and situations about which they have been obliged to write. Since they have inherited a world without values and since they have had no choice but to find their material in that world, they have had to deal with valuelessness; and that can never form the basis of a successful literature.

The absence of a set of attitudes and values, both in themselves and in their society, has left its mark on the work of nearly all the new writers I have discussed in this book. It is behind the failure of that portion of *The Naked and the Dead* which has to do with the philosophical evil of war; and it is clearly epitomized in the emptiness of the central character, Lieutenant Hearn. In *The Gallery* it is behind the failure of the "Portraits" to dramatize fully Burns's undramatized assertions in the "Promenades"; and once again the dilemma of the novel is represented in the dilemma of a character — the neurotic Lieutenant Hal. The absence of genuine values led Shaw in *The Young Lions* to concoct false values and to superimpose them upon his material. Miller in *That Winter* was guilty of much the same offense, although in a large part of the book he avoided the problem of values simply by falling back on the skillful manipulation of trivia. The weakness of all of Vidal's novels between *Williwaw* and *A Search for the King* is that the material presented in them is not valuable enough to dramatize successfully the issues which Vidal wished to set forth. The emptiness of Jim Willard in *The City and the Pillar* vitiates the tragedy of his homosexual dream; the emptiness of Bill Giraud in *The Season of Comfort* vitiates the drama of his struggle against his mother. The same emptiness in Kit and Port Moresby in *The Sheltering Sky* made it impossible for Bowles to motivate or dignify their destruction; and in *Other Voices, Other Rooms* and *A Long Day's Dying* the metaphorical complexities and mythical parallels serve merely to disguise the triviality of the characters and situations.

Yet it would be a mistake to assume, as I may seem to have assumed, that the failure of values is a mechanical and lifeless formula which can be applied in laboratory isolation to the work of the new writers. If I have applied it in isolation and as a formula, I have done so purely in the interests of analysis and in order to compress a great many ideas and observations into a single working principle. Actually, the failure of values is only part of the total problem facing these writers. There are other issues which have as much bearing on their dilemma and which are more concretely the results of their circumstances as writers and the intellectual climate of their age.

The war years gave many of the new writers an opportunity to leave the country, stay away for a time, and come back again. They were able, as few Americans are, to watch the fading of their old attitudes and to prepare their minds for a fresh perspective. Returning from Europe and the Pacific, they were, in a sense, returning exiles, more knowledgeable and less provincial than they had been. If what they found at home had offered them a new contact with experience, they might have been afforded what Louis Bromfield has called "the sense of criticism and of valuation" needed for fresh writing. But the country they returned to was much the same country they had left; and it was not greatly different from the country which had been responsible for the vehement exile of the Lost Generation.

Businessmen still made up the bulk of the population. People were still paying homage to the machine, still scrambling after goods and wealth to the neglect of their sensibilities. The average citizen retained his inscrutable apathy toward matters of social injustice, morals, art, and affairs abroad. People who were old enough to have been outraged by Sinclair Lewis were living as if *Babbitt* and *Main Street* had never been written. Life in America was as aesthetically starved as ever, still without a true culture and a standard of adult values. The ingredients for another all-out war of artistic secession were there, but the will to revolt was not. The most aborting truth was that it had all been done before.

Social protest had been for the generation of Mencken and Lewis what negation and loss had been for the generation of Hemingway, Fitzgerald, and Dos Passos—a frame of art, a means of ordering the material of life into the material of art. In the years after 1910, protest depended upon

the recollection of a time when values were relatively secure and the immediate apprehension of a time when values were in transition — when machine
ethics and machine culture was vulgarizing Main Street and provincialism
was giving way to a cheap and artificial urbanity. For the writers who
attacked the American way of life in *Civilization in the United States* in
1921, it depended upon a belief in aesthetic values over the values of mass
production, the European way over the American. But by the end of the
second war, the transitional phase was over; the machine age was a going
concern; and the values of the machine had become such an integral part
of the national culture that not only was protest redundant but the perspective necessary for protest had ceased to exist.

And as American life was formulated, so also was American literature.
The literary movements that sprang up in Chicago and Greenwich Village
before 1920 were energized by a sense of new beginnings. Writers were
consciously breaking with the past and asserting the unique experience of
life in the modern age. If the best books and poems of the time protested
the evils of industrialism and the paralysis of industrial man, it was because writers were at last discovering the truth of industrialism and beginning to sense the dominant sickness of the age. They were experimenting
with new forms and techniques, new ideas and a new language, because
the world was new; and they were held together by their common devotion to the cause of art because not only was that cause threatened but
the impact of artistic change was moving them all in the same direction
toward the same goal. By the middle 1940's, however, the age of awakening had become the age of somnolence. There had been the brief concern
for the Depression victims of the 1930's; but the literature of economics
and the people had been short-lived and had failed to leave an important
mark on new writing. The "experimentalists" of the 1920's were the true
literary forefathers of the present generation; but their experiments were
now established; and young writers seemed unable to make new ones.

Lacking the focus of negation and loss, a new world to discover, and a
single perspective for protest, the new writers are deprived as well of group
solidarity. They form no distinct generation in the old sense; they champion no cause; they share no common aim; they are impelled by no awareness of a common artistic mission. It is the sum of their rejections that
even though they have never known the values that were lost for them
thirty years ago, they cannot make a new or substitute value of their art.
For them the religion of art belongs with all the other dead faiths. It
was good for a time when writers functioned on the periphery of life,
when there was a side for art and a side for life. But it is of no use in a
time when the position of the writer, if it is defined at all, is somewhere
near the bottom of the list of artisans and almost at the top of the list
of tradesmen. Besides, they have seen the religion of art become in their

time a blind alley, a coterie dogma with restrictive bylaws that threaten to smother the thing they were invented to preserve; they have seen pedantry, obscurantism, and snobbery sprout like anemic flowers from the dead health of Stein and Joyce. They have learned that after the innovators come the specialists and after the specialists the imitators and that after a movement has spent itself there can only come the incestuous, the archaeologists, and the ghouls.

But perhaps more than anything else they have learned that they no longer need the protection of one another. The revolt of their predecessors required the strategy of a complex military maneuver. They were attacking the past by invading the present; and there were enemies in both camps. There was poverty in the beginning—the persistent affliction of the young of Grub Street and Greenwich Village in all ages; the reactionary element in power; the philistinism of the press and the popular magazines; the babbittry of the folks back home; comstockery; prohibition; and the general public resistance to change. Today the anti-literary elements have been to a great extent overridden; or perhaps they have simply faded into the background for lack of opposition. A young writer can produce his novel today without first having to defend himself for being a writer; and he can stay at home to do it. His greatest disadvantage is that, being alone, he is denied access to the free interplay of ideas that can only be had through association with other writers; and he is likely to find it hard in isolation to preserve his singular function amid those other functions which are carried on around him and which, because of their difference of aim, are necessarily opposed to his. . . .

The old beacons burn dimly

21

Luigi Barzini, Jr.   **Americans Are Alone in the World**

Luigi Barzini, Jr., is a leading Italian journalist who studied in America and worked as a reporter in the United States before becoming publisher of Il Globo, *Italy's leading economic newspaper. In 1965, his book* The Italians *became a best-seller in this country. At present he is a member of the Italian parliament. His book on America, which was a result of a trip to the United States in the early 1950's, is an appraisal of the country, with some criticisms of its people. In the following selection, Barzini discusses the paradox of abundance. He echoes an important contemporary idea that abundance is not enough. For related ideas, see Galbraith, Berle, Dedijer.*

A strange perplexity seems to corrode the bold assurance of the American people, as if, by different roads, through different experiences, for sometimes contradictory reasons, they had all arrived at the same dead end, the old people in Los Angeles bored with mechanical comforts, the inventor who hopefully pursues nature's elusive secrets, the State Department officials who endlessly dig the quarry of mimeographed facts, the staff officers who test and adopt new wonderful weapons.

It is as if everybody realized that the rainbow ends nowhere and there is no pot of gold to be found. Perhaps one of the most obvious examples of this· contradictory aspect of American life is the New York traffic. For more than half a century, every resource of United States industry, billions of dollars, human lives, endless research, patience, and ingenuity have been dedicated to producing more and more cars, faster, cheaper, more powerful models, with the final result that in New York everybody walks. Another example which foreigners notice is the elephantiasis of American newspapers. Such is the publishers' wealth and power, who can make use of so many modern devices for gathering and printing news, opinions, pictures, cartoons (the best correspondents everywhere, telecommunications of all kinds, river-like delivery of mass agency news, syndicated features of all quality, taste, and weight, fast machinery to print mountains of copies an hour), such is also the wealth of the market and the abundance of advertising, that newspapers have become unwieldy paper mattresses, impenetrable jungles, filled with overlong and overdetailed news stories, some of which are extremely good but lost in a confusion of brassieres, corsets, candies, mink coats, television sets and new automobiles.

Only an experienced reader can cut his way to the things he wants. Newcomers are easily lost. This, in the country which believes itself to worship the practical, the concise, the predigested, the timesaving in everything. Or take American popular magazines which have reached such technical perfection and such large circulations that they must be planned, written, illustrated, and made up many months before publication. Christmas scenes are painted· by sweating artists in the summer, bathing-suited models shiver in January beach scenes. All contents are as old the day they appear as those in magazines which used to be found in dentists' waiting rooms in the days when publishing speed was practically unknown.

Another illustration of the same contradictions is the American scientists' complaints (which one sees often in magazines or hears from their own voices) who have discovered that funds, large laboratories, well-paid and competent staffs seldom uncover great truths, because all the important discoveries still seem to be made by solitary workers pursuing fixed ideas in their dingy little laboratories, with practically no staff and little money.

The dead end is the discovery, which everyone makes sooner or later, that abundance is not enough. Nothing, of course, can be done without adequate means. The solitary scientist must have time, some laboratory space and enough money for his requirements. But means are not enough to reach the goal. There is no way to buy success, certainty, truth and peace. There is no way to build a foolproof word machine, supplied with the latest accessories, automatic pacts, clauses, agreements, to prevent war. There is no way to fight a war with machines, even very expensive machines, without getting killed. Abundance not only solves few problems but makes them all more complicated and obscure, as extremely rich men have discovered who tried to live human and pleasant lives. It was easier to edit a newspaper when one had not too much copy. It was easier to make a good picture when technical means were few and budgets were low. It was easier to shape a foreign policy when one did not have limitless means and when one trimmed one's ambitions to the size of one's power. This discovery casts a shadow over the life of everyone, in the United States, whether they are conscious of it or not. One often hears friends recall how beautiful and hopeful the world was years ago when they could still believe they were on the threshold of a new happy era when all man's problems were to vanish like ghosts at the stroke of midnight.

The United States is still filled with the same old books that teach everything: how to make love, how to make friends, how to dress with style, how to write a novel, a play, a film script, a short story, how to get fat or thin, how to tap one's secret sources of energy, how to cure all diseases with faith, diets, massages, or confessions. Girls still buy the many books that teach them to acquire charm and beauty through will power, I was told by a clerk in a Grand Central Station bookstore, but most of them now know that the chances of changing their appearance or their personality are slim, as the commuters who buy guides to gardening know that they will never grow the cabbagelike flowers shown in the illustrations. "The girls now know," he said, "that the woman who studies how to enter a room with poise and grace, as shown in Chapter One, will probably stumble on the carpet, overturn a table, and pour tomato juice on her dress. The girl who wants to be charming at all costs possibly may be avoided like poison."

The same sadness of the defeated gardener and the ugly girl can be felt in the words of the editors of *Fortune* who wrote a book, which was widely distributed by the United States Information Service, called *U.S.A. The*

Permanent Revolution: "What is the aim of our propaganda? Friendship? To many Americans this is the end-all. And nothing has done us more grievous harm—for we are offended terribly when love is not forthcoming from others. It is quite impossible anyway. We have only to look at India; since their departure, the British, who never gave a damn whether anybody liked them or not, have become increasingly popular, while we, who did our best to expedite that departure, are becoming increasingly unpopular."

Love blossoms unjustly in the garden of the British who did not buy the book on "how to do it," and love avoids that of the Americans.

This, I think, is the American crisis, the setting of a wonderful certainty. The dream of a better future is always there to warm the heart: the dream of a peaceful, just, healthy, well-fed, free, rich, brotherly world, which somehow should be generated by their sacrifices, sorrow, and blood; but it is no more than a dream now, in which people are sometimes afraid to believe, whereas before it was a concrete itinerary and a timetable for history. There are things which technique, money, abundance, research, diligence alone do not change. Perhaps old man Kettering secretly suspects that without books or a new philosophy he will never discover the secret of why the grass is green. President Eisenhower now knows that aid to foreign countries, no matter how abundant, will not defeat Russia. Arthur Sulzberger now knows that the New York *Times* cannot really contain all the news that is fit to print. Dr. Gallup now knows that there is no way to find out exactly what people will do in the future. The old beacons of American life are burning dimly. The old guideposts cannot be trusted any more. But were they the only beacons and the only guideposts?

Alienation and the intellectual

Sidney Hook	**Statement on America and the Intellectuals**	**22**

Sidney Hook, teacher and philosopher, was born in New York City in 1902. After graduating from The City College of New York in 1923, he attended Columbia University, which awarded him a Ph.D. in 1927. He started his career as a public school teacher and was appointed to the faculty of New York University in 1927. His many writings include John Dewey, an Intellectual Portrait *(1939)*, John Dewey, Philosopher of Science and Freedom *(1950)*, The Quest for Being *(1961)*. *As a leading thinker on the pragmatist movement, he is well qualified to describe the role of the intellectual in America, as he does in the following selection. For related ideas, see Bell, Barzun, Larrabee.*

I cannot understand why American intellectuals should be apologetic about the fact that they aré limited in their effective historical choice between endorsing a system of total terror and *critically* supporting our own imperfect democratic culture with all its promises and dangers. For after all within our culture they are not *compelled* to choose whereas in the Soviet world neutrality or even silence is treason. Surely, this should count for something even with those who, although dependent upon the protective security of our relatively free culture for their neutralism and cultivation of purity, regard its struggle for survival as a vulgar battle of ideologies. Nor is it clear to me why an appreciation of the values of American life is incompatible with vigorous criticism of its many deficiencies and with determined efforts to enhance both its chances of survival and the quality of its cultural experience by more enlightened domestic and foreign policies. And if there are any seers or prophets among us, let them make their visions known.

The political and moral issues of our time are no different for the intellectual classes, the writers, artists and scholars, than they are for the working classes who recognize that even under the dislocations of our mixed economy, they enjoy more bread and freedom than the working classes anywhere else in the world. If anything, one expects the intellectuals to see even more clearly that the relative autonomy of their craft is threatened by Soviet totalitarianism more completely than by any other social system in history.

I must also confess to some perplexity in understanding laments about the "alienation" of the creative artist in American culture if this means that he faces more obstacles to doing significant work or finding an appreciative audience than was the case fifty or a hundred years ago. Surely, compared with his forebears, he can have no complaint on the score of creature comforts, which he certainly deserves no less than other human beings. The notion circulated in some quarters that university life is the Golgotha of the intellectual spirit is absurd. It seems to me that the creative life in America suffers more from mediocrity than from frustration. Equally bewildering is the view that mass culture or the popular arts constitute a profound menace to the position of American intellectuals. Cer-

This article appeared in *Partisan Review* (September-October 1952) under the title "Our Country and Our Culture." © 1952 by *Partisan Review*. Reprinted by permission of *Partisan Review* and the author.

tainly those who love cream more than their work may drown in it. The only sense I can find in the violent garrulities of Ortega y Gasset is that the mass "kind of man" who threatens the individual, is the man who lurks inside of anyone who fears to be himself. That mass "kind of man" in one form or another has always existed. And he sometimes is present in the man who strives and strains to be different as distinct from one who genuinely feels and thinks differently from his fellows.

There are all kinds of alienations in the world and one can get startling effects by confusing them. Hegel understood by self-alienation the process of dialectical development by which the individual consciousness progresses from innocence to maturity, from the simplicity of bare perception to the richly funded comprehension of a complexly interrelated system. Remove the mystification about the Absolute Self, drop the consolatory, religious overtones about the meaningfulness of the Whole, and what we get in the language of a barbarous literary psychology is an account of the travail of spiritual growth in any culture—not only for the artist but for every human being.

Marx's notion of self-alienation is historically circumscribed and has much less sweep than Hegel's. It applies primarily to the worker who is compelled to labor at something which neither expresses nor sustains his own needs and interests as a person. The unalienated man for Marx is the creative man. It is anyone who, under an inner compulsion, is doing significant work wrestling with a problem or striving to articulate a vision. The artist for Marx is the unalienated man par excellence to the extent that he does not produce *merely* a commodity. Remove the Utopianism of believing that all work in an industrial society can make a call on man's creative capacities, and of imagining that everybody, once a market economy disappears, will be able to do creative work, and what Marx is really saying is not obscure. The more truly human a society is, the more will it arrange its institutions to afford opportunities for creative fulfillment through uncoerced work. Man humanizes himself through work, which in association with others, is the source of speech. Man is dehumanized by *forced* work. There are some echoes of Rousseauistic myth in this and by a strange un-Marxian lapse Marx refers to a society in which there is no forced labor as a more natural society. From this point of view, the workers attending a conveyor belt, feeding a machine, endlessly filing orders or names are far more alienated than those intellectuals who have chosen their vocations and enjoy some freedom in setting their own goals or selecting their tasks.

There is a third conception of alienation popular with some sociologists and Bohemians which is applied to the artist who breaks with the conventions or norms of his family, society, or class. He is pitied and sometimes pities himself because he has no market or patron or reputation on the assumption that this is a necessary consequence of his non-conformity despite the fact that other non-conformists created their own audience and following and feel unalienated in the Marxian sense even when hostile critics ignore or rage against them. This is the most popular conception of the alienated artist in America and the shallowest. Why it is so popular I do not know unless it be that many individuals mistake the indifference of the world or their private creative agonies—which may very well be due to lack of creative capacity or to an ambition altogether incommensurate to their talents—for unerring signs of election to an alienated elite. But all a free culture can do is to provide opportunities for revolt: it cannot guarantee professional success.

No one knows the secret of significant creativity. We do know it cannot be mass produced and that it cannot emerge under conditions of extreme privation. But since the material lot of American artists has improved considerably in the last few decades and since the cultural atmosphere in America is much more receptive to the notion of total dedication to a creative calling—the son's announcement that he refuses to enter business or a profession but wants to be a writer, artist or musician no longer causes a family crisis—I must confess I do not know why the American arts are more anemic than the arts abroad *if* they are. And I suspect that no one else knows. Certainly, American work in science, scholarship and medicine does not lag behind European achievements. The hypothesis that mass culture and the popular arts—the Hollywood trap!—threaten the emergence of a significant culture of vitality and integrity because they constitute a perpetual invitation to a sell-out seems very far-fetched. Unless one is an incurable snob (I am old enough to remember intense discussions by otherwise intelligent people as to whether the cinema is an art), the forms of mass culture and the popular arts should serve as a challenge to do something with them. There are "sell-outs" of course but there are two parties to every "sell-out." The writer who "sells out" to Hollywood or the slicks cannot absolve himself of responsibility on the ground that he wouldn't be able to live as plushily as if he did. Why should he? I shall be accused of saying that I am sentencing artists and writers to starvation. But if scholars can live Renan's life of "genteel poverty" and do important work so can those who don't go to Hollywood.

Finally, I see no specific virtue in the attitude of conformity or non-conformity. The important thing is that it should be voluntary, rooted in considered judgment, an authentic expression of some value or insight for which the individual is prepared to risk something. 'Conformity' or 'non-conformity' are relational terms. Before evaluating them I should like to know *to and with what* a person is conforming or not conforming and *how*. Under the Weimar Republic, Stefan George, Spengler and Hitler were non-conformists: under the Czarist regime Dostoevsky in his most fruitful years was a conformist. To the greatest of men the terms 'conformist' or 'non-conformist' have singularly little relevance—Shakespeare, Milton, Goethe, Plato, Aristotle, Kant, or Dewey.

Particularly inexplicable to me is the final question whether the American intellectual should continue the tradition of critical non-conformism. The social function of the American intellectual is to think, and to act in such a way that the results of his thinking are brought to bear upon the great issues of our time. The cardinal attribute of the life of thought—its proper virtue—is the capacity to discriminate, to make relevant distinctions. He is no more un-American when he is intelligently critical of the United States than he is chauvinistic when he is intelligently appreciative. Many American intellectuals are unaware of the extent to which the social climate and objective possibilities for a democratic welfare state have improved in the last twenty years. Some still think of socialism as a good in itself. Having made a religion of a form of economy, they are incapable of learning from experience. They comfort themselves with a superior terminological intransigence in the belief that their sincerity atones for their stupidity. Their opposite numbers now regard socialism as an evil in itself. Socialism is no longer a form of economy for them, but the principle of welfare or social control itself. Like the most orthodox of Marxists they believe that any economy uniquely entails one political way of life. Fortunately, more and more intellectuals are beginning to understand what they could have learned from John Dewey long ago, that democratic process is more important than any predetermined program, and that persons and values are the test of adequate social relations not conversely.

Outside their own immediate craft too many intellectuals are irresponsible, especially in politics. They don't know enough, don't think enough, and are the creatures of fashion. It is sufficient for the majority to believe anything, for them to oppose it. They are too conscious of "public relations." Some are exhibitionists who are always washing their hands in public, Mary Magdalenes making a cult of purity. The lowest form of intellectual life is led by left bank American expatriates who curry favor with Sartrian neutralists by giving them the lowdown on the cultural "reign of terror" (sic!) in America.

Most American intellectuals still do not understand the theory, practice, and tactics of the Communist movement. Because McCarthy has made wild and irresponsible charges, too many are inclined to dismiss the Communist danger in its total global impact as relatively unimportant. American intellectuals were more frightened of Franco in 1936 and of Hitler in 1933 than they are of Stalin today. In 1933 and 1936 they did *not* say that, after all, there were few Fascists in America, fewer Fascists than there ever were of Communists since 1919. As country after country has come under Stalin's knife, concern in the colleges, in literary circles, even scientific quarters has *not* increased. The term "anti-Communist" has not got the same overtones as "anti-Fascist." It is not enough to say that McCarthy and reactionary demagogues have ruined the term "anti-Communist." Why didn't the Communists ruin the term "anti-Fascist"? They were just as vehement in their anti-Fascism as McCarthy is in his anti-Communism and even more irresponsible, because they called men like Dewey, Kallen, and Norman Thomas "fascists."

The task of the intellectual is still to lead an intellectual life, to criticize what needs to be criticized in America, without forgetting for a moment the total threat which Communism poses to the life of the free mind. Our own vigilantes and reactionaries are much more like witches and straw scarecrows than are the paid and underpaid agents of the Kremlin who constitute the membership of the Communist Parties in all countries.. They can be cleared out of the way by a little courage and a sense of humor. They have nuisance value especially because of their effects abroad.

We face grim years ahead. The democratic West will require the critical support, the dedicated energy and above all, the intelligence, of its intellectuals if it is to survive as a free culture. With the possible exception of the technical arts and their theoretical ancillaries, great creative visions, conforming or non-conforming, can today flourish only in the soil of a free culture. It was not always so. But modern totalitarianism is not the same as ancient absolutisms.

Let the neutralists of the world remember. In the West non-conformists, no matter how alienated, can always win a hearing, even if they do not win a place in the Academy or earn the Order of Merit. In the land of Purges and Brainwashing, the only thing a non-conformist can earn is a bullet in the neck. This is the historical premise of our age whose recognition is binding on all humanists whether they are democratic socialists or civil libertarian conservatives or members of the alienated avant-garde.

C. Wright Mills   The Power Elite   **23**

*C. Wright Mills was born in Waco, Texas, in 1916. He was educated at
the University of Texas and the University of Wisconsin, receiving his Ph.D.
from the latter in 1941. He was a professor of sociology at Columbia University until his death. His works include* The New Men of Power *(1948),*
White Collar *(1951),* The Causes of World War III *(1958), and* The Sociological Imagination *(1959). The following selection posits that power in
American society now resides in three big elite groups: the political, the
economic, and the military. President Eisenhower in his valedictory address
to the nation expressed his concern about the "power elite" described by
Mills. For related ideas, see Brogan, Henry, Brooks.*

Within American society, major national power now resides in the economic, the political, and the military domains. Other institutions seem off
to the side of modern history, and, on occasion, duly subordinated to these.
No family is as directly powerful in national affairs as any major corporation; no church is as directly powerful in the external biographies of young
men in America today as the military establishment; no college is as powerful in the shaping of momentous events as the National Security Council. Religious, educational, and family institutions are not autonomous
centers of national power; on the contrary, these decentralized areas are
increasingly shaped by the big three, in which developments of decisive
and immediate consequence now occur.

Families and churches and schools adapt to modern life; governments
and armies and corporations shape it; and, as they do so, they turn these
lesser institutions into means for their ends. Religious institutions provide
chaplains to the armed forces where they are used as a means of increasing the effectiveness of its morale to kill. Schools select and train men for
their jobs in corporations and their specialized tasks in the armed forces.
The extended family has, of course, long been broken up by the industrial
revolution, and now the son and the father are removed from the family,
by compulsion if need be, whenever the army of the state sends out the
call. And the symbols of all these lesser institutions are used to legitimate

the power and the decisions of the big three.

The life-fate of the modern individual depends not only upon the family into which he was born or which he enters by marriage, but increasingly upon the corporation in which he spends the most alert hours of his best years; not only upon the school where he is educated as a child and adolescent, but also upon the state which touches him throughout his life; not only upon the church in which on occasion he hears the word of God, but also upon the army in which he is disciplined.

If the centralized state could not rely upon the inculcation of nationalist loyalties in public and private schools, its leaders would promptly seek to modify the decentralized educational system. If the bankruptcy rate among the top five hundred corporations were as high as the general divorce rate among the thirty-seven million married couples, there would be economic catastrophe on an international scale. If members of armies gave to them no more of their lives than do believers to the churches to which they belong, there would be a military crisis.

Within each of the big three, the typical institutional unit has become enlarged, has become administrative, and, in the power of its decisions, has become centralized. Behind these developments there is a fabulous technology, for as institutions, they have incorporated this technology and guide it, even as it shapes and paces their developments.

The economy—once a great scatter of small productive units in autonomous balance—has become dominated by two or three hundred giant corporations, administratively and politically interrelated, which together hold the keys to economic decisions.

The political order, once a decentralized set of several dozen states with a weak spinal cord, has become a centralized, executive establishment which has taken up into itself many powers previously scattered, and now enters into each and every cranny of the social structure.

The military order, once a slim establishment in a context of distrust fed by state militia, has become the largest and most expensive feature of government, and, although well versed in smiling public relations, now has all the grim and clumsy efficiency of a sprawling bureaucratic domain.

In each of these institutional areas, the means of power at the disposal of decision makers have increased enormously; their central executive powers have been enhanced; within each of them modern administrative routines have been elaborated and tightened up.

As each of these domains becomes enlarged and centralized, the consequences of its activities become greater, and its traffic with the others increases. The decisions of a handful of corporations bear upon military and political as well as upon economic developments around the world. The decisions of the military establishment rest upon and grievously affect political life as well as the very level of economic activity. The decisions made within the political domain determine economic activities and military programs. There is no longer, on the one hand, an economy, and, on the other hand, a political order containing a military establishment unimportant to politics and to money-making. There is a political economy linked, in a thousand ways, with military institutions and decisions. On each side of the world-split running through central Europe and around the Asiatic rimlands, there is an ever-increasing interlocking of economic, military, and political structures. If there is government intervention in the corporate economy, so is there corporate intervention in the governmental process. In the structural sense, this triangle of power is the source of the interlocking directorate that is most important for the historical structure of the present.

The fact of the interlocking is clearly revealed at each of the points of crisis of modern capitalist society—slump, war, and boom. In each, men of decision are led to an awareness of the interdependence of the major institutional orders. In the nineteenth century, when the scale of all institutions was smaller, their liberal integration was achieved in the automatic economy, by an autonomous play of market forces, and in the automatic political domain, by the bargain and the vote. It was then assumed that out of the imbalance and friction that followed the limited decisions then possible a new equilibrium would in due course emerge. That can no longer be assumed, and it is not assumed by the men at the top of each of the three dominant hierarchies.

For given the scope of their consequences, decisions—and indecisions—in any one of these ramify into the others, and hence top decisions tend either to become co-ordinated or to lead to a commanding indecision. It has not always been like this. When numerous small entrepreneurs made up the economy, for example, many of them could fail and the consequences still remain local; political and military authorities did not intervene. But now, given political expectations and military commitments, can they afford to allow key units of the private corporate economy to break down in slump? Increasingly, they do intervene in economic affairs, and as they do so, the controlling decisions in each order are inspected by agents of the other two, and economic, military, and political structures are interlocked.

At the pinnacle of each of the three enlarged and centralized domains, there have arisen those higher circles which make up the economic, the political, and the military elites. At the top of the economy, among the corporate rich, there are the chief executives; at the top of the political order, the members of the political directorate; at the top of the military establishment, the elite of soldier-statesmen clustered in and around the Joint Chiefs of Staff and the upper echelon. As each of these domains has coincided with the others, as decisions tend to become total in their consequence, the leading men in each of the three domains of power—the warlords, the corporation chieftains, the political directorate—tend to come together, to form the power elite of America.

They accept

24

William H. Whyte, Jr.   The Organization Man

William Hollingsworth Whyte, editor and writer, was born in Westchester, Pennsylvania, in 1917 and graduated from Princeton University in 1939. He has done editorial work on a number of magazines, including Fortune, *and has also been active in work on conservation problems. He was editor of and contributor to* The Exploding Metropolis *(1958), and is a frequent magazine contributor. The following selection criticizes the "social ethic" which produces an "organization man," "the man in the gray flannel suit," which became a cliche in the 1950's. For related ideas, see Reisman, Wheelis, Warner, Brogan, Henry.*

Let us now broaden our view to organization man in general and ask what this climate of thought portends. If, as I believe, the people I have been examining in this book are representative of the main stream of organization life, one thing seems clear. If ever there was a generation of technicians, theirs is it. No generation has been so well equipped, psychologically as well as technically, to cope with the intricacies of vast organizations; none has been so well equipped to lead a meaningful community life; and none probably will be so adaptable to the constant shifts in environment that organization life is so increasingly demanding of them. In the better sense of the word, they are becoming the interchangeables of our society and they accept the role with understanding. They are all as they say, in the same boat.

But where is the boat going? No one seems to have the faintest idea; nor, for that matter, do they see much point in even raising the question. Once people liked to think, at least, that they were in control of their destinies, but few of the younger organization people cherish such notions. Most see themselves as objects more acted upon than acting—and their future, therefore, determined as much by the system as by themselves.

In a word, they *accept,* and if we do not find this comforting at least we should recognize that it would be odd if they did not feel this confidence. For them society has in fact been good—very, very good—for there has been a succession of fairly beneficient environments: college, the paternalistic, if not always pleasant, military life, then, perhaps, graduate work through the G.I. Bill of Rights, a corporation apprenticeship during a period of industrial expansion and high prosperity, and, for some, the camaraderie of communities like Park Forest. The system, they instinctively conclude, is essentially benevolent.

No one should begrudge them the prosperity that has helped make them feel this way. If we have to have problems, after all, the adversities of good times are as worthy as any to have to worry about. Nor should we regard the emphasis on co-operation as a reversal of our national character. When the suburbanites speak of re-establishing the spirit of the frontier communities, there is a truth in their analogy. Our country was born as a series of highly communal enterprises, and though the individualist may have opened the frontier, it was the co-operative who settled it. So throughout our history. Our national genius has always lain in our adaptability, in our distrust of dogma and doctrine, in our regard for the opinion of others, and in this respect the organization people are true products of the American past. "The more equal social conditions become," De Tocqueville, no friend of conformity, presciently observed, "the more men display this reciprocal disposition to oblige each other."

And there is the crux. When De Tocqueville wrote this a century ago it was the double-edged nature of this disposition that haunted him. He understood its virtue; he was an aristrocrat and he confessed that he missed the excellence of the few in the good of the many, but he saw clearly that our egalitarianism and our ease of social co-operation were the great fruits of democracy. We could not sustain these virtues without suffering their defects. But could we keep them in balance? De Tocqueville made a prophecy. If America ever destroyed its genius it would be by intensifying the social virtues at the expense of others, by making the individual come to regard himself as a hostage to prevailing opinion, by creating, in sum, a tyranny of the majority.

And this is what the organization man is doing. He is doing it for what he feels are good reasons, but this only makes the tyranny more powerful, not less. At the very time when the pressures of our highly organized society make so stringent a demand on the individual, he is himself compounding the impact. He is not only other-directed, to borrow David Riesman's concept, he is articulating a philosophy which tells him it is right to be that way.

My charge against the Social Ethic, then, is on precisely the grounds of contemporary usefulness it so venerates. It is not, I submit, suited to the needs of "modern man," but is instead reinforcing precisely that which least needs to be emphasized, and at the expense of that which does. Here is my bill of particulars.

It is redundant. In some societies individualism has been carried to such extremes as to endanger the society itself, and there exist today examples of individualism corrupted into a narrow egoism which prevents effective co-operation. This is a danger, there is no question of that. But is it today as pressing a danger as the obverse—a climate which inhibits individual initiative and imagination, and the courage to exercise it against group opinion? Society is itself an education in the extrovert values, and I think it can be rightfully argued that rarely has there been a society which has preached them so hard. No man is an island unto himself, but how John Donne would writhe to hear how often, and for what reasons, the thought is so tiresomely repeated.

It is premature. To preach technique before content, the skills of getting along isolated from why and to what end the getting along is for, does not produce maturity. It produces a sort of permanent prematurity, and this is true not only of the child being taught life adjustment but of the organization man being taught well-roundedness. This is a sterile concept, and those who believe that they have mastered human relations can blind themselves to the true bases of co-operation. People don't co-operate just to co-operate; they co-operate for substantive reasons, to achieve certain goals, and unless these are comprehended the little manipulations for morale, team spirit, and such are fruitless.

And they can be worse than fruitless. Held up as the end-all of organization leadership, the skills of human relations easily tempt the new administrator into the practice of a tyranny more subtle and more pervasive than that which he means to supplant. No one wants to see the old authoritarian return, but at least it could be said of him that what he wanted primarily from you was your sweat. The new man wants your soul.

It is delusory. It is easy to fight obvious tyranny; it is not easy to fight benevolence, and few things are more calculated to rob the individual of his defenses than the idea that his interests and those of society can be wholly compatible. The good society is the one in which they are most compatible, but they never can be completely so, and one who lets The Organization be the judge ultimately sacrifices himself. Like the good society, the good organization encourages individual expression, and many have done so. But there always remains some conflict between the individual and The Organization. Is The Organization to be the arbiter? The Organization will look to its own interests, but it will look to the individual's *only as The Organization interprets them.*

It is static. Organization of itself has no dynamic. The dynamic is in the individual and thus he must not only question how The Organization interprets his interests, he must question how it interprets its own. The bold new plan he feels is necessary, for example. He cannot trust that The Organization will recognize this. Most probably, it will not. It is the nature of a new idea to confound current consensus—even the mildly new idea. It might be patently in order, but, unfortunately, the group has a vested interest in its miseries as well as its pleasures, and irrational as this may be, many a member of organization life can recall instances where the group clung to known disadvantages rather than risk the anarchies of change.

It is self-destructive. The quest for normalcy, as we have seen in suburbia, is one of the great breeders of neuroses, and the Social Ethic only serves to exacerbate them. What is normalcy? We practice a great mutual deception. Everyone knows that they themselves are different—that they are shy in company, perhaps, or dislike many things most people seem to like—but they are not sure that other people are different too. Like the norms of personality testing, they see about them the sum of efforts of people like themselves to seem as normal as others and possibly a little more so. It is hard enough to learn to live with our inadequacies, and we need not make ourselves more miserable by a spurious ideal of middle-class adjustment. Adjustment to what? Nobody really knows—and the tragedy is that they don't realize that the so-confident-seeming other people don't know either . . .

Contrast in the economic spheres

John Kenneth Galbraith   **The Affluent Society**   **25**

John Kenneth Galbraith, Canadian by birth, was educated at the University of California and is now Professor of Economics at Harvard. He has held a number of public posts in which he has served with distinction, most recently as Ambassador to India. He was elected head of Americans for Democratic Action in 1967. He is also the author of American Capitalism *(1952) and* The Great Crash, 1929 *(1954). Here, Professor Galbraith describes the disparity between the wealthy private sector of the economy and the impoverished public sector and points the way for greater American concern with that public sector. The publication of* The Affluent Society *during the tranquil years of the Eisenhower administration introduced a new issue into American political life and anticipated in an important way the President's later request for goals for American society. For related ideas, see Harrington, Berle, Barzun, Dedijer, Nairn, Communist Party, U.S.A.*

The final problem of the productive society is what it produces. This manifests itself in an implacable tendency to provide an opulent supply of some things and a niggardly yield of others. This disparity carries to the point where it is a cause of social discomfort and social unhealth. The line which divides our area of wealth from our area of poverty is roughly that which divides privately produced and marketed goods and services from publicly rendered services. Our wealth in the first is not only in startling contrast with the meagerness of the latter, but our wealth in privately produced goods is, to a marked degree, the cause of crisis in the supply of public services. For we have failed to see the importance, indeed the urgent need, of maintaining a balance between the two.

This disparity between our flow of private and public goods and services is no matter of subjective judgment. On the contrary, it is the source of the most extensive comment which only stops short of the direct contrast being made here. In the years following World War II, the papers of any major city—those of New York were an excellent example—told daily of the shortages and shortcomings in the elementary municipal and metropolitan services. The schools were old and overcrowded. The police force was under strength and underpaid. The parks and playgrounds were insufficient. Streets and empty lots were filthy, and the sanitation staff was underequipped and in need of men. Access to the city by those who work there was uncertain and painful and becoming more so. Internal transportation was overcrowded, unhealthful, and dirty. So was the air. Parking on the streets had to be prohibited, and there was no space elsewhere. These deficiencies were not in new and novel services but in old and established ones. Cities have long swept their streets, helped their people move around, educated them, kept order, and provided horse rails for vehicles which sought to pause. That their residents should have a nontoxic supply of air suggests no revolutionary dalliance with socialism.

The discussion of this public poverty competed, on the whole, successfully, with the stories of ever-increasing opulence in privately produced goods. The Gross National Product was rising. So were retail sales. So was personal income. Labor productivity had also advanced. The automobiles that could not be parked were being produced at an expanded rate. The children, though without schools, subject in the playgrounds to the affectionate interest of adults with odd tastes, and disposed to increasingly

From *The Affluent Society* by John Kenneth Galbraith. Reprinted by permission of the publisher, Houghton Mifflin Company. Pp. 251–253.

imaginative forms of delinquency, were admirably equipped with television sets. We had difficulty finding storage space for the great surpluses of food despite a national disposition to obesity. Food was grown and packaged under private auspices. The care and refreshment of the mind, in contrast with the stomach, was principally in the public domain. Our colleges and universities were severely overcrowded and underprovided, and the same was true of the mental hospitals.

The contrast was and remains evident not alone to those who read. The family which takes its mauve and cerise, air-conditioned, power-steered, and power-braked automobile out for a tour passes through cities that are badly paved, made hideous by litter, blighted buildings, billboards, and posts for wires that should long since have been put underground. They pass on into a countryside that has been rendered largely invisible by commercial art. (The goods which the latter advertise have an absolute priority in our value system. Such aesthetic considerations as a view of the countryside accordingly come second. On such matters we are consistent.) They picnic on exquisitely packaged food from a portable icebox by a polluted stream and go on to spend the night at a park which is a menace to public health and morals. Just before dozing off on an air mattress, beneath a nylon tent, amid the stench of decaying refuse, they may reflect vaguely on the curious unevenness of their blessings. Is this, indeed, the American genius?

Deficient sense of self

Allen Wheelis   **The Quest for Identity**   **26**

Allen Wheelis has a private practice in psychiatry and psychoanalysis in San Francisco and is also on the staff of the Mt. Zion Psychiatric Clinic. A graduate of the University of Texas, he received his medical training at the College of Physicians and Surgeons of Columbia University, New York City. From 1943 to 1946 he served as Medical Officer in the U.S. Navy. He has been a Fellow of the Menninger Foundation School of Psychiatry,

a staff member of the Austen Riggs Center, Stockbridge, Massachusetts,
and is a graduate of the New York Psychoanalytic Institute. He has also
been an instructor in the San Francisco Psychoanalytic Institute. For re-
lated ideas, see Brogan, Riesman, Whyte.

With increasing frequency in recent years a change in the character of
the American people has been reported and described. The change is within the lifetime of most persons of middle or advanced years, and the process of change is still underway. The social character of ourselves and our
children is unmistakably different from what we remember of the character of our grandparents.

Our grandparents had less trouble than we do in finding themselves.
There were lost souls, to be sure, but no lost generation. More commonly then than now a young man followed his father, in character as in
vocation, and often so naturally as to be unaware of having made a choice.
Though the frontier was gone, there was still, for those who needed it,
the open west. Sooner rather than later one found his calling; and, having
found it, failure did not readily cause one to reconsider, but often was a
goad to greater effort. The goal was achievement, not adjustment; the
young were taught to work, not to socialize. Popularity was not important,
but strength of character was essential. Nobody worried about rigidity of
character; it was supposed to be rigid. If it were flexible you couldn't
count on it. Change of character was desirable only for the wicked.

Many of us still remember the bearded old men: the country doctor, the
circuit rider, the blacksmith, the farmer. They were old when we were
young, and they are dead now. We remember the high shoes, the heavy
watch chain, the chewing tobacco, the shiny black suit on Sunday. The
costume and make-up may still be seen, as they turn up in plays now and
then. The character that went with them is disappearing, and soon even
its memory will be lost.

Nowadays the sense of self is deficient. The questions of adolescence—
"Who am I?" "Where am I going?" "What is the meaning of life?"
—receive no final answers. Nor can they be laid aside. The uncertainty
persists. The period of being uncommitted is longer, the choices with which
it terminates more tentative. Personal identity does not become fixed,
does not, therefore, provide an unchanging vantage point from which to
view experience. Man is still the measure of all things, but it is no longer
the inner man that measures; it is the other man. Specifically, it is the
plurality of men, the group. And what the group provides is shifting
patterns, what it measures is conformity. It does not provide the hard
inner core by which the value of patterns and conformity is determined.
The hard inner core has in our time become diffuse, elusive, often fluid.
More than ever before one is aware of the identity he appears to have,

and more than ever before is dissatisfied with it. It doesn't fit, it seems alien, as though the unique course of one's life had been determined by untoward accident. Commitments of all kinds—social, vocational, marital, moral—are made more tentatively. Long-term goals seem to become progressively less feasible.

Identity is a coherent sense of self. It depends upon the awareness that one's endeavors and one's life make sense, that they are meaningful in the context in which life is lived. It depends also upon stable values, and upon the conviction that one's actions and values are harmoniously related. It is a sense of wholeness, of integration, of knowing what is right and what is wrong and of being able to choose.

During the past fifty years there has been a change in the experienced quality of life, with the result that identity is now harder to achieve and harder to maintain. The formerly dedicated Marxist who now is unsure of everything; the Christian who loses his faith; the workman who comes to feel that his work is piecemeal and meaningless; the scientist who decides that science is futile, that the fate of the world will be determined by power politics—such persons are of our time, and they suffer the loss or impairment of identity.

Identity can survive major conflict provided the supporting framework of life is stable, but not when that framework is lost. One cannot exert leverage except from a fixed point. Putting one's shoulder to the wheel presupposes a patch of solid ground to stand on. Many persons these days find no firm footing; and if everything is open to question, no question can be answered. The past half century has encompassed enormous gains in understanding and in mastery; but many of the old fixed points of reference have been lost, and have not been replaced.

The change in social character is often described as a decline of individualism; but individualism means many things, and not all of them have declined. Individualism means self-reliance, productive self-sufficiency, following one's chosen course despite social criticism, and bearing personally the risks of one's undertakings; and all of these are on the wane. Ours is an age of reliance on experts, of specialized production, of deference to public opinion, and of collective security. But individualism means, also, the awareness of individuality, and this has increased. For accompanying the other changes there has occurred an extension of awareness.

Modern man has become more perceptive of covert motivations, in both himself and others. Areas of experience formerly dissociated from consciousness have become commonplace knowledge. Passivity, anxiety, disguised hostility, masochism, latent homosexuality—these are not new with the present generation; what is new is the greater awareness of them. We deride the affectations which this heightened awareness so facilely serves— the "parlor psychiatry," the "curbstone interpretation"—but overlook the

emergent fact of extended awareness of which the affectation is sympto-
matic. As man has lost his sense of identity he has, paradoxically, discovered more of those elements of his nature out of which identity may
be formed, the raw materials with which to build. In losing the whole he
has found some of the previously lost parts.

This extended awareness is both cause and effect of the loss of identity.
It is a cause for the reason that identity is harder to achieve if renegade
motivations have free access to consciousness. If one is able to deny with
finality those lurking tendencies that run counter to the dominant trends
of personality, then it is easier to know who one is and where one stands.
This is of relevance in comparing the unsure man of today with his very
sure grandfather. His sense of identity is less firm, but the elements he
is called upon to integrate are more numerous and less homogeneous. The
identity of his grandfather was like the log cabin of the frontier; it was
small and dark, but it was put up with dispatch and was sturdy and snug.
The grandson is fumbling as a builder, and keeps hankering to turn the
whole job over to a professional architect; but it is to be noted that his
job is harder. The materials with which he must work are more variegated.
Their proper integration would achieve not a log cabin, but a more complicated and interesting structure, admitting more light and air and providing more room for living.

The extended awareness is also an effect of the loss of identity for the
reason that, being unsure of who one is and where one stands, it be-
hooves one to be more alert and perceptive. A firm sense of identity
provides both a compass to determine one's course in life and ballast to
keep one steady. So equipped and provisioned, one can safely ignore
much of the buffeting. Without such protection more vigilance is needed;
each vicissitude, inner and outer, must be defined and watched.

A change has occurred, also, in the dimensions of our existence. During
this century, it is said, our lives have been both lengthened and narrowed.
This makes reference to our longer life expectancy and to the increasing
industrialization that is thought to diminish the meaning of life by the kind
of work it imposes. The increased life span is indisputable, and doubtless
much clerical and assembly line work is monotonous. Yet in a somewhat
different sense the dimensional change is just the opposite of that proposed:
our lives have been enriched cross-sectionally and diminished longitudinally.

In our time the range and variety of experience has been enormously
extended. It is less integrated and less stable, but it is far wider in scope.
Fifty years ago the great orchestras could be heard in only a few cities;
now they are heard, by radio and recording, in every village across the
continent. Comparable changes have occurred in the availability of all the
arts. Better means of communication enable us to experience meanings
that occur at great distances, better methods of travel to experience per-

sons and areas heretofore inaccessible. Though these experiences are more easily had by the rich, they are to a notable degree available, also, to the assembly-line worker whose life is thought to be so impoverished. A war in Korea, a play on Broadway, a new philosophy in France—all are experienced more quickly and more widely than ever before.

Nor has the depth or meaningfulness of this experience been diminished. When radios became common it was sometimes predicted that the musical taste of the nation would be depraved by the constant din of jazz. In fact, the relatively small amount of serious music that was broadcast along with the jazz developed the musical appreciation of millions. Serious music is now understood and valued by a far higher proportion of the people than would have been possible without the advent of radio. "Twenty years ago you couldn't sell Beethoven out of New York," reports a record salesman. "Today we sell Palestrina, Monteverdi, Gabrielli, and renaissance and baroque music in large quantities." Parallel developments could be cited for countless other areas of experience. The gain in breadth of experience has generally been accompanied by a gain, also, in depth. Not only is the man of today constantly informed of a larger number of world events than was his grandfather; he understands them better. And within his own home he understands his children better. In all of these ways our lives have been cross-sectionally enriched.

But as our span of years has increased, our span of significant time has diminished. In some measure we have lost the sense of continuity with past and future. More and more quickly the past becomes outdated, and if we look back two or three generations the character and values of our forebears become as strange to us as their beards and high collars. Family portraits no longer hang in homes; there is no place for them in modern houses. And as we have lost touch with the past, so we have lost touch with the future. We know that we are in motion but do not know where we are going, and hence cannot predict the values of our children. Our grandfathers are likely to have dreamt of leaving as legacy a tract of land which would stay in the family and be maintained by their descendants; of building a house that would endure and be lived in after they were gone; of a profession that would become a tradition and be carried on by sons; of a name that would be wrought in iron over the carriage gate, the prestige of which would be shared and furthered by all who bore it. Seeing how these dreams have come to naught in us, we no longer try to direct or even to foresee the values of our descendents. We cannot now, with loving foresight, further their ends; for we do not know what ends they will pursue, nor where. We feel lucky if we can give our children an education. The founders of this country had a lively sense of the future, knew that posterity would vindicate their revolution, their moving west, their capitalism, their competition, their church. We—

who have no idea of what posterity will honor — live more largely in the present.

Becker has pointed out that this is an age in which we cannot feel that we understand anything until we know its history. As we become more aware of how things change, it becomes more important to know how they developed, how they got to be the way they are. But this does not mean that we feel more related to the past and future. It is rather the other way round: our feeling of estrangement in time and of the transience of the present prompts the historical approach. The historical approach is a symptom of our trouble. We are trying to recapture the sense of continuity, to find again the durable patterns of life — hoping we shall not lose altogether our connections with those who have lived before and those who will live after.

**Switching to the American
way of business**

27

U.S. News & World Report   **Is the World Going American?**

U.S. News & World Report aims at a business audience and is primarily concerned with topics of interest to such an audience. The selection which follows — one of a series — is from a compilation of reports from around the world showing how the adoption of American commercial methods has affected other nations. "Americanization," in this article, is seen in a limited and special way. It should be noted that here America becomes synonymous with technology. For related ideas, see Toynbee, Brogan, Barzini, Dedijer, Henry.

Something like a modern revolution — a switch to the American way of doing things — is stirring the world. The daily lives of millions of people in one nation after another are being changed.

This is happening at a time when Communists — both Chinese and Soviet — are driving hard to sell their system. In day-to-day affairs, close to peoples' lives, Reds are having scant success.

Regional Editors for "U.S. News & World Report," stationed abroad, now find that American ways of buying and selling, American habits in

Reprinted from *U.S. News & World Report* (March 23, 1959), published at Washington.

eating and dressing are being widely accepted and imitated. The same is not true of Soviet manners and customs. Even in countries where the Communist vote is high—such as France and Italy—the very people who vote Communist are showing a preference for the American mode of living.

Everywhere people are demanding—and getting—more of the things that have given Americans the highest standard of living in the world. As a result, vast, untapped markets are opening up. American ways of reaching these markets are being adopted.

Installment buying, almost unknown to consumers in Europe and Asia a short time ago, is becoming commonplace. Assembly-line production in country after country is being geared up to meet the rising demands, set free by credit buying, for goods that will make life easier and pleasanter: home appliances, automobiles, radio and television sets. Shopping has become simpler through supermarkets, self-service stores and mail-order firms, as merchants compete for their share of the boom.

You see signs everywhere that nations abroad are moving into a period of growth not unlike that which spread through the U.S. with the birth of the "motor age" early in the century. And the tempo of change is increasing.

The speed with which Britain is becoming Americanized surprises many Americans and annoys some Britons.

Basically, the big changes in the British way of life in the past decade hinge on two ideas, common in U.S.: self-service shopping and liberalized consumer financing. . . .

The "American revolution" is taking place in the stronghold of French tradition, the French home. Labor-saving devices, mostly French made but based on American ideas, are replacing hand drudgery. . . .

Perhaps the most American thing about West Germany is a sense of bustle and urgency in the cities. People are busy and they act as though they enjoy it. This is a marked contrast to the sullen, driven attitude with which the people in Communist East Germany plod about their daily tasks. . . .

In Italy, it is in cities and industrial areas that U.S. influence is most evident, even though, in many cases, these are the same places where Communists are politically strong.

Life is changing, becoming more American, for young and old alike. Women are enjoying increased freedom. More of them are taking jobs in commerce and industry, fewer are hiring out as maids, cooks and seamstresses. They drive cars, wear slacks, smoke in public—all things that would have been strange 10 years ago. Family-arranged marriages are not so common as they used to be, and the American custom of "dating" is being accepted. The first drive-in movie has just started outside of Rome. It is a success, and more are planned around other urban centers. . . .

Nowhere in the Orient have American ideas been more enthusiastically adopted than in Japan. Sparked by the introduction of installment buying, 1 out of 3 Japanese bought something on credit last year. Total sales of consumer goods on credit last year came to more than a billion dollars. Television sets accounted for a lot of that. Next came automobiles, refrigerators, radios and sewing machines.

Programs for Japan's 1.5 million TV sets—there were only 2,000 sets in the country in 1953—are mostly American imports or local imitations. Toll highways, to take care of the increasing number of cars, are being extended and new ones are being built, including an expressway in the heart of Tokyo. Parking is a problem, and parking meters are being installed.

American styles, particularly for casual wear, have largely replaced the traditional kimono for women in Japanese cities. And youngsters of both sexes don blue jeans for their play hours. Slacks are popular with teenagers.

In their homes, too, Japanese are taking to such American foods as popcorn, canned juices, potato chips and bread. And, in Tokyo, homes themselves are changing. Big apartment units are replacing the small, low houses of the city, giving many streets an American appearance. . . .

There are traffic jams, and parking meters now in Nairobi, capital of Kenya in East Africa, where Mau Mau terrorists raged only two years ago. Americans are popular. One nationalist leader, who seeks independence from Britain for the natives, has said: "Africans like the personal attitudes of Americans—they find Americans easy to get along with."

Johannesburg, in the Union of South Africa—with its skyscrapers, miles of modern apartment buildings and industrial suburbs—looks more like an American city than any community in Europe or elsewhere in Africa. . . .

In the Western Hemisphere, Soviet agents are at present concentrating their subversive drives on the countries of Latin America, including the islands of the Caribbean. Large "have not" populations in these lands would seem to furnish good ground for Communist propaganda and infiltration. But here, as in the rest of the free world, it's the American influence which is creating a real revolution in the daily lives of people.

This revolution is most apparent in the large cities—capitals and seaports. Here you see many signs of American ideas at work, American ways being copied, American-style clothing is worn by men and women. American cars crowd the streets, looking for a spot by an American parking meter. . . .

The American Way: "Wave of the Future"?

Most U.S. spokesmen who carry on the fight of ideas against Communists agree that the success of the "American revolution" abroad represents a victory in the "cold war." But the victory may have its price, they warn.

George V. Allen, the career diplomat who heads the United States Information Agency, has this to say:

"People may feel their way of life is being insidiously undermined by what they regard as irresistible encroachments by America on their way of doing things. We are not consciously pushing this Americanism as an instrument of the cold war. It's just happening.

"But," Mr. Allen goes on, "to the extent that the so-called American cult does represent the real attitude and progress of the U.S., I welcome it, because I like America to be regarded as 'the wave of the future.' "

And the wave seems to be gathering force and speed. — *Copyright 1959 U.S. News & World Report, Inc.*

Religiousness without religion

Will Herberg   **Protestant-Catholic-Jew**   **28**

Will Herberg, born in New York City in 1907, attended Columbia University, from which he was granted a Ph.D. in 1932. At present, he is Professor of Judaic Studies at Drew University. In his early years, Herberg was an exponent of Marxism; he describes as the critical point in his life the time that he came under the influence of Reinhold Niebuhr and renounced Marxism. His works include Judaism and Modern Man *(1951) and a contribution to* Roman Catholicism and the American Way of Life *(1960). In the following selection, Herberg suggests that religion in America represents a departure from the traditional Christian-Jewish complex. He sees it as a civic religion dedicated to the American way of life. For related ideas, see Cox, Fuchs, Gabriel.*

The ultimate ambiguity of the present religious situation in this country is obvious on the face of it. Every manifestation of contemporary American religion reveals diverse sides, of varying significance from the standpoint of Jewish-Christian faith. No realistic estimate of the present religious situation is possible unless this fundamental ambiguity is recognized.

The new status of religion as a basic form of American "belonging," along with other factors tending in the same direction, has led to the virtual disappearance of anti-religious prejudice, once by no means uncommon in our national life. The old-time "village atheist" is a thing of the past, a folk curiosity like the town crier; Clarence Darrow, the last of the "village atheists" on a national scale, has left no successors. The present generation can hardly understand the vast excitement stirred up in their day by the "atheists" and "iconoclasts" who vied for public attention less than half a century ago, or imagine the brash militancy of the "rationalist" movements and publications now almost all extinct. Religion has become part of the ethos of American life to such a degree that overt anti-religion is all but inconceivable.

The same factors that have led to the virtual disappearance of overt anti-religion have also made for a new openness to religion and what religion might have to say about the urgent problems of life and thought. In many ways the contemporary mind is more ready to listen to the word of faith than Americans have been for decades.

Yet it is only too evident that the religiousness characteristic of America today is very often a religiousness without religion, a religiousness with almost any kind of content or none, a way of sociability or "belonging" rather than a way of reorienting life to God. It is thus frequently a religiousness without serious commitment, without real inner conviction, without genuine existential decision. What should reach down to the core of existence, shattering and renewing, merely skims the surface of life, and yet succeeds in generating the sincere feeling of being religious. Religion thus becomes a kind of protection the self throws up against the radical demand of faith.

Where the other-directed adjustment of peer-group conformity operates, the discrepancy becomes even more obvious. The other-directed man or woman is eminently religious in the sense of being religiously identified and affiliated, since being religious and joining a church or synagogue is, under contemporary American conditions, a fundamental way of "adjusting" or "belonging." But what can the other-directed man or woman make of the prophets and the prophetic faith of the Bible, in which the religion of the church he joins is at least officially grounded? The very notion of being "singled out," of standing "over against" the world, is deeply repugnant to one for whom well-being means conformity and adjustment. Religion is valued as conferring a sense of sociability and "belonging," a sense of being really and truly *of* the world and society, a sense of reassurance; how can the other-directed man then help but feel acutely uncomfortable with a kind of religion—for that is what biblical faith is—which is a declaration of permanent resistance to the heteronomous claims of society, community, culture, and cult? The other-directed man generally protects himself against this profoundly disturbing aspect of biblical faith by refusing to understand it; indeed, insofar as he is other-directed, he really cannot understand it. The religion he avows is still formally the Christian or Jewish faith rooted in the prophetic tradition; it is, however, so transformed as it passes through the prism of the other-directed mind that it emerges as something quite different, in many ways, its opposite. The other-directed man, no matter how religious, simply cannot understand an Elijah or an Amos, a Jesus or an Isaiah; nor can he conceivably feel any warmth of admiration for these "zealots of the Lord." Zeal, nonconformity, uncompromising witness are so "unsociable," so terribly "unadjusted"! The very purpose of the other-directed man's built-in radar apparatus is to protect him against such perils; it protects him so well that it makes the prophetic faith of the Bible almost unintelligible to him. The Christianity or Judaism he understands—and which he finds, or convinces himself that he finds, in church or synagogue—is something very different; it is an other-directed gospel of adjustment, sociability, and comfort, designed to give one a sense of "belonging," of being at home in the society and the universe. It is thus not too much of a paradox to assert that many of the inner-directed "unbelievers" of the nineteenth century in a sense stood closer to, or at least less distant from, authentic biblical faith than do so many of the religious people of our time, whose religion comes to them as an aspect of other-directed conformism and sociability.

Equally dubious from the standpoint of Jewish-Christian faith is that aspect of the present religious situation which makes religion in America so thoroughly American. On the one side this means that no taint of foreignness any longer adheres to the three great American "faiths." Catholics, Jews, Lutherans, and others, who remember how formidable an obstacle to the preservation and communication of their faith the taint of foreignness once was, will not be altogether ungrateful for this development. And all Americans may be thankful for the new spirit of freedom and tolerance in religious life that the emergence of the tripartite system of three great "religions of democracy" has engendered; it makes increasingly difficult the sinister fusion of religious prejudice with racist or nationalist chauvinism. But on the other side, the "Americanization" of religion has meant a distinct loss of the sense of religious uniqueness and universality: each of the three "faiths," insofar as the mass of its adherents are concerned, tends to regard itself as merely an alternative and variant form of being religious in the American way. This is true even of rank-and-file American Catholics, whose official theology places the strongest possible emphasis on the uniqueness and universality of the Roman Catholic Church as the "one true church"; this is true even of the vast majority of American Jews, who possess so pronounced a sense of worldwide Jewish kinship.

The common ground between Judaism and Christianity, and on another
level between Protestantism and Catholicism, is real and important, sufficiently real and important, indeed, to make it possible to speak significantly of Jewish-Christian faith in a way that no one could conceivably
speak of Jewish-Buddhist or Christian-Hindu faith; yet the very existence
of this common ground makes the unique and distinctive witness of each
communion, even the advocacy of universal claims where such are felt to
be justified, all the more necessary for the life of faith. Insofar as the
"Americanness" of religion in America blunts this sense of uniqueness and
universality, and converts the three religious communions into variant expressions of American spirituality (just as the three religious communities
are understood to be three subdivisions of American society), the authentic
character of Jewish-Christian faith is falsified, and the faith itself reduced
to the status of an American culture-religion.

This American culture-religion is the religious aspect of Americanism,
conceived either as the common ground of the three "faiths" or as a kind
of super-religion embracing them. It will be recalled that President Eisenhower declared "recognition of the Supreme Being" to be "the first, the
most basic expression," not of our historical religions, although undoubtedly Mr. Eisenhower would agree that it is, but of . . . *Americanism.*
Americanism thus has its religious creed, evoking the appropriate religious
emotions; it may, in fact, be taken as the civic religion of the American
people.

But civic religion has always meant the sanctification of the society and
culture of which it is the reflection, and that is one of the reasons why
Jewish-Christian faith has always regarded such religion as incurably idolatrous. Civic religion is a religion which validates culture and society,
without in any sense bringing them under judgment. It lends an ultimate
sanction to culture and society by assuring them that they constitute an
unequivocal expression of "spiritual ideals" and "religious values." Religion becomes, in effect, the cult of culture and society, in which the
"right" social order and the received cultural values are divinized by being
identified with the divine purpose. Any issue of *Christian Economics,* any
pronouncement of such organizations as Spiritual Mobilization, will provide sufficient evidence of how Christian faith can be used to sustain the
civic religion of "laissez-faire capitalism." Similar material from Catholic
and Jewish sources comes easily to hand, from "liberal" quarters as well
as from "conservative." On this level at least, the new religiosity pervading America seems to be very largely the religious validation of the
social patterns and cultural values associated with the American Way of
Life.

In a more directly political sense, this religiosity very easily comes to
serve as a spiritual reinforcement of national self-righteousness and a spirit-

ual authentication of national self-will. Americans possess a passionate awareness of their power and of the justice of the cause in which it is employed. The temptation is therfore particularly strong to identify the American cause with the cause of God, and to convert our immense and undeniable moral superiority over Communist tyranny into pretensions to unqualified wisdom and virtue. In these circumstances, it would seem to be the office of prophetic religion to raise a word of warning against inordinate national pride and self-righteousness as bound to lead to moral confusion, political irresponsibility, and the darkening of counsel. But the contemporary religious mood is very far indeed from such prophetic transcendence. Aside from occasional pronouncements by a few theologians or theologically-minded clergymen, religion in America seems to possess little capacity for rising above the relativities and ambiguities of the national consciousness and bringing to bear the judgment of God upon the nation and its ways. The identification of religion with the national purpose is almost inevitable in a situation in which religion is so frequently felt to be a way of American "belonging." In its crudest form, this identification of religion with national purpose generates a kind of national messianism which sees it as the vocation of America to bring the American Way of Life, compounded almost equally of democracy and free enterprise, to every corner of the globe; in more mitigated versions, it sees God as the champion of America, endorsing American purposes, and sustaining American might. "The God of judgment has died."

Insensibly, this fusion of religion with national purpose passes over into the direct exploitation of religion for economic and political ends. A good deal of the official piety in Washington, it is charged, is of this kind, and much of the new religiousness of businessmen and business interests throughout the country. Certainly, when we find great corporations such as U.S. Steel distributing Norman Vincent Peale's *Guideposts* in huge quantities to their employees, when we find increasing numbers of industrial concerns placing "plant chaplains" on their staffs, we are not altogether unjustified in suspecting that considerations of personnel policy have somehow entered into these good works of religion. On another level, there seems to be a concerted effort to turn President Eisenhower's deep and sincere religious feeling into a political asset. How otherwise are we to interpret the paragraph in the resolution officially adopted by the Republican National Committee on February 17, 1955, in which it is declared: "He [President Eisenhower], in every sense of the word, is not only the political leader, but the spiritual leader of our times"? The fusion of political and spiritual leadership in the person of one national leader is in accord with neither the American democratic idea nor the tradition of Jewish-Christian faith; yet the statement of the Republican National Committee, making explicit the political exploitation of the "President's religion," seems to have aroused no comment in American religious circles. If indeed religion is the "spiritual" side of being an American, why should not the President of the United States be hailed as the "spiritual leader of our times"?

Religion is taken very seriously in present-day America, in a way that would have amazed and chagrined the "advanced" thinkers of half a century ago, who were so sure that the ancient superstition was bound to disappear very shortly in the face of the steady advance of science and reason. Religion has not disappeared; it is probably more pervasive today, and in many ways more influential, than it has been for generations. The only question is: What kind of religion is it? What is its content? What is it that Americans *believe in* when they are religious?

"The 'unknown God' of Americans seems to be faith itself." What Americans believe in when they are religious is, as we have already had occasion to see, religion itself. Of course, religious Americans speak of God and Christ, but what they seem to regard as really redemptive is primarily religion, the "positive" attitude of *believing*. It is this faith in faith, this religion that makes religion its own object, that is the outstanding characteristic of contemporary American religiosity. Daniel Poling's formula: "I began saying in the morning two words, 'I believe' — those two words *with nothing added* . . ." (emphasis not in original) may be taken as the classic expression of this aspect of American faith.

On the social level, this faith in religion involves the conviction, quite universal among Americans today, that every decent and virtuous nation is religious, that religion is the true basis of national existence and therefore presumably the one sure resource for the solution of all national problems. On the level of personal life, the American faith in religion implies not only that every right-minded citizen is religious, but also that religion (or faith) is a most efficacious device for getting what one wants in life. "Jesus," the Rev. Irving E. Howard assures us, "recommended faith as a technique for getting results. . . . Jesus recommended faith as a way to heal the body and to remove any of the practical problems that loom up as mountains in a man's path."

As one surveys the contemporary scene, it appears that the "results" Americans want to get out of faith are primarily "peace of mind," happiness, and success in worldly achievement. Religion is valued too as a means of cultural enrichment.

Prosperity, success, and advancement in business are the obvious ends for which religion, or rather the religious attitude of "believing," is held to be useful. There is ordinarily no criticism of the ends themselves in terms of the ultimate loyalties of a God-centered faith, nor is there much concern about what the religion or the faith is all about, since it is not the content of the belief but the attitude of believing that is felt to be operative.

Almost as much as worldly success, religion is expected to produce a kind of spiritual euphoria, the comfortable feeling that one is all right with God. Roy Eckardt calls this the cult of "divine-human chumminess" in which God is envisioned as the "Man Upstairs," a "Friendly Neighbor," Who is always ready to give you the pat on the back you need when you happen to feel blue. "Fellowship with the Lord is, so to say, an extra emotional jag that keeps |us| happy. The 'gospel' makes [us] 'feel real good.' " Again, all sense of the ambiguity and precariousness of human life, all sense of awe before the divine majesty, all sense of judgment before the divine holiness, is shut out; God is, in Jane Russell's inimitable phrase, a "livin' Doll." What relation has this kind of god to the biblical God Who confronts sinful man as an enemy before He comes out to meet repentant man as a Savior? Is this He of Whom we are told, "It is a fearful thing to fall into the hands of the living God" (Heb. 10.31)? The measure of how far contemporary American religiosity falls short of the authentic tradition of Jewish-Christian faith is to be found in the chasm that separates Jane Russell's "livin' Doll" from the living God of Scripture.

The cultural enrichment that is looked for in religion varies greatly with the community, the denomination, and the outlook and status of the church members. Liturgy is valued as aesthetically and emotionally "rewarding," sermons are praised as "interesting" and "enjoyable," discussions of the world relations of the church are welcomed as "educational," even theology is approved of as "thought provoking." On another level, the "old-time religion" is cherished by certain segments of the population because it so obviously enriches their cultural life.

But, in the last analysis, it is "peace of mind" that most Americans expect of religion. "Peace of mind" is today easily the most popular gospel that goes under the name of religion; in one way or another it invades and permeates all other forms of contemporary religiosity. It works in well with the drift toward other-direction characteristic of large sections of American society, since both see in adjustment the supreme good in life. What is desired, and what is promised, is the conquest of insecurity and anxiety, the overcoming of inner conflict, the shedding of guilt and fear, the translation of the self to the painless paradise of "normality" and "adjustment"! Religion, in short, is a spiritual anodyne designed to allay the pains and vexations of existence.

It is this most popular phase of contemporary American religiosity that has aroused the sharpest criticism in more sophisticated theological circles. The Most Rev. Patrick A. O'Boyle, Catholic archbishop of Washington, has warned that although "at first glance piety seems to be everywhere . . ." many persons appear to be "turning to religion as they would to a benign sedative to soothe their minds and settle their nerves." Liston Pope emphasizes that the approach of the "peace of mind" school is not only "very dubious on psychological grounds," but its "identification [with] the Christian religion . . . is of questionable validity." Roy Eckardt describes it as "religious narcissism," in which "the individual and his psycho-spiritual state occupy the center of the religious stage" and piety is made to "concentrate on its own navel." I have myself spoken of it as a philosophy that would "dehumanize man and reduce his life to the level of sub-human creation which knows neither sin nor guilt." It encourages moral insensitivity and social irresponsibility, and cultivates an almost lascivious preoccupation with self. The church becomes a kind of emotional service station to relieve us of our worries: "Go to church—you'll feel better," "Bring your troubles to church and leave them there" (slogans on subway posters urging church attendance). On every ground, this type of religion is poles apart from authentic Jewish-Christian spirituality which, while it knows of the "peace that passeth understanding" as the gift of God, promotes a "divine discontent" with things as they are and a "passionate thirst for the future," in which all things will be renewed and restored to their right relation to God.

The burden of this criticism of American religion from the point of view of Jewish-Christian faith is that contemporary religion is so naively, so innocently *man-centered*. Not God, but man—man in his individual and corporate being—is the beginning and end of the spiritual system of much of present-day American religiosity. In this kind of religion there is no sense of transcendence, no sense of the nothingness of man/and his works before a holy God; in this kind of religion the values of life, and life itself, are not submitted to Almighty God to judge, to shatter, and to reconstruct; on the contrary, life, and the values of life, are given an ultimate sanction by being identified with the divine. In this kind of religion it is not man who serves God, but God who is mobilized and made to serve man and his purposes—whether these purposes be economic prosperity, free enterprise, social reform, democracy, happiness, security, or "peace of mind." God is conceived as man's "omnipotent servant," faith as a sure-fire device to get what we want. The American is a religious man, and in many cases personally humble and conscientious. But religion as he understands it is not something that makes for humility or the uneasy conscience: it is something that reassures him about the essential rightness of everything American, his nation, his culture, and himself; something that validates his goals and his ideals instead of calling them into question; something that enhances his self-regard instead of challenging it; something that feeds his self-sufficiency instead of shattering it; something that offers him salvation on easy terms instead of demanding repentance and a "broken heart." Because it does all these things, his religion, however sincere and well-meant, is ultimately vitiated by a strong and pervasive idolatrous element.

Returning from a five-month visit to the United States, Bishop Eivind Berggrav, the eminent Norwegian Lutheran churchman, reported his impressions of religious life in America. He not only defended American churches against the charge of "materialism" and "activism," so often leveled against them by European observers; he also testified that "American Christianity is real, true, and personal." He found the American churches in a "period of youthful vigor," representing "a family rather than an individual Christianity," in which the congregation was a true "organism of fellowship." While he foresaw a future period of "crisis" for the American churches, he confessed himself much impressed by them and their genuine vitality.

Similar testimonies may be noted in the comments of other European churchmen, Catholic as well as Protestant. With all their criticism of American religion, they find in America religious life a vigor and a closeness to the people, a pervasive sense of the importance of religion, that is most impressive.

Yet this is the same American religion that, seen from another angle, we have found to be so empty and contentless, so conformist, so utilitarian, so sentimental, so individualistic, and so self-righteous. Each judgment has its validity and is necessary to correct and supplement the other. Both may be summed up by saying that Americans are "at one and the same time, one of the most religious and most secular of nations."

Americans fill the houses of worship, but their conceptions, standards, and values, their institutions and loyalties, bear a strangely ambiguous relation to the teachings that the churches presumably stand for. The goals and values of life are apparently established autonomously, and religion is brought in to provide an enthusiastic mobilization of human resources for the promotion of the well-being of the individual and society. Of the very same Americans who so overwhelmingly affirm their belief in God and their membership in the historic churches, a majority also affirm, without any sense of incongruousness, that their religion has little to do with their politics or business affairs, except to provide an additional sanction and drive. Most of the activities of life—education, science, entertainment—could be added to the list; they too apparently operate under their own rules, with religion invoked as a "spiritual" embellishment and a useful sustaining force. This is not felt as in any sense a disparagement of religion; it is merely America's way of defining for itself the place of religion and the church in the total scheme of things. But this way of looking at things is precisely the way of secularism, for what is secularism but the practice of the absence of God in the affairs of life? The secularism characteristic of the American mind is implicit and is not felt to be at all inconsistent with the most sincere attachment to religion. It is, nevertheless, real and pervasive, and in this sense Handlin is certainly right in saying that America is growing more secularist, at the very time when in another sense, in the sense of affiliation and identification and of the importance attributed to religion, America is becoming increasingly more religious.

So thoroughly secularist has American religion become that the familiar distinction between religion and secularism appears to be losing much of its meaning under present-day conditions. Both the "religionists" and the "secularists" cherish the same basic values and organize their lives on the same fundamental assumptions — values and assumptions defined by the American Way of Life. What really seems to distinguish one from the other is that the explicit secularism of the avowed secularists is suspicious of, sometimes even hostile to, institutional religion and its influence in public life, while the implicit secularism pervading American religion identifies itself wholeheartedly with the religious institutions of the nation. The tension between the two is no less sharp, though the issues that divide them are rather different than the simple distinction between religion and secularism would imply.

The widespread secularism of American religion, in which religion is made to provide the sanctification and dynamic for goals and values otherwise established, is often difficult for Europeans to understand, since in Europe the confrontation between secularism and religion tends to be much more explicit and well defined. In the United States explicit secularism — hostility or demonstrative indifference to religion — is a minor and diminishing force; the secularism that permeates the American consciousness is to be found within the churches themselves and is expressed through men and women who are sincerely devoted to religion. The witness to authentic Jewish-Christian faith may well prove much more difficult under these conditions than when faith has to contend with overt and avowed unbelief.

The spirit of secularism has always been pervasive and powerful and has always had its effect on religious institutions. The unique feature of the present religious situation in America is that this secularism is being generated out of the very same conditions that are, in part at least, making for the contemporary religious revival. The sociological factors that underlie the new urge to religious identification and affiliation are also factors that enhance the secularization of the religiousness they engender. It is not secularism as such that is characteristic of the present religious situation in this country but secularism within a religious framework, the secularism of a religious people.

Yet we must not see the picture as all of one piece. Within the general framework of a secularized religion embracing the great mass of American people, there are signs of deeper and more authentic stirrings of faith. Duncan Norton-Taylor, in his comments on the new religiousness of businessmen, may not be altogether wrong in noting that "particularly among the younger men, there *is* a groping for a spiritual base." Norman Thomas, though recognizing that the "return to religion," which is "one of the significant phenomena of our confused and troubled times," is a "phenomenon of many and contradictory aspects," nevertheless finds it, in part at least, "definitely characterized by an awareness of, or search after God." Certainly among the younger people, particularly among the more sensitive young men and women on the campuses of this country, and in the suburban communities that are in so many ways really continuous with the campus, there are unmistakable indications of an interest in, and concern with, religion that goes far beyond the demands of mere social "belonging." These stirrings are there; they are not always easily identified as religion on the one hand, or easily distinguishable from the more conventional types of religiousness on the other — but they constitute a force whose range and power should not be too readily dismissed. Only the future can tell what these deeper stirrings of faith amount to and what consequences they hold for the American religion of tomorrow.

But even the more conventional forms of American religion, for all their dubiousness, should not be simply written off by the man of faith. Even in this ambiguous structure there may be elements and aspects — not always those, incidentally, that seem most prepossessing to us today — which could in the longer view transform the inner character of American religion and bring it closer to the faith it professes. Nothing is too unpromising or refractory to serve the divine will. After all, the God Who is able to make the "wrath of man" to praise Him (Ps. 76.10) is surely capable of turning even the intractabilities and follies of religion into an instrument of His redemptive purpose.

Dominant qualities in architecture

James Marston Fitch   **The "American" in**   **29**
                                   American Architecture

James Marston Fitch is an architect who was educated at the University of Alabama and Tulane. He is presently professor of architecture at Columbia University. His works include American Buildings *(1948),* Treasury of American Gardening *(1956), and* Walter Gropius *(1960). In the following*

From *Architecture and the Esthetics of Plenty* by James Marston Fitch (New York: Columbia University Press, 1961), pp. 3–13.

selection, Fitch describes the effect of three dominant qualities on American architecture. They are acquisitiveness, plasticity, and productivity. For related ideas, see Hassan, Goodrich, Rostow.

What is American about American architecture? The question is easier to ask than to answer—especially if, as is so often the case nowadays, we are really trying to isolate those aspects of our national life which are uniquely good rather than merely unique. So we had best rephrase the question: Does American architecture display qualities which we can safely describe as characteristic, irrespective of whether or not we can be proud of them? This we can answer affirmatively. There are many areas in which our architecture is easily distinguishable from that of the rest of the world. The single family house, for example, shares with its foreign contemporaries the basic elements of plan (rooms for sleeping, bathing, cooking, resting, etc.); the same general types of furnishings (tables, chairs, beds, etc.); the same utilities (gas, electricity, water). And yet the way in which these elements are organized into a whole gives our houses certain qualities which we can call "typically American." The use of large areas of unprotected glass, the window wall, is one such. The large size of garage and motor court and the degree of mechanization in the kitchen are others. Middle-class houses in São Paulo or Helsinki will also have glass, garages and mechanical equipment. But the *concentration* of these elements is far higher in our houses than in the rest of the world; and this purely quantitative factor makes for qualitative differences—though of course the differences are seldom as important and almost never as favorable as we should like to imagine.

It is even more hazardous to attempt to generalize upon the purely formal aspects of American architecture since, during the three and a half centuries of its history, it has employed so many idioms, so many various means of expression. Visually, it presents a pattern of bewildering complexity; this complexity is, however, but a reflection of Western experience generally. Fortunately for our purposes, the basic *qualities* of a national architecture are much more permanent than the *forms* it assumes at any moment. And from this point of view, three dominant qualities seem to have been always present in our architecture. They are:

1. Acquisitiveness—its tendency to rely upon imported forms.
2. Plasticity—its lack of inertia, its ability to react to external stimuli, to adapt itself to rapid rates of change.
3. Productivity—its ability to modify the new form to some average level of mass taste, adapt it to mass production, then produce it seriatim indefinitely.

American architecture was acquisitive from its very inception. It began with borrowed means and has borrowed ever since. Architectural forms

and building techniques were acquired in two ways. First, from the settlers themselves who, in wave after wave of English, French, Dutch, Swedish, German, Italian, and Middle European immigration, naturally brought
with them their own familiar tools and techniques, their own esthetic standards. The second source of new forms was more generalized: from the
first, American architecture showed itself extremely sensitive to world fashions, to the styles of the European centers. And then, from the beginning
of the nineteenth century, the development of transportation and communication made the broadcasting of these changing fashions ever easier. They
were registered on the American scene with the speed and accuracy of a
seismograph. Scott had but to write a novel, Ruskin to read a paper, or
Norman Shaw to build a new country house for the impulse to be at once
reflected in our architecture here.

This acquisitiveness was undoubtedly characteristic. But can it be proved
unique? Obviously, no other country had comparable immigration, but
immigrant taste, while pervasive, was never as decisive as the international
fashions of the upper class. Certainly, the stylistic gyrations of the last 150
years have been more quickly felt and widely echoed in America than in
stagnant areas like Spain or southern Italy. But Paris, London, and Berlin
were also swayed by these fashions: in fact, one or the other of them was
the source of most vogues. Gothic Revival churches, Italianate villas and
Art Nouveau subway kiosks were forms actually invented there and only
subsequently imported to America. Only recently, in forms like skyscrapers
or abstract expressionist art, can America be said to have started a vogue.

The unique property of American acquisitiveness seems thus to be its
scale. We undoubtedly have built more Gothic churches, Tuscan villas and
Art Nouveau subway kiosks than other lands. But they have not been
"better," so that our leadership is largely statistical. Of course, even here
a difference in degree becomes ultimately a difference in kind. For if the
building industry is intensely active, as it always has been in America, then
these exotic stimuli become more quickly imbedded and more widely distributed in the whole body of its concepts and practices. Thereby they
affect future as well as contemporaneous forms. And this brings us to a
second quality of American architecture: its plasticity.

It began, as we have seen, with a series of imported forms, none of them
particularly well suited to the climate or economic conditions of the New
World. And of course it began in a landscape in which no pre-existing concepts or technologies held sway. (The only exception to this would be the
Spanish in the Southwest, who found settled cultures of a relatively high
order with a building technique not unlike their own.) Thus, on the one
hand, there was in colonial America every incentive to radical modification
of inherited building technologies and forms; and on the other, no inertia
of a cultural or economic nature to resist it. Under these conditions,

American architecture developed a remarkable ability to adapt itself to change. This quality becomes especially evident when the rate of change itself accelerated with the expansion of the original colonies across the Appalachian barrier at the end of the eighteenth century.

The opening of the West confronted the building industry with new demands. Changes in climate, in available building materials, in the speed of construction required, and the short length of tenure anticipated—all of these placed a premium on flexibility, adaptability, plasticity in both process and final product. Nor have these forces diminished; to the contrary, they have steadily increased, especially in the years since the Second World War. They have produced a new kind of obsolescence in the field. Buildings which are still perfectly sound physically are technologically so obsolete that it is more economical to wreck than to remodel them.

This quality of plasticity, then, is characteristically American: to what extent is it unique? Here again the answer is not easy. Despite our rapid rates of both growth and change, one can always find examples of identical change as early, or even earlier, in Western Europe. We have come to think of steel and concrete as being peculiarly American materials. Yet both Bessemer steel and Portland cement are English inventions; and the discovery of reinforced concrete is French. Moreover, the application of these materials to structural problems predates ours by decades. England was building daring iron bridges before 1800, and her beautiful iron railway sheds were a commonplace by the 1830s, when our railway system was scarcely begun. The Crystal Palace was English, and the Eiffel Tower was French; these were for decades the largest and the tallest modern structures in the world. In the application of metal to more orthodox architectural problems, Labrouste's magnificent libraries in Paris—the Ste. Geneviève (1850) and the Nationale (1858–68)—appeared years before any similar use in this country.

The same thing must be said about many amenities now commonly held to be American. Steam heating was common in English greenhouses long before it appeared in the American home. All the elements of the bathroom—pump, running water and plumbing—were English before they were American. Faraday and Kelvin did the theoretical spadework for the electric refrigerator, though the refrigerator using natural ice for food preservation does seem to be indisputably an American invention. The list could be continued indefinitely. How does it happen, then, that all these characteristic features of modern architecture are so commonly regarded as American?

It seems to me that the answer must lie, not in who used these elements *first*, but in who used them *most*. In Western Europe they appeared early but remained alone, isolated phenomena which did not substantially affect subsequent practice. (It is almost as difficult to get a central heating plant or a bathroom in France or England today as it would have been in 1850.) In America, on the other hand, these features were adopted and absorbed into the very tissue of theory and practice. They became as integral a feature of the building as its floor or roof. (I do not mean to imply that there are not, even now, plenty of buildings in this country which have neither plumbing nor heating, but rather that they are generally recognized as shameful departures from the norm.)

Here, it seems to me, we come closer to a quality in American architecture which is unique; its tendency not merely to respond to change but to respond in *depth*, from top to bottom, throughout the nation's whole structure. Its genius seems to lie, not so much in invention as in application. And this brings us to a third, and to my mind most important, characteristic of our architecture and the industry which produces it: its powers of productivity. If it is acquisitive, and if these acquisitions are to be effectively put to work, then it must operate on a massive scale, be organized on an industrial basis geared to rapid change, to serve an expanding market which is never (except for periodic depressions) saturated. To accomplish this—to put into widest use the new concept, the new structural system or the new piece of equipment—it is always necessary to modify it to meet two sets of requirements: those of the industrial process itself and those imposed by the standards of taste of the American people.

This entire process has always been conditioned, in America, by a fact of immense significance: labor has always been scarce and hence expensive, while materials have always been plentiful and relatively cheap. This ratio of labor to material costs seems to have held as well in 1781 (Jefferson, in Paris, found he could get printing done for a fourth of what he had been asked in the United States) as in 1950. It is, moreover, the exact reverse of conditions in Europe and the rest of the world, where the cost of labor is low relative to the cost of materials. Finally, the relation between these two ratios has been constant throughout our history. For architecture this has important implications, since the American ratio is an incentive towards industrial production, while the other tends towards the persistence of handicraft.

Of all the areas colonized by an exploding Europe since the sixteenth century, North America alone offered no native populations which could be exploited or enslaved. Thus, unlike other colonists in South America, India, or Africa, the Americans were confronted by a labor shortage from the start. Our deliberate destruction of the small original Indian population and our subsequent introduction of Negro slaves did little to abate it. This made it mandatory that Americans build America with their own hands and, in the very process, reconstruct their building techniques as well as their very character.

The Patent Office presents an impressive record of our response to this situation. No machine was ever too expensive to build, out of no matter what materials, if it promised to increase the productivity—i.e., reduce the unit cost—of labor. This drive towards rationalization has dominated our building activity from the very beginning and gives to our architecture certain formal qualities which may be described as distinctive, if not unique.

In structure, for example, we have always avoided the load-bearing, mass masonry which was our dominant heritage from Europe. The reason was simple: it demanded too much labor and there was no way of reducing the labor component until reinforced concrete came into common use around 1900. Thus we find no masonry tradition in the United States; I doubt if there are fifty genuine masonry vaults or domes in the whole country. (The masonry walls which we see in most buildings are not load-bearing—on the skyscraper they are mere curtains—and even where they do carry a load, they require a skeletal trussed roof or floor to complete the enclosure.)

The structural form which we did adopt, and which we have cultivated intensively ever since, is the skeleton. There were two great virtues to skeletal structures. The first was purely technical: it was more efficient than mass masonry in resisting loads and, because of its specialized curtain walls, could be made much more effective in repelling climatic attack. The second virtue was economic. The skeleton was *possible* in America, as nowhere else in the modern world, because ample supplies of the proper materials, wood and steel, were at hand. But it was *desirable* because the skeleton frame and its curtain walling are subject to a high degree of rationalization. The economies in labor were so pronounced that it has remained for three centuries our most popular structural form.

It is instructive to observe how quickly these forces began to operate in colonial building. The English settlers brought with them the concept of a skeletal structural system as expressed in late medieval wood-framed houses and barns. Its members were all hand worked, and it was fairly primitive from both a structural and an environmental point of view. Its members were heavy, crude, and inexact. Its walling, which merely filled the interstices, did not protect the skeleton itself from the great extremes of the New England climate, and it rapidly deteriorated as a result.

Radical modifications of this structural system were called for, and they were not long in appearing. The first steps were towards the lightening and simplification of the skeleton and the development of a continuous skin or sheath of either clapboards or shingles with which to protect the skeleton from the elements. Although it was possible to split shingles by hand, clapboards and floorboards had to be sawed; sawing would also speed up the production of structural timbers. Thus, though there was no tradition of sawmills in England (they had, as a matter of fact, been forbidden), we find waterpowered sawmills appearing as early as 1633 at the

Falls of Piscataqua, on the line between New Hampshire and Maine. In the succeeding century and a half, a giant lumber industry was to rise, spurred on by the appearance of the steam-powered sawmill at the end of the eighteenth century. However, the development of that authentically American structure, the balloon-framed wooden house, was delayed until the 1830s by the exorbitant cost of handmade nails. Until machine-made nails appeared, the skeleton had to be put together with pegs or mortise and tenon; these connections required bulky framing members and they were often hand hewn. But with the appearance of the wire-cut nail, hand-worked members disappeared almost at once. The entire structure was immeasurably lightened, and site labor greatly reduced. By 1840, in the Midwest, the typical frame house was built completely of milled elements.

But, long before the elements were completely machine-made, the fabrication of hand-sawed and even hand-adzed wooden structures was also being rationalized. Thus, there are records of prefabricated house frames being made as early as 1578. The Louisiana French were shipping them to the West Indies as early as 1727. A prefabricated house was stolen from a Natchez, Mississippi, wharf in 1791; and the Utopian community of the Rappists at Economy, Pennsylvania, erected 200 identical dwelling houses in the years 1824-1830, prefabricating them from a single set of shop drawings. By the time of the California Gold Rush, prefabricated houses were being manufactured in Chicago and shipped out to San Francisco by boat. Houses are not as completely fabricated even today as they obviously could be, due to the resistance of the *rentier* element in building financing: but even so, the proportion of labor done on the site has been reduced to a fraction of its former amount and could readily be reduced to almost zero if builders so desired.

In its development and exploitation of the wood frame, America is almost unique. Only the Japanese have approached us in this respect. But, though their walls are models of rationalized construction, surpassing ours in their clarity and grace, their roof framing is clumsy and inefficient. For some odd reason, they never discovered the truss, relying upon very heavy cribbing to support their roofs. Hence their wooden skeletons are, from a qualitative point of view, inferior to ours. While we cannot claim to have invented the truss (the Romans used it in their basilicas), we have certainly brought it to its highest level of development. With it, we devised a completely three-dimensional skeletal framing system.

The most significant American contribution to the field of skeletal structure, however, has been in metal rather than wood. Here again our contribution has been more in the area of exploitation than invention since, as we have seen, England pioneered in the manufacture and use of cast iron, wrought iron, and steel structural members. Our adoption of the metal-framed building was entirely logical. We had had over two centuries of experience with the wooden skeleton when the metal frame became possible. The two materials are roughly similar in their structural behavior, both having high resistance to tensile as well as compressive loading. And, as it turned out, we had enormous supplies of iron ore and of coal wherewith to smelt it. Hence our transition to metal was easy and—because of the enormous expansion of the mid-nineteenth century—very rapid.

The first substitutions of metal for wood occurred in precisely those areas where its greater strength and predictability were most appreciated: in mills, factories, and railroad bridges. We find metal columns, beams, and trusses in New England textile mills in 1835; prefabricated non-load-bearing cast iron curtain walls in New Orleans, St. Louis, and Pottsville (Pa.) at about the same time. And we find the two combined in an all-metal building in New York by 1850. There was a slight decline in the years after the Civil War, when several disastrous fires proved that though iron did not burn like wood, it melted and collapsed even faster. But fireproofing techniques were evolved and the completely articulated steel frame found its most typical—though by no means most brilliant—expression in the skyscraper. This building type, together with the elevator which made it possible, can certainly be reckoned as uniquely American.

Today, the cubical steel skeleton of the skyscraper dominates the American skyline, both literally and conceptually. Its particular form is the one which we have cultivated to the exclusion of all others, even in many buildings which are not multi-story and need not be cubical. Yet it is efficient and economical only within the reference frame of American conditions. In the abstract, it is neither. The criterion of structural efficiency is that the minimum material does the maximum work. In this light, the cubical skeleton is only moderately efficient. Suspended structures like the George Washington Bridge or stressed skin structures like the molded plywood speedboat have a much more favorable ratio of material to work. Nor is the skyscraper frame economical except in relation to the high cost of labor and the plentitude of steel in this country. In most parts of the world, the steel frame is prohibitively expensive. So great is the prestige of this particular steel form that we even duplicate it in concrete, though the unique potentials of this material are best exploited in shell structures, as the steel-poor countries of Latin America and Europe are so brilliantly demonstrating.

Thus, beyond some point not easily determined, the most characteristic quality of American architecture—its power of rationalization—displays serious limitations. While, relative to the rest of the world, it always produces a statistical predominance (most skyscrapers, most bathrooms, most heating plants) and in many respects a high average level, rationalization tends to inhibit qualitative superiority of design. There seems to be a cyclical effect in rationalization, especially in these days of intensive mechanization. This permits us, at one stage, to appropriate the best of existing ideas and leap into world leadership with their concrete application. But the very process of "tooling up" introduces a rigidity into the picture which, at another point of the spiral, acts to slow down qualitative advance. This is precisely what happened to Henry Ford. He completed the first production line assembly in the world before 1920 and with it was catapulted into absolute priority in his field. Yet within a decade he had lost it to the competition with newer and more flexible production lines.

Though they have many problems, less massively industrialized countries than our own do not suffer from this liability. In a quantitative sense their systems support fewer architects than does ours, but they do at the same time offer these designers greater freedom of action. They produce fewer buildings, and many of these are low by any standard; but some of them are very high by any standard. And it is due to this paradox that Rio de Janiero and Mexico City, Milan and Stockholm often produce more stimulating modern architecture today than New York or Chicago. This fact should expose a widely held American fallacy that statistical superiority leads automatically to qualitative preeminence. Unfortunately, in design, at least, this does not follow. There is a necessary correlation between building many skyscrapers and building the best. But this proposition cannot be read backwards: to have the most skyscrapers is no automatic *guarantee* of having the best.

Moreover, it must be observed that a scarcity of materials seems often to have a benign effect on both design and workmanship, while abundance leads often to vulgarity. This is especially evident in metal-poor countries like Italy. Here steel is very expensive. It can only be used where nothing else will do, as in trains and automobiles; and here the sheer brilliance with which Italian engineers wring the last milligram of performance out of each millimeter of material is an exciting experience for the designer to witness. The Italians, like most of the rest of the world, actually have only one material out of which to build: reinforced concrete. Because of this, they are *forced* to exploit its potentials to the utmost, using 3-inch thick shells to span great voids where American practice would call for 24-inch beams and 8-inch slabs. In social life poverty has nothing to commend it; but in design its astringent discipline often stimulates the designer's imagination beyond the power of plenty.

These, in greatly capsuled form, are the qualities which make American architecture American. On close examination, it becomes apparent that only one is possibly unique, and it by no means uniquely good. There is much cause for pride in the past of American architecture and some reason for confidence in its future, but no excuse at all for being complacent about it.

30

Ihab Hassan   Radical Innocence

Ihab Habib Hassan was born in Cairo, Egypt, in 1925. He was educated at
the University of Cairo and the University of Pennsylvania, from which he
received his Ph.D. in 1953. He has taught at Rensselaer Polytechnic Insti-
tute and Wesleyan, where he is currently professor of English. He is a
frequent contributor of articles on avant-garde literature to many publica-
tions. The following selection, reflecting in a particular way Henry Bamford
Parkes's notion of American innocence, suggests that the hero in contempo-
rary American novels is characterized by a "radical innocence" and that
the important theme is "recoil" — that is, privatism and disengagement.
The same "recoil" might be seen in the techniques and subject of contem-
porary painting and sculpture. For related ideas, see Aldridge, Goodrich,
Schlesinger, Jr., Larrabee, Kouwenhoven.

It is the privilege of every age to consider its predicament unique, and
it is its hope that the predicament may prove the most gravid history has
known. Such illusions are not always idle; for they are the stuff of which
men make the record of their speeding days, heightening their moment
with some articulate show of pride, wonder, or despair. In the end, such
illusions are but the human way of stating: "We are here!"

We are indeed here, past the meridian of the twentieth century, a dev-
astating war behind us, and a war we dare not call by any name lowering
ahead. Yet it is time, perhaps, we called a halt to the melodrama of fis-
sion and fusion, of grim threats and endless lamentation. Poised at the
edge of the Space Age, we have no recourse but to choose life over death,
turning our attention to this time and to this place, to the actions of man
and to his works which make time and place an habitation for his spirit.

We are here: precisely the cry literature has articulated with the fullest
resonances throughout the ages. If that were the only statement contemporary American fiction made, it should have been reason enough to rescue
it from the vulgar interest or stylish indifference with which it is greeted.
But the contemporary American novel does not only aver our presence: it
explores and enlarges the modalities of our *being*. "To be alive, to be the

From Ihab Hassan, *Radical Innocence: The Contemporary American Novel* (Princeton
University Press, 1961), pp. 3–6, 62–66. Reprinted by permission.

whole man alive: that is the point," D. H. Lawrence wrote with the wisdom that qualifies itself by excess. "And at its best, the novel, and the novel supremely, can help you. It can help you not to be a dead man in life." Professors of the view that the novel is defunct — professors, that is, of their own weary sophistication — condemn current fiction as a spent form, irrelevant to the goals of a Supersociety committed to a galactic adventure, and therefore no longer receptive to the piteous heroics of the individual soul. Such a view reveals that myopia is indeed the most pronounced trait of utopian vision; and though we can no more refute it than we can refute a nightmare or a prophecy, we can put its judgment to question by inquiring into a more vital matter: the nature of the contemporary self in action and reaction, in stress and freedom, in assent and denial, sallying forth to confront experience and recoiling again to preserve its sanity or innocence.

The actions and recoils of the contemporary self engage that dense area of reality wherein our epochal consciousness and our literary forms meet. The movements of the self suggest the regions of tension and repose in our cultural life. Such movements have been the primary business of the novel since the Knight of the Mournful Countenance jogged down the road with fat Sancho by his side. The hero, while life still beats in his fictive heart, mediates between self and world in that imaginative dialectic form we have agreed to identify as the novel.

But what image of the hero does contemporary American fiction project, giving the novel its shape and our world its particular substance? No single answer, of course, will tell the whole story. Still, a beginning may be made by imagining the reactions of a venerable and literate Martian to some current titles — merely the titles — on our bookshelves: *The Victim, Dangling Man, The Naked and the Dead, The Heart Is a Lonely Hunter, Invisible Man, A Long Day's Dying, The Color of Darkness, A Good Man Is Hard to Find, The End of Pity, A Tree of Night, Lie Down in Darkness,* etc. We should not hold it entirely against our visitor if his initial reaction should be that the Planet Earth is on the way to self-demolition. Obviously, a dark impulse of *resistance* permeates contemporary letters. Novelists are not afraid to admit it. A Christain writer like Flannery O'Conner and a radical novelist like Norman Mailer concur that violence and distortion must be the means of projecting a vision to which society is hostile. They would further agree that the contemporary world presents a continued affront to man, and that his response must therefore be the response of the rebel or victim, living under the shadow of death.

Such a response goes far beyond the assumptions of mere opposition, and it bears no witness to the charges of neutrality or disaffiliation. The contemporary "opposing self," to be sure, has the powers of indignant "perception," has the "intense and adverse imagination of the culture in which it has its being" that Lionel Trilling astutely perceived in the novel of the last hundred and fifty years. But the contemporary self is also post-Romantic. It was not only born, like Little Dorrit, in a prison, and it has not only made of its prison, like Axel, a fortress and mausoleum. It has been also discovering the strange secrets of all prisons: that though their doors are never locked, no prisoner wishes to escape; that all avenues of escape lead to the same cell; that nothing may really exist beyond prison walls; that every gaoler is merely another prisoner in disguise. The contemporary self recoils, *from* the world, *against* itself. It has discovered absurdity. The parable used by Saul Bellow as an epigraph to his novel, *The Victim,* sums up this terrible recognition. The story is that of the wealthy merchant in the *Arabian Nights* who sat down under a tree to eat his dates in peace.

> When he had ended eating the dates he threw away the stones with force and lo! an Ifrit appeared, huge of stature and brandishing a drawn sword, wherewith he approached the merchant and said, "Stand up that I may slay thee even as thou slewest my son!" Asked the merchant, "How have I slain thy son?" and he answered, "When thou atest dates and threwest away the stones they struck my son full in the breast as he was walking by, so that he died forthwith."

Yet if the contemporary self is in recoil, it is not, we hope and believe, cravenly on the run. Its *re-coil* is one of the resources of its awareness, a strategy of its *will.* As we shall have occasion to see, its most tortured gestures of opposition proclaim its involvement in the world it opposes, and its most desperate forms of surrender probe the heart of the religious life in our time. "If the modern temper, as distinct from the romantic, lies in the admission that men are mortal," Wright Morris says, "this admission determines the nature of the raw material with which the artist must work. An element of despair, a destructive element, is one of the signs by which we shall know him—the other is the constructive use to which this element is put."

Both elements, we believe, emerge in the new figure of the hero in contemporary American fiction. Precisely what the new hero stands for, no one can yet define. He is not exactly the liberal's idea of the victim, not the conservative's idea of the pariah, not the radical's idea of the rebel. Or perhaps he is all of these and none in particular. Sometimes one aspect of his makeup is underscored, sometimes another. His capacity for pain seems very nearly saintly, and his passion for heresy almost criminal. But flawed in his sainthood and grotesque in his criminality, he finally appears as an expression of man's quenchless desire to affirm, despite the voids and vicissitudes of our age, the human sense of *life!*

It is this quality of his passion, of his awareness, that we have chosen to call *radical innocence.* Radical, first, because it is inherent in his character, and goes to the root or foundation of it. But radical, too, because it is extreme, impulsive, anarchic, troubled with vision. The new hero brings the brilliant extremities of the American conscience and imagination to bear on the equable tenor of our present culture. His stance questions the "mystic centrality" of our day, which Richard Chase so ably condemned in *The Democratic Vista,* and his fate testifies to the continuance of "the vivid contradictions and anomalies that in the past have engaged the A- merican mind." His innocence, therefore, does not merely revert to those simplicities which, rightly or wrongly, have been identified with vision in America. His innocence, rather, is a property of the mythic American Self, perhaps of every anarchic Self. It is the innocence of a Self that re- fuses to accept the immitigable rule of reality, including death, an aborigi- nal Self the radical imperatives of whose freedom cannot be stifled. There is something in the quality of that innocence to remind us of the *ignoble* savage, the archaic and roguish character, say, of the Winnebago Trickster who, as Jung described him, "is a faithful copy of an absolutely undif- ferentiated human consciousness, corresponding to a psyche that has hardly left the animal level." But the innocence we speak of also has a divine element in it; has, like Dionysus, that inner energy of being, creative and sacrificial, which D. H. Lawrence hoped to find in the American Adam. The disparity between the innocence of the hero and the destructive char- acter of his experience defines his concrete, or existential, situation. This does not add up to an orthodox notion of American innocence—the no- tion is radical—but it is one, we believe, that can help to make the new hero more intelligible. . . .

The movement from the surface images to the hidden motives in our culture is subtle and continuous. There are no sudden gaps. But the dis- tance is nevertheless great, and it is experienced every day by the individ- ual in anguish or puzzled resentment.

When World War II came to an end soon after the holocausts at Hiroshima and Nagasaki, and millions of young men climbed out of uni- form, a new age was ushered in. The men who went to war went, at best, with mixed idealism; they were not, it is often said, as innocent as their fathers who were sent from a Midwestern farm to a trench of the Marne. In retrospect, some of us may be inclined to feel as Edmund Wilson did in 1957 that "both Roosevelt and the country at large were moved mainly by the irresistible instinct of power to expand itself. . . ." Whatever the "real" motive may have been, the men who went to war finished what they or someone else had started, and they returned to put America in a position of unquestionable world eminence. The age of so- called comfort and conformity had begun. Other generations followed them—those who fought at Korea, those who are now entering colleges or have just graduated from them—and following their seniors, accelerated the established trend. A feeling of some intensity, an awareness of urgency and even power, was evident for a few years after 1945. But the feeling, which we sense in the best war novels, seems to have dissipated itself— with the possible exception of Norman Mailer, none of the "war novelists" commands our attention any longer. The new age often demanded another kind of novel and the image it projected began imperceptibly to bemuse the "veterans" whose youthful memories found their origin in the Depression.

"Ours is a society with more built-in tranquilizers of more different sorts than any that has ever existed," Russell Lynes recently said in his witty exposé, *A Surfeit of Honey*. The statement might well serve as a standard keynote of contemporary culture. The diversity of works, flip or erudite, blithe or somber, on the subject of mass society betrays the extent to which we are fascinated by the aspect we offer to the world at the same time that we are made vaguely uneasy by its consequences. We cannot bring ourselves to believe that this is quite the way we are. And indeed the composite image of ourselves, made up of slogans and stock responses, seems more ludicrous than terrifying. It is the image of an organization man in gray flannel suit who foregoes the ulcerous rewards of executive suite, preferring to lead the good life in the suburbs (or, if his paycheck allows, in exurbia), pottering about a house with a cracked picture window looking into the crack of another picture window (or Doing-It-Himself, whatever it may be, in the backyard, with regulation brogans and blue jeans on), and viewing with a mixture of apathy and wise disaffiliation the coming caesars of our imperial state, the hidden persuaders and clowns of commerce on Madison Avenue, U.S.A., and the exploding metropolis on whose far fringes our Quiet American has found his corner of Shangri-La. Together with his family as with himself, he expects any day now Erma, the ambidextrous automaton, to fulfill all his physical needs at home; meanwhile, there is the astonished and astonishing muse of TV to provide his spiritual sustenance. and when the evening is done, he can sleep with an easy conscience, after the usual dose of Miltown, in the knowledge that when he wakes up at least one of the insolent chariots in his two-car garage will be ready to transport him to another appointment with a white-collar day. In this other-directed paradise, where everyone is another to someone else and nothing to himself, The American Adam can obviously have no knowledge of evil, except perhaps that which is vicariously rendered on his stereophonic set by Eartha Kitt: "I wanna be evil, I wanna be bad" (the awful daring of a moment's surrender to Mickey Spillane is no longer fashionable). Happy, adjusted, prosperous, without an enemy or thought in the world, the American Adam fulfills his manifest destiny in the republic of consumers united under God.

This is not a serious image of America. But ironic or preposterous as it may seem, it contains the partial and perverse truth every cliché contains. The portrait also supports Aldous Huxley when he says, in *Brave New World Revisited,* that the odds for us in America are now more in favor of a benevolent, dehumanized utopia such as Huxley described thirty years ago than of the totalitarian nightmare Orwell predicted by 1984. One thing is certain: the septic surface image of our culture is far removed from anything we have traditionally considered, and still believe, to be crucial to our moral life, let alone to our instinctual needs. In this orgiastic technological fantasy in which our lives are led for us, it is all too easy to assume that basic human needs are altered or radically modified. Basic needs merely go undergound; the distance between reality and illusion multiplies; and men brave heavier psychic and spiritual penalties as they try to reconcile the sharpening polarity of self and world. Obviously, all is not well in God's country. And however skillfully we disguise the fact from ourselves, we are even now improvising new defenses for our flattened egos. Culture itself retreats from the unreality of its surface image, allowing men to pursue their lives on various levels of uniformity and dissent. Where the first imaginary level of culture presents unrelieved homogeneity, the second evidences encouraging human discrepancies. The second level, one might say, harbors values still powerless to be born.

Since David Riesman gave currency in *The Lonely Crowd* to the term "other-directed," we have not ceased to wonder how well or ill our new slogan becomes us — Riesman himself, despite his lucid and critical intelligence, tends to be elusive on this score. Members of an older generation find it difficult to condone the accent on adjustment and security, the lack of ambition and independence, which the younger generation exhibits. They are not pleased that the aggressive Protestant Ethic of work and initiative on which the American Dream was predicated is giving way to the more unctuous Social Ethic defined by William S. Whyte, Jr., in *The Organization Man,* as "that contemporary body of thought which makes morally legitimate the pressures of society against the individual." Whyte's definition is not without bias, but it serves to remind us that while we still pay lip service to the go-getter virtues embodied in the American Dream, we have in effect renounced these for the relaxed fringe benefits of communal existence. What has happened, in effect, is that the insatiable American Faust has gone epicurean. The situation has interesting implications, and it involves us in strange paradoxes. Worshippers of the bitch-goddess of success, whom the American conscience repeatedly censured, become worshippers of leisure and the small household gods. The decision to withdraw from the public realm, dramatized by *The Man in the Gray Flannel Suit,* leaves that realm open to the demonic and the obsessed. The Faustian spirit still finds its incarnation, as it always has, in science, about which the layman knows less and less, and finds its incarnation in the State, over which the layman has diminishing controls.

Obviously, what we are witnessing on this secondary level of culture is a double form of recoil: recoil from the compulsive materialism of the American tradition and also from the enforced homogeneity of contemporary life. The recoil manifests itself, ineffectually, as a search for privatism in the midst of conformity and for contentment in the midst of frenetic bustle—the old search for human innocence in the midst of a rat race. The other manifestation of recoil in contemporary America has gone by various names, disaffiliation, apathy, silence, coolness, and is supposedly common among youth of college age. An international study of youth in various cultures conducted by James Gillespie and Gordon Allport suggests that Americans now put a lower premium on such patent American values as ambition and competitiveness than some "backward" countries do. A symposium in *The Nation,* entitled "The Careful Young Men," leaves us with the impression of a cautious, sane, and skeptical generation who will neither pluck the stars from their sockets nor yet detonate the cobalt bomb under our feet. But despite the fact that our war with them is apt to be simply the old-fashioned war of generations rooted in different climes of childhood—the war of the generations and the battle of the sexes are perhaps the only wars we can still afford—despite the petulant accusations we level at them and the abject confessions we make of our own failures, we are finally bound to recognize that enlightened disengagement is complicit in moral apathy and therefore in guilt. The implications of this idea are recognized with a modest success in Richard Frede's recent novel of college life, *Entry E.* "Indifference. An inability to get emotionally involved in anything," as the Dean puts it, leads young Bogard to commit a crime by default of positive action. Frede's novel is somewhat thin, and it is not entirely finished as a moral work of the imagination but, like *The Man in the Gray Flannel Suit,* it deftly isolates a popular dilemma of the times. Frede finally goes farther than Wilson when he intimates that beyond privatism lurks the shadow of indifference, and so the assumption of guilt for the very ills privatism seeks to escape. Clearly, the opportunities of commitment we ignore under the pretense of sophisticated realism are also the rights we abdicate in the name of disengagement. Recoil, on this level, becomes simply relaxation. . . .

John M. Blum · Exegesis of the Gospel of Work,
Success and Satisfaction
in Recent American Culture

31

*John Morton Blum was born in New York in 1921. He was educated at
Harvard University, where he received his Ph.D. in 1950. He has been a
professor of history at a number of institutions, including M.I.T., Yale,
and Cambridge, where he is currently Pitt Professor of American History
and Institutions. His writings include* Joe Tumulty and the Wilson Era
(1951), Woodrow Wilson and the Problems of Morality *(1956), and* The
National Experience *(1963). In the selection which follows, Blum considers
the effect of affluence and abundance upon the traditional values of work,
thrift, and success, as exemplified in the Horatio Alger stories. The Protestant ethic of work and achievement is receiving a great deal of attention
at this time because of the new leisure and the increasing meaninglessness
of work. For related ideas, see Rostow, Sproat, Cox, McConnell.*

Early in the twentieth century . . . the problem of sufficient production
no longer existed within the United States. The nation's superb natural
endowment had always contained the promise of abundance. The massive
movement of peoples to the country and westward within it had provided
a necessary pool of labor and a market for goods. The advantages of a
free society and a vast, free market had encouraged the accumulation and
investment of capital. · As enterprise flourished, American business had
completed the organization of conditions of plenty. The consolidation of
industry made possible the efficiencies of integration and diversification,
the acceleration of technology, and the professionalization of management.
The twentieth century was still young when Henry Ford and Frederick
Taylor, devoted disciples of the gospel of work, accomplished their prod-
igies of production, when during World War I the United States supplied
not only its own ordinary and emergency needs but also the extraordinary
demands of most of western Europe. Certainly by 1915, probably years
earlier, the nation had in hand the resources and the techniques to furnish
luxuries as well as necessities for a far larger population than it contained.

"Exegesis of the Gospel of Work, Success and Satisfaction in Recent American Culture," *Trends in Modern American Society,* Clarence Morris (ed.). (Philadelphia: University of Pennsylvania Press, 1962), pp. 17–36.

By that time the cult of work, thrift and success had lost some of its following. Labor was persuaded that the earth would spin just as swiftly if the work day were nearer eight than ten hours. The owners of the machines that helped to encourage that persuasion still resisted it, often with the argument that hard work never hurt anybody, but some of them were also in their own ways violating the cult. Vacations had become more common and longer. More sons and daughters of wealth were deliberately unemployed. With success, moreover, frugality frequently yielded to ostentation.

Though conditions had changed, and the culture, too, the idea of work survived the era of its basic relevance. Theodore Roosevelt, by any measure a national hero in 1903, then told one audience that work was "absolutely necessary; . . . no man can be said to live in the true sense of the word, if he does not work." At times self-consciously a Jeremiah, he attacked most viciously the idleness and folly of the rich. In a similar vein, Thorstein Veblen chose the leisure class as the particular target for his censures, reserving his fondest blessings for the "engineers," creatively productive men whose fulfillment came from work.

Roosevelt and Veblen were members of a generation that lived through the stage of mechanization which carried the United States once and for all across the brink of industrial abundance. The engineers, by the time Veblen arranged their apotheosis, had already worked their powerful magic on the price system; and the strenuous life, when Roosevelt lived it, had to spend its furious energies seeking adventures as substitutes for productive labor. Yet those who in their youth had covenanted with the gospel of work clung, not surprisingly, to their obsolescent ethic.

So strong was the national faith that it instructed at least one later generation. Twenty years after Roosevelt's most successful campaign, the chairman of the board of a large corporation employed Algerine language to explain the promotion of a company officer. "I'd put it this way," he said. "Albert Salt was the best office boy we ever had, the best clerk we ever had, the best salesman we ever had, the best purchasing agent we ever had, and he never knew when the whistle blew." Such incantations struck notes to which the middle class still responded. The popular novels and stories of the 1920's, repeating the success theme, held up to Albert Salt and his would-be companions a mirror in which they could admire themselves. The same novels suggested that indolence and elegance alike encouraged licentiousness, a disease to which artists and intellectuals, presumably marginal workers at best, were particularly subject. Greenwich Village and the Left Bank were the havens of exiles, as one of them recalled, who were fleeing the culture of their high schools, the still virulent cult of work. Even Franklin during the 1920's was rather less popular as a symbol than was Albert Salt, for unlike him, Franklin had a cultivated taste for wine and women, rest and speculation. Those diversions from productive work and careful thrift were the undoing of Sam Dodsworth. As middle class readers pitied him, so they esteemed without stint that most virtuous of American engineers, Herbert Hoover, an Albert Salt of an heroic scale.

Esteem was the ultimate article of the total faith. Work and thrift, pluck and luck brought success which earned man status. That progression was central to the creed which faced a shattering challenge during the 1920's when Americans were shown a short-cut to esteem — a short-cut, moreover, that reckoned thrift a vice. With the problem of production solved, industry's next problem was sales, and its next solution, advertising, which had to reach and stimulate the national market. In order to teach Americans to buy more than they needed, though rarely as much as their growing enterprises were producing, advertising had to disseminate an abbreviated image of the good life. It sold esteem.

Of course it also sold many other good things. Advertisements for soap sold cleanliness; for orange juice, health; for mouth wash, romantic love. But most of all advertising sold success. These clothes, that furniture, this correspondence course, those houses, and especially these automobiles were made the appurtenances of success. Ownership brought success itself, ordinarily in company with beautiful woman, and ownership was simplified. One could buy today and pay tomorrow in regular, small installments. No need to wait, no need to save, and the interest rate, while hideous, was hidden.

As the advertising profession has so often claimed, its techniques exposed demands and did not create them. The exposure necessarily associated available and marketable commodities with more remote and sometimes impalpable aspirations. Powerful aspirations, after all, long predated the layouts that translated sex into antiperspirants, appetite into electric grills, and vigor into breakfast cereals. So, too, and emphatically, with status. If success had not already become an American fetish, advertising could scarcely have invented it. The triumph of advertising derived from divorcing esteem from sweat and denial.

Similarly advertising encouraged waste. Alfred Sloan understood the situation exactly. Just as General Wood had realized that the drift of population to the cities would give Sears, Roebuck a larger stake in retail stores than in mail-order catalogues, so Sloan realized that mechanization permitted General Motors to manufacture cars much faster than its customers could use them up. As one executive put it, "The old factors of wear and tear can no longer be depended upon to create a demand." Neither could beauty or performance alone, but advertising could hasten obsolescence, and though some company engineers were unhappy, G.M. made fashion the pavement of its road to glory. As with automobiles, so with many consumer items, the date and packaging determined the measure of esteem.

Yet here again advertising was rather more revealing than revolutionary. Waste, as David Potter has pointed out, had always attended American experience in abundance. The nation had condoned a profligate use of land and minerals and a reckless spoilage of timber, water, even air. Indeed a willingness to waste may have been an indispensable part of the essential spirit of bullish speculation that force-fed innovation and over-built facilities in expectations of unending growth. These expectations in turn supplied the means for their own ultimate satisfaction. But if waste had long existed, and with importance, it had not been counted a quality of success. Rascals were spendthrift, but good men, wise and frugal, until advertising drew a beard on savers and shaved clean the purchasers of fashion.

In attaching esteem to ownership, as it did, advertising substituted a static value for the kinetic attributes of the Alger story. The fact of acquisition replaced the process of achievement. The success image lost its motion. This was a portentous but possibly essential change, for the professionalization of American life, especially of American business, had increasingly separated the Alger myth from reality.

Whatever the absolute values of work and thrift, they had become in themselves weaker and weaker levers for success. As the studies of William Miller demonstrate, in business as well as in law and politics, the elite of each generation since the early nineteenth century had been recruited in increasing proportion from the ranks of the children of the elite, children blessed with the advantages of economic security, higher education, and influential friends. Careers in America remained more open to talent than they did in any other society, education remained more readily available, and self-made men still received invitations to join old and exclusive clubs; but the percentage of those who were born to families of farmers or work-ingmen, and yet rose past the level of farmers or foremen, was diminishing continuously. This deceleration of social mobility, a function of the institutionalizing of American life, threatened to destroy the old success image and, with it, one fetching promise of the past.

By redefining the image, the hucksters distorted it, to be sure, but they also preserved it. The Alger story was among other things only one expression of a larger image of a society of opportunity, plenty, and human dignity. Madison Avenue, contriving a new recipe from old ingredients, simply associated opportunity and dignity with shared abundance. That association made the standard of living as well as the nature of work a gauge of esteem, perhaps especially of self-esteem. With high wages, a laborer, however mean his job, could be fashionable, and therefore, in his view and that of many others, successful.

Under the pressure of advertising, the conspicuous consumption and conspicuous leisure that had so worried Veblen gradually became aspirations of Americans in all walks of life. Those who so aspired, including a sizable fraction of the middle class, suffered special frustrations during the great depression. Beginning with the New Deal, however, there has been a broad redistribution of wealth, public provision of marginal economic security, and a rapid growth of labor unions. Along with these developments, the extraordinary economic recovery that the war effort spurred and the continuing prosperity of the postwar years have placed the expectations advertising nurtured within the range of probable fulfillment for the majority of an affluent society. Perhaps necessarily, ownership and fashion now weigh far more in the scales of the image of success than do industry and thrift.

Along with other twentieth-century developments, advertising affected earlier ideas about work. Artificial obsolescence was a continuing charge against the integrity of a product and consequently against the satisfactions of manufacturing it. There could be small sense of purpose in making something only to have it sold and thrown away. Doubtless mechanization itself, as Ortega observed, cost laborers much of their involvement in their jobs and perhaps all of their identification with their products. Advertising, by acclaiming waste, at the very least exaggerated the resulting loss of dignity in work. Albert Salt never knew when the whistle blew, but he was an office worker. His counterpart at a punching machine, employed in a routinized job fabricating a disposable artifact distinguished primarily by its salability, heard the whistle loud and clear. So also increasingly did office and professional workers whose own functions were made more and more mechanized, more and more specialized, more and more routine. The Algerine view of virtuous industry could not persist where labor lacked mission and work lacked joy.

Perhaps just in time, the changing culture endorsed the ready compensations of more income and more leisure, luxuries that a bountiful technology made possible. Advertising did not destroy the old cult. Rather, it expressed the values of a society in which there were no real problems of production. The culprit, if there was a culprit, goes often by the name of progress. There are still no major problems of production. The national stock of resources and skills can amply satisfy the foreseeable needs of a growing population for consumer and producer goods and for national defense. There are other problems, of course — problems of social goals and social organizations, problems of pace and allocation, problems of priorities for individuals, for neighborhoods, and for the whole nation. Many of these defy easy solution, but none can be solved primarily by more or harder work as Alger's generation thought of work. Like higher real wages, greater leisure has probably come to stay.

Indeed under contemporary conditions the old exhortations are no longer convincing. Johnny wants to buy a Chevrolet, not a sewing machine, and his mother, whose pension is now generous, approves. She is also not so sure that hard work never hurt anybody. That may have been true of picking cranberries and turning the grindstone, physical work out in the fresh air. Johnny will do well to mow the lawn. But hard work at a desk or in a laboratory or with a group of people, work involving primarily intellectual or interpersonal skills and their application, can hurt almost anyone who fails to find the time for rest and recreation. Johnny's modern benefactor is doubtless at his office every year more nearly sixteen hundred than thirty-six hundred hours, and Johnny knows it. Johnny has still the right stuff in him. He goes to school, loves his mother, heeds the example of his elders, wants to become a useful and prosperous lawyer or engineer, but he considers Alger's Johnny (if he must consider him) "out, man, way out." He has no compelling cause for thinking otherwise.

Entirely apart from its relation to success, work, of course, provided satisfaction for a fortunate few. They derived from it a sense of identification and fulfillment, a sense of self and self-expression. Such satisfaction, however, was elusive, even when goods and leisure were less plentiful than they have become. Work without dignity had little to recommend it except as a means for survival. Furthermore, identification and fulfillment escaped men from every stratum of society, including many who rose relentlessly from tier to tier.

Such men, as Ralph Waldo Emerson once suggested, wanted either an instinct for recognizing their personal genius or an opportunity for giving it release. "A man is a beggar who only lives to be useful," Emerson wrote, and beggars there had to be while the economy commanded the bulk of human energy and the culture condemned an unproductive use of time. Beggars there still are in a routinized economy where fewer and fewer jobs afford scope for self-expression. Consequently, for most of the laboring force, less work for more pay comes as an unmitigated gain.

The apparent agencies for that gain, rather than the oppressive jobs, naturally evoke the workers' loyalties. On that account the labor union receives the grateful allegiance accorded to political machines seventy years ago. Today's locals, like yesterday's precinct houses, are clubs, whose members are true to each other and to their leaders, united against their opponents, hostile or uncomprehending toward criticism. Today's union officials, like yesterday's bosses, take care of their following and also of themselves, sometimes with scant regard for means, in rare but troubling cases with small regard for law. When they are attacked, whether justly or unjustly, their constituents also feel embattled, and consequently respond like partisan fans outraged by an unfavorable call at second base, whatever the umpire's vision or wisdom. The rank and file of labor are not dishonest, but they are devoted, and they are apprehensive of change lest change reduce their share in plenty, their share in the appurtenances of success. They value the results their leaders get; they are less concerned with process.

That is precisely the attitude also of a host of men whose overalls have an Ivy cut—teachers not the least. They value the income from their jobs or the prestige of their professions; they are not involved in work, but in success. Their lack of satisfaction is regrettable, for it breeds unhappiness, but it is not immoral, and it is most decidedly not attributable to abundance or to advertising. It has yet to be demonstrated that comfort damages character, and it is manifest that the cult of work often honored labor less for itself than for its utility in achieving status.

There is, however, a pathos in the lives of those who seek success by sending dollars out in chase of goods. John Maynard Keynes was surely right about deficits and depressions, but a society made up of men attempting to spend their way to status is scarcely a beguiling goal for 1984. It is all too clear that the salesmen of fashion have dealt in envy, not in satisfaction. Yet only a romantic nostalgia can dignify a subsistence culture. Conformity did not develop because of abundance. Indeed, abundance threatens it, for as Martin Mayer has said, conformity is the special burden of impoverished communities where people work to exhaustion and have neither the money nor the leisure to express their tastes. In contrast, the fashions of affluence, for all their fraudulence, at least have variety and sometimes even elegance.

What those fashions lack is the capacity to provide lasting satisfaction to either their producers or their consumers. And that capacity is, among other things, an attribute of style—of an excellence of purpose, form and execution that endures while vogues decline. It is a lack of style that permits the expensive vulgarity now imitated on a wider scale than Veblen's nightmares contemplated. Here advertising, ambassador extraordinary to vogue, exemplifies the problem, for advertising rarely ministers to style. That function has no commercial basis, for by enduring, style rejects the claims of artificial obsolescence, and those who, with style, find lasting satisfactions of their own, need not indulge the whims of salesmen of esteem. Those salesmen, their clients, and the media they employ have displayed small sense of obligation to propose a separation of fashion from esteem, or of status from the image of success. Indeed probably the obligation is not theirs, for neither advertising nor its servants should be expected to renounce the profits of a gospel preached so many years. Alger, after all, did not let Johnny drown.

Style, in any event, is not susceptible to mass production. The man who recognizes it, like the man who contrives it, does so alone. It is akin to what Emerson meant by genius, the disciplined expression of a creative instinct. Only exploration of the self and of its world can disclose that kind of genius, that path to style and to satisfaction. But such exploration, which demands spare time, is not universally rewarding. For those who resist it, leisure can be frightening at worst and at best drudgery, from which one escape is pointless or compulsive work. Yet leisure, far better than toil, can help uncover genius and give it vent, can bring a man to design a style of his own.

Leisure, moreover, the most common coin of national plenty, has often been in recent years the medium of inflating opportunity. In spite of all the confusions imbedded in the culture to which Madison Avenue adheres, there is impressive quantitative evidence that Americans have seized their chance to spend their wealth for time and tools to use it. There are, most obviously, the power saws in the cellars and the dry flies on the lakes; there are the gardens, the sailboats, the skis, the bedrolls from Albany unfurled in Montana. For hundreds of the growing thousands who can acquire them, these are more than diversions, more than toys. They are instead the instruments of a process chosen to engage a legitimate pride in skill or a poignant rapport with nature. Those satisfactions are neither mean nor silly nor, in the balance, expensive. They are, in Emerson's sense of the word, the very essence of genius.

Other quantities measure different satisfactions. There are the palettes and pianos, the titles in soft covers, the records, the tents for summer symphony and theater. Never anywhere have intellectuals had larger audiences, the arts more patrons, or patrons wider choice. Leisure and abundance have set off an explosion of high culture throughout America, and hundreds of the growing thousands who paint or play or listen have found both joy and style in the processes of their minds. That represents a genuine success—a success devoid of status and achieved during a leisure curiously akin to work.

The quality as well as the quantity of goods and leisure Americans consume has been rising. Perhaps there has been no relative increase in the number of great artists. Certainly ugliness still abounds. But with abundance there has been a discernible education of taste and a mounting demand for beauty. There is evidence of these changes in architecture, city planning, and commerical design. There is also evidence in the offerings of the movies, television, and the printed media. So, for example, the incidental music of the omnipresent westerns has been acquainting children with subtle harmonies their parents rejected as discord.

Refinement, as always, has proceeded through stages, and the sophisticated, as always, have tended to deplore its pace, but pessimism need not accompany their meritorious impatience. Culture, as it were, has moved in the pattern that George Fitzhugh ascribed to labor. There has been at the bottom an unavoidable mudsill of slaves to the vulgar and the banal. Yet each cultural quake has lifted mudsill and mountain peak alike. As

one American recently reminded British critics who deplore the horrid and
the sham they see across the ocean, the cultural tribulations of Americans
are not their own alone, but the shared experience of mass society in this
century. Compared to other peoples, Americans have done well. Indeed,
under conditions of plenty, conspicuous emulation has proved to be an
effective agency for communicating gradually the advancing standards of
an intellectual elite.

A better agency of communication is education, through which leisure
has scored its largest triumphs. Half a century ago illiteracy thrived on
child labor. Now both are substantially erased. American children have
the spare time to learn to read, though the means they employ may sometimes be inefficient, and the time to go at least through secondary school,
though not all of them elect to. Most of the marginally talented can find
the time and means for college, and more would do so were there available the necessary public funds and private motivations.

For all its shortcomings, the national performance in education has set
significant precedents during the past fifty years. The elongation of schooling has depended upon a distribution of general wealth in the form of
leisure and facilities to individuals of less than average means, including
those in communities of less than average standing. Those individuals who
have labored at their leisure have confirmed the promise inherent in the
fading cult of work. Their productive use of time has opened to them
opportunities for both kinds of success—for the careers that society esteems
and, more important though less honored, for the satisfactions that
trained minds achieve.

The gospel of work always made an allowance for education as a factor
in the success of esteem. "Learning," Franklin said, "whether speculative
or practical, is . . . the natural source of wealth and honor." Alger's Johnny's mother insisted on her son's completing school. Though it was the
success of satisfaction that meant more to Emerson, education, in school
or out, was in his view the dowser for the genius for which he sought
release. "Half engaged in the soil, pawing to get free," he wrote a century
ago, "man needs all the music that can be brought to disengage him . . .
If trade with its money; if Art with its portfolios; if Science with her
telegraphs through the deeps of space and time can set his dull nerves
throbbing . . . make way and sing." The kind of education he endorsed
pointed that way. It exposed, thus inviting adventure, which then with
experience made discipline the haversack of discovery.

Without denying education that non-directive inspiration, Alfred North
Whitehead demanded for it a sharper aim. "Culture should be for action,"
he wrote; and formal liberal education, he believed, taught men to act,
for it whetted their perceptions and instilled a sense of manner. It taught
them style, in Whitehead's phrase, "the last acquirement of the educated

mind, . . . also the most useful." "With style," he wrote, "you attain your end and nothing but your end. With style the effect of your activity is calculable."

Useful for men who take their satisfaction in their work, style in Whitehead's sense is no less useful for those who must seek like rewards in leisure. The very abundance of spare time invites action disciplined by education, action no less fulfilling because it is essentially private. "Style," Whitehead concluded, "is the ultimate morality of the mind." With it, a new freedom of time makes possible a new plenty, not of more goods and services, but of creative experiences that set man's dull nerves throbbing, and lift him beyond Emerson's depths of space and time.

In an age of leisure, the want of a liberal education, the absence of a morality of the mind, too frequently converts spare time to anguish, especially because society persists in unthinking incantation of the values of the cult of work. The resulting perplexities have disturbed particularly those at or near retirement. Lacking a positive, private mission, most elder men and women have suffered from a sense of uselessness that derives from equating both use and good with work. American society has been rich enough to support advances in medicine and public health that have lengthened life expectancies, and rich enough to provide generous, almost universal pensions. American culture, however, has yet to develop a corollary gerontology. The aged especially need to understand the uses of productive leisure, and today's children will be aged very soon.

Even sooner many of them, trained to operate the complex machines, mechanical or organizational, of a sophisticated economy, will reach a ceiling of responsibility and performance beyond which lies the risk overwhelming ennui. Such was the brief experience just fifteen years ago of most men now middle-aged—the men who mastered radar and then sat with Mister Roberts, preferring danger to another night alone. Most of them still dread to sit alone. Their peacetime radar conquered, they fly from the privacy they fear to another flickering scope or to the empty company of togetherness. There they meet their wives, resourceless fugitives from time saved by electricity and prepackaged foods. They waste their leisure as their forebears wasted abundant land and water. So also will their sons and daughters if education emphasizes trades.

An advanced technology perforce demands longer and better schooling of technicians to manipulate its engines and its laws, but a leisure culture demands much more. It needs to educate its citizens to use their time; it needs to teach them a morality of the mind, or, as aimless artisans a century ago corrupted work, and thus themselves, they will corrupt their leisure, and thus their opportunity and their society's.

So many Americans have found themselves in leisure that there is strong reason to believe that in the future, few need be lost. But education has to help much more than it yet has. It cannot wait for cultural quakes; it must precipitate them. It cannot wait for languid and complacent office holders to offer assistance for a function they do not begin to understand. It must instruct them, and their constituents.

"It is shocking," Walter Lippmann wrote not long ago, "and indeed something in the way of a disgrace, that this country, which . . . is so rich, has not had the purpose or the will . . . or a sufficiently responsible sense of the future to provide an adequate school system." It is also shocking, and equally a disgrace, that educators have so often measured their crisis in bricks and mortar and aspirant Ph.D.'s.

There is a greater urgency. There is need to demonstrate that a system productive of wealth can also produce satisfying individuality. There is need to prove that men welcome freedom from want because they value freedom to discover and to express themselves. Any rich society can, if it will, suffuse its members with fashionable goods. Any can inflate its members' traffic in purchasable esteem. Any can give them time to spare. Leisure time is susceptible to massive use in contemplation and creativity, but leisure time has yet to be directed to those ends by a gospel of confidence, a gospel as powerful and pervasive as the outmoded cult of work.

It can be. It can be if educators transfigure the gospel of work by elucidating the best meaning of success. In so doing they will propound a gospel of leisure for men to believe and to follow. Its chapters lie deep and sure within the culture. They have been for decades the core of the content and of the purpose of liberal education, of the arts and sciences and newer social sciences which society can now ill afford to deny to any boy or girl.

The message of these arts and sciences, taught with the conviction and the vigor, the duration and universality that once attended instruction in the cult of work, opens for exploration the boundless life of the mind. That is the cradle to Emerson's genius, by which each individual first finds and then differentiates himself. That is the crucible of Whitehead's style, which directs the actions of each differentiated man. Only such men are finally successful, for only they are satisfied. Only such men, in the last analysis, are free. They will not long remain so if they suffer the contemporary Algers their wasteful affluence. They have instead to teach the new, the now inclusive leisure class to work to find the private satisfactions so abundant in their plentitude of time.

Rachel Carson   A Fable for Tomorrow   **32**

Rachel Louise Carson, scientist and writer, was born in Springdale, Pennsylvania, in 1907 and died in 1966. She changed from an English to a science major and received her Bachelor's degree in 1929 from the Pennsylvania College for Women. She did her postgraduate work at Johns Hopkins University and in 1936 became an aquatic biologist with the United States Bureau of Fisheries, a position she held until the end of her life. Her book The Sea Around Us *(1951) was a best-seller and established her national reputation. In the following selection, Miss Carson, perhaps prophetically, describes the ultimate destruction of America's natural environment. Although her position is attacked as extreme, she did awaken the nation to a new concern for its physical environment. For related ideas, see Nairn, Galbraith.*

There was once a town in the heart of America where all life seemed to live in harmony with its surroundings. The town lay in the midst of a checkerboard of prosperous farms, with fields of grain and hillsides of orchards where, in spring, white clouds of bloom drifted above the green fields. In autumn, oak and maple and birch set up a blaze of color that flamed and flickered across a backdrop of pines. Then foxes barked in the hills and deer silently crossed the fields, half hidden in the mists of the fall mornings.

Along the roads, laurel, viburnum and alder, great ferns and wildflowers delighted the traveler's eye through much of the year. Even in winter the roadsides were places of beauty, where countless birds came to feed on the berries and on the seed heads of the dried weeds rising above the snow. The countryside was, in fact, famous for the abundance and variety of its bird life, and when the flood of migrants was pouring through in spring and fall people traveled from great distances to observe them. Others came to fish the streams, which flowed clear and cold out of the hills and contained shady pools where trout lay. So it had been from the days many years ago when the first settlers raised their houses, sank their wells, and built their barns.

From *Silent Spring* by Rachel Carson. Reprinted by permission of the publisher, Houghton Mifflin Company. Pp. 1-3.

Then a strange blight crept over the area and everything began to change. Some evil spell had settled on the community: mysterious maladies swept the flocks of chickens; the cattle and sheep sickened and died. Everywhere was a shadow of death. The farmers spoke of much illness among their families. In the town the doctors had become more and more puzzled by new kinds of sickness appearing among their patients. There had been several sudden and unexplained deaths, not only among adults but even among children, who would be stricken suddenly while at play and die within a few hours.

There was a strange stillness. The birds, for example—where had they gone? Many people spoke of them, puzzled and disturbed. The feeding stations in the backyards were deserted. The few birds seen anywhere were moribund; they trembled violently and could not fly. It was a spring without voices. On the mornings that had once throbbed with the dawn chorus of robins, catbirds, doves, jays, wrens, and scores of other bird voices there was now no sound; only silence lay over the fields and woods and marsh.

On the farms the hens brooded, but no chicks hatched. The farmers complained that they were unable to raise any pigs—the litters were small and the young survived only a few days. The apple trees were coming into bloom but no bees droned among the blossoms, so there was no pollination and there would be no fruit.

The roadsides, once so attractive, were now lined with browned and withered vegetation as though swept by fire. These, too, were silent, deserted by all living things. Even the streams were now lifeless. Anglers no longer visited them, for all the fish had died.

In the gutters under the eaves and between the shingles of the roofs, a white granular powder still showed a few patches; some weeks before it had fallen like snow upon the roofs and the lawns, the fields and streams.

No witchcraft, no enemy action had silenced the rebirth of new life in this stricken world. The people had done it themselves.

This town does not actually exist, but it might easily have a thousand counterparts in America or elsewhere in the world. I know of no community that has experienced all the misfortunes I describe. Yet every one of these disasters has actually happened somewhere, and many real communities have already suffered a substantial number of them. A grim specter has crept upon us almost unnoticed, and this imagined tragedy may easily become a stark reality we all shall know. . . .

Michael Harrington   The Other America   **33**

*Michael Harrington was born in 1928 in St. Louis, Missouri, and educated
at Holy Cross College and Yate University Law School. He received a
Master's degree in English literature in 1949 from the University of Chicago. He was editor of* The Catholic Worker *from 1951 to 1955 and is
now a writer and contributor to such magazines as* Dissent *and* New America. *He was co-editor of* Labor in a Free Society. *In the following selection, poverty in the United States is described as a "culture," a "way of
life." The book from which this selection is taken can be said to have
sparked "the war on poverty." For related ideas, see Galbraith, Berle,
Brooks, Dedijer.*

The United States in the sixties contains an affluent society within its
borders. Millions and tens of millions enjoy the highest standard of life
the world has ever known. This blessing is mixed. It is built upon a peculiarly distorted economy, one that often proliferates pseudo-needs rather
than satisfying human needs. For some, it has resulted in a sense of spiritual emptiness, of alienation. Yet a man would be a fool to prefer hunger
to satiety, and the material gains at least open up the possibility of a
rich and full existence.

At the same time, the United States contains an under-developed nation,
a culture of poverty. Its inhabitants do not suffer the extreme privation of
the peasants of Asia or the tribesmen of Africa, yet the mechanism of the
misery is similar. They are beyond history, beyond progress, sunk in a
paralyzing, maiming routine.

The new nations, however, have one advantage: poverty is so general
and so extreme that it is the passion of the entire society to obliterate it.
Every resource, every policy, is measured by its effect on the lowest and
most impoverished. There is a gigantic mobilization of the spirit of the
society: aspiration becomes a national purpose that penetrates to every
village and motivates an historic transformation.

But this country seems to be caught in a paradox. Because its poverty
is not so deadly, because so many are enjoying a decent standard of life,

Reprinted with permission of The Macmillan Company from *The Other America* by
Michael Harrington. © Michael Harrington, 1962. Pp. 169–186.

there are indifference and blindness to the plight of the poor. There are even those who deny that the culture of poverty exists. It is as if Disraeli's famous remark about the two nations of the rich and the poor had come true in a fantastic fashion. At precisely that moment in history where for the first time a people have the material ability to end poverty, they lack the will to do so. They cannot see; they cannot act. The consciences of the well-off are the victims of affluence; the lives of the poor are the victims of a physical and spiritual misery.

The problem, then, is to a great extent one of vision. The nation of the well-off must be able to see through the wall of affluence and recognize the alien citizens on the other side. And there must be vision in the sense of purpose, of aspiration: if the word does not grate upon the ears of a gentile America, there must be a passion to end poverty, for nothing less than that will do. . . .

Perhaps the most important analytic point to have emerged in this description of the other America is the fact that poverty in America forms a culture, a way of life and feeling, that it makes a whole. It is crucial to generalize this idea, for it profoundly affects how one moves to destroy poverty.

The most obvious aspect of this interrelatedness is in the way in which the various subcultures of the other America feed into one another. This is clearest with the aged. There the poverty of the declining years is, for some millions of human beings, a function of the poverty of the earlier years. If there were adequate medical care for everyone in the United States, there would be less misery for old people. It is as simple as that. Or there is the relation between the poor farmers and the unskilled workers. When a man is driven off the land because of the impoverishment worked by technological progress, he leaves one part of the culture of poverty and joins another. If something were done about the low-income farmer, that would immediately tell in the statistics of urban unemployment and the economic underworld. The same is true of the Negroes. Any gain for America's minorities will immediately be translated into an advance for all the unskilled workers. One cannot raise the bottom of a society without benefiting everyone above.

Indeed, there is a curious advantage in the wholeness of poverty. Since the other America forms a distinct system within the United States, effective action at any one decisive point will have a "muliplier" effect; it will ramify through the entire culture of misery and ultimately through the entire society.

Then, poverty is a culture in the sense that the mechanism of impoverishment is fundamentally the same in every part of the system. The vicious circle is a basic pattern. It takes different forms for the unskilled workers, for the aged, for the Negroes, for the agricultural worker, but in each case the principle is the same. There are people in the affluent society who are poor because they are poor; and who stay poor because they are poor.

To realize this is to see that there are some tens of millions of Americans who are beyond the welfare state. Some of them are simply not covered by social legislation: they are omitted from Social Security and from minimum wage. Others are covered, but since they are so poor they do not know how to take advantage of the opportunities, or else their coverage is so inadequate as not to make a difference.

The welfare state was designed during that great burst of social creativity that took place in the 1930's. As previously noted its structure corresponds to the needs of those who played the most important role in building it: the middle third, the organized workers, the forces of urban liberalism, and so on. At the worst, there is "socialism for the rich and free enterprise for the poor," as when the huge corporation farms are the main beneficiaries of the farm program while the poor farmers get practically nothing; or when public funds are directed to aid in the construction of luxury housing while the slums are left to themselves (or become more dense as space is created for the well-off).

So there is the fundamental paradox of the welfare state: that it is not built for the desperate, but for those who are already capable of helping themselves. As long as the illusion persists that the poor are merrily free-loading on the public dole, so long will the other America continue unthreatened. The truth, it must be understood, is the exact opposite. The poor get less out of the welfare state than any group in America.

This is, of course, related to the most distinguishing mark of the other America: its common sense of hopelessness. For even when there are programs designed to help the other Americans, the poor are held back by their own pessimism.

On one level this fact has been described in this book as a matter of "aspiration." Like the Asian peasant, the impoverished American tends to see life as a fate, an endless cycle from which there is no deliverance. Lacking hope (and he is realistic to feel this way in many cases), that famous solution to all problems — let us educate the poor — becomes less and less meaningful. A person has to feel that education will do something for him if he is to gain from it. Placing a magnificent school with a fine faculty in the middle of a slum is, I suppose, better than having a run-down building staffed by incompetents. But it will not really make a difference so long as the environment of the tenement, the family, and the street counsels the children to leave as soon as they can and to disregard schooling.

On another level, the emotions of the other America are even more profoundly disturbed. Here it is not lack of aspiration and of hope; it is a matter of personal chaos. The drunkenness, the unstable marriages, the violence of the other America are not simply facts about individuals. They are the description of an entire group in the society who react this way because of the conditions under which they live.

In short, being poor is not one aspect of a person's life in this country, it is his life. Taken as a whole, poverty is a culture. Taken on the family level, it has the same quality. These are people who lack education and skill, who have bad health, poor housing, low levels of aspiration and high levels of mental distress. They are, in the language of sociology, "multiproblem" families. Each disability is the more intense because it exists within a web of disabilities. And if one problem is solved, and the others are left constant, there is little gain.

One might translate these facts into the moralistic language so dear to those who would condemn the poor for their faults. The other Americans are those who live at a level of life beneath moral choice, who are so submerged in their poverty that one cannot begin to talk about free choice. The point is not to make them wards of the state. Rather, society must help them before they can help themselves.

**Afraid to be all the things
she can be**

Morton Hunt   **Her Infinite Variety**   **34**

Morton Magill Hunt was born in Philadelphia, Pennsylvania, in 1920. He received his Bachelor's degree from Temple University in 1941 and did graduate study at the University of Pennsylvania. He has been a writer and editor of magazines for a number of years, beginning with Look *(1946– 1947), and has done profiles for* The New Yorker. *Among his writings are* The Natural History of Love *(1959),* Mental Hospital *(1962), and* The Talking Cure *(1964). He is a frequent contributor to many periodicals. The following selection deals with the "paradox" of the American woman: she has almost everything that women through all history have wanted,*

Pp. 4–8, "Introduction" to *Her Infinite Variety*, by Morton Hunt. Copyright © 1962 by Morton M. Hunt. Reprinted by permission of Harper & Row, Publishers, Inc.

and yet she is not content with her lot. For related ideas, see Friedan;
Schlesinger, Jr.; Whyte; Wheelis; Cox; Schlesinger, Sr.; Von Borch.

Several years ago, while writing a history of love, I was struck by the
curious paradox of modern American woman: she has almost everything
that thoughtful and intelligent women have wanted and lacked for many
centuries, yet there are many indications that she is not really content
with herself or her place in contemporary life. The emancipated middle-
class American woman—free to train her mind and use it, free to move
about unchaperoned in her society, free to marry for personal joy, free
even to accept or refuse her mate's passion at night—is more nearly a
complete human being than any Western woman, save a handful of queens,
viragos, and salonières, since the days of the Roman Empire. Yet far
from being completed and fulfilled by all this, it appears that she is often
unsure of what to do with her freedoms, distracted and intimidated by
her many opportunities, fearful that she may lose her femininity if she
experiments too far with them, and fretful, bored, and discontented when
she limits herself to safe, traditional ways. In brief, she is afraid to be
all the things she can be, and dissatisfied to be only some of them.

All this is true, to be sure, only of some modern women, not all.
Opinions as to the frequency of discontent differ, but Margaret Mead
conservatively estimates that over one-quarter of the women in the United
States are "definitely disturbed" about their lot as women, the proportion being greater among those very middle-class pace setters who are the
most favored and emancipated. If one were to include lesser levels of
disturbance of which women are not clearly or consciously aware, the
figures would be far higher.

But what troubles them in this earthly female's paradise? Many things
—most of which cluster about the several bewildering different roles a
woman can now play in life, and the conflicts among them. She can be
primarily a seductress, but that grates against her functions as a loving
mother or an efficient businesswoman; she can be a community worker
or a careerist, but either of these takes her away from her home and her
children; any and all of these roles, furthermore, seem to get in the way
of her being her husband's lover, let alone his companion—both of which
functions are, in turn, somewhat inconsistent with being his housekeeper.
Is she a person, her own person, at all, or merely an ill-assorted aggregate of satisfactions of other people's needs? And which kind of person,
whether her own or theirs, should she choose to be, and why?

In a medieval French barony, a frontier American settlement, or an
Inca village, there were specified sets of activities and duties which a girl
anticipated and grew into; whatever the hardships or shortcomings in
these several patterns, each of them was at least unambiguous. Woman's
chief problem was how to play her part well; modern woman has the

prior and additional problem of which part or parts to choose, and how to combine them without disaster or else give up some of them without bitterness. "Somehow we must *find* ourselves," bravely proclaims a young woman writing to me from Wharton, Texas, "we must learn our personal abilities and limitations, proceed carefully through the maze of things to be done, picking the few that genuinely fulfill us"—but she does not know what they are. Anne Lindbergh's *Gift from the Sea* was one of the great best-sellers of the 1950's because it poetically pleaded that woman's life was too complicated, and needed pruning and the rediscovery of its essentials; but she, too, gave no answers.

In more formal sociological language, Dr. Florence R. Kluckhohn of Harvard University writes, "Women give every evidence of being extremely ambivalent and confused about their roles as women, their expectations for themselves, and their responsibilities to others." *What to be* is a problem that men do not face and women in the past never knew; it troubles modern women to a degree their husbands rarely realize, even after living with them for years. An old friend of mine learned from me of my intention to write a book on this subject, and with kindly concern tried to dissuade me. "No doubt some women can't cope with the conflicting demands made upon them," he wrote, " and can't solve the problem of evolving a means of fulfilling themselves, but I feel they are a small minority and require individual professional care." Then, apparently, he showed the letter to his wife, for he added in a chastened marginal note, "Seems I should have asked my spouse. She says the 'small minority' is 100 percent, and furthermore *she* hasn't found a solution and doesn't know anyone who has."

Woman's confusion is no trivial matter. Some pessimists have held that her present freedoms and conflicts are responsible for a host of social ailments: alcoholism and neurosis in herself, waning potency in her husband, delinquency in her children, and such other assorted ills as ulcers, divorce, teen-age immorality, and suburban conformity. More fairly, the eminent sociologist Talcott Parsons has written that "the feminine role is a conspicuous focus of the strains inherent in our social structure." The health of society, of the family, and of woman all interact upon each other; woman is not wholly or largely to blame for present social problems, but she is an integral part of whatever has produced them.

The very forces that make women fearful of using their intellectual abilities, for instance, have also prevented them from serving their society well and relieving some of its problems. The shortage of physicians is an example: three-quarters of Russian doctors are women, as against a little over 6 percent of American doctors. Russian women have fewer of the amenities of life, but they are serving their society better, perhaps as a result. Ironically, though, American woman's decision to limit herself to domesticity hurts her more than anyone else, by virtually ending her purposeful life at about forty-five, when she still has thirty years to spend — decades which are a slow shriveling rather than a harvest time. The paradox of American woman that I stated a moment ago can be restated thus: out of her very satisfactions she makes her dissatisfactions, and out of her disregard of society's needs there sooner or later comes her failure to meet her own needs.

The strains and maladaptations of modern woman's life are all implicit in one question she never quite answers. Each child, as he grows up, asks himself, "Who, or what, am I?," but modern woman never really finds out. If she is not sure who she is, plenty of people have been ready to tell her who she ought to be. She is urged by some to preserve her figure, by others to improve her mind, and by still others to be fertile and earthy. She is told to quit envying men and competing with them, and to get back into the kitchen and nursery, but Hollywood actresses, lady novelists, women delegates to the United Nations, and female fashion buyers are held up to her as examples of successful women. She can choose her medicine from a wide-ranging pharmacopeia: Simone de Beauvoir's polemic *The Second Sex* assures her that women will never know genuine happiness until the system of marriage is done away with and every woman is fully independent of the male; psychoanalyst Marynia Farnham proclaims in *Modern Woman: The Lost Sex* that she will only find real peace and happiness by returning to sewing, baking, fertility, and dependency, forgoing all the delusive pleasures of emancipation; and hundreds of others offer solutions over the whole intervening range.

All of the more extreme answers offered are, to tell the truth, simple rather than difficult; they narrow down, define, crystallize, specialize. And because they are simple and clearcut, they have a great surface appeal. But my thesis is that in the long run they tend to be maladaptive and disappointing. The hundreds of research studies I read, the thousand-odd statements I collected from American women, the file cabinet I filled with notes and documents showing the effects on their lives, and the lives of those around them, of divers modes of adjustment, have led me to think that there is a better answer, though surely not a simple one. Quite briefly, it is this: under the conditions of modern life, the only choice that will lastingly satisfy a growing number of middle-class women is the conscious effort to play many roles and perform many functions harmoniously, the mature decision in favor of the complicated life and of full development.

Herbert Von Borch   The Unfinished Society

35

Herbert Von Borch was born in China in 1909 where his father was then serving as a German diplomat. He studied at the Universities of both Berlin and Frankfort and received his Ph.D. in 1933 from the University of Heidelberg. He presently lives in Washington, D.C., and is the American correspondent for the German paper Die Welt. *Among his other books are* Authority and Resistance *(1954) and* Kennedy, the New Style in World Politics *(1961), both published in Germany. In the selection which follows, the role of women, especially the matriarchal aspects, are described. For related ideas, see Hunt; Friedan; Schlesinger, Jr.; Cox.*

Women's emancipation took place later in the United States than in the Old World. But, like the American industrial revolution, the erotic revolution in America outpaced everything of the same order in Europe. Even at the point of departure, women were at an advantage in America. They had a scarcity value which they never enjoyed in Europe. This explains the indissoluble association of a romantic concept of love with the instituition of marriage which has become the obvious, yet exceedingly fragile, frame into which love in America must ever be forced. . . .

Because of the original scarcity value of women, "romantic love" became the powerful and undisputed norm for young Americans of both sexes, and "romantic love" culminating in marriage became the natural pattern of sex relations. "True love," all evidence to the contrary notwithstanding, has been regarded ever since, both as spontaneously generated (instead of being prepared by family arrangement) and permanent. Young girls never had to regard themselves as adjuncts to a dowry, since that social practice did not exist; this was no bad starting point for the later emancipation of women, however extensive the authority of the *paterfamilias* in the early Puritan regime of the New England settlers.

The influence of Puritanism on American values cannot, or course, be overestimated, even if is more honored in the breach than in the observance. Nevertheless, it would be wrong to ascribe to the New England

Puritans of the seventeenth and eighteenth centuries a fanatical hostility to everything sexual. Unlike Catholicism, Puritanism never upheld the ideal of virginity or of priestly continence. For Puritans, marriage was a civil contract, which is why they countenanced divorce. Their ministers married and eagerly obeyed the Biblical prescription to be fruitful and multiply, evidently unburdened by any sense of sin. Marriages in the Puritan colonies took place so unbelievably early — the girls often at fourteen or fifteen, the men under twenty — that there could be no problem at all of premarital relations. Strict Puritans refused sexual pleasure on Sundays; since this was regarded as a restriction, one may draw conclusions as to the rest of the week. The determining factor was not asceticism but morality: only procreation justifies sexuality. Historians of civilization believe that only when Puritanism was allied with late nineteenth-century Victorianism was that prudish fustiness developed which is now meant by "puritanical."

On the other hand, the role of Puritanism is unmistakable in the way love is monopolized by marriage. Romantic love — regarded as the most genuine type of love — should not be hidden from society; but it may be acknowledged before the world only in the form of marriage. Hence, the frequency of remarriage among divorced persons. The trinity of romantic love, marriage monopoly and Puritan work ethos, incidentally, is not best suited to develop the faculty of charming frivolity. That is why European descriptions of America have always denied its people any talent for love, and legends have developed on the subject — for instance, the legend of the native frigidity of the American woman.

The matriarchal features of contemporary American society make one forget that here, too, woman had to fight for her rights for a whole century. Her present position of equality can be regarded as one of the most successful revolutions in world history — perhaps even too successful, as many women may secretly think. For the high price which American woman has had to pay for her ascent is that she may no longer be weak. She has shed this attribute of Eve, and, logically, the upper-class concept of a lady has finally had to be sacrificed too. She could not well retain the weapon of weakness and at the same time accumulate so much political, economic and erotic power as she has accumulated in the space of a few generations.

If it is sometimes said that the American woman is not only the wealthiest, physically healthiest, best dressed and most independent woman in the world, but also the most unhappy, this certainly has some connection with the surrender of the weapon of weakness. This surrender is paid for in the coin of neuroses. But this too may be only a transition to a new equilibrium which the victorious woman is striving to achieve. . . .

Sociologists distinguish four separate revolutions leading to the present position of women. The same phases exist in Europe too, but in all of them the American woman has by far overshot the European mark.

The first was the revolution resulting in votes for women—but not until 1920—and the right to equal education and access to leadership in politics and industry. Today women hold high government office, they are ambassadors, public prosecutors, bankers, general managers and, at least, vice-presidents of great firms. Woman's ascent in the modern professional and labor world is truly staggering. Generally speaking, the distinction between man and woman as far as economic efficiency is concerned has almost disappeared. It is only logical that in a recent discussion about the prospects of a woman becoming President of the United States, the only impediment suggested was that she could not very well fulfill the presidential role of commander in chief of the armed forces. . . .

The second revolution was the sexual revolution in the narrower sense, the revolt against the dual "standard" in morals, which permitted to man what it forbade to woman. (But since in any case extra-marital relations were not of such frequent occurrence, the conquest in this domain was not so great.) The specific victory consists in the re-evaluation of the sexual claims of woman within the marriage, to which we have already referred.

Thirdly, there took place a revolution in manners; women were permitted to smoke in public, even in the street, to drink, to dress just as casually as the men, to bare their bodies in a most unpuritanical way, to drive cars and pilot planes.

The fourth revolution took place in the home (particularly in the kitchen); it consisted in the release of woman from the creaturely, never-ending burdens of the household through the mechanization of household appliances and the availability of built-in labor services in the form of frozen and canned foods. This, in turn, hastened the economic revolution. . . .

Despite all these newly won powers, or perhaps precisely because of them, the indications are that the forty-five million married women in the United States are not really able to enjoy their ascendancy. Neuroses, as reported by doctors, the frightening number of abortions (even among married women, as the third Kinsey report showed), divorces, increasing alcoholism (especially in suburbia, those idyllic settlements surrounding the cities, where other stimulants are absent), have raised the question of why, at the height of her triumph, the American woman is not happier. What appears as the "decline of the American male" seems to be for her, too, no untrammeled pleasure.

The anti-feminists have their answer ready: the man-like woman, this new Amazon of a technological civilization, this he-woman (the counterpart of the she-man) has overreached herself. She has become delirious in her power. The reality must be both less simple and less alarming. If only because American civilization is based emphatically on monogamy, the woman, however independent she may be, will in the first place seek the married status, that is, the man. She will also, supported by a sophisticated — and democratized — cosmetics and fashion industry, take trouble to look attractive, to be, if possible, slim, long-legged, provocative and paying tribute to the absurd bosom-fetishism of the film world. But that is not all.

This society, in which woman has succeeded in conquering such an outstanding position, nevertheless remains basically masculine, suffused with power impulses, with power conflicts of an almost violent nature. It is not easy for a woman who wishes to retain her independence to affirm herself in this society. What is hardest is to fulfill the incredible variety of functions incumbent upon her, without failing in the unavoidable, biological duty which the feminist movement underestimated, that of being simply a woman.

Modern American society offers the most extreme contrast to the old Chinese cultural pattern. Whereas in the latter, a woman was respected and influential the older she grew, in America the young glamour girl who kindles the romantic ardor which leads irresistibly to marriage is the self-prescribed ideal, after which there can be nothing but gradual decline. Not to depart too sharply from this narrow beauty cliché even as the years relentlessly take their toll, and at the same time to play the many parts which emancipation have brought her — that is an existence which truly deserves the description which a social analyst has used as a chapter heading, "the ordeal of the American woman." According to this scholar, the modern American woman "leads simultaneously a multiplicity of lives, playing at once the role of sexual partner, mother, home manager, hostess, nurse, shopper, figure of glamour, supervisor of the children's schooling and play and trips, culture audience and culture carrier, club-woman, and often worker and careerist." Adlai Stevenson, for his part, presents the position of the educated woman as stripped of all romanticism since the dying out of the servant class. In former times, he says, such women would talk art and philosophy late into the night; now they are so tired that their eyes close as soon as the dishes are put away. They used to write poetry; now they write laundry lists.

Adolf Berle, Jr.   The American Economic Republic

36

Adolf A. Berle, Jr. was born in Boston in 1895 and educated at Harvard. He has taught at Columbia University since 1928 as Professor of Law and has lectured throughout the United States. He has received many honorary degrees. In addition, he has had a distinguished career in public service, his posts including those of Assistant Secretary of State from 1938 to 1944, and Ambassador to Brazil from 1945 to 1946. He served as consultant on President Kennedy's task force on Latin American policy. He is a prolific writer and has published widely. Among his extensive writings are The Modern Corporation and Private Property *(with G. C. Means) (1937),* The 20th Century Capitalist Revolution *(1954),* Power without Property *(1959), and* Latin America: Diplomacy and Reality *(1962). Here, the author discusses the moral assumptions underlying American economic institutions. For related ideas, see Galbraith, Parkes, Harrington, Dedijer, Communist Party, U.S.A.*

With nations as with individuals, as they think, so are they. The vital current that has brought the American social-economic system to unlimited heights of production and, on the material side, to unequaled comfort for all but a small fragment of its large population was not materialist, but ethical. It does not matter that the body of ethics is differently stated — or left unstated — by the American community. The body exists, and has terrific force.

The conception that the strong should help the weak, that the prosperous should carry a greater portion of the load than the poor, is not an economic conception. It is an attempt to give form to the old socialist maxim "From each according to his capability, to each according to his need." Yet it was that conception that caused the United States to adopt the graduated income tax and to make it the heart of the American tax system. Economic reasoning was only a secondary consideration when the policy was adopted of giving tax exemption to philanthropic institutions. The widespread practice of private philanthropy, developed when the Protestant ethic was more readily understood, carried itself forward into the

tax laws of the United States and of most of the American states. As a
result, your and my gifts to religious or philanthropic institutions are de-
ducted from the income on which we pay taxes. Even the last stronghold
of pure economic motivation—the corporation which operates an enterprise for profit and, in theory, for profit only—in most states now has
the statutory power to give to philanthropy a small portion (conventionally,
5%) of its income for philanthropic purposes, and to deduct that income
when it pays taxes to the federal government. The law likewise encourages
in a variety of ways the setting up of the pension trusts which, as we
have seen, are social devices to insulate men from certain kinds of misfortune, notably sickness and poverty-stricken old age. And all of these
were preceded by federal, state, and local taxation to support the first
great system of free public education, first at the primary, later at the
secondary, level, that the world had ever seen.

No one contends that the ideals implicit in this current of American
thought have been realized; probably they never will be realized. If indeed
they approach realization, new vistas of possibility will have been opened.
The pursuit of enduring values can be as long as the span of history.
The pursuit of eternal values is, by its terms, unending. With each achievement, however tiny, farther horizons appear. Necessity of action in matters
which heretofore went unnoticed becomes obvious, just as the Protestant
ethic of the nineteenth century pushed toward wider and deeper education
even as it disregarded the economic misery of great sectors of the population.

The point here made is this: the preoccupation of American democracy
with selfless goals—that is, goals not related to direct individual advantage
on this earth—accounts for the surprising and quite measurable social-
economic achievements of the United States. Specifically, it accounts for
the fact that this country has the highest gross national product, both aggregate and per capita, of any country (in 1962 this product was running
at the rate of 550 billions' worth of goods and services measured in 1960
dollars, actually produced and paid for). Preoccupation with something
like a fair, or, at any rate, a very wide, distribution of the benefits was
determinative: the job could not have been done without it. A wide distribution of income is essential to a mass market. The American corporate
system could not have emerged without this distribution. But wide distribution was not undertaken in order to achieve mass markets so that corporations could be larger. It was the result of the vital, essentially modern,
insistence, first, that human beings should not go hungry and unhoused,
and, second, as that goal approached realization, that they should have
opportunity for comfort and diversion as well. This last, probably, proceeded from an undefined general feeling that any system limiting comfort,
diversion, and luxury to a single group was essentially unfair, if not immoral. As in every system, someone looked at his more prosperous or

more powerful neighbor and said, substantially, "Why he, and not me?" The prosperous, in fact, asked the same questions of themselves—or at least enough of them did so that there was no invincible resistance.

In part, in the American economic system this was due to a piece of historical luck. Elsewhere in the world—for example, Europe—answers to the question "Why he, and not me?" were ready-made by historical tradition. This king was legitimate because he was descended from Louis Capet or John of Gaunt and he held power by that fact and by the grace of God. The noblemen entrusted with estates and wealth were a class set apart. Too close scrutiny of the historical origins of their entry into that class was not encouraged; at all events, the hierarchic system of rank and fortune, of family position and inherited stance, was accepted. This had its uses in maintaining a degree of order. If the mutual obligations between the classes were well and truly observed, probably it made life tolerable for great masses of people who otherwise would have been in difficulties. But it did not conduce to wide distribution either of power or of wealth. And it certainly did not encourage, let alone assist, any man in the lower class to hope that by merit or ability he or his children could reach an upper and more favored class.

The American economic system never really encountered this, though there are remnants of the old tradition in racial antagonisms and in some of the Southern states. Even in its royalist colonial period, the growing population of America paid little attention to the strata of European civilization. For one thing, when you are struggling with wilderness and weather, you are not preoccupied with social theory. You are thinking of getting a field plowed and a harvest reaped, of making a road passable, of having enough laid up for the winter to see you through. Adam delved and Eve span and so did a gentleman if he expected to survive. Not all, but most of the country grew in the face of that experience. It is of interest to see the same process going on in the Soviet Union today. Communist hierarchy, rank, and ideology are strongest in Moscow and European Russia. But, travelers tell us, in the huge and not wholly clement Siberian portions of the Soviet Union—destined in their time to be immensely more important than European Russia—dogma and hierarchy alike are taken far less seriously.

Whatever the cause, the American colonies indulged the British class system only in mild degree. When the Jeffersonian revolution took place in 1800, the remnants of it were discarded. In economic terms, the result was to set up a powerful political force which caused the American political-economic system to devote a continuous and growing part of its production toward nonindividualist "selfless" ends. This presently appeared as a powerful force in its economic development, and is today a crucial factor both in maintaining balance (avoiding economic crises) and in increasing the distribution and in calling into existence the production which is at present the salient phenomenon of the American system.

Let us not claim that the transcendental margin is peculiar to the American social-economic system. Actually, it can be identified in greater or less degree in most effective economic systems of modern times — and perhaps of ancient times as well. But in the United States the transcendental margin was continuously greater, and expanded more consistently, than in most other contemporary systems. It generated greater productivity, and greater intellectual resources for still further expansion. In the post-World War II period, it has become a decisive influence.

The conclusions may be summarized.

The American economic system and indeed all economic systems are not ends in themselves. Certainly they cease to be so when they have provided for the elementary necessities of the population which created them. They reflect the value system of the community in which they operate.

That value system, and the intensity with which it is pursued, is a coefficient of the productivity of the system. Specifically, it can determine whether the economic system produces, per capita, more or less.

Likewise, the value system will determine the allocation of its product — to education or cathedrals as against automobiles or office buildings, and as between consumption and consumer goods and capital and instruments of production.

Capital is the capacity to mobilize labor, technique, and things to create or add to existing instruments of production. Such capacity may be derived from power or from money, or possibly both. To some extent power may be used in place of money, but at the sacrifice of human life and liberty.

To grow and become more productive, an economic system must devote a substantial portion of its resource and production to achieve ends transcending the calculation of individual material advantage. This is the "transcendental margin."

The ends and the extent of the margin of resources allocated to them are determined by the value system of the community. In the United States, the operative value system is determined by public consensus more or less freely arrived at by the entire community, and expressed through the political mechanism of the democratic state, in association with nonstatist institutions.

Betty Friedan   The Feminine Mystique   **37**

Betty Friedan is a native of Peoria, Illinois, and a graduate of Smith College. She has also done graduate work in psychology. Miss Friedan, whose book became a best-seller, defines "the feminine mystique" as the notion that a woman can only fulfill herself as a wife and mother. In the following selection, the signs of the American woman's discontent are described: divorce, neurosis, and unhappiness. For related ideas, see Schlesinger, Jr.; Hunt; Von Borch; Wheelis.

. . . The year American women's discontent boiled over, it was also reported *(Look)* that the more than 21,000,000 American women who are single, widowed, or divorced do not cease even after fifty their frenzied, desperate search for a man. And the search begins early — for seventy per cent of all American women now marry before they are twenty-four. A pretty twenty-five-year-old secretary took thirty-five different jobs in six months in the futile hope of finding a husband. Women were moving from one political club to another, taking evening courses in accounting or sailing, learning to play golf or ski, joining a number of churches in succession, going to bars alone, in their ceaseless search for a man.

Of the growing thousands of women currently getting private psychiatric help in the United States, the married ones were reported dissatisfied with their marriages, the unmarried ones suffering from anxiety and, finally, depression. Strangely, a number of psychiatrists stated that, in their experience, unmarried women patients were happier than married ones. So the door of all those pretty suburban houses opened a crack to permit a glimpse of uncounted thousands of American housewives who suffered alone from a problem that suddenly everyone was talking about, and beginning to take for granted, as one of those unreal problems in American life that can never be solved — like the hydrogen bomb. By 1962 the plight of the trapped American housewife had become a national parlor game. Whole issues of magazines, newspaper columns, books learned and frivolous, educational conferences and television panels were devoted to the problem.

Even so, most men, and some women, still did not know that this problem was real. But those who had faced it honestly knew that all the superficial remedies, the sympathetic advice, the scolding words and the cheering words were somehow drowning the problem in unreality. A bitter laugh was beginning to be heard from American women. They were admired, envied, pitied, theorized over until they were sick of it, offered drastic solutions or silly choices that no one could take seriously. They got all kinds of advice from the growing armies of marriage and child-guidance counselors, psychotherapists, and armchair psychologists, on how to adjust to their role as housewives. No other road to fulfillment was offered to American women in the middle of the twentieth century. Most adjusted to their role and suffered or ignored the problem that has no name. It can be less painful, for a woman, not to hear the strange, dissatisfied voice stirring within her.

It is no longer possible to ignore that voice, to dismiss the desperation of so many American women. This is not what being a woman means, no matter what the experts say. For human suffering there is a reason; perhaps the reason has not been found because the right questions have not been asked, or pressed far enough. I do not accept the answer that there is no problem because American women have luxuries that women in other times and lands never dreamed of; part of the strange newness of the problem is that it cannot be understood in terms of the age-old material problems of man: poverty, sickness, hunger, cold. The women who suffer this problem have a hunger that food cannot fill. It persists in women whose husbands are struggling interns and law clerks, or prosperous doctors and lawyers; in wives of workers and executives who make $5,000 a year or $50,000. It is not caused by lack of material advantages; it may not even be felt by women preoccupied with desperate problems of hunger, poverty or illness. And women who think it will be solved by more money, a bigger house, a second car, moving to a better suburb, often discover it gets worse. . . .

Nathan Glazer
and Daniel P. Moynihan

Beyond the Melting Pot

38

Nathan Glazer was born in New York City in 1923. He received his Bachelor's degree from the City College of New York in 1944 and his Master's from the University of Pennsylvania in the same year. In 1962 he received his Ph.D. from Columbia University and is presently a member of the Department of Sociology, University of California, Berkeley. He started his career as an editor of Commentary *magazine and has also served as consulting editor for Random House, New York. Other writings of his are* The Lonely Crowd, *with David Riesman (1950), and* The Social Basis of American Communism *(1961).*

Daniel P. Moynihan, author of the Moynihan Report on the Negro Family, *was born in Tulsa, Oklahoma, in 1927. He graduated from Tufts College and received his Ph.D. from Fletcher School of Law and Diplomacy. He was an assistant secretary during Averill Harriman's governorship of New York and went on to the United States Department of Labor as Assistant Secretary during the Kennedy administration. He is currently on the faculty of M.I.T., studying urban problems.*

In the selection that follows, Glazer and Moynihan discuss the significance of New York City to America as a background for a discussion of the homogeneity of ethnic groups in America. Their book refutes a long-standing idea that America homogenizes national and religious minorities. For related ideas, see Malcolm X, Cox, Fuchs, Herberg, Baltzell.

. . . The only New York image that has permanently impressed itself on the national mind is that of Wall Street—a street on which nobody lives. Paris may be France, London may be England, but New York, we continue to reassure ourselves, is *not* America.

But, of course, it *is* America: not all of America, or even most, but surely the most important single part. As time passes, the nation comes more under the influence of the city—consider the effect of television in the past fifteen years. As time passes, the nation comes more to resemble the city: urban, heterogeneous, materialist, tough; also, perhaps, ungovern-

Reprinted from *Beyond the Melting Pot* by Nathan Glazer and Daniel P. Moynihan by permission of The M.I.T. Press, Cambridge, Massachusetts. Copyright 1963 by The Massachusetts Institute of Technology and the President and Fellows of Harvard College. Pp. 2-17, 310-315.

able, except that somehow it is governed, and not so badly, and with a considerable measure of democracy. . . .

New York's culture is what it is presumably because it is the cultural capital of the richest and most important nation in the world. If America's culture is important, New York's culture must be important, and this would be true even if New York were all Anglo-Saxon and Protestant. And yet, the fact that the city is one-quarter Jewish, and one-sixth Italian, and one-seventh Negro — this also plays some part in the cultural history of New York. Ethnic identity is an element in all equations. . . .

The census of 1960 showed that 19 per cent of the population of the city were still foreign-born whites, 28 per cent were children of foreign-born whites, another 14 per cent were Negro, 8 per cent were of Puerto Rican birth or parentage. Unquestionably, a great majority of the rest (31 per cent) were the grandchildren and great-grandchildren of immigrants, and still thought of themselves, on some occasions and for some purposes, as German, Irish, Italian, Jewish, or whatnot, as well as of course Americans.

Of the foreign-stock population (immigrants and their children), 859,000 were born in Italy or were the children of Italian immigrants; 564,000 were from the U.S.S.R. (these are mostly Jews); 389,000 from Poland (these too are mostly Jews); 324,000 from Germany; 312,000 from Ireland; 220,000 from Austria; 175,000 from Great Britain; almost 100,000 from Hungary; more than 50,000 from Greece, Czechoslovakia, Rumania, and Canada; more than 25,000 from Yugoslavia; around 10,000 from the Netherlands, Denmark, Finland, and Switzerland; more than 5,000 from Portugal and Mexico. There were more than a million Negroes, and more than 50,000 of other races, mostly Chinese and Japanese. From almost every country in the world there are enough people in the city to make up communities of thousands and tens of thousands with organizations, churches, a language, some distinctive culture. . . .

But now what does it mean for New York that most of its population is composed of people who think of themselves — at least at some times, for some purposes — as Jews, Italians, Negroes, Germans, Irishmen, Puerto Ricans? Is New York different, because of this fact, from London, Paris, Moscow, Tokyo? . . .

The heterogeneity of New York is of the masses — numbers so great that Negroes are not exotic, as they are in Paris, Puerto Ricans not glamorous representatives of Latin American culture, as they might be in London, Italians not rare representatives of a great nation, as they are in Tokyo. Here the numbers of each group are so great, so steady and heavy a presence, that it takes an effort of mind to see that all these group names describe a double aspect: those one sees around one, and those in some other country, on some other continent, with a different culture. . . .

Perhaps the meaning of ethnic labels will yet be erased in America. But it has not yet worked out this way in New York. It is true that immigrants to this country were rapidly transformed, in comparison with immigrants to other countries, that they lost their language and altered their culture. It was reasonable to believe that a new American type would emerge, a new nationality in which it would be a matter of indifference whether a man was of Anglo-Saxon or German or Italian or Jewish origin, and in which indeed, because of the diffusion of populations through all parts of the country and all levels of the social order, and because of the consequent close contact and intermarriage, it would be impossible to make such distinctions. This may still be the most likely result in the long run. After all, in 1960 almost half of New York City's population was still foreign-born or the children of foreign-born. Yet it is also true that it is forty years since the end of mass immigration, and new processes, scarcely visible when our chief concern was with the great masses of immigrants and the problems of their "Americanization," now emerge to surprise us. The initial notion of an American melting pot did not, it seems, quite grasp what would happen in America. At least it did not grasp what would happen in the short run, and since this short run encompasses at least the length of a normal lifetime, it is not something we can ignore. . . .

Ethnic groups then, even after distinctive language, customs, and culture are lost, as they largely were in the second generation, and even more fully in the third generation, are continually recreated by new experiences in America. The mere existence of a name itself is perhaps sufficient to form group character in new situations, for the name associates an individual, who actually can be anything, with a certain past, country, race. But as a matter of fact, someone who is Irish or Jewish or Italian generally has other traits than the mere existence of the name that associates him with other people attached to the group. A man is connected to his group by ties of family and friendship. But he is also connected by ties of *interest*. The ethnic groups in New York are also *interest groups.*

This is perhaps the single most important fact about ethnic groups in New York City. When one speaks of the Negroes and Puerto Ricans, one also means unorganized and unskilled workers, who hold poorly paying jobs in the laundries, hotels, restaurants, small factories or who are on relief. When one says Jews, one also means small shopkeepers, professionals, better-paid skilled workers in the garment industries. When one says Italians, one also means homeowners in Staten Island, the North Bronx, Brooklyn, and Queens. . . .

We have tried to show how deeply the pattern of ethnicity is impressed on the life of the city. Ethnicity is more than an influence on events; it is commonly the source of events. Social and political institutions do not merely respond to ethnic interests; a great number of institutions exist for the specific purpose of serving ethnic interests. This in turn tends to perpetuate them. In many ways, the atmosphere of New York City is hospitable to ethnic groupings: it recognizes them, and rewards them, and to that extent encourages them.

This is not to say that no individual group will disappear. This, on the contrary, is a recurring phenomenon. The disappearance of the Germans is a particularly revealing case. . . .

It is a good general rule that except where color is involved as well the specifically *national* aspect of most ethnic groups rarely survives the third generation in any significant terms. The intermarriage which de Crèvecoeur described continues apace, so that even the strongest national traditions are steadily diluted. The groups do not disappear, however, because of their *religious* aspect which serves as the basis of a subcommunity, and a subculture. Doctrines and practices are modified to some extent to conform to an American norm, but a distinctive set of values is nurtured in the social groupings defined by religious affiliation. This is quite contrary to early expectations. It appeared to de Crèvecoeur, for example, that religious as well as national identity was being melted into one by the process of mixed neighborhoods and marriage:

> . . . This mixed neighborhood will exhibit a strange religious medley, that will be neither pure Catholicism nor pure Calvinism. A very perceptible indifference even in the first generation, will become apparent; and it may happen that the daughter of the Catholic will marry the son of the seceder, and settle by themselves at a distance from their parents. What religious education will they give their children? A very imperfect one. If there happens to be in the neighborhood any place of worship, we will suppose a Quaker's meeting; rather than not shew their fine clothes, they will go to it, and some of them may attach themselves to that society. Others will remain in a perfect state of indifference; the children of these zealous parents will not be able to tell what their religious principles are, and their grandchildren still less.
>
> Thus all sects are mixed as well as all nations; thus religious indifference is imperceptibly disseminated from one end of the continent to the other; which is at present one of the strongest characteristics of the Americans.

If this was the case in the late eighteenth century, it is no longer. Religious identities are strongly held by New Yorkers, and Americans generally, and they are for the most part transmitted by blood line from the original immigrant group. A great deal of intermarriage occurs among nationality groups of the three great religious groups, of the kind Ruby Jo Kennedy described in New Haven, Connecticut under the general term of the Triple Melting Pot, but this does not weaken religious identity. When marriages occur between different religions, often one is dominant, and the result among the children is not indifference, but an increase in the numbers of one of the groups. . . .

The white Protestants are a distinct ethnic group in New York, one that has probably passed its low point and will now begin to grow in numbers and probably also in influence. It has its special occupations, with the customary freemasonry. This involves the banks, corporation front offices, educational and philanthropic institutions, and the law offices who serve them. It has its own social world (epitomized by, but by no means confined to, the *Social Register*), its own churches, schools, voluntary organizations and all the varied institutions of a New York minority. These are accompanied by the characteristic styles in food, clothing, and drink, special family patterns, special psychological problems and ailments. For a long while political conservatism, as well as social aloofness, tended to keep the white Protestants out of the main stream of New York politics, much in the way that political radicalism tended to isolate the Jews in the early parts of the century. Theodore Roosevelt, when cautioned that none of his friends would touch New York politics, had a point in replying that it must follow that none of his friends were members of the governing classes.

There has been a resurgence of liberalism within the white Protestant group, in part based on its growth through vigorous young migrants from outside the city, who are conspicuous in the communications industry, law firms, and corporation offices of New York. These are the young people that supported Adlai Stevenson and helped lead and staff the Democratic reform movement. The influence of the white Protestant group on this city, it appears, must now grow as its numbers grow.

In this large array of the four major religio-racial groups, where do the Puerto Ricans stand? Ultimately perhaps they are to be absorbed into the Catholic group. But that is a long time away. The Puerto Ricans are separated from the Catholics as well as the Negroes by color and culture. One cannot even guess how this large element will ultimately relate itself to the other elements of the city; perhaps it will serve, in line with its own nature and genius, to soften the sharp lines that divide them.

Protestants will enjoy immunities in politics even in New York. When the Irish era came to an end in the Brooklyn Democratic party in 1961, Joseph T. Sharkey was succeeded by a troika (as it was called) of an Irish Catholic, a Jew, and a Negro Protestant. The last was a distinguished clergyman, who was at the same time head of the New York City Council of Protestant Churches. It would have been unlikely for a rabbi, unheard of for a priest, to hold such a position.

Religion and race define the next stage in the evolution of the American peoples. But the American nationality is still forming: its processes are mysterious, and the final form, if there is ever to be a final form, is as yet unknown.

39

Lloyd Goodrich

Lloyd Goodrich, director of the Whitney Museum of American Art in New York City, was born in Nutley, New Jersey, in 1897. He has studied and served in a variety of capacities, all of them related to the arts. Among his books are those written about American artists, Thomas Eakins *(1923),* Max Weber *(1949), and* Albert P. Ryder *(1959). He is a frequent contributor to literary and art periodicals. In the following selection, which traces the modern movement in American art from the Armory show of 1913 to the present, he discusses those features that characterize American art. He reflects a recently expressed sentiment of Governor Nelson Rockefeller that American art, because it represents an important area of freedom, has an exciting future. For related ideas, see Fitch, Roper, Hassan, Kouwenhoven, Aldridge.*

[American] abstract art received an impetus from the 1913 Armory Show and many early modernists experimented with it. But most of them after a few years returned to more representational styles, and by about 1925 this first wave of abstraction had passed, except for a few individuals. It had not been, as in Europe, the product of long historical evolution, and our art world was not yet ready for so extreme a departure from representation. More nativist trends intervened — the American scene and social-content schools. For more than a decade, advanced styles were much less practised here than abroad. Not until the middle 1930s did the second wave of abstraction begin to gather force.

Futurism, not represented in the Armory Show, had few exponents aside from Stella, although one would have expected its doctrines of dynamism and speed to appeal to Americans. Though Duchamp, Picabia and Man Ray launched a proto-dada movement in New York in 1915, dada had no deep roots here. Surrealism had few representatives until the arrival of several of its European leaders in the 1930s. But surrealism's exploration of the unconscious mind had a wide effect on artists who were not orthodox surrealists, freeing them from external realism in subject-matter and releasing new elements of fantasy and free imagery.

By far the most widespread form of modernism in America from the

From *Art in America* (No. 4, 1963) pp. 24–27. Reprinted by permission of the publisher.

Armory Show to World War II was expressionism. Expressionism is a broad word with ill-defined boundaries, but the only one to cover the myriad varieties of art which are not predominantly realistic on the one hand nor abstract on the other, and whose common element is the expression of emotions related in some degree to the real world. Expressionism's wide prevalence in this country can be linked to certain historic factors: the continuing tradition of romanticism in the American mind; our partiality for art which embodies emotions arising from specific realities; our preference for personal expression as against formalism; and the increasingly important role played in our art by certain national and racial elements, especially German, Russian and Jewish, particularly sympathetic to free emotional expression.

All these varieties of modernism were international. But in the middle 1920s, partly in reaction against modernism, came a wave of nationalism, a conscious rediscovery and exploration of America, still an untouched continent for most 20th-century American artists. This paralleled the literary explorations of Dreiser, Sherwood Anderson, Sinclair Lewis, Faulkner and Wolfe. Regionalists such as Benton, Wood and Curry returned to the rural Midwest and South, and immersed themselves in their people, landscape and folkways. Articulate champions of native values, they celebrated the flavor and old-fashioned virtues of what they considered the heartland of America. At the same time, Eastern painters of the American scene such as Hopper, Burchfield and Marsh pictured the city and small town with a more drastic realism, a full acceptance of the ugly aspects of our country, but also with a deep emotional attachment. Their portrait of the city, compared with the good-humored gusto of the Henri group, revealed its elements of vulgarity, monotony and human misery — new notes of pessimism and satire. Their version of the American landscape included all those characteristic and often grotesque man-made features shunned by their tender-minded predecessors the impressionists. In the work of such artists, aspects of the United States never touched before were assimilated into art. In a general way the American scene painters were a continuation of the interrupted tradition of 19th-century genre; but with little conscious influence, and with greater maturity, realism and emotional depth.

The depression of the 1930s, the rise of fascism, and increasing world tensions brought to artists as to everyone else a new realization of the ills of our times. A surge of social-protest art, ranging ideologically from socialist idealism to party-line conformity, swept the country, producing the first full-scale pictorial attack on our social system. This school dominated the art world of the mid-1930s; in no other nation did artists say so frankly, loudly and persistently what was wrong with their country. And many of them did so while on the federal payroll — an example of democratic freedom of expression unique in modern history. It is noteworthy that for the first time there appeared an influence from Latin American—in this case Mexico, through Rivera and Orozco.

Regionalism with its accompanying chauvinism and isolationism could not survive in the modern world; and as for the social-protest school, world events after 1939 rendered its message obsolete. As dominant movements they were replaced by the trend to abstraction. But the American scene and social schools together achieved the most far-reaching visual exploration and evaluation of our civilization to date, and made an enormous contribution to our national self-knowledge. While the mass of their work is now of interest mainly as ideological history, the best of it ranks among the most vital achievements of American art, and I believe will be more highly valued in the future than at present. And social content and the American scene are still important ingredients of present-day art, with individual exponents such as Hopper, Burchfield, Shahn, Evergood and Levine who are among our strongest figures. To such artists the world in which they live, its actualities, issues and human meanings, are essential elements out of which to create art.

In spite of the current predominance of abstraction, an interesting feature of American art today is the number and strength of representaional artists. I do not mean academicians, who still cling to 19th-century viewpoints, but non-academic artists who speak in more or less representational language. These artists have profited by the discoveries of modern art, especially its emphasis on plastic values, but they believe that there need be no conflict between the representation of reality and the creation of plastic design, any more than there was in the great art of the past.

Over the past twenty years the prevailing trend has been toward abstraction, which dominates the present as the American scene and social schools did the 1930s. The word abstraction, like expressionism, today covers a multitude of concepts and styles, and many degrees of relationship or non-relationship to natural forms. As compared to the pioneer abstract movement of 1913 to 1925, contemporary abstract painting and sculpture in this country is much more independent of European sources. There has been ample time for the principles of abstraction to become widely accepted and acclimatized, and for a whole generation to attain maturity within the abstract idiom. Our artists have evolved individual styles of a wide variety, and original forms of great power and richness.

With all the diversity of our abstract art today, a few general characteristics can be discerned. One is its strongly expressionist tendency. With a few notable exceptions it includes relatively little formalism, purism or geometrical style. Freeform abstraction is much more widely practised than formal abstraction, and considerably more inventive. In this, one can see our traditional indifference to the classic virtues. The most widespread current tendency, what has been generally called abstract expressionism, stems from older expressionism in its subjectivity and emotionalism, its fluidity and freedom, and the dominant role it gives to color and to the sensuous impact of materials. Forms have been reduced to the most elemental, traditional concepts of design have been dispensed with, direct physical sensation has been given primacy, and conscious composing has been replaced by more intuitive methods, in which the actual materials and their manipulation, and the process of creation itself, play a large part in determining the final result.

The advanced abstract school is international, but it has some of its strongest representatives in the United States. It is indeed the first international movement in which Americans have not only participated fully on their home grounds, but are in the advance guard. In this new art form, in which traditional values are at a minimum and personal creativeness is the chief criterion, American artists are more on a par with their European colleagues than in any preceding period. Our advanced artists, it seems to me, are conducting a more fundamental exploration into the physical and sensuous sources of art than the pioneer modernists of forty years ago, who were more dependent on European leadership. In a sense they can be considered as a new native manifestation of primitivism; and indeed, in their discarding of traditional forms, their drive to rebuild art on its basis in the senses, they are a logical result of the primitivist tendency that has marked modern art for the past fifty years or more. With all their occasional over-simplifications, vacancies and brutalities, they are standing on their own feet more than any previous advanced school in this country.

Representationalism, expressionsism, abstraction, and all their innumerable variations—I doubt if there was ever a nation or a period whose art was more diverse than that of the United States today. The swift, successive revolutions of the past half-century, occurring in an artistic community conservative at the beginning, have resulted in the phenomenon of an advance guard, a middle guard and a rear guard all existing simultaneously. Some of our strongest artists, like their 19th-century predecessors, have remained relatively unaffected by current movements. We have individuals and whole schools of many different viewpoints, all having their measure of validity.

In spite of this variety, some generalizations are possible. Our art is still individualistic, produced for private collectors, museums and the art public, with a minimum of official patronage. Whatever vital public art is being done is mostly for business and industry. Subject-matter in general is personal, contemporary and indigenous; historical, religious or complex intellectual content is rare. The predominant artistic languages are naturalism, expressionism and abstraction, the latter with a strong expressionist bent; formalism in either representational or abstract schools is exceptional. Our art has no deep roots in its own past; while our artists may consider certain of their ancestors especially sympathetic, for the greater tradition they look in Europe, the Orient, or primitive cultures. Any continuing relations with the American past are largely unconscious. As to basic innovations in artistic concepts, we have so far made few contributions as fundamental as those of the chief European masters of this century. But in recent years we have begun to create forms that are more original and less dependent on European example than at any time in our history. No other nation today, I believe, exhibits more general artistic vitality, more varied or more widely diffused, or with greater possibilities for the future.

What qualities of our contemporary art can be called characteristically American? Those artists who consciously base their art on the contemporary American world, interpreted naturalistically or expressionistically, and who are therefore the most obviously American, see and express their native subject-matter in highly individual ways, from Hopper's, Wyeth's, and Burchfield's naturalism to Shahn's and Levine's imaginative, symbolic commentary on our society. In other artists whose subject-matter is less specifically native we also find qualities that seem characteristically American: Marin's dynamism and perennial freshness, as native as Homer; Weber's intense expression of the Jewish element in the American mind; Davis' powerful calligraphy, creating patterns that are as native as jazz.

In the more abstract forms American characteristics also seem unmistakable — the ingenious and often captivating uses of new materials and techniques: Calder's introduction of motion into a hitherto static art, and his inventiveness and gaiety; Pollock's direct physical impact and powerful rhythms; Roszak's poetic transformations of motifs from sea and desert into compelling imagery; Tobey's mystical feeling for space and vitalizing light.

Even the most advanced school seems to me to express, in purely abstract terms, many characteristics of present-day America. The artists' return to primary physical sensation has its parallels in many fields of our national life. Their emphasis on creation as action is analogous to the free improvisations of jazz. The speed, impact and explosiveness of their art expresses these attributes of our era and country. Their floating forms seem related to our air age, and the patterns they create recall the earth's patterns as seen from above. Their open compositions, their sense of space, seem to reflect the space and openness of America. Even the big scale of their works — so romantically ill-adapted to our living conditions — suggests the bigness of our land.

All these varied qualities seem to me as clearly products of our culture as the simpler virtues of our 19th-century art. As to any "American" common denominator, any single quality that underlies all, I do not believe that it exists, or if it does, that it can be isolated by us who are so close to the contemporary scene. What we have are many diverse qualities that can be called characteristically American. This diversity, this lack of any simple unity, are factors that sometimes make our contemporary art scene bewildering not only to the public but to the cognoscenti, who side violently with one side or the other. But this pluralistic art of ours is the fitting expression of a democratic society, free and fluid, allowing wide scope to individualism. It is paradoxical but encouraging that in a society as standardized as ours in material ways, where we see the same films and listen to the same radio and television programs, there should be such variety of artistic creation and opinion.

The scientific-technological élite

Jules Henry   **Culture against Man**   **40**

Jules Henry studied under Franz Boas and Ruth Benedict at Columbia University, where he received his doctorate in anthropology. He is currently Professor of Anthropology and Sociology at Washington University in St. Louis and also serves as a consultant to the National Institute of Mental Health and the World Health Organization. In the following selection, Professor Henry discusses the role of the scientific and engineering élite and "fun" and "fear" in the society. For related ideas, see Bell, Goodman, Mills, Whyte, Dedijer.

The Cultural Maximizers

All great cultures, and those moving in the direction of greatness, have an élite which might be called the *cultural maximizers* whose function is to maintain or push further the culture's greatness and integration. In ancient Israel, where the pivot of greatness was religion, these were the Prophets. In Rome, as among the Dakota Indians also, the cultural maximizers united within themselves qualities of violence and statesmanship, for they had to be warriors as well as wise men. The functions of a cultural maximizer include organization (i.e., maintaining the level of integration of the culture as it is) and contributing certain qualitative features necessary to the continuance of the cultural life. His function is never to alter the culture radically. He may help to give more intense expression to features that already exist, but he never wants to bring about a fundamental change. Thus, those who have the capacity to maximize culture in this sense are among the élite in all highly developed civilizations.

In our own culture there is no group that deserves more recognition, and hence a position among the élite, than the scientists and engineers. They are the central power from which emanate the new technical ideas and industrial products so necessary to the continuation of our culture. Insofar as they are able to expand the array of lethal weapons so necessary to a warlike people, they are in the truest sense cultural maximizers.

In America the scientifically trained élite is one of the most mobile segments of the population. Because of their scarcity relative to the demand for them, and because, as with other American workers, their institutional loyalties are weak, large sums are spent by industry to attract them, and they are offered many psychic rewards. In the advertisements for scientists and engineers is the essence of the American dream—the dream that every American is supposed to realize in his lifetime work, but which is approximated only by the élite. A few examples will give the flavor:

The following is a third-of-a-page advertisement [from the *New York Times*, 1956], addressed to "electronic and mechanical engineers and physicists":

An invitation to a better
way of life . . . from MELPAR

> The Washington D.C. Area provides a stimulating environment for professional and intellectual growth under conditions of minimum stress. Melpar laboratories are located in Northern Virginia, suburban to the Nation's Capitol. The area enjoys the country's highest per capita income, is free of heavy industry, and virtually depression proof. Cultural, recreational, and educational facilities abound. Housing is fine and plentiful.
>
> Should you join Melpar you would tie your own professional growth to that of a Company which has doubled in size every 18 months for the past decade. Melpar maintains a policy of *individual recognition* which enables our engineers to progress according to their own time tables, not prearranged ones. Performance primarily determines advancement. Age, tenure, length of experience are only secondary considerations. . . .

The chance to grow, to achieve recognition for performance as an individual—precisely what is denied most workers—is offered the élite as a special lure; such inducements are not found in advertisements for most other jobs. The phenomenal growth of this company is interesting, because one of the commonest words in advertisements directed to cultural maximizers is "expand." It is a rare advertisement that emphasizes permanence or stability as such, since in the circles in which the élite move, expansion *is* stability. That is to say, cultural maximizers in America abhor stability; what interests them, or better, what drives them, is expansion, and the permanence of their world is seen in terms of its limitless growth. But in actuality, "growth" does not quite cover the case for cultural maximizers, for growth does not of itself imply the outward-in-all-directions-at-once kind of increase that fires their imagination. Rather, their phantasy is the expanding universe of the astronomers, and that is also their concept of stability.

International Business Machines placed this advertisement in the *New York Times;* it was arranged as if spelled out on a Scrabble board:

```
        D
    ELECTRONIC
        V   E
    ENGINEERS
        L   E
        O   A
        P   R
        M   C
        E   H
        N
        T
```

How to spell out a winning future . . .

. . . .

The IBM engineer is confident of his future because he knows that digital computer development, design, and manufacture is perhaps the one "unlimited" field in electronics today . . . and that IBM is an acknowledged world leader in this permanently significant field.

Ideas . . . ideas . . . and more ideas are the raw materials of successful engineering. And at IBM you expand your ideas in a small team, where they are immediately recognized and rewarded. IBM's awareness of each engineer's individual performance is expressed in the great number of challenging positions awaiting men who prove their abilities at IBM.

Right now there are career openings at IBM that offer *you* every opportunity to grow in professional stature to the fullest extent of *your* abilities.

Here the feeling of expansiveness is communicated through an emphasis on having ideas—an experience largely irrelevant to the work-life of men on the assembly line. Shrewdly, IBM's advertisement (which reads as if it had been composed after running a thousand answers to a questionnaire on "What do you most desire in a job?" through an electronic sorter to find out what words appeared most often) emphasizes immediate recognition and reward of ideas by the company, an experience reserved almost exclusively for cultural maximizers.

Another of the world's giant corporations placed the following advertisement:

ENGINEERS

What are the attractions at General Electric? To men who think ahead, this expanding department offers the opportunity to pioneer in the creation and development of important, new projects, plus the advantages of living in Utica, at the gateway to the Adirondacks.

Within easy reach of your home you'll find 5 golf courses . . . over 8,000 acres of parks . . . an unspoiled countryside of lakes noted for fishing and swimming.

Openings for Experienced

Mechanical engineers—for creating new airborne equipment to operate under prodigious conditions of shock, (etc.) . . . The "Specs" will be written *after* your job is done. We want mechanical engineers with vision, horse sense and the courage of their convictions.

Electrical engineers—These projects from science fiction require rational dreamers who possess a high starting and operating torque.

Through the advertisements, many of them a quarter of a page or more in size, run the themes of challenge, creativity, initiative, personal growth, expansion, novelty, individuality, the taking of responsibility, stimulation through professional on-the-job contacts, and achievement. The majority of American jobs, however, are remote from these. What is most striking is that realization of these things should be offered as *inducements:* the very form of the advertisements is an acknowledgment that in America most jobs are not challenges, that no creativity or initiative is desired.

But what of these "dreamers" with "high starting and operating torque"? Do their dreams come true? For a very large number of the Ph.D.'s entering the American industrial system they do not. With its characteristic detachment the Bureau of Labor Statistics states the case:

The figures . . . indicate that more than two-thirds of the scientists who left the government, private industry, or a foundation for another type of employment entered educational institutions. *The largest numbers entering education from other types of employment came from private industry.*

The fact that the universities were able to compete successfully with other types of employers in attracting and retaining scientists is noteworthy in view of the low salary levels prevailing in educational institutions. Apparently, the advantages of university employment, such as *freedom of research,* are sufficiently strong to countervail, in the minds of many scientists, the economic handicaps such employment imposes. [Italics supplied.]

Their figures show also that while two-fifths of the scientists whose first position is in private industry take one in a university for their second, only 16 per cent of the Ph.D.'s whose first job is on a campus take their second in industry. As a matter of fact, "the |scientist| recruits into . . . industry have come in large numbers from the ranks of *newly created* doctors of philosophy rather than from among scientists already established as educators." |Italics supplied.|

Thus, it is hard experience that teaches the young, and usually deeply committed, scientist that industry is not the place for him. Attracted at first by the startling pay and the lure of pleasant living, he finds these are no compensation for personality loss. *Executive Life* tells the same story:

> "A help-wanted ad we ran recently," one executive explains, "asked for engineers who would 'conform to our work patterns.' Somebody slipped on that one. He actually came out and said what's really wanted around here."

In view of the relative hysteria that has arisen in connection with our shortage of scientists and engineers it might be well to stop for a moment and review some stimulating observations on scientists and engineers gleaned from the *New York Times* over the years. I start with Devon Francis' *Some Dreams F.O.B. Detroit:*

> . . . much of the time they sit at their desks performing such grubby tasks as redesigning an engine camshaft or doing surgery on a rear axle because the company sales department has decreed a change to meet competition. (*N.Y. Times* Magazine, Oct. 25, 1959.)

Vance Packard in *The Waste Makers* has also pointed to the subjection of scientific and engineering brains to the whims of the market. An advertising executive commenting on the recruitment practices of companies looking for scientists and engineers, observed:

> . . . many recruitment ads failed to give a valid picture of the employer —a factor that tends to increase engineering turnover. The average engineer changes jobs about once every two and one half years, according to the study |carried out by his agency|. (*N.Y. Times,* Jan. 27, 1961.)

As a matter of fact the companies themselves are aware of the deceptions, for in attempting to pirate researchers from one another they use appeals like the following:

> "If those glamorous projects you were promised you'd work on haven't materialized. . . ."
> |These appeals| are typical of a barrage of newspaper help-wanted advertisements that appeared today |in Los Angeles| before 3,000 participants in a joint national meeting of the American Rocket Society and the Institute of Aeronautical Sciences. . . .

The advertising barrage was part of the most intensive talent-raiding episodes in recent industrial history. Large corporations constantly engage in the process colloquially called "body-snatching." (*N.Y. Times,* June 16, 1961.)

All of this enables us to make a discovery in connection with the present panic in America over the lack of scientific brains in industry; for we see now that when industry does get scientists it cannot hold them, because it interferes with their autonomy and growth. This élite shows the same tidal movement as the plebe, and for the same reasons. The difference is that this élite can get out of the industrial system, but the plebe cannot. The university, with its unpainted walls, its preposterous architecture, poor lighting, petty politics, status hunger, and trailing clouds of pipe smoke is still a refuge of the human spirit. Of course, as consulting fees mount and professors rush around garnering them, even this function of the university becomes problematic—as does the existence of the "human spirit." Professors have no immunity against the effects of the high-rising standard of living.

Fear in America

Most American workers have learned to put the constantly rising standard of living in place of progressive self-realization. Only the élites—the professionals, the corporation executives, and the successful businessmen—have a real chance to express the most highly rewarded cultural drives or to try in their occupational lives for some kind of self realization not comprehended within the retail price index. On the outer fringes of this group are millions of "little men" who struggle along in their own businesses and whose failures are numbered in the ever-increasing tens of thousands. They are the men who yearn to "go in business for myself," and who, though animated by the drives of the élite, also have other, more intimate, possibly more determining motives.

When a man goes into business for himself he is moved not only by the élite drives but also by the wish to have self-respect, to not have somebody else tell him what to do, to be able to work when he pleases and stop when he pleases. Being his own boss means keeping for himself what he makes and using his own ideas rather than somebody else's. In short, "my own boss" means that the little man controls himself rather than being controlled by someone who has no interest in him other than a pecuniary one. To be used up for somebody else's drive realization goes against his grain; he wants to survive in his own interest and not be consumed in somebody else's; he wants to be protected.

It is because going into business for one's self expresses such deeply rooted yearnings that the traditional American drama of big and little business has its perennial appeal. In it something big (Big Business) is always pushing somebody small and helpless around and depriving him of his right to life and self, and Americans respond to the drama with vigor and passion because most of them feel pushed around. While it is true that the restraints exercised on the economy by the great concentrations of industrial capital are real, the repeated congressional investigations of big business and the plight of little business reflect widespread folk anxieties. The following from "Teen-Agers Views of Big Business" gives the tone:

> "Big Businesses run everything in America—they have all the money." This reaction of a 16-year-old high school girl in Tucson, Arizona, sums up the attitude of many of our young people toward big business. . . .
> Nearly 31 per cent of those interviewed thought of big business in a negative sense, as sort of a giant monopoly spread across all America. They feared the future will see all free enterprise swallowed up in one or two gigantic trusts. The consensus was that in the next decade and a half there will be one or two large companies representing each individual industry.

The opinions of this cross-section of American youth reflect fear of the enormously ramifying network of controls exercised over the American economy by big business. While the giant American enterprises help raise the standard of living, contribute brilliantly to the élan of American capitalism and are necessary for its survival, and represent in some ways the approaching climax of a creative type of economic organization, they nevertheless fill many Americans with a feeling of mingled anxiety, hostility, and dependence. Thus, although the teenagers previously quoted are angry at and fearful of big business, the majority of the boys are yet eager to become dependent on it:

> Only one out of eight young men in high school expects or has any desire to go into business for himself. The majority hopes to find security and success in positions with important national companies. The "reach for the sky" dream of American youth seems to have suffered a setback in the period since the end of World War II. Young men would rather put their trust in management of large concerns than set out on their own.

This is self-renunciation again—only this time the American does it because he is intelligently afraid to try his hand alone.

Anyone can readily understand why youth should feel as it does about starting out on its own, for even without their intuitive sense of the limited chances of survival, there is the obvious reality that new and little businesses die off rapidly. The new man and the little one are forced to go into businesses which are the easiest to enter and where, therefore, competition is keen, profits low, and business mortality high. Even in boom times, it is difficult to gain a foothold, for then big business borrows the loose money available in order to finance expansion, thus making money hard for others to come by and compelling them to pay higher interest than big business. For these and other reasons, nearly half of new business never reaches its second birthday.

A further factor that gives big business increasing advantage over the new and the little man is the capacity of big business, aided by social psychology and psychoanalysis, to channel unconscious cravings into consumption. Since the new man and the little one often lack the financial resources necessary to do this, they cannot move with as much assurance as the big enterprise into areas as yet unexploited, and where the chances of success may be greater. In this way, big business, with its new capacity for diversification — the ability of one enormous enterprise to expand in a variety of directions with a variety of new goods and services — and with the money to finance advance market research, is reducing the possible areas of success for the little man. To all of this must be added the natural reluctance of banks to lend money to new ventures by little people.

Thus, the man who seeks to be "independent" by starting his own business cannot make a free choice of what he shall do, and having made his enforced choice, he has about a 50 per cent chance of surviving. If he survives, he will remain small and earn a modest income.

Thus, the little businessman stands out in the open, fearful of other little men and of the large enterprises. But his fear is not of economic destruction only; what he fears also is loss of the remnants of his self-hood embodied in his business. In this he is little different from the worker, for the protection a worker wants from his union is not only against low pay, insecurity, and poor working conditions: what he wants also is a safeguard against humiliation, for that is spiritual murder.

Out of the fears inherent in technological drivenness have arisen unique economic institutions. The giant corporations' drive to diversification is an expression not only of the will to profit but of the fear of loss of markets. The trade unions arose out of the fear of the arbitrary, humiliating power of employers. The vast quantity and quite unbelievable quality of American advertising expresses not only the will to riches but also the fear of competition and consumer indifference. Thus, technological drivenness derives much of its motive power from fear. But we can go even further than this and say that the economy *relies* on fear. Take away fear of competition, of failure, of loss of markets, of humiliation, of becoming obsolete, and the culture would stop; take away the fear the union man has of the boss and the union would blow away.

But it is not merely fear of one another that keeps us driving hard; there is also the Great External Fear — fear of the Soviet Union. Without it the automobile industry would drop to almost half its size, the aircraft industry would dwindle to a shadow, and numberless businesses that supply them or live on the paychecks of their workers would shrink or vanish. Without the Great External Fear, indeed, Latin America, India, Southeast Asia, and the Near East would starve at our gates while we continued to digest our billions. Thus fear impels us to maximize production at home and abroad and casts us in the role of reluctant Samaritan.

It is now possible to understand better why some scientific talent leaves American industry. Industries that hire most of the engineers and scientists depend heavily on military contracts, and since they must produce the instruments of attack and defense against the Great Fear, they are often compelled to concentrate on fear-created technical problems. Most of the advertisements for scientists specify the particular mechanism or problem on which the scientist is expected to work and sometimes a company actually specifies in detail, as on an examination, precisely what the Ph.D. is expected to do. For example:

1. How does the AGC bandwidth affect the accuracy of the angle-tracking radars?
2. What are the statistical factors to be considered in calculating the detection probability of a search radar?
3. What is the effect of atmosphere turbulence on high gain antenna performance?
4. How is the sidelobe level of radar antenna affected by random perturbations of phase and amplitude over the aperture?

If you have answers to any of these four related questions, then we would like to talk to you.

We are looking for engineers and physicists with inquisitive and imaginative minds. . . .

To a scientist it must seem that such meticulous statement of the problem implies a lack of interest in "inquisitive and imaginative minds," as the editors of *Fortune* point out.

In the course of evolution it has appeared that the greatest asset of an organism is its potentiality for "adaptive radiation," the capacity to develop new forms to suit new conditions of life. What we see in a fear-ridden human being is loss of adaptability, a tendency to become frozen in unchanging patterns of behavior and thought. As far as scientists are concerned, the record of their departure from industry for the campus speaks for itself: quite a few are unwilling to suffer the loss of adaptation potential required by the fear-dependent milieu in which they must work. Of course, fear-*dependent* does not mean fear-*ridden,* but the consequences are the same. Though it is not implied that the drafting and thinking rooms of industry are atremble with the Great Fear, what is clear is that the Great Fear dictates the problems and accounts for the uniformity of scientific offerings in the advertisements for scientists. A further paradox inheres in a drive for a knowledge that is dictated by fear; for in the long run, the product of fear is a certain vital ignorance — an ignorance of all that does not help allay the fear, that does not contribute to attack or defense against an enemy.

Fear has served the animal kingdom well; without it, oysters, apes, and man would perish. Yet when fear penetrates all aspects of culture and becomes a dominant driving force, the culture freezes in fixed attitudes of attack and defense, all cultural life suffers, and the Self nearly dies in the cold.

Fun in America

But really the Self does not die, given half a chance. Even poor, sick, aged, depersonalized, bedridden patients in a bare public hospital preserve . . . a spark of Self that can be blown into a flame, for Nature has endowed all life with a capacity to seize any opportunity to stay alive. This capacity for "adaptive radiation" is a primal endowment of the cell and dies with it. The Self is the spiritual manifestation of this capacity in man.

Fun in America is an adaptive radiation, for it is the expression of the American's determination to stay alive. It is an underground escape from the spiritual Andersonville in which technological drivenness has imprisoned us. In fun the American saves part of his Self from the system that consumes him. Fun, in its rather unique American form, is grim resolve. When the foreigner observes how grimly we seem to go about our fun, he is right; we are as determined about the pursuit of fun as a desert-wandering traveler is about the search for water, and for the same reason.

But though fun revives people so that they can carry on with work in which they have no interest and out of which they get little psychic reward, fun in America is also a clowning saboteur undermining the very system fun was meant to sustain. For having fun is the precise opposite of what is necessary to keep the system driving hard. The system needs students who will work at "tough subjects," and it needs executives who will take work home and find their principal pleasure in driving hard on the job. But since fun is opposed to all this, it undermines the system; it is impossible to educate children to want fun ("Learning can be fun!") and not expect the fun ideal to eventually blow the ideal of hard work to pieces, and with it the system hard work supports.

In this way, by its curious dialectic, the Self still manages to save itself. To wring "heaps of fun" from a culture that is harsh in so many ways is an American adaptive radiation. Europeans think we work too hard at having fun, but we know better.

Fun is a creature out of the Id, the repository of all untamed instinctual cravings that surge within us. Within every man and woman, says Freud, is an Id, a volcano of seething impulse, held in check only by society, whose controls become our conscience, our Super Ego. In contrast to the Id, which urges us to seek only pleasure, the Super Ego commands that we work hard, save, and control our impulse life. But nowadays, as the Super Ego values of hard work, thrift, and abstemiousness no longer pay off, and technological drivenness presses the Self so hard; nowadays, when the high-rising standard of living has become a moral ideal, the Id values of fun, relaxation, and impulse release are ascendant. Only a people who have learned to decontrol their impulses can consume as we do. So the consequence of technological drivenness is the creation of a people who, though reared to support it—by being trained to heroic feats of consumption—are quietly undermining it by doing the least they can rather than the most, not only because it is hard to get anything out of the system but also because they have stayed up so late the night before having fun!

**Art establishes
the basic human truth**

John F. Kennedy

**Remarks at Amherst College
upon Receiving
an Honorary Degree**

41

President John F. Kennedy was, in Lewis Mumford's words, "the first American President to give art, literature, and music a place of dignity and honor in our national life." He was convinced, says Arthur Schlesinger, "that the health of the arts was vitally related to the health of society." Consequently, beginning with his inauguration—where, for the first time an American poet, Robert Frost, was invited to participate—President Kennedy led the nation in honoring its artists. Not only were they welcomed at his inauguration—over fifty were on the rostrum when he took the oath—but, during his three years as president, American artists from all fields of endeavor were invited to the White House to meet with and/or perform for visiting Chiefs-of-State. The nation was thus able to display— on its most appropriate platform—the best of its civilization. But President Kennedy went further. A consultant to the arts was created to explore all the areas in which government impinged on the arts—in the design of stamps, coins, and medals, in the erection of public buildings and in tariff and tax policy which might present obstacles to the artist and artistic creations. He rehabilitated the Presidential Medal of Freedom to give visible evidence of the nation's desire to honor those "whose talent enlarges the

public vision of the dignity with which life can be graced and the fullness
with which it can be lived."

In the selection which follows—taken from an address given at Amherst
on the day he received a Doctor of Laws degree and dedicated the Robert
Frost Library—President Kennedy defines the singular role of the poet in
our society and goes on to offer his vision of the American promise. For
related ideas, see Parkes, Goodrich, Kouwenhoven.

. . . The problems which this country now faces are staggering, both at
home and abroad. We need the service, in the great sense, of every educated man or woman to find 10 million jobs in the next 2½ years, to
govern our relations—a country which lived in isolation for 150 years, and
is now suddenly the leader of the free world—to govern our relations with
over 100 countries, to govern those relations with success so that the balance of power remains strong on the side of freedom, to make it possible
for Americans of all different races and creeds to live together in harmony,
to make it possible for a world to exist in diversity and freedom. All this
requires the best of all of us.

Therefore, I am proud to come to this college whose graduates have recognized this obligation and to say to those who are now here that the
need is endless, and I am confident that you will respond.

Robert Frost said:

Two roads diverged in a wood, and I—
I took the one less traveled by,
And that has made all the difference.

I hope that road will not be the less traveled by, and I hope your commitment to the Great Republic's interest in the years to come will be
worthy of your long inheritance since your beginning.

This day devoted to the memory of Robert Frost offers an opportunity
for reflection which is prized by politicians as well as by others, and even
by poets, for Robert Frost was one of the granite figures of our time in
America. He was supremely two things: an artist and an American. A
nation reveals itself not only by the men it produces but also by the men
it honors, the men it remembers.

In America, our heroes have customarily run to men of large accomplishments. But today this college and country honors a man whose contribution was not to our size but to our spirit, not to our political beliefs
but to our insight, not to our self-esteem, but to our self-comprehension.
In honoring Robert Frost, we therefore can pay honor to the deepest
sources of our national strength. That strength takes many forms, and the

Public Papers of the Presidents of the United States, John F. Kennedy, 1963. (Washington: U.S. Government Printing Office, 1964), pp. 816–818.

most obvious forms are not always the most significant. The men who create power make an indispensable contribution to the Nation's greatness, but the men who question power make a contribution just as indispensable, especially when that questioning is disinterested, for they determine whether we use power or power uses us.

Our national strength matters, but the spirit which informs and controls our strength matters just as much. This was the special significance of Robert Frost. He brought an unsparing instinct for reality to bear on the platitudes and pieties of society. His sense of the human tragedy fortified him against self-deception and easy consolation. "I have been," he wrote, "one acquainted with the night." And because he knew the midnight as well as the high noon, because he understood the ordeal as well as the triumph of the human spirit, he gave his age strength with which to overcome despair. At bottom, he held a deep faith in the spirit of man, and it is hardly an accident that Robert Frost coupled poetry and power, for he saw poetry as the means of saving power from itself. When power leads man towards arrogance, poetry reminds him of his limitations. When power narrows the areas of man's concern, poetry reminds him of the richness and diversity of his existence. When power corrupts, poetry cleanses. For art establishes the basic human truth which must serve as the touchstone of our judgment.

The artist, however faithful to his personal vision of reality, becomes the last champion of the individual mind and sensibility against an intrusive society and an officious state. The great artist is thus a solitary figure. He has, as Frost said, a lover's quarrel with the world. In pursuing his perceptions of reality, he must often sail against the currents of his time. This is not a popular role. If Robert Frost was much honored during his lifetime, it was because a good many preferred to ignore his darker truths. Yet in retrospect, we see how the artist's fidelity has strengthened the fibre of our national life.

If sometimes our great artists have been the most critical of our society, it is because their sensitivity and their concern for justice, which must motivate any true artist, makes him aware that our Nation falls short of its highest potential. I see little of more importance to the future of our country and our civilization than full recognition of the place of the artist.

If art is to nourish the roots of our culture, society must set the artist free to follow his vision wherever it takes him. We must never forget that art is not a form of propaganda; it is a form of truth. And as Mr. MacLeish once remarked of poets, there is nothing worse for our trade than to be in style. In free society art is not a weapon and it does not belong to the sphere of polemics and ideology. Artists are not engineers of the soul. It may be different elsewhere. But democratic society — in it, the highest duty of the writer, the composer, the artist is to remain true to himself and to let the chips fall where they may. In serving his vision of the truth, the artist best serves his nation. And the nation which disdains the mission of art invites the fate of Robert Frost's hired man, the fate of having "nothing to look backward to with pride, and nothing to look forward to with hope."

I look forward to a great future for America, a future in which our country will match its military strength with our moral restraint, its wealth with our wisdom, its power with our purpose. I look forward to an America which will not be afraid of grace and beauty, which will protect the beauty of our natural environment, which will preserve the great old American houses and squares and parks of our national past, and which will build handsome and balanced cities for our future.

I look forward to an America which will reward achievement in the arts as we reward achievement in business or statecraft. I look forward to an America which will steadily raise the standards of artistic accomplishment and which will steadily enlarge cultural opportunities for all of our citizens. And I look forward to an America which commands respect throughout the world not only for its strength but for its civilization as well. And I look forward to a world which will be safe not only for democracy and diversity but also for personal distinction. . . .

Gracious dying

42

Jessica Mitford   **The American Way of Death**

Jessica Mitford was born in England in 1917 and is a member of the celebrated Mitford family. She has contributed articles to many publications, and her books include Daughters and Rebels *(1960). In the following selection, Miss Mitford takes a different tack from the satiric approach used by her countryman Evelyn Waugh in his discussion of American death practices in* The Loved One. *She is concerned with the commercialization and consumerism of dying in America. For related ideas, see Galbraith, Cox, Herberg.*

From *The American Way of Death*, pp. 15–19; copyright © 1963 by Jessica Mitford. Reprinted by permission of Simon & Schuster, Inc.

O death, where is thy sting? O grave, where is thy victory? Where, indeed. Many a badly stung survivor, faced with the aftermath of some relative's funeral, has ruefully concluded that the victory has been won hands down by a funeral establishment—in a disastrously unequal battle.

Much has been written of late about the affluent society in which we live, and much fun poked at some of the irrational "status symbols" set out like golden snares to trap the unwary consumer at every turn. . . .

If the Dismal Traders (as an eighteenth-century English writer calls them) have traditionally been cast in a comic role in literature, a universally recognized symbol of humor from Shakespeare to Dickens to Evelyn Waugh, they have successfully turned the tables in recent years to perpetrate a huge, macabre and expensive practical joke on the American public. It is not consciously conceived of as a joke, of course; on the contrary, it is hedged with admirably contrived rationalizations.

Gradually, almost imperceptibly, over the years the funeral men have constructed their own grotesque cloud-cuckoo-land where the trappings of Gracious Living are transformed, as in a nightmare, into the trappings of Gracious Dying. The same familiar Madison Avenue language, with its peculiar adjectival range designed to anesthetize sales resistance to all sorts of products, has seeped into the funeral industry in a new and bizarre guise. The emphasis is on the same desirable qualities that we have all been schooled to look for in our daily search for excellence: comfort, durability, beauty, craftsmanship. The attuned ear will recognize too the convincing quasi-scientific language, so reassuring even if unintelligible.

So that this too, too solid flesh might not melt, we are offered "solid copper—a quality casket which offers superb value to the client seeking long-lasting protection," or "the Colonial Classic Beauty—18 gauge lead coated steel, seamless top, lap-jointed welded body construction." Some are equipped with foam rubber, some with innerspring mattresses. Elgin offers "the revolutionary 'Perfect-Posture' bed." Not every casket need have a silver lining, for one may choose between "more than 60 color matched shades, magnificent and unique masterpieces" by the Cheney casket-lining people. Shrouds no longer exist. Instead, you may patronize a grave-wear couturiere who promises "handmade original fashions— styles from the best in life for the last memory—dresses, men's suits, negligees, accessories." For the final, perfect grooming: "Nature-Glo—the ultimate in cosmetic embalming." And, where have we heard that phrase "peace of mind protection" before? No matter. In funeral advertising, it is applied to the Wilbert Burial Vault, with its 3/8-inch precast asphalt inner liner plus extra-thick, reinforced concrete—all this "guaranteed by Good Housekeeping." Here again the Cadillac, status symbol par excellence, appears in all its gleaming glory, this time transformed into a pastel-colored funeral hearse.

You, the potential customer for all this luxury, are unlikely to read the lyrical descriptions quoted above, for they are culled from *Mortuary Management* and *Casket and Sunnyside,* two of the industry's eleven trade magazines. For you there are ads in your daily newspaper, generally found on the obituary page, stressing dignity, refinement, high-caliber professional service and that intangible quality, *sincerity.* The trade advertisements are, however, instructive, because they furnish an important clue to the frame of mind into which the funeral industry has hypnotized itself.

A new mythology, essential to the twentieth-century American funeral rite, has grown up — or rather has been built up step by step — to justify the peculiar customs surrounding the disposal of our dead. And, just as the witch doctor must be convinced of his own infallibility in order to maintain a hold over his clientele, so the funeral industry has had to "sell itself" on its articles of faith in the course of passing them along to the public.

The first of these is the tenet that today's funeral procedures are founded in "American tradition." The story comes to mind of a sign on the freshly sown lawn of a brand-new Midwest college: "There is a tradition on this campus that students never walk on this strip of grass. This tradition goes into effect next Tuesday." The most cursory look at American funerals of past times will establish the parallel. Simplicity to the point of starkness, the plain pine box, the laying out of the dead by friends and family who also bore the coffin to the grave — these were the hallmarks of the traditional funeral until the end of the nineteenth century.

Secondly, there is the myth that the American public is only being given what it wants — an opportunity to keep up with the Joneses to the end. "In keeping with our high standard of living, there should be an equally high standard of dying," says the past president of the Funeral Directors of San Francisco. "The cost of a funeral varies according to individual taste and the niceties of living the family has been accustomed to." Actually, choice doesn't enter the picture for the average individual, faced, generally for the first time, with the necessity of buying a product of which he is totally ignorant, at a moment when he is least in a position to quibble. In point of fact the cost of a funeral almost always varies, not "according to individual taste" but according to what the traffic will bear.

Thirdly, there is an assortment of myths based on half-digested psychiatric theories. The importance of the "memory picture" is stressed — meaning the last glimpse of the deceased in open casket, done up with the latest in embalming techniques and finished off with a dusting of make-up. A newer one, impressively authentic-sounding, is the need for "grief therapy," which is beginning to go over big in mortuary circles. A historian of American funeral directing hints at the grief-therapist idea when speaking of the new role of the undertaker — "the dramaturgic role, in which the undertaker becomes a stage manager to create an appropriate atmosphere and to move the funeral party through a drama in which social relationships are stressed and an emotional catharsis or release is provided through ceremony.''

Lastly, a whole new terminology, as ornately shoddy as the satin rayon casket liner, has been invented by the funeral industry to replace the direct and serviceable vocabulary of former times. Undertaker has been supplanted by "funeral director" or "mortician." (Even the classified section of the telephone directory gives recognition to this; in its pages you will find "Undertakers—see Funeral Directors.") Coffins are "caskets"; hearses are "coaches," or "professional cars"; flowers are "floral tributes"; corpses generally are "loved ones," but mortuary etiquette dictates that a specific corpse be referred to by name only—as, "Mr. Jones"; cremated ashes are "cremains." Euphemisms such as "slumber room," "reposing room," and "calcination—the *kindlier* heat" abound in the funeral business.

If the undertaker is the stage manager of the fabulous production that is the modern American funeral, the stellar role is reserved for the occupant of the open casket. The decor, the stagehands, the supporting cast are all arranged for the most advantageous display of the deceased, without which the rest of the paraphernalia would lose its point—*Hamlet* without the Prince of Denmark. It is to this end that a fantastic array of costly merchandise and services is pyramided to dazzle the mourners and facilitate the plunder of the next of kin.

Grief therapy, anyone? But it's going to come high. According to the funeral industry's own figures, the *average* undertaker's bill in 1961 was $708 for casket and "services," to which must be added the cost of a burial vault, flowers, clothing, clergy and musician's honorarium, and cemetery charges. When these costs are added to the undertaker's bill, the total average cost for an adult's funeral is . . . closer to $1,450. . . .

43

Arthur M. Schlesinger, Jr.   The Crisis of American Masculinity

Arthur Meier Schlesinger, Jr., son of the eminent historian, was born in Columbus, Ohio, in 1917 and graduated from Harvard in 1938. He has had a distinguished career as a writer, historian, and public servant—most recently as an adviser to President John F. Kennedy. He is presently Professor of History at the University of the City of New York. He received the Pulitzer prize for history for his Age of Jackson *in 1946. His distinguished list of books also includes* The Age of Roosevelt *(4 volumes, 1957—1961). In the following selection (which originally appeared in* Esquire, *November, 1958) examples of current literature and drama are used to suggest that male and female roles are being increasingly merged in the American household. The consequences, suggests Mr. Schlesinger, is that the male is becoming more and more uncertain about his virility. For related ideas, see Wheelis, Hunt, Von Borch, Cox.*

What has happened to the American male? For a long time, he seemed utterly confident in his manhood, sure of his masculine role in society, easy and definite in his sense of sexual identity. The frontiersmen of James Fenimore Cooper, for example, never had any concern about masculinity; they were men, and it did not occur to them to think twice about it. Even well into the 20th century, the heroes of Dreiser, of Fitzgerald, of Hemingway remain men. But one begins to detect a new theme emerging in some of these authors, especially in Hemingway: the theme of the male hero increasingly preoccupied with proving his virility to himself. And by mid-century, the male role had plainly lost its rugged clarity of outline. Today men are more and more conscious of maleness not as a fact but as a problem. The ways by which American men affirm their masculinity are uncertain and obscure. There are multiplying signs, indeed, that something has gone badly wrong with the American male's conception of himself.

On the most superficial level, the roles of male and female are increasingly merged in the American household. The American man is found as never before as a substitute for wife and mother—changing diapers, wash-

"The Crisis of American Masculinity" by Arthur M. Schlesinger, Jr., from *The Politics of Hope*, 1963, pp. 237–246. Reprinted by permission of the publisher, Houghton Mifflin Company. First published in *Esquire Magazine*.

ing dishes, cooking meals, and performing a whole series of what once were considered female duties. The American woman meanwhile takes over more and more of the big decisions, controlling them indirectly when she cannot do so directly. Outside the home, one sees a similar blurring of function. While men design dresses and brew up cosmetics, women become doctors, lawyers, bank cashiers, and executives. "Women now fill many 'masculine' roles," writes the psychologist Dr. Bruno Bettelheim, "and expect their husbands to assume many of the tasks once reserved for their own sex." Women seem an expanding, aggressive force, seizing new domains like a conquering army, while men, more and more on the defensive, are hardly able to hold their own and gratefully accept assignments from their new rulers. A recent book bears the stark and melancholy title *The Decline of the American Male.*

Some of this evidence, it should be quickly said, has been pushed too far. The willingness of a man to help his wife around the house may as well be evidence of confidence in masculinity as the opposite; such a man obviously does not have to cling to masculine symbols in order to keep demonstrating his maleness to himself. But there is more impressive evidence than the helpful husband that this is an age of sexual ambiguity. It appears no accident, for example, that the changing of sex — the Christine Jorgensen phenomenon — so fascinates our newspaper editors and readers; or that homosexuality, that incarnation of sexual ambiguity, should be enjoying a cultural boom new in our history. Such developments surely express a deeper tension about the problem of sexual identity.

Consider the theater, that faithful mirror of a society's preoccupations. There have been, of course, popular overt inquiries into sexual ambiguities, like *Compulsion* or *Tea and Sympathy.* But in a sense these plays prove the case too easily. Let us take rather two uncommonly successful plays by the most discussed young playwrights of the United States and Great Britain — Tennessee Williams' *Cat on a Hot Tin Roof* and John Osborne's *Look Back in Anger.* Both deal with the young male in a singular state of confusion and desperation. In *Cat on a Hot Tin Roof,* Brick Pollitt, the professional football player, refuses to sleep with his wife because of guilty memories of his relations with a dead teammate. In *Look Back in Anger,* Jimmy Porter, the embittered young intellectual who can sustain a relationship with his wife only by pretending they are furry animals together, explodes with hatred of women and finds his moments of happiness roughhousing around the stage with a male pal.

Brick Pollitt and Jimmy Porter are all too characteristic modern heroes. They are, in a sense, castrated; one is stymied by fear of homosexuality, the other is an unconscious homosexual. Neither is capable of dealing with the woman in his life: Brick surrenders to a strong woman, Jimmy destroys a weak one. Both reject the normal female desire for full and reciprocal love as an unconscionable demand and an intolerable burden. Now not many American males have been reduced to quite the Pollitt-Porter condition. Still the intentness with which audiences have watched these plays suggests that exposed nerves are being plucked — that the Pollitt-Porter dilemma expresses in vivid and heightened form something that many spectators themselves feel or fear.

Or consider the movies. In some ways, the most brilliant and influential American film since the war is *High Noon*. That remarkable movie, which invested the Western with the classic economy of myth, can be viewed in several ways: as an existentialist drama, for example, or as a parable of McCarthyism. It can also be viewed as a mordant comment on the effort of the American woman to emasculate the American man. The sheriff plainly did not suffer from Brick Pollitt's disease. But a large part of the story dealt with the attempt of his girl to persuade him not to use force — to deny him the use of his pistol. The pistol is an obvious masculine symbol, and, in the end, it was the girl herself, in the modern American manner, who used the pistol and killed the villain. (In this connection, one can pause and note why the Gary Coopers, Cary Grants, Clark Gables, and Spencer Tracys continue to play romantic leads opposite girls young enough to be their daughters; it is obviously because so few of the younger male stars can project a convincing sense of masculinity.)

Psychoanalysis backs up the theater and the movies in emphasizing the obsession of the American male with his manhood. "Every psychoanalyst knows," writes one of them, "how many emotional difficulties are due to those fears and insecurities of neurotic men who are unconsciously doubting their masculinity." "In our civilization," Dr. Theodor Reik says, "men are afraid that they will not be men enough." Reik adds significantly: "And women are afraid that they might be considered only women." Why is it that women worry, not over whether they can fill the feminine role, but whether filling that role is enough, while men worry whether they can fill the masculine role at all? How to account for this rising tide of male anxiety? What has unmanned the American man?

There is currently a fashionable answer to this question. Male anxiety, many observers have declared, is simply the result of female aggression: what has unmanned the American man is the American woman. The present male confusion and desperation, it is contended, are the inevitable consequence of the threatened feminization of American society. The victory of women is the culmination of a long process of masculine retreat, beginning when Puritanism made men feel guilty about sex and the frontier gave women the added value of scarcity. Fleeing from the reality of femininity, the American man, while denying the American woman juridical equality, transformed her into an ideal of remote and transcendent purity with overriding authority over the family, the home, the school, and culture. This habit of obeisance left the male psychologically disarmed and vulnerable when the goddess stepped off the pedestal and demanded in addition equal economic, political, and legal rights. In the last part of the 19th century, women won their battle for equality. They gained the right of entry into one occupation after another previously reserved for males. Today they hold the key positions of personal power in our society and use this power relentlessly to consolidate their mastery. As mothers, they undermine masculinity through the use of love as a technique of reward and punishment. As teachers, they prepare male children for their role of submission in an increasingly feminine world. As wives, they complete the work of subjugation. Their strategy of conquest is deliberately to emasculate men — to turn them into Brick Pollitts and Jimmy Porters.

Or so a standard indictment runs; and no doubt there is something in it. American women have unquestionably gained through the years a place in our society which American men have not been psychologically prepared to accept. Whether because of Puritanism or the frontier, there has been something immature in the traditional American male attitude toward women — a sense of alarm at times amounting to panic. Almost none of the classic American novels, for example, presents the theme of mature and passionate love. Our 19th-century novelists saw women either as unassailable virgins or abandoned temptresses — never simply as women. One looks in vain through *Moby Dick* and *The Adventures of Huckleberry Finn,* through Cooper and Poe and Whitman, for an adult portrayal of relations between men and women. "Where," Leslie Fiedler has asked, "is the American *Madame Bovary, Anna Karenina, Wuthering Heights,* or *Vanity Fair?"*

Yet the implication of the argument that the American man has been unmanned by the emancipation of the American woman is that the American man was incapable of growing up. For the 19th-century sense of masculinity was based on the psychological idealization and the legal subjection of women; masculinity so spuriously derived could never — and should never — have endured. The male had to learn to live at some point with the free and equal female. Current attempts to blame "the decline of the American male" on the aggressiveness of the American female amount to a confession that, under conditions of free competition, the female was bound to win. Simple observation refutes this supposition. In a world of equal rights, some women rise; so too do some men; and no pat generalization is possible about the sexual future of society. Women have gained power in certain ways; in others, they have made little progress. It is safe to predict, for example, that we will have a Roman Catholic, perhaps even a Jew, for President before we have a woman. Those amiable prophets of an impending American matriarchy (all men, by the way) are too pessimistic.

Something more fundamental is involved in the unmanning of American men than simply the onward rush of American women. Why is the American man so unsure today about his masculine identity? The basic answer to this is plainly because he is so unsure about his identity in general. Nothing is harder in the whole human condition than to achieve a full sense of identity—than to know who you are, where you are going, and what you mean to live and die for. From the most primitive myths to the most contemporary novels—from Oedipus making the horrified discovery that he had married his mother, to Leopold Bloom and Stephen Dedalus searching their souls in Joyce's Dublin and the haunted characters of Kafka trying to make desperate sense out of an incomprehensible universe—the search for identity has been the most compelling human problem. That search has always been ridden with trouble and terror. And it can be plausibly argued that the conditions of modern life make the quest for identity more difficult than it has ever been before.

The pre-democratic world was characteristically a world of status in which people were provided with ready-made identities. But modern Western society—free, equalitarian, democratic—has swept away all the old niches in which people for so many centuries found safe refuge. Only a few people at any time in human history have enjoyed the challenge of "making" themselves; most have fled from the unendurable burden of freedom into the womblike security of the group. The new age of social mobility may be fine for those strong enough to discover and develop their own roles. But for the timid and the frightened, who constitute the majority in any age, the great vacant spaces of equalitarian society can become a nightmare filled with nameless horrors. Thus mass democracy, in the very act of offering the individual new freedom and opportunity, offers new moral authority to the group and thereby sets off a new assault on individual identity. Over a century ago Alexis de Tocqueville, the perceptive Frenchman who ruminated on the contradictions of equality as he toured the United States in the 1830's, pointed to the "tyranny of the majority" as a central problem of democracy. John Stuart Mill, lamenting the decline of individualism in Great Britain, wrote: "That so few now dare to be eccentric marks the chief danger of the time." How much greater that danger seems a century later!

For our own time has aggravated the assault on identity by adding economic and technological pressures to the political and social pressures of the 19th century. Modern science has brought about the growing centralization of the economy. We work and think and live and even dream in larger and larger units. William H. Whyte, Jr., has described the rise of "the organization man," working by day in immense business concerns, sleeping by night in immense suburban developments, deriving his fantasy life from mass-produced entertainments, spending his existence not as an individual but as a member of a group and coming in the end to feel guilty and lost when he deviates from his fellows. Adjustment rather than achievement becomes the social ideal. Men no longer fulfill an inner sense of what they *must* be; indeed, with the cult of the group, that inner sense itself begins to evaporate. Identity consists not of self-realization but of smooth absorption into the group. Nor is this just a matter of passive acquiescence. The group is aggressive, imperialistic, even vengeful, forever developing new weapons with which to overwhelm and crush the recalcitrant individual. Not content with disciplining the conscious mind, the group today is even experimenting with means of violating the subconscious. The subliminal invasion represents the climax of the assault on individual identity.

It may seem a long way from the loss of the sense of self to the question of masculinity. But if people do not know *who* they are, it is hardly surprising that they are no longer sure what sex they are. Nigel Dennis' exuberant novel *Cards of Identity* consists of a series of brilliant variations on the quest for identity in contemporary life. It reaches one of its climaxes in the tale of a person who was brought up by enlightened parents to believe that there was no such thing as pure male or female—everyone had elements of both—and who accepted this proposition so rigorously that he (she) could not decide what his (her) own sex was. "In what identity do you intend to face the future?" someone asks. "It seems that nowadays," comes the plaintive reply, "one must choose between being a woman who behaves like a man, and a man who behaves like a woman. In short, I must choose to be one in order to behave like the other." If most of us have not yet quite reached that condition of sexual chaos, yet the loss of a sense of identity is obviously a fundamental step in the decay of masculinity. And the gratification with which some American males contemplate their own decline should not obscure the fact that women, for all their recent legal and economic triumphs, are suffering from a loss of identity too. It is not accidental that the authors of one recent book described modern woman as the "lost sex."

If this is true, then the key to the recovery of masculinity does not lie in any wistful hope of humiliating the aggressive female and restoring the old masculine supremacy. Masculine supremacy, like white supremacy, was the neurosis of an immature society. It is good for men as well as for women that women have been set free. In any case, the process is irreversible; that particular genie can never be put back into the bottle. The key to the recovery of masculinity lies rather in the problem of identity. When a person begins to find out *who* he is, he is likely to find out rather soon what sex he is.

For men to become men again, in short, their first task is to recover a sense of individual spontaneity. And to do this a man must visualize himself as an individual apart from the group, whatever it is, which defines his values and commands his loyalty. There is no reason to suppose that the group is always wrong: to oppose the group automatically is nearly as conformist as to surrender to it automatically. But there is every necessity to recognize that the group is one thing and the individual—oneself—is another. One of the most sinister of present-day doctrines is that of *togetherness*. The recovery of identity means, first of all, a new belief in apartness. It means a determination to resist the overpowering conspiracy of blandness, which seeks to conceal all tension and conflict in American life under a blanket of locker-room affability. And the rebirth of spontaneity depends, at bottom, on changes of attitude *within* people—changes which can perhaps be described, without undue solemnity, as moral changes. These changes will no doubt come about in as many ways as there are individuals involved. But there are some general suggestions that can be made about the techniques of liberation. I should like to mention three such techniques: satire, art, and politics.

Satire means essentially the belief that nothing is sacred—that there is no person or institution or idea which cannot but benefit from the exposure of comedy. Our nation in the past has reveled in satire; it is, after all, the nation of Abraham Lincoln, of Mark Twain, of Finley Peter Dunne, of H. L. Mencken, of Ring Lardner. Indeed, the whole spirit of democracy is that of satire; as Montaigne succinctly summed up the democratic faith: "Sit he on never so high a throne, a man still sits on his own bottom." Yet today American society can only be described as a pompous society, at least in its official manifestations. Early in 1958 Mort Sahl, the night-club comedian, made headlines in New York because he dared make a joke about J. Edgar Hoover! It was not an especially good joke, but the fact that he made it at all was an encouraging sign. One begins to feel that the American people can only stand so much reverence—that in the end our native skepticism will break through, sweep aside the stuffed shirts and the stuffed heads and insist that platitudes are platitudinous and the great are made, among other things, to be laughed at. Irony is good for our rulers; and it is even better for ourselves because it is a means of dissolving the pomposity of society and giving the individual a chance to emerge.

If irony is one source of spontaneity, art is another. Very little can so refresh our vision and develop our values as the liberating experience of art. The mass media have cast a spell on us: the popular addiction to prefabricated emotional cliches threatens to erode our capacity for fresh and direct aesthetic experience. Individual identity vanishes in the welter of machine-made reactions. But thoughtful exposure to music, to painting, to poetry, to the beauties of nature, can do much to restore the inwardness, and thereby the identity, of man. There is thus great hope in the immense cultural underground of our age—the paper-bound books, the long-playing records, the drama societies, the art festivals, the new interest in painting and sculpture. All this represents a disdain for existing values and goals, a reaching out for something more exacting and more personal, an intensified questing for identity.

And politics in a true sense can be a means of liberation—not the banal politics of rhetoric and self-congratulation, which aims at burying all real issues under a mass of piety and platitude; but the politics of responsibility, which tries to define the real issues and present them to the people for decision. Our national politics have become boring in recent years because our leaders have offered neither candid and clear-cut formulations of the problems nor the facts necessary for intelligent choice. A virile political life will be definite and hard-hitting, respecting debate and dissent, seeking clarity and decision.

As the American male develops himself by developing his comic sense, his aesthetic sense, and his moral and political sense, the lineaments of personality will at last begin to emerge. The achievement of identity, the conquest of a sense of self—these will do infinitely more to restore American masculinity than all the hormones in the test tubes of our scientists. "Whoso would be a *man*," said Emerson, "must be a nonconformist"; and, if it is the present writer who adds the italics, nonetheless one feels that no injustice is done to Emerson's intention. How can masculinity, femininity, or anything else survive in a homogenized society, which seeks steadily and benignly to eradicate all differences between the individuals who compose it? If we want to have *men* again in our theaters and our films and our novels—not to speak of in our classrooms, our business offices, and our homes—we must first have a society which encourages each of its members to have a distinct identity.

**An ethnically
heterogeneous establishment**

E. Digby Baltzell   **The Protestant Establishment**   **44**

E. Digby Baltzell, a former naval officer in World War II, is a graduate of the University of Pennsylvania who received his Ph.D. from Columbia University. He is currently an associate professor of sociology at the University of Pennsylvania. In the following selection, the author discusses the

end of the domination of American society by the White Anglo-Saxon Pro-
testants. He views the election of John F. Kennedy to the Presidency as
the end of WASP domination, at least in the Democratic Party. For re-
lated ideas, see Fuchs, Herberg, Glazer and Moynihan, Toynbee, Warner,
Gabriel, Cox.

There was every reason to believe that the Eisenhower victory in 1952 was needed to restore a sense of responsibility and power within the Republican Party and a measure of tranquillity among the people as a whole. At the same time, however, the members of the intellectual community, who had been more enthusiastic about Adlai Stevenson than about any other Presidential candidate in the twentieth century with the possible exception of Woodrow Wilson, were deeply depressed. There were exceptions, among them Walter Lippman who, as has been pointed out above, thought the country needed a Republican victory, especially in order to rid itself of McCarthyism. "If Eisenhower had lost in 1952," he said when interviewed in 1961, "the Republicans would have followed McCarthy. After being out of power for 20 years, they would have gone mad."

The two Republican terms in the White House have usually been attributed less to the party than to the charismatic leadership of President Eisenhower and his ability to appeal to all the people. They were also due, I think, to a deep yearning in this country, as well as in many other Western democracies, for a return to conservatism. Witness, for instance, the postwar leadership of such tory conservatives as Macmillan, deGaulle and Adenauer in Europe. The Republican Party, however, while it represents a combined establishment of business as well as a majority of the members of the old-stock upper class, still has not been able, like the Tories in England for instance, to establish itself as the majority party, in spite of the conservative mood of the people.

In the meantime, the Democrats are still the established party politically. By 1960, when they returned to power under the leadership of John F. Kennedy, the Democrats had come to represent a political tradition which had been in the process of developing in this country in the course of almost three decades, and especially since the re-election of Franklin Roosevelt in 1936 (and this tradition stretched even farther back as a minority movement under the leadership of Theodore Roosevelt and Woodrow Wilson). Adlai Stevenson, one of the more philosophically mature conservatives to come upon the American political scene in this century, described this development as follows, in 1952:

> The strange alchemy of this has somehow converted the Democrats into
> the truly conservative party of this country—the party dedicated to con-

From *The Protestant Establishment*, pp. 294–301, by E. Digby Baltzell. © Copyright 1964 by E. Digby Baltzell. Reprinted by permission of Random House, Inc.

serving all that is best, and building solidly and safely on these foundations. The Republicans, by contrast, are behaving like the radical party
— the party of the reckless and the embittered, bent on dismantling institutions which have been built solidly into our social fabric. . . . Our social
security system and our Democratic party's sponsorship of the social
reforms and advances of the past two decades [are] conservatism at its
best. Certainly there could be nothing more conservative than to change
when change is due, to reduce tensions and wants by wise changes, rather
than to stand pat stubbornly, until like King Canute we are engulfed by
relentless forces that will always go too far.

John F. Kennedy's victory in 1960 represented a return to power of an
essentially conserving political tradition. The fighting faiths of one generation have a way of becoming conservative assumptions in the next. A
decade after Adlai Stevenson made the statement quoted above, Walter
Lippmann wrote, in the New York *Herald Tribune,* as follows: "Though
Mr. Kennedy is a progressive and a liberal, he is also a profound conservative, and only the befuddled theorists find that strange and hard to
understand." In other words, President Kennedy stood for both continuity
and change, the essence of any dynamic conservatism. The symbolic significance of his being sent to the White House by the American people in
the 1960's has already been discussed in an earlier chapter. Several things,
however, should be emphasized here.

In the first place, the fact that President Kennedy was the first non-
Protestant to enter the White House in our history was of great importance. It was of even more importance that the Kennedy administration
represented both the second generation of Democratic majority-party rule
as well as the first generation of American political leadership to have
grown up entirely in the twentieth century. Thus President Eisenhower
calmly reigned as representative of a generation still dominated by the
Protestant establishment, which was slowly passing from the stage, while
President Kennedy represented a younger and more heterogeneous generation of American political leaders who were just coming to power (within
both political parties, of course). McCarthyism, for example, was surely
oriented toward exposing the past rather than planning for the future. In
many ways McCarthy was the product of America's last innocent generation's fratricidal fight over its adherence to already-lost illusions. It was
no wonder, in an era which witnessed the Rosenberg, Oppenheimer and
Hiss cases, the Yalta re-evaluations and the Korean and Cold wars, that
cries of conspiracy and treason filled the air and opened wide the door to
one form or another of McCarthyism. Perhaps Eisenhower was needed to
calm the hysteria of an old, tired and disillusioned generation of leaders
who would not, and perhaps could not, face the future and were consequently engaged in a schizophrenic conflict over their pasts. Indeed it was
no accident that the affluent fifties began with the purposeless publicity-

seeking of McCarthy and ended with a nation-wide debate, in the pages of the Luce publications as well as in formal hearings in the Congress, over our lack of a sense of National Purpose. It will be no easy task, but perhaps the generational change in leadership which marked the election of 1960 will eventually produce a renewed sense of purpose in America.

The Two Democratic Generations

The new generation of Democrats differed in almost every way from the generation of Franklin Roosevelt. For the two generations came to maturity in very different worlds. Roosevelt's generation was born in an age of innocence and security at the turn of the century, when an Anglo-Saxon establishment ruled the nation and the world; they went away to college, where they naturally assumed the leadership due their social position (the "Gold Coast" ruled Harvard); they went away to training camps like Plattsburgh, where Ivy League gentlemen prepared to be officers in the last idealistic war to end all wars; they turned to the Democratic Party under Wilson, especially after the party of their fathers deserted the ideals for which they had fought; having discovered sex and Freud, they went on an irresponsible spree in the twenties; and finally, armed with the easy optimism of John Dewey if not Marxism, they led a brilliant and idealistic reform movement against poverty and economic insecurity at home and then produced the unconditional surrender of "all the evil forces in the outside world" in the Second War, only to be faced with an era of reaction in the late forties and fifties, often articulately led by conservative ex-New Dealers, as well as ex-Marxists and ex-Communists of the more extreme Right.

The Democrats of the second generation were very different men, bred in a very different world. Coming to maturity in an urban, Augustan age, marked by fierce, and often cynically manipulative, struggles for power, they were far removed from rural and republican America where amateur aristocrats, from Washington and Jefferson to the two Roosevelts, were called, like Cincinnatus of republican Rome, to serve the nation in time of need. Forced to struggle for power like the Caesars of old, they tended to be realists rather than idealists, professionals rather than gentlemen-amateurs. They were born during the war which spelled the beginning of the end of the Pax Britannica and they came to maturity during the Depression years, when established authority was rapidly retreating before the fanatic ideologists of fascism and communism abroad and the New Deal and Liberty League at home; they went to college, where leadership was awarded to the swift rather than the polite, and where the "Gold Coast" was rapidly vanishing or being relegated to an inconspicuous and minor role; and, above all, they went to war with no illusions, and were trained as officers in a highly competitive atmosphere of talented men from diverse ethnic backgrounds (the aviators of this generation were the product of the most aristocratic, rather than castelike, selective process this nation, or the world, had ever witnessed). They came back from all parts of a war-torn world to rise to the top in a postwar era in which all illusions, if not ideals, were surely dying. Thus their spiritual and intellectual mood, whether they were gentiles or Jews, was far closer to the neo-orthodox Christianity of Reinhold Niebuhr (or his spiritual kin, Martin Buber, the existentialist Jew) than to the optimistic and naturalistic scientism of John Dewey. Perhaps Arthur M. Schlesinger, Jr., the Court Philosopher of the Kennedy Administration, has best expressed the conservative mood of his generation in the following paragraph:

> But the Christian millennium calls for a catastrophic change in human nature. Let us not sentimentalize the millennium by believing we can attain it through scientific discovery or through the revision of our economic system. We must grow up now and forsake the millennial dream. . . . Given human imperfection, society will continue imperfect. Problems will always torment us, because all important problems are insoluble: that is why they are important. The good comes from the continuing struggle to try and solve them, not from the vain hope of their solution.

And, ironically enough, this second generation of philosophically conservative realists, struggling to defend our traditional freedoms in a cold war which will surely last for more than a generation, were opposed by a radicalism on the Right which was crying out for unconditional surrender, in the utopian style of Rooseveltian idealism.

But perhaps the most important difference between the two generations was the fact that, while the Protestant patricians of Roosevelt's generation sincerely believed in assimilating the members of minority groups into the main stream of American economic life and leadership, they were at the same time incapable of accepting the members of minority groups as their social equals. Although both Franklin and Eleanor Roosevelt sincerely wanted to complete the melting pot, they were never really at ease socially with the Farleys, the Flynns or the Al Smiths. It was not so much a matter of ethnic snobbery, as it was that their backgrounds and education were so divergent. The Roosevelts were, of course, very close to their Dutchess County neighbors, the Morgenthaus, who were after all of the old-stock and German generation within the Jewish community. Yet on the whole, there was just a touch of the condescending Lady Bountiful in Eleanor Roosevelt, which was entirely in accord with her Victorian background. Thus Ambassador Kennedy, who always deeply resented being referred to as an "Irish American," once expressed his feelings toward Mrs. Roosevelt in the following blunt statement to the press: "She bothered us more on our jobs in Washington to take care of the poor little nobodies than all the rest of the people down there put together. She's always sending me a note to have some little Susie Glotz to tea at the Embassy." And although Franklin Roosevelt was continually amused by the wit and brilliance of Kennedy's mind, in the last analysis he preferred to relax with what Jim Farley, with a touch of resentment, once called the "Hasty Pudding Cabinet" as he watched them sail away for a brief vacation with the President on Vincent Astor's yacht.

What one generation begins is often left to the next generation to complete. The New Deal revolution marked the beginning of both an ethnic democracy and an ethnic *elite* in this country. The Kennedy Administration brought to Washington a talented and extremely ambitious group of leaders and their families who represented the beginning of an ethnically heterogeneous *establishment*. The men who surrounded Kennedy on the New Frontier, as has been pointed out in an earlier chapter, were surely social peers of great ethnic diversity. There was, moreover, no old-stock dominance or ethnic condescension. The minority-group members among them, a generation or more removed from Roosevelt's ethnic associates, shared a common educational background at the best universities (most often Harvard) with their friends of the old-stock establishment.

Perhaps of even greater importance, I think, was the fact of their having shared a common war experience. Most of them were officers in hierarchical organizations which were, at the same time, led by the most ethnically heterogeneous elite in the nation's history. Indeed, it is hard to believe that shallow ethnic prejudices could have survived in the minds of men, whether from Back Bay, Park Avenue, Brooklyn or the Bronx, who had once shared the risks and dangers of war together in the intimate atmospheres of the ward room on a carrier in the South Pacific, or in the officers' mess of a bomber squadron in Britain. In fact, I visualized the possibility of an ethnically mixed establishment, which underlies the theory of American leadership developed in this book, during my own experiences in the ward rooms and officers' clubs of the South Pacific. At any rate, the American ideal of equality of opportunity in a hierarchically organized social structure had never been so nearly realized as in the selection of reserve officers who led our armed forces during the Second World War. It is hard to believe that down in Washington on the New Frontier the accidents of birth meant much to leaders of men who had shared a common war experience, a common educational background and common ideals about our democracy. As an artist friend — son of a clergyman who was Dean of the Princeton Chapel for many years, classmate of John F. Kennedy at an Officers' Candidate School in the Navy, and a veteran of over twenty months of the Pacific war — said to me some six months before the President's assassination: "I love everything about the New Frontier, and whatever Kennedy does, whether I agree or not, seems part of me and of my generation."

My beautiful black
brothers and sisters

The Autobiography of Malcolm X

45

*A veritable flood of literature on civil rights and the Negro, seen as "issues"
or as "problems," threatens to overwhelm the reader. We use a selection
from* The Autobiography of Malcolm X *to show the Negro as a "creation"
of White America. This selection deals with the white American's robbery
of the Negro's dignity and pride. The attempt to regain that pride and
dignity is the most powerful moving force in the Negro community today.
The account by Malcolm X of his self-debasement is, therefore, entirely
appropriate as an example of what Americans have "created." At the same
time, it serves as an appropriate introduction to any understanding of the
militancy of young Negroes today.*

*Malcolm X, born Malcolm Little in Omaha, Nebraska, in 1926 was—
until shortly before his murder in 1965—the most celebrated apostle of
Elijah Muhammed, leader of the Black Muslim movement in the United
States. He broke with the Muslims in 1964 and founded The Organization
of Afro-American Unity. After what Nat Hentoff has called "a stunning
journey to Mecca," Malcolm discovered "that white was not a color but
an attribute." We believe that Malcolm X was one of those special and
rare persons in history who never stopped learning and growing. And because his* Autobiography *is a reflection of that fact, we believe it is a classic American document. For related ideas see, Wheelis, Gabriel, Baltzell,
Glazer and Moynihan, Slaikeu.*

Shorty soon decided that my hair was finally long enough to be conked.
He had promised to school me in how to beat the barbershops' three- and
four-dollar price by making up congolene, and then conking ourselves.

I took the little list of ingredients he had printed out for me, and went
to a grocery store, where I got a can of Red Devil lye, two eggs, and two
medium-sized white potatoes. Then at a drugstore near the poolroom, I
asked for a large jar of vaseline, a large bar of soap, a large-toothed comb
and a fine-toothed comb, one of those rubber hoses with a metal spray-

head, a rubber apron and a pair of gloves.

"Going to lay on that first conk?" the drugstore man asked me. I proudly told him, grinning, "Right!"

Shorty paid six dollars a week for a room in his cousin's shabby apartment. His cousin wasn't at home. "It's like the pad's mine, he spends so much time with his woman," Shorty said. "Now, you watch me—"

He peeled the potatoes and thin-sliced them into a quart-sized Mason fruit jar, then started stirring them with a wooden spoon as he gradually poured in a little over half the can of lye. "Never use a metal spoon; the lye will turn it black," he told me.

A jelly-like, starchy-looking glop resulted from the lye and potatoes, and Shorty broke in the two eggs, stirring real fast—his own conk and dark face bent down close. The congolene turned pale-yellowish. "Feel the jar," Shorty said. I cupped my hand against the outside, and snatched it away. "Damn right, it's hot, that's the lye," he said. "So you know it's going to burn when I comb it in—it burns *bad*. But the longer you can stand it, the straighter the hair."

He made me sit down, and he tied the string of the new rubber apron tightly around my neck, and combed up my bush of hair. Then, from the big vaseline jar, he took a handful and massaged it hard all through my hair and into the scalp. He also thickly vaselined my neck, ears and forehead. "When I get to washing out your head, be sure to tell me anywhere you feel any little stinging," Shorty warned me, washing his hands, then pulling on the rubber gloves, and tying on his own rubber apron. "You always got to remember that any congolene left in burns a sore into your head."

The congolene just felt warm when Shorty started combing it in. But then my head caught fire.

I gritted my teeth and tried to pull the sides of the kitchen table together. The comb felt as if it was raking my skin off.

My eyes watered, my nose was running. I couldn't stand it any longer; I bolted to the washbasin. I was cursing Shorty with every name I could think of when he got the spray going and started soap-lathering my head.

He lathered and spray-rinsed, lathered and spray-rinsed, maybe ten or twelve times, each time gradually closing the hot-water faucet, until the rinse was cold, and that helped some.

"You feel any stinging spots?"

"No," I managed to say. My knees were trembling.

"Sit back down, then, I think we got it all out okay."

The flame came back as Shorty, with a thick towel, started drying my head, rubbing hard. *"Easy* man *easy!"* I kept shouting.

"The first time's always worst. You get used to it better before long. You took it real good, homeboy. You got a good conk."

When Shorty let me stand up and see in the mirror, my hair hung down in limp, damp strings. My scalp still flamed, but not as badly; I could bear it. He draped the towel around my shoulders, over my rubber apron, and began again vaselining my hair.

I could feel him combing, straight back, first the big comb, then the fine-toothed one.

Then, he was using a razor, very delicately, on the back of my neck. Then, finally, shaping the sideburns.

My first view in the mirror blotted out the hurting. I'd seen some pretty conks, but when it's the first time, on your *own* head, the transformation, after the lifetime of kinks, is staggering.

The mirror reflected Shorty behind me. We both were grinning and sweating. And on top of my head was this thick, smooth sheen of shining red hair—real red—as straight as any white man's.

How ridiculous I was! Stupid enough to stand there simply lost in admiration of my hair now looking "white," reflected in the mirror in Shorty's room. I vowed that I'd never again be without a conk, and I never was for many years.

This was my first really big step toward self-degradation: when I endured all of that pain, literally burning my flesh with lye, in order to cook my natural hair until it was limp, to have it look like a white man's hair. I had joined that multitude of Negro men and women in America who are brainwashed into believing that the black people are "inferior"—and white people "superior"—that they will even violate and mutilate their God-created bodies to try to look "pretty" by white standards. . . .

Soon after that, Minister Lemuel Hassan urged me to address the brothers and sisters with an extemporaneous lecture. I was uncertain, and hesitant—but at least I had debated in prison, and I tried my best. (Of course, I can't remember exactly what I said, but I do know that in my beginning efforts my favorite subject was Christianity and the horrors of slavery, where I felt well-equipped from so much reading in prison.)

"My brothers and sisters, our white slavemaster's Christian religion has taught us black people here in the wilderness of North America that we will sprout wings when we die and fly up into the sky where God will have for us a special place called heaven. This is white man's Christian religion used to *brainwash* us black people! We have *accepted* it! We have *embraced* it! We have *believed* it! We have *practiced* it! And while we are doing all of that, for himself, this blue-eyed devil has *twisted* his Christianity, to keep his *foot* on our backs . . . to keep our eyes fixed on the pie in the sky and heaven in the hereafter . . . while *he* enjoys *his* heaven right *here* . . . on *this earth* . . . in *this life*."

Today when thousands of Muslims and others have been audiences out before me, when audiences of millions have been beyond radio and television microphones, I'm sure I rarely feel as much electricity as was then generated in me by the upturned faces of those seventy-five or a hundred Muslims, plus other curious visitors, sitting there in our storefront temple with the squealing of pigs filtering in from the slaughterhouse just outside.

In the summer of 1953—all praise is due to Allah—I was named Detroit Temple Number One's Assistant Minister.

Every day after work, I walked, "fishing" for potential converts in the Detroit black ghetto. I saw the African features of my black brothers and sisters whom the devilish white man had brainwashed. I saw the hair as mine had been for years, conked by cooking it with lye until it lay limp, looking straight like the white man's hair. Time and again Mr. Muhammad's teachings were rebuffed and even ridiculed. . . . "Aw, man, get out of my face, you niggers are crazy!" My head would reel sometimes, with mingled anger and pity for my poor blind black brothers. I couldn't wait for the next time our Minister Lemuel Hassan would let me speak: "We didn't land on Plymouth Rock, my brothers and sisters—Plymouth Rock landed on *us!*" . . . "Give *all* you can to help Messenger Elijah Muhammad's independence program for the black man! . . . This white man always has controlled us black people by keeping us running to him begging, 'Please, lawdy, please, Mr. White Man, boss, would you push me off another crumb down from your table that's sagging with riches. . . .'

". . . my *beautiful,* black brothers and sisters! And when we say 'black,' we mean everything not white, brothers and sisters! Because *look* at your skins! We're all black to the white man, but we're a thousand and one different colors. Turn around, *look* at each other! What shade of black African polluted by devil white man are you? You see me—well, in the streets they used to call me Detroit Red. Yes! Yes, that raping, red-headed devil was my *grandfather!* That close, yes! My *mother's* father! She didn't like to speak of it, can you blame her? She said she never laid eyes on him! She was *glad* for that! I'm *glad* for her! If I could drain away *his* blood that pollutes *my* body, and pollutes *my* complexion, I'd do it! Because I hate every drop of the rapist's blood that's in me!

"And it's not just me, it's *all* of us! During slavery, *think* of it, it was a *rare* one of our black grandmothers, our great-grandmothers and our great-great-grandmothers who escaped the white rapist slavemaster. That rapist slavemaster who emasculated the black man . . . with threats, with fear . . . until even today the black man lives with fear of the white man in his heart! Lives even today still under the heel of the white man!

"*Think* of it—think of that black slave man filled with fear and dread, hearing the screams of his wife, his mother, his daughter being *taken*—in the barn, the kitchen, in the bushes! *Think* of it, my dear brothers and sisters! *Think* of hearing wives, mothers, daughters, being *raped!* And you were too filled with *fear* of the rapist to do anything about it! And his vicious, animal attacks' offspring, this white man named things like 'mulatto' and 'quadroon' and 'octoroon' and all those other things that he has called us—you and me—when he is not calling us *'nigger'!*

"Turn around and look at each other, brothers and sisters, and *think* of this! You and me, polluted all these colors—and this devil has the arrogance and the gall to think we, his victims, should *love* him!"

I would become so choked up that sometimes I would walk in the streets until late into the night. Sometimes I would speak to no one for hours, thinking to myself about what the white man had done to our poor people here in America. . . .

Every time I spoke at our Temple One, my voice would still be hoarse from the last time. My throat took a long time to get into condition.

"Do you know *why* the white man really hates you? It's because every time he sees your face, he sees a mirror of his crime—and his guilty conscience can't bear to face it!

"Every white man in America, when he looks into a black man's eyes, should fall to his knees and say 'I'm sorry, I'm sorry—my kind has committed history's greatest crime against your kind; will you give me the chance to atone?' But do you brothers and sisters expect any white man to do that? *No, you know* better! And why won't he do it? Because he *can't* do it! The white man was *created* a devil, to bring chaos upon this earth. . . ."

In late 1959, the television program was aired. "The Hate That Hate Produced"—the title—was edited tightly into a kaleidoscope of "shocker" images . . . Mr. Muhammad, me, and others speaking . . . strong-looking, set-faced black men, our Fruit of Islam . . . white-scarved, white gowned Muslim sisters of all ages . . . Muslims in our restaurants, and other businesses . . . Muslims and other black people entering and leaving our mosques. . . .

Every phrase was edited to increase the shock mood. As the producers intended, I think people sat just about limp when the program went off.

In a way, the public reaction was like what happened back in the 1930's when Orson Welles frightened America with a radio program describing, as though it was actually happening, an invasion by "men from Mars."

No one now jumped from any windows, but in New York City there was an instant avalanche of public reaction. It's my personal opinion that the "Hate . . . Hate . . ." title was primarily responsible for the reaction. Hundreds of thousands of New Yorkers, black and white, were exclaiming "Did you hear it? Did you see it? Preaching *hate* of white people!"

Here was one of the white man's most characteristic behavior patterns—where black men are concerned. He loves himself so much that he is startled if he discovers that his victims don't share his vainglorious self-opinion. In America for centuries it had been just fine as long as the victimized, brutalized and exploited black people had been grinning and begging and "Yessa, Massa" and Uncle Tomming. But now, things were different. First came the white newspapers—feature writers and columnists: "Alarming" . . . "hate-messengers" . . . "threat to the good relations between the races" . . . "black segregationists" . . . "black supremacists," and the like.

And the newspapers' ink wasn't dry before the big national weekly news magazines started: "Hate-teachers" . . . "violence-seekers" . . . "black racists" . . . "black fascists" . . . "anti-Christian" . . . "possibly Communist-inspired. . . ."

It rolled out of the presses of the biggest devil in the history of mankind. And then the aroused white man made his next move.

Since slavery, the American white man has always kept some handpicked Negroes who fared much better than the black masses suffering and slaving out in the hot fields. The white man had these "house" and "yard" Negroes for his special servants. He threw them more crumbs from his rich table, he even let them eat in his kitchen. He knew that he could always count on them to keep "good massa" happy in his self-image of being so "good" and "righteous." "Good massa" always heard just what he wanted to hear from these "house" and "yard" blacks. "You're such a good, *fine* massa!" Or, "Oh, massa, those old black nigger fieldhands out there, they're happy just like they are; why, massa, they're not intelligent enough for you to try and do any better for them, massa—"

Well, slavery time's "house" and "yard" Negroes had become more sophisticated, that was all. When now the white man picked up his telephone and dialed his "house" and "yard" Negroes—why, he didn't even need to instruct the trained black puppets. They had seen the television program; had read the newspapers. They were already composing their lines. They knew what to do.

I'm not going to call any names. But if you make a list of the biggest Negro "leaders," so-called, in 1960, then you've named the ones who began to attack us "field" Negroes who were sounding *insane,* talking that way about "good massa."

"By no means do these Muslims represent the Negro masses—" That was the first worry, to reassure "good massa" that he had no reason to be concerned about his fieldhands in the ghettoes. "An irresponsible hate cult" . . . "an unfortunate Negro image, just when the racial picture is improving—"

They were stumbling over each other to get quoted. "A deplorable reverse-racism" . . . "Ridiculous pretenders to the ancient Islamic doctrine" . . . "Heretic anti-Christianity—"

The telephone in our then small Temple Seven restaurant nearly jumped off the wall. I had a receiver against my ear five hours a day. I was lis-

tening, and jotting in my notebook, as press, radio, and television people
called, all of them wanting the Muslim reaction to the quoted attacks of
these black "leaders." Or I was on long-distance to Mr. Muhammad in
Chicago, reading from my notebook and asking for Mr. Muhammad's
instructions.

I couldn't understand how Mr. Muhammad could maintain his calm and
patience, hearing the things I told him. I could scarcely contain myself.

My unlisted home telephone number somehow got out. My wife Betty
put down the phone after taking one message, and it was ringing again.
It seemed that wherever I went, telephones were ringing.

The calls naturally were directed to me, New York City being the major
news-media headquarters, and I was the New York minister of Mr.
Muhammad. Calls came, long-distance from San Francisco to Maine . . .
from even London, Stockholm, Paris. I would see a Muslim brother at
our restaurant, or Betty at home, trying to keep cool; they'd hand me the
receiver, and I couldn't believe it, either. One funny thing—in all that
hectic period, something quickly struck my notice: the Europeans never
pressed the "hate" question. Only the American white man was so plagued
and obsessed with being "hated." He was so guilty, it was clear to me,
of hating Negroes.

"Mr. Malcolm X, why do you teach black supremacy, and hate?" A
red flag waved for me, something chemical happened inside me, every time
I heard that. When we Muslims had talked about "the devil white man"
he had been relatively abstract, someone we Muslims rarely actually came
into contact with, but now here was that devil-in-the-flesh on the phone—
with all of his calculating, cold-eyed, self-righteous tricks and nerve and
gall. The voices questioning me became to me as breathing, living devils.

And I tried to pour on pure fire in return. "The white man so guilty
of white supremacy can't hide *his* guilt by trying to accuse The Honorable
Elijah Muhammad of teaching black supremacy and hate! All Mr.
Muhammad is doing is trying to uplift the black man's mentality and the
black man's social and economic condition in this country.

"The guilty, two-faced white man can't decide *what* he wants. Our
slave foreparents would have been put to death for advocating so-called
'integration' with the white man. Now when Mr. Muhammad speaks of
'separation,' the white man calls us 'hate-teachers' and 'fascists'!

"The white man doesn't *want* the blacks! He doesn't *want* the blacks
that are a parasite upon him! He doesn't *want* this black man whose
presence and condition in this country expose the white man to the world
for what he is! So why do you attack Mr. Muhammad?"

I'd have *scathing* in my voice; I *felt* it.

"For the white man to ask the black man if he hates him is just like
the rapist asking the *raped,* or the wolf asking the *sheep,* 'Do you hate

me?' The white man is in no moral *position* to accuse anyone else of
hate!

"Why, when all of my ancestors are snake-bitten, and I'm snake-bitten,
and I warn my children to avoid snakes, what does that *snake* sound like
accusing *me* of hate-teaching?"

"Mr. Malcolm X," those devils would ask, "why is your Fruit of Islam
being trained in judo and karate?" An image of black men learning anything suggesting self-defense seemed to terrify the white man. I'd turn
their question around: "Why does judo or karate suddenly get so ominous
because black men study it? Across America, the Boy Scouts, the YMCA,
even the YWCA, the CYP, PAL—they *all* teach judo! It's all right, it's
fine—until *black men* teach it! Even little grammar school classes, little
girls, are taught to defend themselves—"

"How many of you are in your organization, Mr. Malcolm X? Right
Reverend Bishop T. Chickenwing says you have only a handful of
members—"

"Whoever tells you how many Muslims there are doesn't know, and
whoever does know will never tell you—"

The Bishop Chickenwings were also often quoted about our "anti-Christianity." I'd fire right back on that:

"Christianity is the white man's religion. The Holy Bible in the white
man's hands and his interpretations of it have been the greatest single
ideological weapon for enslaving millions of nonwhite human beings. Every
country the white man has conquered with his guns, he has always paved
the way, and salved his conscience, by carrying the Bible and interpreting
it to call the people 'heathens' and 'pagans'; then he sends his guns, then
his missionaries behind the guns to mop up—"

White reporters, anger in their voices, would call us "demagogues,"
and I would try to be ready after I had been asked the same question
two or three times.

"Well, let's go back to the Greek, and maybe you will learn the first
thing you need to know about the word 'demagogue.' 'Demagogue' means,
actually, 'teacher of the people.' And let's examine some demagogues. The
greatest of all Greeks, Socrates, was killed as a 'demagogue.' Jesus Christ
died on the cross because the Pharisees of His day were upholding their
law, not the spirit. The modern Pharisees are trying to heap destruction
upon Mr. Muhammad, calling him a demagogue, a crackpot, and fanatic.
What about Gandhi? The man that Churchill called 'naked little fakir,'
refusing food in a British jail? But then a quarter of a billion people, a
whole subcontinent, rallied behind Gandhi—and they twisted the British
Lion's tail! What about Galileo, standing before his inquisitors, saying
'The earth *does* move!' What about Martin Luther, nailing on a door his
thesis against the all-powerful Catholic church which called him 'heretic'?

We, the followers of The Honorable Elijah Muhammad, are today in the ghettoes as once the sect of Christianity's followers were like termites in the catacombs and the grottoes—and they were preparing the grave of the mighty Roman Empire!"

I can remember those hot telephone sessions with those reporters as if it were yesterday. The reporters were angry. I was angry. When I'd reach into history, they'd try to pull me back to the present. They would quit interviewing, quit their work, trying to defend their personal white devil selves. They would unearth Lincoln and his freeing of the slaves. I'd tell them things Lincoln said in speeches, *against* the blacks. They would drag up the 1954 Supreme Court decision on school integration.

"That was one of the greatest magical feats ever performed in America," I'd tell them. "Do you mean to tell me that nine Supreme Court judges, who are past masters of legal phraseology, couldn't have worked their decision to make it stick as *law?* No! It was trickery and magic that told Negroes they were desegregated—Hooray! Hooray!—and at the same time it told whites 'Here are your loopholes.' " . . .

Mr. Muhammad would come quickly to the stand, looking out over the vacuum-quiet audience, his gentle-looking face set, for just a fleeting moment. Then, "As-Salaikum-Salaam—"

"WA-ALAIKUM-SALAAM!"

The Muslims roared it, as they settled to listen. From experience, they knew that for the next two hours Mr. Muhammad would wield his two-edged sword of truth. In fact, every Muslim worried that he overtaxed himself in the length of his speeches, considering his bronchial asthmatic condition.

"I don't have a degree like many of you out there before me have. But history don't care anything about your degrees.

"The white man, he has filled you with a fear of him from ever since you were little black babies. So over you is the greatest enemy a man can have—and that is fear. I know some of you are afraid to listen to the truth—you have been raised on fear and lies. But I am going to preach to you the truth until you are free of that fear. . . .

"Your slavemaster, he brought you over here, and of your past everything was destroyed. Today, you do not know your true language. What tribe are you from? You would not recognize your tribe's name if you heard it. You don't know nothing about your true culture. You don't even know your family's real name. You are wearing a *white man's* name! The white slavemaster, who *hates* you!

"You are a people who think you know all about the Bible, and all about Christianity. You even are foolish enough to believe that nothing is *right* but Christianity!

"You are the planet Earth's only group of people ignorant of yourself, ignorant of your own kind, of your true history, ignorant of your enemy! You know nothing at *all* but what your white slave-master has chosen to tell you. And he has told you only that which will benefit himself, and his own kind. He has taught you, for *his* benefit, that you are a neutral, shiftless, helpless so-called 'Negro.'

"I say '*so-called*' because you are *not* a '*Negro.*' There is no such thing as a race of '*Negroes.*' You are members of the Asiatic nation, from the tribe of *Shabazz!* 'Negro' is a false label forced on you by your slave-master! He has been pushing things onto you and me and our kind ever since he brought the first slave shipload of us black people here—"

When Mr. Muhammad paused, the Muslims before him cried out, "Little Lamb!" . . . "All praise is due to Allah!" . . . "*Teach,* Messenger!" He would continue.

"The *ignorance* we of the black race here in America have, and the *self-hatred* we have, they are fine examples of what the white slavemaster has seen fit to teach to us. Do we show the plain common sense, like every other people on this planet Earth, to unite among ourselves? No! We are humbling ourselves, sitting-in, and begging-in, trying to *unite* with the slavemaster! I don't seem able to imagine any more ridiculous sight. A thousand ways every day, the white man is telling you 'You can't live here, you can't enter here, you can't eat here, drink here, walk here, work here, you can't ride here, you can't play here, you can't study here.' Haven't we yet seen enough to see that he has no plan to *unite* with you?

"You have tilled his fields! Cooked his food! Washed his clothes! You have cared for his wife and children when he was away. In many cases, you have even suckled him at your *breast!* You have been far and away better Christians than this slavemaster who *taught* you his Christianity!

"You have sweated blood to help him build a country so rich that he can today afford to give away millions—even to his *enemies!* And when those enemies have gotten enough from him to then be able to attack him, you have been his brave soldiers, *dying* for him. And you have been always his most faithful servant during the so-called 'peaceful' times—

"And, *still,* this Christian American white man has not got it in him to find the human *decency,* and enough sense of *justice,* to recognize us, and accept us, the black people who have done so much for him, as fellow human beings!"

"YAH, Man!" . . . "*Um-huh!*" "*Teach,* Messenger!" . . . "*Yah!*" . . . "*Tell 'em!*" . . . "You *right!*" . . . "Take your *time* up there, little Messenger!" . . . "Oh, *yes!*"

Others besides the Muslims would be shouting now. We Muslims were less extroverted than Christian Negroes. It would sound now like an old-fashioned camp meeting.

"So let us, the black people, *separate* ourselves from this white man slavemaster, who despises us so much! You are out here begging him for some so-called *'integration!'* But what is this slave-master white, *rapist,* going about saying! He is saying *he* won't integrate because black blood will *mongrelize* his race! *He* says that — and look at *us!* Turn around in your seats and look at each other! This slavemaster white man already has *'integrated'* us until you can hardly find among us today any more than a very few who are the black color of our foreparents!''

"God-a-mighty, the man's right!'' . . . *"Teach,* Messenger — '' *"Hear* him! *Hear* him!''

"He has left such a little black in us," Mr. Muhammad would go on, "that now he despises us so bad — meaning he despises *himself,* for what he has *done* to us — that he tells us that *legally* if we have got *one drop* of black blood in us, that means you are all-black as far as his laws are concerned! Well, if that's all we've got left, we want to *reclaim* that one drop!''

Mr. Muhammad's frail strength could be seen to be waning. But he would teach on:

"So let us *separate* from this white man, and for the same reason *he* says — in time to save ourselves from any more *'integration!'*

"Why *shouldn't* this white man who likes to think and call himself so good, and so generous, this white man who finances even his enemies — why *shouldn't* he subsidize a separate state, a separate territory, for we black people who have been such faithful slaves and servants? A separate territory on which we can lift *ourselves* out of these white man's *slums* for us, and his *breadlines* for us. And even for *those* he is complaining that we cost him too much! We can do something for *ourselves!* We never have done what we *could* — because we have been brainwashed so well by the slavemaster white man that we must come to him, begging him, for everything we want, and need — ''

After perhaps ninety minutes, behind Mr. Muhammad, every minister would have to restrain himself from bolting up to his side, to urge him that it was enough. He would be pressing his hands tightly against the edges of the speaker's stand, to support himself.

"We black people don't *know* what we can do. You never can know what *anything* can do — until it is set *free,* to act by itself! If you have a cat in your house that you pamper and pet, you have to free that cat, set it on its *own,* in the woods, before you can see that the cat had it *in* him to shelter and feed itself!

"We, the black people here in America, we never have been *free* to find out what we really can *do!* We have knowledge and experience to pool to do for ourselves! All of our lives we have farmed — we can grow our own food. We can set up factories to manufacture our own necessities! We can build other kinds of businesses, to establish trade, and commerce — and become independent, as other civilized people are—

"We can *throw off* our brainwashing, and our self-hate, and live as *brothers* together . . .

". . . some land of our *own!* . . . Something for *ourselves!* . . . leave this white slavemaster to *himself. . . .*"

Mr. Muhammad always stopped abruptly when he was unable to speak any longer.

The standing ovation, a solid wall of sound, would go on unabating. . . .

Our crumbling citadels of virtue

46

John P. Sisk   The Fear of Immorality

John P. Sisk was born in Spokane, Washington, in 1914 and educated at Gonzaga University and the University of Washington. He has been a member of the English department of Gonzaga since 1938, four years of which time he served in the U.S. Army Air Force in World War II. He is presently Professor and Chairman of the English Department at Gonzaga. A prolific essayist, his numerous writings have appeared in Commonweal, American, Thought, Ramparts, Prairie Schooner, *and* The Shakespeare Quarterly. *His short novel,* A Trial of Strength, *won the Carl Forman Award in 1961 in an international contest sponsored by Harcourt, Brace and Collins. The selection which follows is one of a series having to do with contemporary American Civilization. Professor Sisk states that his primary concern is with "society's efforts to handle information and control itself," and especially with how these efforts are reflected in popular art and culture. Professor Sisk posits a change in American morality—from impulse restraint to impulse gratification. He relates this change to the growth of a radical right. For related ideas, see Gabriel, Fuchs, Slaikeu.*

A fear that the moral center of things is about to give way is as natural to the American as suspicion of big government. You can always get an audience in America with a variation on the theme that everything is going

From *Commonweal* (December 18, 1964), pp. 415–418. Reprinted by permission of the publisher.

to pot: fundamentalists enthral congregations with it; politicians get elected
with it; right-wingers extract oil money with it. America is by nature a
place where one opens one's morning paper with a combination of antici-
pation and dread: who, by way of a vicuña coat, a block of stock, an
irresistible call girl, is the latest to assault the crumbling citadels of virtue?

Most periods have had their share of commentators who were convinced
that they were living in the moral fag-end of things. Even the optimistic
Whitman caught a whiff of the Gilded Age and mistook it, at least momentarily, for the Waste Land. It is worth remembering also the extent
to which one's sense of the moral tone of one's time is dependent on
communication facilities. In the age of Telstar immorality gets a mislead-
ingly good and fast press. We learn about it more quickly, react to it
more quickly, experience its public repercussions more quickly. News of
immorality is almost the "noise" of modern communication media: the
operational racket they create simply in the act of existing as media.

Allowing for these considerations, we are at the moment sufficiently immoral by standards still publicly recognized (however seldomly practiced)
to be concerned and afraid. And all men, not only Americans, are afraid
of immorality. As individuals men may sin with great gusto or indulge
in fantasies of release from moral bonds or define freedom for themselves
in terms that oppose current moral norms. But, as sinners in act or fantasy, they depend on a containing moral framework to give structure and
security to their lives, much as gangsters depend on a police system to
maintain the public order without which their own disorder would be impossible. Immorality rampant points to disorder and chaos; it threatens
the freedom of individual sinners. A corrupt establishment is not simply
hypocritical when it defers publicly to a moral code it violates in private:
the very coherence of things is at stake.

Certainly Americans have ample historical reason for their own fear of
immorality. Behind our moral anxiety, and the reforming spirit with which
it expresses itself, lies the myth of a Promised Land and of a virginity
that must be kept unsullied if the Promised Land is to be entered. To be
an American, then, is to be tensed with perfectionism: to be susceptible
to exhortations to reach for the ultimate, and to be continually dismayed
as effort after effort falls short. Extremes of idealism and cynicism, of ex-
ultation and despair, are characteristically found among us cheek-by-jowl.
Dreaming of an impossible innocence, we are haunted by intimations of
corruption and suffer from a compulsion to unmask it. Thus in a muck-
raker's paradise we live from crisis to crisis.

And even now, when the American Dream has been secularized and
eroticized, we are greatly determined by a traditional morality of rigorous
devotion to duty, self-denial, rigid control of impulse and suspicion of
sensuous pleasure. Our national sense of well-being, our sense of direction,

is conditioned by this sense of being morally on a tight rein. But over the past hundred years, and especially in this century, the morality of self-denial, of frugality and impulse-control, has been undermined by the values that have made possible, and been made possible by, a rising standard of living and the exigencies of the gross national product. The result, as anthropologist Jules Henry has pointed out in *Culture Against Man,* is "the first phase of the psychic revolution of modern times."

The prime agent of this revolution, though hardly the cause, is advertising, which attacks powerfully and subversively the old morality and attempts to replace it with an ethic of consumption and impulse-release. The latter can be called a morality because it persuades the consumer with moral imperatives, however disguised: one ought to pass the buck back into circulation, one ought to buy, because more consumption means more production, means more jobs, means a higher standard of living, means a happier and more united people, means a stronger nation and the ultimate triumph of America and the Christian West over the godless Russians, etc.

The subversion of the conventional morality may not have been especially subtle, yet it appears to have taken in some of the admen themselves (to say nothing of their clients), who often speak and write as though they subscribe passionately to the old restrictive, conserving moral order. Actually, of course, the old morality is used against itself through a transvaluation of terms. Note this, for instance, in beer, wine and whiskey advertisements, which make skillful use of symbols identified with the old impulse-inhibiting morality: grass-roots family gatherings, the great out-of-doors, the classics, historical figures and events, traditional decor and architectural settings, and the like.

Of course, other forces were at work subverting the traditional morality long before the modern adman made his appearance. To understand why men fear immorality it is also necessary to understand that at any particular time this fear may be in part a fear of life. Ideally, a moral system, like an artist's discipline, is aimed at the effective utilization and release of available forces. But if some forces are inordinately feared, the over-inhibiting moral system that results may contain the dynamics of its own subversion.

Much of American literature is the record of a subversive attack on conventional morality in the interests of a freer and fuller life. Many of the subversives are the authors of the classics we revere and even proudly associate with our conventional moral system: Emerson, Thoreau, Twain, Whitman, Melville, James—to say nothing of the older twentieth-century writers who have now receded far enough into the past to begin to benefit from the respectability of history.

One of the most familiar figures in our literature is the sensitive young

man from the farm, the small town or the slum neighborhood who finds
the moral system of his home stifling and so takes to the road, searching
for new standards that will make possible a satisfactory release of his
life's forces. Characteristically, the release involves a heroic abandonment
of the old sexual mores, which are symbolic of all those forces in the conventional morality that stand in the way of self-discovery.

Henry Miller and the more uninhibited Beat writers, around whom the
octopus of history has already wrapped a tentacle, seemed not too long
ago to be the ultimate in this sort of subversiveness, yet in effect they
bizarrely teamed up with Madison Avenue in celebrating an uninhibited
release of impulse—a fact that gives some substance to the adman's habit
of speaking of himself as a creative person. And indeed, one must concede
that advertising is the popular and hyperbolic poetry made out of an indiscriminate yearning to be released to a fuller life—an ambiguous poetry
in which it is never quite clear whether sexual release is a symbol of release generally or is itself the ultimate release.

In any event, our moral anxiety is understandable. We have ambivalent
feelings about the writer's vision of the released life, and we sense that
we are on a dangerously loose rein as, urged on by the advertiser, we consume prodigiously and the gross national product increases. The conventional morality is built into our culture, which means that it is built into
our nervous systems, and it dies hard.

A great deal of the anxiety is not even moral in a strict sense; it is an
anxiety about security and control. Our fear of our immorality, especially
our fear of sexual immorality, expresses our fear of uncontrolled power,
our modern sense of living on a powder keg, a fear that underlines the
sheer living convenience of what we think of as the conventional morality.
Thus while a time of moral anxiety may be a time of blind groping it
may just as characteristically be a time of revival movements. Hence a
good deal of the nation's energy that is left over after heroic acts of consumption is devoted to pursuing the emotional and psychological comforts
of the old morality of impulse control.

One of the important functions of people in high places—in government,
religion, law, industry, education and communication—is that of inducing
in the public the belief that the conventional morality is still protectively
in force, despite the fact that these are often the same people who are
instigating or administering forces that subvert it. The burden of the
people's moral expectation on people in high places is especially great in
America, not only because of the habit of identifying the national well-
being with a widely violated code of morality but because the public looks
to its leaders to protect it while it indulges itself with affluence.

One of the most effective means an American has for keeping a grip on
the conventional morality, and therefore on himself, is his expression of

the compulsion to reform according to the patterns of a morally pastoral condition in which the nation's strength is believed to be rooted. Reform, one of the most important means by which a democracy renews itself, is not only a way of correcting real or imagined evils but of relieving moral anxiety by proving in action the relevancy and strength of traditional standards. A catalogue of recent or current targets of the reforming spirit would have all the variety of the American scene itself, and would range from racial discrimination through the mortuary business to the nudity of animals.

Reform can come from the Left or the Right, from liberals or conservatives, from intellectuals or anti-intellectuals. But the most spectacular reform movement at the present time is that of the Radical Right. Its appeal and power cannot be understood apart from the prevailing moral anxiety and the tendency of that anxiety to gather to itself all other anxieties about threats to order and security. In the fundamentalism of the Radical Right the American fear of immorality moves close to panic. The predicament of the Radical Right—and to a degree it is the national predicament—is that in its centers of power it is thoroughly committed to the values and forces that are subverting the conventional restrictive morality upon which it believes itself to be taking a stand. The Radical Right would like an economy of abundance structured with the impulse-denying morality of an economy of scarcity—but then so would a great many of us who think of ourselves as liberal or moderate. We can thank the Radical Right (and books like Galbraith's *The Affluent Society*) for underlining our dilemma.

Our native conviction that politics is by nature a corrupt activity does not keep political argument in America from being both an aspect of, and an attempt to relieve, our morally anxious reforming spirit. Contending parties address themselves to one another and to the public in terms of a moral crusade, and vie with one another in their championship of the conventional morality as they condemn each other's moral defections. The rhetoric of the political convention is often indistinguishable from that of a revival meeting. It is generally more effective to accuse an entrenched administration of moral turpitude than of political incompetence (indeed, the two are widely believed synonymous).

Americans often seem incapable of entertaining political ideas or of understanding themselves in terms of differing political commitments unless political issues and facts are assigned places in a conventional moral melodrama. This is the American trait in that very American book, *The Conscience of a Conservative,* in which the complex economic, social, political and moral issues of our time are reduced to a heroic conflict between the conservative conscience and the liberal immoralities that offend it. The whole tone of the liberal-conservative debate frequently suggests that of a socio-political Council of Trent. This moralism in our politics (so easily confused with real moral seriousness) may obscure more issues than it clarifies; nevertheless, in this manner politics becomes a device for giving us at least the illusion of being sustained by our moral roots.

But no less important to us now in our efforts to maintain our connections with our moral origins is Russia. In *Russia and the West under Lenin and Stalin* former ambassador Kennan has pointed our how our relations with hostile nations are complicated by our practice of reducing such relations to simplistic moral terms. The conflict of West and East, which in our minds is almost hopelessly confused with our fear of the poor, is characteristically conceived as a conflict between the acceptors and rejectors of the conventional morality—in Kennan's terms, a conflict between the center of all virtue and the embodiment of all evil. Russia (whose recent leader reacted to a Hollywood display of flesh exactly as an American raised on the conventional morality might have been expected to) thus becomes the supreme immorality, gathering to itself all those fears that immorality inspires in us. The act of rising to that fear is easily and habitually identified as an act of moral revival and has the exhilarating integrative effect on persons and groups that moral revivals generally have.

To oppose this passionate integration, precarious and deceptive as its basis may be, is to oppose a powerful aggregate of forces. But if it is not opposed we may find in the end that Russia has harmed us less by the threat of her bombs or her rate of economic growth or her territorial expansion than by having encouraged us to play a part with her in an international melodrama in which, conceiving ourselves as crusaders, our faculties for self-criticism atrophy. Our fear of immorality, in other words, belongs at home, and if we examine it closely and honestly enough we may discover what we are really afraid of.

The means we employ to revive in ourselves the comforts of the conventional morality keep us from realizing how much that morality is responsible for our anxiety—and not simply because it induces the anxieties of perfectionism but because of serious flaws in it that time has been revealing. We like to believe that our trouble stems from our defection from the Christian morality that made America great. But in that very belief, expressing as it does an endorsement of something, less for itself, than for its material dividends, we catch a glimpse of the unpleasant truth: that the moral system that helped make America great is much too simply identified as the Christian moral system.

What we define as the conventional morality is, in America, involved with egoistic, anti-social impulses, with a moralized energetic pursuit of material well-being, with an initially strengthening but ultimately crippling conviction of divine election, with the gradual metamorphosis of a Puritan God into the hidden hand of *laissez faire* economics. The conventional morality was oriented to property rather than social justice, to freedom rather than fraternity, to the individual rather than the person. In the conventional morality the "economical" virtues were glorified (frugality replacing charity) with the result not so much that economic life was made more moral as that morality was made to serve economic ends.

Even the economic determinism of the Social Darwinists was argued in moral terms, as though the God who had led us out of the wilderness into the Promised Land was Himself a classical liberal. We see this confusion of morality and economics now in the Radical Right, for whom the income tax is above all a moral outrage. Indeed, the conventional morality has been so "economized" that one's first suspicion about a morally indignant American is not that his sense of social justice has been outraged but that his pocketbook or his property rights have been threatened in some way.

The irony of the conventional morality is the prominence it has given to exactly those impulse-denying virtues that, given America's material potential, energy, geographic isolation and technological skill, were bound to result in affluence. But we have discovered that affluence, unlike a Promised Land, is not a terminal state. We can only have it by having continually more of it, which means a progressively greater emphasis on consumption and the virtues of impulse-release. Our trouble, then, is not so much that we have abandoned the conventional morality as that we have stayed with it while it worked out its logic on us.

Thus our moral anxiety, our fear of immorality, goes deeper than the fear that the conventional morality is being abandoned; it is a fear that there may be no salvation in a return to it. We have been living morally on borrowed time, and more and more this fact is forcing itself into the national consciousness. More and more the conditions of the age reveal to us our human involvement with one another and force us to see the terrible impracticality of uncharitableness. The times are trying to make us accept the prescriptions of Christian morality that our conventional morality has habitually de-emphasized or ignored. In the meantime we suffer from a kind of double bad conscience: we feel guilty about the violation of traditional admonitions to inhibit impulse, and we feel guilty about the failure in charity that is institutionalized in the traditional morality we consciously look to for salvation.

Put another way, our problem is one of reconciling living with loving. If living is to be measured by consumption, then loving, which subordinates consumption to charitable concern for persons, easily appears as a threat to living. But if loving is the only real living, then to refuse loving is the ultimate immorality. The fear of immorality then may be at bottom a fear of both living and loving. The best of our reformers are moving towards this realization; most of the others continue (often quite innocently) to induce the fervors of moral reform in order to hide from themselves the reasons for their anxiety.

Arthur L. Slaikeu   A Profile of Courage   **47**

The Reverend Arthur L. Slaikeu has been pastor of the first Baptist Church in Lincoln, Nebraska, since 1958. He has also served churches in Aberdeen, South Dakota, and Salina, Kansas. Born in Iowa, The Reverend Slaikeu was graduated from high school in Luck, Wisconsin, and from the University of Minnesota in 1941. In 1943, he earned the Bachelor of Theology Degree from the Eastern Baptist Theological Seminary in Philadelphia. John Brown University awarded him a Doctor of Divinity Degree in 1959. He is currently secretary of the Ministers' Council of the American Baptist Convention, and a member of the Board of Directors of the American Baptist Foreign Missions Society.

This sermon was preached from manuscript during the regular Sunday morning service, November 24, 1963. According to the Reverend Slaikeu, the congregation numbered about 500, only slightly larger than usual. For related ideas, see Malcolm X, Gabriel, Sisk, Fuchs.

It seems now that it must have been weeks ago, but it was only two days ago that we sat in numb and unbelieving silence before our radio and television sets and listened to the tragic words that reached us. The President is dead! The President is dead! The evil plot of Lee Oswald, a committed but apparently undisciplined communist, had developed as he planned. From a 6th-story window of a warehouse in Dallas, Texas, he had awaited the approach of the limousine that carried the President of our country. And when President Kennedy's head moved into the cross hairs of the telescopic sight of Oswalds's high-powered rifle, the assassin squeezed the trigger that fired the shots, and thirty minutes later we heard the words, "The President is dead." Our beloved President was dead! Friday, November 22, 1963, has now become a black day that will forever live in infamy for every citizen of our land.

The tragic Friday through which we have just come reminds us of another

"A Profile of Courage," Charles J. Stewart and Bruce Kendall (eds.), *A Man Named John F. Kennedy* (Glen Rock, N.J.: Paulist Press, 1964), pp. 52 – 63. Reprinted by permission of the publisher.

tragic Friday in American history, Friday, April 14, 1865. On that day President Lincoln held his last Cabinet meeting. The Civil War was fast drawing to a close. President Lincoln asked General Grant if he had had any late news from Sherman. His reply was in the negative. Lincoln replied that it would come soon, and he knew it would be favorable, for he said, "Last night I had a familiar dream." It was the same dream that he had had before Sumter, before Bull Run, before Murpheesboro, Vicksburg and Wilmington. The President dreamed that in a strange indescribable ship he seemed to be moving rapidly toward a dark and undefined shore.

That night, John Wilkes Booth shot President Lincoln as he watched a play in Ford Theater. The President was carried across the street from the theater to a poor rooming house where he was laid on a bed in a small back room. He never regained consciousness. Secretary of the Navy Gideon Welles described the scene. "The giant sufferer," writes Welles, "lay diagonally across the bed, which was not long enough for him. His slow, full respiration lifted the clothes with each breath that he took. His features were calm and striking."

"It was a dark and gloomy night," the historian Commager has told us, "and rain fell at dawn. Crowds remained in the street looking in vain for hope from the watchers who came out for a breath of air. A little before half-past seven, the great heart ceased to beat."

Welles continues, "I went after breakfast to the Executive Mansion. There was a cheerless, cold rain, and everything seemed gloomy. On the avenue in front of the White House were several hundred colored people, mostly women and children, weeping and wailing their loss. The crowd did not seem to diminish through the whole of that cold, wet day. They seemed not to know what was to be their fate since their great benefactor was dead, and their hopeless grief," said Welles, "affected me more than almost anything else, though strong and brave men wept when I met them on the street."

Since last Friday, many of us have known what it means to weep as those men wept, and for a similar reason. The tragic assassination of President Kennedy in Dallas makes us recall a similar event that took place in Jackson, Mississippi, just a few months ago. It was just past midnight on Tuesday, June 21, 1963, when Medgar Evers, a Negro freedom leader, father of three, drove into the driveway of his little home in Jackson. As he stepped from his car, from a honeysuckle thicket 150 yards away, came a shot that tore into the Negro's back, plowed through his body, and lodged in the kitchen counter of his own little home. Mr. Evers' wife and children were waiting for him. They heard the shot and hurried out into the driveway, to find their husband and father staggering toward them and finally falling in the driveway in a puddle of blood. His wife reached down and cradled his head in her arms. His children kept crying, "Daddy, get up, please get up.'' But he couldn't get up. He died shortly.

Medgar Evers died as President Kennedy died. There is a striking similarity between the death of 46-year old President Kennedy and the death of 37-year old Medgar Evers, a greater similarity than may at first seem apparent. I know one was killed by an American rifle with a telescopic sight and the other was killed by a European rifle with a telescopic sight. One was shot at 100 yards from a warehouse and the other at 150 yards from a honeysuckle patch. One left a wife and two children. The other left a wife and three children. The skin of the one man was white and the skin of the other man was black, but both were killed because they were believers in freedom, and they dared to battle for their beliefs. In each case the killer's weapon was found soon after it had been used. Both Kennedy and Evers were veterans, and their bodies will finally rest in the same cemetery, Arlington Memorial Cemetery, in Washington. But there, or about there, the comparison between the death of these two men seems to end, because the killer of our President has been apprehended, and in all likehood will be convicted and will be brought to justice. But the killer of that Negro freedom leader is still at large, six months after his dastardly deed.

The one who killed the President may be a communist, an atheist, who says that he hates America. But the one who killed Medgar Evers, in all likelihood, says he is a loyal American citizen, a man who believes in states' rights, a respectable citizen in his community, a member of a Christian church, if you can call any segregated church a Christian church. And the killer of Medgar Evers, in all likelihood, is in church this morning, as you and I are in church.

The murder of President Kennedy will never be forgotten, but most of us have long since forgotten the murder of Medgar Evers. Of course, one was our President and the other was only a Negro freedom leader, but both were persons, and both were American citizens. And one loved life just as much as the other, and the widow and three little children of Medgar Evers will miss their husband and daddy just as much as Jacqueline Kennedy, Caroline and "John-John" will miss theirs.

Now I don't mean to say that the murder of a common citizen like you or me is a crime of the same magnitude as the assassination of our beloved President. But I want to sound a solemn warning to you this morning, a warning that I wish could be winged to every citizen in our land. For I believe that the same forces that killed Evers killed Kennedy, and I further believe that those forces pose a serious threat to the existence of our nation and to the preservation of our freedom.

Because I believe this, I ask you, then, to consider two things this morning. First, what I believe to be our number one national problem, and secondly, the way that I believe this problem must be faced. First of all,

I want you to think about what I believe is our number one national problem. There are many ways in which it could be stated. But I cannot help
but favor the statement of the analyst who described it as "the conflict
between the rational and the irrational elements in our society."

Americans, as you know, are born moralists. Our statesmen are preachers. Notice I did not claim that our preachers are statesmen. But our
statesmen are preachers. Oh, how we lecture to the nations of the world.
We have told them how to achieve freedom. We can tell them how to
run their lands. How many peace plans we have given to the world. We
seem to think that we Americans are the very essence of the ethical, and
that we are the great founders and the defenders of law and of freedom.
But the assassination of our President by one of our own citizens has made
us sober, and we cannot escape asking some condemning questions.

Why have we assassinated more heads of State in the United States of
America than any other civilized nation in the world? Why has there been
a 114% increase in crime in our country in the past 12 years? In 1962,
more than two million crimes of rape, murder, burglary, larceny, and theft
were committed. How can a society like ours produce a citizen like Lee
Oswald, a man who is sane, but a man who killed the President of his
own country? How could he do it? This is the question we are asking.
Shall we say he was irrational? Does this describe the assassin of our
President adequately? One of the problems of our country is irrationality.
But we need also to face the fact that there is a strata of violence in the
makeup of America.

I do not mean the violence of our criminals, but I refer to the quiet
violence of our sadistic comics, our television serials, our movies, our Broadway plays, our best-selling novels, and our lurid magazines. When I think
of the fare that is offered the minds of Americans through the mass media
of entertainment, I am not surprised that so many home quarrels end in
murder, and that so many have tried to settle their own personal problems
through attempts at suicide.

We have had a taste of violence in our own fair city this week. The pep
rally on Thursday night before the Oklahoma game defied the law enforcement forces of our city. And don't say that it was fun or that it was funny.
For I tell you that people who will join a mob to defy one law for fun
can just as easily be mobilized to join another mob that will defy law because of hatred. The oranges that we saw thrown on the playing field at
the Oklahoma game yesterday afternoon were thrown in fun. But part of
the fun was the fun of violence and the fun of lawlessness. Those who
tore down the goalposts of the Nebraska stadium were friends of our school
and citizens of our state. But they were not only enjoying the heady wine
of victory. They were tingling with the poisonous taste of violence.

But perhaps we would be more comfortable if we would leave Nebraska and journey southward to see what our nation's number one problem is. We have the problem of irrationality. We have the problem of a strata of violence that runs through American culture, and we have a number one problem of lawlessness. We have seen Governor Orval Faubus of Arkansas, Governor Wallace of Alabama, and Governor Ross Barnett of Mississippi openly defy the Supreme Court, the highest tribunal of our land. And I tell you that when governors follow such a code of conduct, little wonder that radicals bombed a church in Birmingham and killed three little girls. And the next day two white-skinned Eagle Boy Scouts shot two Negro boys, and murdered one of them.

And then we wonder why an American assassin killed our President. It is simply because our birds have come home to roost. We have sowed the wind, and we are reaping the whirlwind. We said nothing when a mob went into a little jail and seized a terrified boy and took him out and lynched him. This was in 1955, and the ones who committed this crime have not yet been brought to justice. We bomb Negro churches. We murder Negro leaders. We kill innocent Negro children, and we never apprehend or punish their killers. And yet, Mayor Thompson, of Jackson, Mississippi, and I am sure he is in somebody's church this morning, and it may well be a Baptist church, calls Jackson the closest place to heaven there is. If Jackson, Mississippi, is heaven I would rather go to hell!

When Ralph Bunche returned from the funeral of Medgar Evers held in Jackson, Mississippi, he said, "Had there been any conscience or sense of decency among the white citizens of Jackson, they would have flocked to the funeral service of Medgar Evers as a mild expression of their shame over the outrage for which they and Jackson must bear responsibility. But they did not come. Then one must conclude that Jackson today has the morality of a jungle." The editor of *Life* magazine, commenting on the statement of Bunche, said, "That is too sweeping, since there are many white moderates in Jackson. But when are they going to make themselves heard?"

The thing that makes our nation suffer today is not the silence of God, but it is the sin of silence on the part of people who know what is right, and do not dare to do it. Who killed President Kennedy? "Oh, Lee Oswald," you might answer, "it's an airtight case." But this is not the answer. Whoever helped spread the germ of hate, of malice, intolerance, injustice and fanaticism, helped create the climate that spawned the assassin who murdered the President of our land last week. Governor Frank Morrison put it well when he said, "It doesn't make much difference who pulled the trigger, but all of us who have held hate or prejudice against our fellow-man — we helped pull the trigger that ended the life of our President."

The number one problem of our nation is the triumph of irrationality against rationality. It is the strata of violence that runs through our society and that is a part of our make-up. And it is the lawlessness that is abroad in the land.

How must our nation's number one problem, then, be faced? I can tell you in a very few words. We will have to face it with courage — courage which Ernest Hemingway has defined as being "grace under pressure." President John F. Kennedy not only wrote a book, *Profiles in Courage,* but as he lived his life he was developing a profile of courage. He was a man of great physical courage, demonstrated well when, as a skipper on a PT boat in the South Pacific, he had his boat slashed in two and sunk by a Japanese destroyer. But he would not let his crew members die. He held their morale together during the night. He towed wounded men to shore. He spent 30 hours in the water until finally he got his men to safety. Little wonder that a man like this would refuse the protection of a bullet-proof bubble, which was not used on his limousine last Friday. He knew that U.N. representative Adlai Stevenson had recently returned from the great state of Texas. He knew the abuse and the indignities that he had suffered there. Our President had been warned against making the trip, but he insisted on making it, because he was a man who had real physical courage.

He was also a man of great moral courage. Were this not true, he never would have become a leader in the great civil rights program that is being adopted in our country. He dared to go against the leadership of his own party in order to do what he thought was right for a disfranchised part of our population. We will always remember his conduct during the crisis over Cuba — a day when he dared to risk not only the existence of this nation, but the existence of civilization as we know it, in order that we may be free. A man of great moral courage and a man of great spiritual courage. Here is a man who did not sack his faith, as so many pseudo-intellectual college sophomores do, because they are such intellectual giants that they can no longer embrace the Christian Faith. Here is a man, saddled with a branch of the Christian Faith which was a political liability to him, but he stayed with it because he believed it was true. He stayed with it, but he didn't surrender his own personal convictions to the Church to which he belonged. The Roman Catholic Church was actively doing its best to get aid for parochial schools and to get an ambassador sent to the Vatican. But President Kennedy opposed the leaders of his own Church. And when he saw that the Roman Catholic leaders of South Vietnam were depriving Buddhists of their rights and of their freedom, he took a stand against the Roman Catholic leadership of that country, and finally helped to bring it to the ground.

He was a man of great courage. He wrote a book, *Profiles in Courage,* and I wish that your boys and girls would read it. I assure you that any boy who reads it and understands it will never be a *hood.* He'll be a great, fearless, self-respecting citizen. We have lost a President who had a profile of courage.

And, what must be the program of courageous men? I find a program outlined very well in Luke 4, 18-19. Jesus was in the Synagogue. He went up and picked up the roll, the Prophecy of Isaiah, and He began to read these words: "The Spirit of the Lord is upon me because He hath anointed me to preach good tidings to the poor. He has sent me to proclaim the release of captives, and the recovering of sight to the blind, to set at liberty those who are oppressed, to proclaim the acceptable year of the Lord." This was the Savior's program, and because it was His program it meant a cross. I find in this simple word, then, in Luke 4, 18-19, a real profile for courage. And the Church has been commissioned to preach the good tidings to the poor.

I conducted a funeral service this past week that thrilled me as no service I have conducted in a long time. The thing that made it so exciting was that the funeral chapel was filled with poor people, and it's so long since I have preached to poor people. Are there no poor people in Lincoln? And if there are, where do they go to church? We never see them here. But we have been commissioned to preach the good tidings to the poor, to proclaim the release of captives, give sight to the blind, and give liberty to them that are bruised; even though they are people who have been bruised by the teeth of a policeman's dog. Or because they have been rolled on the pavement by a fireman's hose. This is the profile of freedom, and the Savior had it. And the Church of Jesus Christ in America today does not have it.

God is still waiting for a generation of Christian people in America who will have a profile of freedom. And I don't have much hope for this generation. Those of you who are still racists and segregationists, you are too old to change, or you would have changed now. I have little hope for you, but I have hope for your children. And I love the songs that some of our kids are singing—a song that says, "If I had a hammer, I'd hammer out justice; I'd hammer out freedom and love for sister and brother all across the land." That old hammer of justice is sounding, bells of freedom are ringing, and I pray God that you and I will have something to do with making freedom ring, and making freedom real in our land.

"Let those who have failed take courage. Though the enemy seem to have won, if he be in the wrong, though his ranks are strong, the battle is not yet done. For sure as the morning follows the darkest hour of the night, no question is ever settled until it is settled right." It was in 1830 that Benjamin Constant, the French philosopher, received a message at the hand of his friends in Paris who were overthrowing the Bourbons. And this is what the message was: "A terrible game is being played here. Our heads are in danger. Come, and add yours."

And I tell you that a terrible game is being played in this land. The stakes are freedom. Our heads—we freedom lovers—our heads are in danger, and I ask you, "Come, and add yours." Have the kind of courage that William Lloyd Garrison had, who coined the saying that is inscribed on the Garrison monument on Commonwealth Avenue in Boston: "I am in earnest. I will not equivocate. I will not excuse. I will not retreat an inch, and I will be heard."

We honor today the memory of a President who had a courage like that; and he, being dead, still speaks.

I have shed my tears since I received the word of the death of the President, and I imagine I will shed some more before I am able to accept it. And you have shed yours, or will. But this can all be just a matter of a wave of emotional sentimentality, and after our tears have been shed there will still be that group of people in our land, and in the city of Lincoln, who are not being given justice. Let's dry our tears, and let's go out and set them free.

**A massive change
in the way men live together**

48

Harvey Cox   **The Secular City**

Harvey Cox has been referred to as "the Reinhold Niebuhr of this generation." Born in Pennsylvania in 1929, he received a Bachelor of History from the University of Pennsylvania and a Bachelor of Divinity from Yale. He is a Baptist theologian, currently on the faculty of the Harvard Divinity School, from which he received his Ph.D. His book The Secular City, *has had a surprising impact and provoked a controversy now available as* The Secular City Debate. *In the following selection, Cox discusses the secularization of modern America and its relation to the city and men and women. For related ideas, see Fuchs; Herberg; Gabriel; Schlesinger, Jr.; Van Borch. Baltzell.*

The Epoch of the Secular City

The rise of urban civilization and the collapse of traditional religion are the two main hallmarks of our era and are closely related movements.

Urbanization constitutes a massive change in the way men live together, and became possible in its contemporary form only with the scientific and technological advances which sprang from the wreckage of religious world-views. Secularization, an equally epochal movement, marks a change in the way men grasp and understand their life together, and it occurred only when the cosmopolitan confrontations of city living exposed the relativity of the myths and traditions men once thought were unquestionable. The ways men live their common life affects mightily the ways they understand the meaning of that life, and vice versa. Villages and cities are laid out to reflect the pattern of the heavenly city, the abode of the gods. But once laid out, the pattern of the polis influences the way in which succeeding generations experience life and visualize the gods. Societies and the symbols by which those societies live influence each other. In our day the secular metropolis stands as both the pattern of our life together and the symbol of our view of the world. If the Greeks perceived the cosmos as an immensely expanded polis, and medieval man saw it as the feudal manor enlarged to infinity, we experience the universe as the city of man. It is a field of human exploration and endeavor from which the gods have fled. The world has become man's task and man's responsibility. Contemporary man has become the cosmopolitan. The world has become his city and his city has reached out to include the world. The name for the process by which this has come about is *secularization*.

What is secularization? The Dutch theologian C. A. van Peursen says it is the deliverance of man "first from religious and then from metaphysical control over his reason and his language." It is the loosing of the world from religious and quasi-religious understandings of itself, the dispelling of all closed world-views, the breaking of all supernatural myths and sacred symbols. It represents what another observer has called the "defatalization of history," the discovery by man that he has been left with the world on his hands, that he can no longer blame fortune or the furies for what he does with it. Secularization is man turning his attention away from worlds beyond and toward this world and this time (*saeculum* = "this present age"). It is what Dietrich Bonhoeffer in 1944 called "man's coming of age."

To some, Bonhoeffer's words still sound shocking, but they really should not. He was merely venturing a tardy theological interpretation of what had already been noticed by poets and novelists, sociologists and philosophers for decades. The era of the secular city is not one of anticlericalism or feverish antireligious fanaticism. The anti-Christian zealot is something of an anachronism today, a fact which explains why Bertrand Russell's books often seem quaint rather than daring and why the antireligious propaganda of the Communists sometimes appears intent on dispelling belief in a "God out there" who has long since been laid to rest.

The forces of secularization have no serious interest in persecuting religion. Secularization simply bypasses and undercuts religion and goes on to other things. It has relativized religious world-views and thus rendered them innocuous. Religion has been privatized. It has been accepted as the peculiar prerogative and point of view of a particular person or group. Secularization has accomplished what fire and chain could not: It has convinced the believer that he *could* be wrong, and persuaded the devotee that there are more important things than dying for the faith. The gods of traditional religions live on as private fetishes or the patrons of congenial groups, but they play no role whatever in the public life of the secular metropolis.

. . . Pluralism and tolerance are the children of secularization. They represent a society's unwillingness to enforce any particular world-view on its citizens. Movements within the Roman Catholic Church culminating in the Second Vatican Council indicate its growing readiness to be open to truth from all sides. Pluralism is breaking out where once a closed system stood.

The age of the secular city, the epoch whose ethos is quickly spreading into every corner of the globe, *is* an age of "no religion at all." It no longer looks to religious rules and rituals for its morality or its meanings. For some religion provides a hobby, for others a mark of national or ethnic identification, for still others an esthetic delight. For fewer and fewer does it provide an inclusive and commanding system of personal and cosmic values and explanations. True, there are some people who claim that our modern age has its secular religions, its political saints, and its profane temples. They are right in a manner of speaking; but to call, for example, nazism or communism "religions" is to obscure a very significant difference between them and traditional religions. It also obscures the fact that nazism was a throwback to a lost tribalism and that every day communism becomes more "secularized" and hence less and less a "religion."

The effort to force secular and political movements of our time to be "religious" so that we can feel justified in clinging to *our* religion is, in the end, a losing battle. Secularization rolls on, and if we are to understand and communicate with our present age we must learn to love it in its unremitting secularity. We must learn, as Bonhoeffer said, to speak of God in a secular fashion and find a nonreligious interpretation of biblical concepts. It will do no good to cling to our religious and metaphysical versions of Christianity in the hope that one day religion or metaphysics will once again be back. They are disappearing forever and that means we can now let go and immerse ourselves in the new world of the secular city. The first step in such an immersion is learning something about its peculiar characteristics. But before we do we must ask more precisely about the other key term we have used in describing the ethos of our time, *urbanization*.

If secularization designates the content of man's coming of age, urbanization describes the context in which it is occurring. It is the "shape" of the new society which supports its peculiar cultural style. In trying to define the term *urbanization,* however, we are confronted with the fact that social scientists themselves are not entirely agreed about what it means. It is clear, however, that urbanization is not just a quantitative term. It does not refer to population size or density, to geographic extent or to a paticular form of government. Admittedly some of the character of modern urban life would not be possible without giant populations concentrated on enormous contiguous land masses. But urbanization is not something that refers only to the city. As Vidich and Bensman have shown in *Small Town in Mass Society,* high mobility, economic concentration, and mass communciations have drawn even rural villages into the web of urbanization.

Urbanization means a structure of common life in which diversity and the disintegration of tradition are paramount. It means a type of impersonality in which functional relationships multiply. It means that a degree of tolerance and anonymity replace traditional moral sanctions and long-term acquaintanceships. The urban center is the place of human control, of rational planning, of bureaucratic organization — and the urban center is not just in Washington, London, New York, and Peking. It is everywhere. The technological metropolis provides the indispensable social setting for a world of "no religion at all," for what we have called a secular style.

The age of the secular, technological city, like all preceding ages, does have its own characteristic *style* — its peculiar way of understanding and expressing itself, its distinctive character, coloring all aspects of its life. Just as the poets and architects, the theologians and the lovers of the thirteenth century all partook of a common cultural substance, so in our time we all share a fund of unspoken perspectives. Just as the straight aisles and evenly clipped hedges of the eighteenth-century formal garden exhibited a style found also in deist theology and in neoclassic verse, so our secular urban culture makes itself felt in all our intellectual projects, artistic visions, and technical accomplishments. . . .

Boston and the United States. We land at Boston's Logan International Airport, not because Boston is either the political or the commercial capital of the United States, but because along the shores of Massachusetts Bay the contrast between the epochs is more pointedly evident than in any other city in America. Boston is at once the oldest city in America and the newest. It is both the historic site of the Puritan colonizers and the launching pad of the new electronic civilization. It combines, in a proportion lacking in any other North American metropolis, just enough Old-

World elegance and space-age streamlining to make it the most transparent American example of the emergence of the secular city.

Martin Myerson and Edward C. Bansfield, two authorities on urban problems, have called Boston "one of the few beautiful cities in America." They suggest that the reason for its special position is that it was built up largely in the pre-industrial period and therefore possesses a great many structures "with the simplicity and charm of an age which could afford nothing less." Also, Boston was governed for a long time by an aristocracy of wealth and taste. It remains true that most of the really beautiful cities of the world were laid out by such people, not by popular referendum. They were designed "by monarchs, nobles and prelates who had absolute power and who cared not a whit for the convenience or welfare of ordinary people."

But Boston, the "good gray lady," had sunk to an abysmally low ebb before her current astonishing rebirth. Picturesque streets became clogged with gasoline buggies. The frontal collision between Yankees and Irish drove many people with money and civic interests to the suburbs. As Mr. Justice Brandeis reported, at the turn of the century the wealthy citizens of Boston told their sons: "Boston holds nothing for you except heavy taxes and political misrule. When you marry, pick out a suburb to build your house in, join the Country Club, and make your life center about your club, your home and your children." The advice was taken not just by the sons of the wealthy, but by everyone with enough savings to flee to Newton or Belmont.

But urban renewal, the great political fact of the 1960s for American cities, has come to Boston in an extra large package. Under one of the most vigorous mayors in her history, aided by one of the toughest urban renewers in the business, Boston has bitten off a huge chunk of self-redevelopment. Early in the process a couple of serious errors were made. The old West End was ruthlessly demolished and its lower-class families scattered to the winds to make room for the futuristic Charles River Park, where both the apartment buildings and the rents charged soar to the upper reaches. A public-housing project on Columbia Point, land reclaimed from the harbor and accessible only over a narrow peninsula, is now also commonly conceded to be a mistake of the first magnitude. But in several other areas, renewal authorities are trying with real success to make up for a bad start. The design for the new Boston City Hall, chosen by an objective jury from 256 entries, has been acclaimed by several architects one of the boldest and most inventive plans yet devised for a civic building in America. In the so-called gray areas of the city, a program called "neighborhood conservation" has begun to replace the bulldozer as the pathway to new metropolitan life. Most significantly, however, the master plan for Boston's redevelopment envisages the preservation of the distinctive character of such sections as Beacon Hill, Back Bay, and North End. This is important. The nourishment of the local color accumulated in diverse quarters *within* a city is just as important as safeguarding variety *among* cities.

But all this activity in the "new" Boston has not simply materialized full-blown out of the brows of Boston's eager urban renewers. The economic basis for it lies mainly in the spectacular growth of a whole new technical and industrial complex in and around Boston. The city and its environs have become what *The New Yorker* has called "the center of a new world." It is the new world of the electronic computer and that peculiar brand of industry which goes along with it: research-oriented, highly skilled bands of specialists working in laboratory-factories on projects which change even faster than automobile designs. The nerve center of this renaissance is Cambridge, just across the Charles River from Boston, but its tentacles spread out for miles in every direction, especially along Route 128, the circumferential highway around Boston that has become synonymous with the electronics industry.

But technopolis in Boston is far from achieved. The tensions between the old and the new are raw and nerve-racking. Wealthy Bostonians, heeding the advice of their fathers, not only left Back Bay but resisted all Boston's efforts to annex them. The town of Brookline presents the most ludicrous anomaly of all. Almost completely surrounded by the City of Boston, it nonetheless clings to its independent status, pretending to spurn all involvement with the corruption of The Hub. Metropolitan Boston exhibits a more serious imbalance between the size of the city proper and the size of the metropolitan area than any other urban region. Suburbanites gleefully utilize the city's harbor, hospitals, and highways, to say nothing of its concerts, films, and theatres. But they retire behind zoning laws and economic ramparts when it comes to the urgent issues of the city itself. Consequently Bostonians groan under an oppressive property-tax burden, which still cannot seem to support an adequate school system, pay the police, or keep the streets clean.

So Boston presents not only a starkly etched contrast of old and young; it also typifies in a particularly glaring way the same crisis faced by every urban region in America — the civic abdication of the middle classes and their withdrawal into a parasitic preserve on the periphery of the city. Like every American city, but in exacerbated form, Boston is impaled on the hyphen in techno-polis. Technically and sociologically, it is a metropolitan region, interdependent in every respect. Politically it is a congeries of fiefdoms and protectorates engaged in the legalized looting of the center city, all the while groping ineffectually with the colossal problems of metropolitan living.

Part of this anarchic miasma stems from the unwillingness of substantial groups within the populace to accept the reality of the secular city. They still want to cling to town and even tribal styles of living. Within the city, clan feuds between Irish, Italian, and Yankee political war parties rage on, while in the suburbs harried escapees from the issues of the inner city deck out their modern homes with wagon wheels and fake colonial furniture. They keep the spotlight shining on the old white church on the green in an effort to convince themselves that they really do live in the simple self-sufficient village founded there three hundred years ago.

But it is all a disastrous self-delusion. Efforts to live in an eighteenth-century town or to maintain the purity and power of the tribe will eventually be exposed for the charades they are. The actual interdependence and technological unity of the urban region will eventually require a political expression.

Besides exemplifying the urban crisis exceptionally well, Boston also portrays with unusual clarity the distinctively American version of the contrast between secularization and secularism. What city better symbolizes a country where a venerable quasi-sacral Protestant culture is just now breathing its last? Its departure, though lamented by some romantics and arcadians, has been greeted by many Protestants with the same relief that European Christians accept the death of "Western Christendom." Protestants may for the first time stand free enough of their culture to be against it or for it selectively, as the guidance of the Gospel suggests. But unfortunately, just as this promising possibility has emerged, the sly temptation of a new sacral society has also appeared. It is the danger of what Martin Marty calls "American shinto." He refers to the "American religion" with three denominations, Catholic—Protestant—Jew, laid open so neatly by Will Herberg and others. It is one of the hidden pitfalls of the present ecumenical movement that we will be urged to remember, *a la* Brotherhood Week posters, that after all we are all Americans and have a common religious heritage.

As Franklin Littell has made potently clear in his book *From State Church to Pluralism,* this "religious past" is really a myth that badly needs demythologizing. People of a variety of religions (and none) came to America for a multiplicity of reasons, not all of them pious. The Protestant sacral culture was imposed on them. The secularization of American society has been a healthy development. It brought about the much-needed emancipation of Catholics, Jews, and others from an enforced Protestant cultural religion. By freeing them it also freed Protestants from important aspects of their culture bondage. It would be too bad if Catholics and Jews, having rightly pushed for the de-Protestantizing of American society and having in effect won, should now join Protestants in reconstituting a kind of tripartite American religion with Americanized versions of Moses, Luther, and Saint Thomas sharing the haloes in its hagiography. At this point, Christians should continue to support the secularization of American society, recognizing that secularists, atheists, and agnostics do not have to be second-class citizens.

We have yet to measure the enormous contribution made by the brief administration of John F. Kennedy to the desacralizing of American society. His election itself marked the end of Protestant cultural hegemony. But in the way he fulfilled the office, in his quiet refusal to function as the high priest of the American religion, Kennedy made an indispensable contribution to the authentic and healthy secularization of our society. He was a supremely political leader. Though there can be little doubt that his Christian conscience informed many of his decisions, especially in the area of racial justice, he stalwartly declined to accept the semireligious halo that Americans, deprived of a monarch who reigns *gratia dei,* have often tried to attach to their chief executive. In thus divesting his office of any sacral significance, Kennedy did, in his place, what the Christians of Eastern Europe do when they seek to distinguish between the political or economic and the ideological claims of Communist regimes.

The secularists of America may be God's way of warning us that the era of sacred societies is over. Christians have contributed to its demise, perhaps more so than most of us realize. By separating pope from emperor and thus granting a certain provisional autonomy to the secular arm, Western Christianity introduced a process which has produced the modern open society and the ecclesiastically neutral or secular state. But, as we have seen, the seeds of secularization go back still further: to the creation story in which man is made responsible for the care of the world; to the separation of the kingly from the prophetic office in Israel; to the New Testament injunctions to respect those in authority so long as they do not make religious claims.

The task of American Christians vis-a-vis their nonreligious fellow citizens is not to browbeat them but to make sure they stay secular. They must be helped to be true to their own premises and not to allow themselves to be perverted into a new fideism, the intolerant religion of secularism. In this respect the decision by the California State Board of Education that the schools should have no hesitance in teaching *about* religion was a welcome one. The board paid its teachers a welcome compliment by suggesting they "are competent to differentiate between teaching about religion and conducting compulsory worship." Significantly, the board added that it would be just as illegal to teach a "point of view denying God" as it would be to "promote a particular religious sect."

This is a decision which points toward maturation in American society. It recognized that the public school is no place for required prayers and hymn-singing. But it also recognizes, as so many disciples of secularism do not, that atheists and agnostics have no more right to propagandize their sectarian views through the schools than anyone else does.

Sex and Secularization

No aspect of human life seethes with so many unexorcised demons as does sex. No human activity is so hexed by superstition, so haunted by residual tribal lore, and so harassed by socially induced fear. Within the breast of urban-secular man, a toe-to-toe struggle still rages between his savage and his bourgeois forebears. Like everything else, the images of sex which informed tribal and town society are expiring along with the eras in which they arose. The erosion of traditional values and the disappearance of accepted modes of behavior have left contemporary man free, but somewhat rudderless. Abhoring a vacuum, the mass media have rushed in to supply a new code and a new set of behavioral prototypes. They appeal to the unexorcised demons. Nowhere is the persistence of mythical and metalogical denizens more obvious than in sex, and the shamans of sales do their best to nourish them. Nowhere is the humanization of life more frustrated. Nowhere is a clear word of exorcism more needed.

How is the humanization of sex impeded? First it is thwarted by the parading of cultural-identity images for the sexually dispossessed, to make money. These images become the tyrant gods of the secular society, undercutting its liberation from religion and transforming it into a kind of neotribal culture. Second, the authentic secularization of sex is checkmated by an anxious clinging to the sexual standards of the town, an era so recent and yet so different from ours that simply to transplant its sexual ethos into our situation is to invite hypocrisy of the worst degree.

Let us look first at the spurious sexual models conjured up for our anxious society by the sorcerers of the mass media and the advertising guild. Like all pagan deities, these come in pairs—the god and his consort. For our purposes they are best symbolized by The Playboy and Miss America, the Adonis and Aphrodite of a leisure-consumer society which still seems unready to venture into full postreligious maturity and freedom. The Playboy and Miss America represent The Boy and The Girl. They incorporate a vision of life. They function as religious phenomena and should be exorcised and exposed.

The Residue of Tribalism. Let us begin with Miss America. In the first century B.C., Lucretius wrote this description of the pageant of Cybele:

> Adorned with emblem and crown . . . she is carried in awe-inspiring state. Tight-stretched tambourines and hollow cymbals thunder all round to the stroke of open hands, hollow pipes stir with Phrygian strain. . . . She rides in procession through great cities and mutely enriches mortals with a blessing not expressed in words. They straw all her path with brass and silver, presenting her with bounteous alms, and scatter over her a snow-shower of roses.

Now compare this with the annual twentieth-century Miss America pageant in Atlantic City, New Jersey. Spotlights probe the dimness like votive tapers, banks of flowers exude their varied aromas, the orchestra blends feminine strings and regal trumpets. There is a hushed moment of tortured suspense, a drumroll, then the climax—a young woman with carefully prescribed anatomical proportions and exemplary "personality" parades serenely with scepter and crown to her throne. At TV sets across the nation throats tighten and eyes moisten. "There she goes, Miss America—" sings the crooner. "There she goes, your ideal." A new queen in America's emerging cult of The Girl has been crowned.

Is it merely illusory or anachronistic to discern in the multiplying pageants of the Miss America, Miss Universe, Miss College Queen type a residuum of the cults of the pre-Christian fertility goddesses? Perhaps, but students of the history of religions have become less prone in recent years to dismiss the possibility that the cultural behavior of modern man may be significantly illuminated by studying it in the perspective of the mythologies of bygone ages. After all, did not Freud initiate a revolution in social science by utilizing the venerable myth of Oedipus to help make sense out of the strange behavior of his Viennese contemporaries? Contemporary man carries with him, like his appendix and his fingernails, vestiges of his tribal and pagan past.

In light of this fertile combination of insights from modern social science and the history of religions, it is no longer possible to see in the Miss America pageant merely an over-publicized prank foisted on us by the advertising industry. It certainly is this, but it is also much more. It represents the mass cultic celebration, complete with a rich variety of ancient ritual embellishments, of the growing place of The Girl in the collective soul of America.

This young woman—though she is no doubt totally ignorant of the fact—symbolizes something beyond herself. She symbolizes The Girl, the primal image, the One behind the many. Just as the Virgin appears in many guises—as our Lady of Lourdes or of Fatima or of Guadalupe—but is always recognizably the Virgin, so with The Girl.

The Girl is also the omnipresent icon of consumer society. Selling beer, she is folksy and jolly. Selling gems, she is chic and distant. But behind her various theophanies she remains recognizably The Girl. In Miss America's glowingly healthy smile, her openly sexual but officially virginal figure, and in the name-brand gadgets around her, she personifies the stunted aspirations and ambivalent fears of her culture. "There she goes, your ideal."

Miss America stands in a long line of queens going back to Isis, Ceres, and Aphrodite. Everything from the elaborate sexual taboos surrounding her person to the symbolic gifts at her coronation hints at her ancient ancestry. But the real proof comes when we find that the function served by The Girl in our culture is just as much a "religious" one as that served by Cybele in hers. The functions are identical—to provide a secure personal "identity" for initiates and to sanctify a particular value structure.

Let us look first at the way in which The Girl confers a kind of identity on her initiates. Simone de Beauvoir says in *The Second Sex* that "no one is *born* a woman." One is merely born a female, and *"becomes* a woman" according to the models and meanings provided by the civilization. During the classical Christian centuries, it might be argued, the Virgin Mary served in part as this model. With the Reformation and especially with the Puritans, the place of Mary within the symbol system of the Protestant countries was reduced or eliminated. There are those who claim that this excision constituted an excess of zeal that greatly impoverished Western culture, an impoverishment from which it has never recovered. Some would even claim that the alleged failure of American novelists to produce a single great heroine (we have no Phaedra, no Anna Karenina) stems from this self-imposed lack of a central feminine ideal.

Without entering into this fascinating discussion, we can certainly be sure that, even within modern American Roman Catholicism, the Virgin Mary provides an identity image for few American girls. Where then do they look for the "model" Simone de Beauvoir convincingly contends they need? For most, the prototype of femininity seen in their mothers, their friends, and in the multitudinous images to which they are exposed on the mass media is what we have called The Girl.

In his significant monograph *Identity and the Life Cycle,* Erik Erikson reminds us that the child's identity is not modeled simply on the parent but on the parent's "super-ego." Thus in seeking to forge her own identity the young girl is led beyond her mother to her mother's ideal image, and it is here that what Freud called "the ideologies of the superego . . . the traditions of the race and the people" became formative. It is here also that The Girl functions, conferring identity on those for whom she is — perhaps never completely consciously — the tangible incarnation of womanhood.

To describe the mechanics of this complex psychological process by which the fledgling American girl participates in the life of The Girl and thus attains a woman's identity would require a thorough description of American adolescence. There is little doubt, however, that such an analysis would reveal certain striking parallels to the "savage" practices by which initiates in the mystery cults shared in the magical life of their god.

For those inured to the process, the tortuous nightly fetish by which the young American female pulls her hair into tight bunches secured by metal clips may bear little resemblance to the incisions made on their arms by certain African tribesmen to make them resemble their totem, the tiger. But to an anthropologist comparing two ways of attempting to resemble the holy one, the only difference might appear to be that with the Africans the torture is over after initiation, while with the American it has to be repeated every night, a luxury only a culture with abundant leisure can afford.

In turning now to an examination of the second function of The Girl — supporting and portraying a value system — a comparison with the role of the Virgin in the twelfth and thirteenth centuries may be helpful. Just as the Virgin exhibited and sustained the ideals of the age that fashioned Chartres Cathedral, as Henry Adams saw, so The Girl symbolizes the values and aspirations of a consumer society. (She is crowned not in the political capital, remember, but in Atlantic City or Miami Beach, centers associated with leisure and consumption.) And she is not entirely incapable of exploitation. If men sometimes sought to buy with gold the Virgin's blessings on their questionable causes, so The Girl now dispenses her charismatic favor on watches, refrigerators, and razor blades — for a price. Though The Girl has built no cathedrals, without her the colossal edifice of mass persuasion would crumble. Her sharply stylized face and figure beckon us from every magazine and TV channel, luring us toward the beatific vision of a consumer's paradise.

The Girl is *not* the Virgin. In fact she is a kind of anti-Madonna. She reverses most of the values traditionally associated with the Virgin — poverty, humility, sacrifice. In startling contrast, particularly, to the biblical portrait of Mary in Luke 1:46-55, The Girl has nothing to do with filling the hungry with "good things," hawking instead an endless proliferation of trivia on TV spot commercials. The Girl exalts the mighty, extols the rich, and brings nothing to the hungry but added despair. So The Girl does buttress and bring into personal focus a value system, such as it is. In both social and psychological terms, The Girl, whether or not she is really a goddess, certainly acts that way.

Perhaps the most ironic element in the rise of the cult of The Girl is that Protestantism has almost completely failed to notice it, while Roman Catholics have at least given some evidence of sensing its significance. In some places, for instance, Catholics are forbidden to participate in beauty pageants, a ruling not entirely inspired by prudery. It is ironic that Protestants have traditionally been most opposed to lady cults while Catholics have managed to assimilate more than one at various points in history.

If we are correct in assuming that The Girl *functions* in many ways as a goddess, then the cult of The Girl demands careful Protestant theological criticism. Anything that functions, even in part, as a god when it is in fact not God, is an idol. When the Reformers and their Puritan offspring criticized the cult of Mary it was not because they were anti-feminist. They opposed anything — man, woman, or beast (or dogma or institution) — that usurped in the slightest the prerogatives that belonged alone to God Almighty. As Max Weber has insisted, when the prophets of Israel railed against fertility cults, they had nothing against fertility. It is not against sexuality but against a cult that protest is needed. Not, as it were, against the beauty but against the pageant.

Thus the Protestant objection to the present cult of The Girl must be based on the realization that The Girl is an *idol*. She functions as the source of value, the giver of personal identity. But the values she mediates and the identity she confers are both spurious. Like every idol she is ultimately a creation of our own hands and cannot save us. The values she represents as ultimate satisfactions — mechanical comfort, sexual success, unencumbered leisure — have no ultimacy. They lead only to endless upward mobility, competitive consumption, and anxious cynicism. The devilish social insecurities from which she promises to deliver us are, alas, still there, even after we have purified our breaths, our skins, and our armpits by applying her sacred oils. She is a merciless goddess who draws us farther and farther into the net of accelerated ordeals of obeisance. As the queen of commodities in an expanding economy, the fulfillment she promises must always remain just beyond the tips of our fingers.

Why has Protestantism kept its attention obsessively fastened on the development of Mariolatry in Catholicism and not noticed the sinister rise of this vampirelike cult of The Girl in our society? Unfortunately, is is due to the continuing incapacity of theological critics to recognize the religious significance of cultural phenomena outside the formal religious system itself. But the rise of this new cult reminds us that the work of the reformer is never done. Man's mind is indeed — as Luther said — a factory busy making idols. The Girl is a far more pervasive and destructive influence than the Virgin, and it is to her and her omnipresent altars that we should be directing our criticism.

Besides sanctifying a set of phony values, The Girl compounds her noxiousness by maiming her victims in a Procrustean bed of uniformity. This is the empty "identity" she panders. Take the Miss America pageant, for example. Are these virtually indistinguishable specimens of white, middle-class postadolescence really the best we can do? Do they not mirror the ethos of a mass-production society, in which genuine individualism somehow mars the clean, precision-tooled effect? Like their sisters, the finely calibrated Rockettes, these meticulously measured and pretested "beauties" lined up on the Boardwalk bear an ominous similarity to the faceless retinues of goose-steppers and the interchangeable mass exercisers of explicitly totalitarian societies. In short, *who* says this is beauty?

The caricature becomes complete in the Miss Universe contest, when Miss Rhodesia is a blonde, Miss South Africa is white, and Oriental girls with a totally different tradition of feminine beauty are forced to display their thighs and appear in spike heels and Catalina swim suits. Miss Universe is as universal as an American adman's stereotype of what beauty should be.

The truth is that The Girl *cannot* bestow the identity she promises. She forces her initiates to torture themselves with starvation diets and beauty-parlor ordeals, but still cannot deliver the satisfactions she holds out. She is young, but what happens when her followers, despite added hours in the boudoir, can no longer appear young? She is happy and smiling and loved. What happens when, despite all the potions and incantations, her disciples still feel the human pangs of rejection and loneliness? Or what about all the girls whose statistics, or "personality" (or color) do not match the authoritative "ideal"?

After all, it is God—not The Girl—who is God. He is the center and source of value. He liberates men and women from the bland uniformity of cultural deities so that they may feast on the luxurious diversity of life He has provided. The identity He confers frees men from all pseudo-identities to be themselves, to fulfill their human destinies regardless whether their faces or figures match some predetermined abstract "ideal." As His gift, sex is freed from both fertility cults and commercial exploitation to become the thoroughly human thing He intended. And since it is one of the last items we have left that is neither prepackaged nor standardized, let us not sacrifice it too hastily on the omnivorous altar of Cybele.

The Playboy, illustrated by the monthly magazine of that name, does for the boys what Miss America does for the girls. Despite accusations to the contrary, the immense popularity of this magazine is not solely attributable to pin-up girls. For sheer nudity its pictorial art cannot compete with such would-be competitors as *Dude* and *Escapade*. *Playboy* appeals to a highly mobile, increasingly affluent group of young readers, mostly between eighteen and thirty, who want much more from their drugstore reading than bosoms and thighs. They need a total image of what it means to be a man. And Mr. Hefner's *Playboy* has no hesitation in telling them.

Why should such a need arise? David Riesman has argued that the responsibility for character formation in our society has shifted from the family to the peer group and to the mass-media peer-group surrogates. Things are changing so rapidly that one who is equipped by his family with inflexible, highly internalized values becomes unable to deal with the accelerated pace of change and with the varying contexts in which he is called upon to function. This is especially true in the area of consumer values toward which the "other-directed person" is increasingly oriented.

Within the confusing plethora of mass media signals and peer-group values, *Playboy* fills a special need. For the insecure young man with newly acquired free time and money who still feels uncertain about his consumer skills, *Playboy* supplies a comprehensive and authoritative guidebook to this forbidding new world to which he now has access. It tells him not only who to be; it tells him *how* to be it, and even provides consolation outlets for those who secretly feel that they have not quite made it.

In supplying for the other-directed consumer of leisure both the norma-
tive identity image and the means for achieving it, *Playboy* relies on a
careful integration of copy and advertising material. The comic book that
appeals to a younger generation with an analogous problem skillfully in-
tersperses illustrations of incredibly muscled men and excessively mammal-
ian women with advertisements for body-building gimmicks and foam-rub-
ber brassiere supplements. Thus the thin-chested comic-book readers of
both sexes are thoughtfully supplied with both the ends and the means
for attaining a spurious brand of maturity. *Playboy* merely continues the
comic-book tactic for the next age group. Since within every identity crisis,
whether in teens or twenties, there is usually a sexual-identity problem,
Playboy speaks to those who desperately want to know what it means to
be a man, and more specifically a *male,* in today's world.

Both the image of man and the means for its attainment exhibit a remarkable consistency in *Playboy.* The skilled consumer is cool and unruf-
fled. He savors sports cars, liquor, high fidelity, and book-club selections
with a casual, unhurried aplomb. Though he must certainly *have* and *use*
the latest consumption item, he must not permit himself to get too attached
to it. The style will change and he must always be ready to adjust. His
persistent anxiety that he may mix a drink incorrectly, enjoy a jazz group
that is passe, or wear last year's necktie style is comforted by an authoritative tone in *Playboy* beside which papal encyclicals sound irresolute.

"Don't hesitate," he is told, "this assertive, self-assured weskit is what
every man of taste wants for the fall season." Lingering doubts about his
masculinity are extirpated by the firm assurance that "real men demand
this ruggedly masculine smoke" (cigar ad). Though "the ladies will swoon
for you, no matter what they promise, don't give them a puff. This cigar
is for men only." A fur-lined canvas field jacket is described as "the
most masculine thing since the cave man." What to be and how to be it
are both made unambiguously clear.

Since being a male necessitates some kind of relationship to females,
Playboy fearlessly confronts this problem too, and solves it by the consistent application of the same formula. Sex becomes one of the items of
leisure activity that the knowledgeable consumer of leisure handles with
his characteristic skill and detachment. The girl becomes a desirable — indeed an indispensable — "Playboy accessory."

In a question-answering column entitled "The Playboy Adviser," queries
about smoking equipment (how to break in a meerschaum pipe), cocktail
preparation (how to mix a Yellow Fever), and whether or not to wear
suspenders with a vest alternate with questions about what to do with girls
who complicate the cardinal principle of casualness either by suggesting
marriage or by some other impulsive gesture toward a permanent relationship. The infallible answer from the oracle never varies: sex must be con-

tained, at all costs, within the entertainment-recreation area. Don't let her get "serious."

After all, the most famous feature of the magazine is its monthly fold-out photo of a *play*mate. She is the symbol par excellence of recreational sex. When playtime is over, the playmate's function ceases, so she must be made to understand the rules of the game. As the crew-cut young man in a *Playboy* cartoon says to the rumpled and disarrayed girl he is passionately embracing, "Why speak of love at a time like this?"

The magazine's fiction purveys the same kind of severely departmentalized sex. Although the editors have recently dressed up the *Playboy* contents with contributions by Hemingway, Bemelmans, and even a Chekhov translation, the regular run of stories relies on a repetitive and predictable formula. A successful young man, either single or somewhat less than ideally married — a figure with whom readers have no difficulty identifying — encounters a gorgeous and seductive woman who makes no demands on him except sex. She is the prose duplication of the cool-eyed but hot-blooded playmate of the fold-out.

Drawing heavily on the fantasy life of all young Americans, the writers utilize for their stereotyped heroines the hero's schoolteacher, his secretary, an old girl friend, or the girl who brings her car into the garage where he works. The happy issue is always a casual but satisfying sexual experience with no entangling alliances whatever. Unlike the women he knows in real life, the *Playboy* reader's fictional girl friends know their place and ask for nothing more. They present no danger of permanent involvement. Like any good accessory, they are detachable and disposable.

Many of the advertisements reinforce the sex-accessory identification in another way — by attributing female characteristics to the items they sell. Thus a full-page ad for the MG assures us that this car is not only "the smoothest pleasure machine" on the road and that having one is a "love-affair," but most important, "you drive it — it doesn't drive you." The ad ends with the equivocal question "Is it a date?"

Playboy insists that its message is one of liberation. Its gospel frees us from captivity to the puritanical "hatpin brigade." It solemnly crusades for "frankness" and publishes scores of letters congratulating it for its unblushing "candor." Yet the whole phenomenon of which *Playboy* is only a part vividly illustrates the awful fact of a new kind of tyranny.

Those liberated by technology and increased prosperity to new worlds of leisure now become the anxious slaves of dictatorial tastemakers. Obsequiously waiting for the latest signal on what is cool and what is awkward, they are paralyzed by the fear that they may hear pronounced on them that dread sentence occasionally intoned by "The Playboy Adviser": "You goofed!" Leisure is thus swallowed up in apprehensive competitiveness, its liberating potential transformed into a self-destructive compulsion to con-

sume only what is *a la mode*. *Playboy* mediates the Word of the most high
into one section of the consumer world, but it is a word of bondage, not
of freedom.

Nor will *Playboy's* synthetic doctrine of man stand the test of scrutiny.
Psychoanalysts constantly remind us how deep-seated sexuality is in the
human being. But if they didn't remind us, we would soon discover it
ourselves anyway. Much as the human male might like to terminate his
relationship with a woman as he would snap off the stereo, or store her
for special purposes like a camel's-hair jacket, it really can't be done. And
anyone with a modicum of experience with women knows it can't be done.
Perhaps this is the reason *Playboy's* readership drops off so sharply after
the age of thirty.

Playboy really feeds on the existence of a repressed fear of involvement
with women, which for various reasons is still present in many otherwise
adult Americans. So *Playboy's* version of sexuality grows increasingly irrelevant as authentic sexual maturity is achieved.

The male identity crisis to which *Playboy* speaks has at its roots a deep-
set fear of sex, a fear that is uncomfortably combined with fascination.
Playboy strives to resolve this antinomy by reducing the proportions of
sexuality, its power and its passion, to a packageable consumption item.
Thus in *Playboy's* iconography the nude woman symbolizes total sexual
accessibility but demands nothing from the observer. "You drive it—it
doesn't drive you." The terror of sex, which cannot be separated from its
ecstasy, is dissolved. But this futile attempt to reduce the *mysterium tre-
mendum* of the sexual fails to solve the problem of being a man. For
sexuality is the basic form of all human relationship, and therein lies its
terror and its power.

Karl Barth has called this basic relational form of man's life *Mitmensch,*
co-humanity. This means that becoming fully human, in this case a human
male, requires not having the other totally exposed to me and my purposes—while I remain uncommitted—but exposing myself to the risk of
encounter with the other by reciprocal self-exposure. The story of man's
refusal so to be exposed goes back to the story of Eden and is expressed
by man's desire to control the other rather than to *be with* the other. It
is basically the fear to be one's self, a lack of the "courage to be."

Thus any theological critique of *Playboy* that focuses on its "lewdness"
will misfire completely. *Playboy* and its less successful imitators are not
"sex magazines" at all. They are basically antisexual. They dilute and dis-
sipate authentic sexuality by reducing it to an accessory, by keeping it at
a safe distance.

It is precisely because these magazines are antisexual that they deserve
the most searching kind of theological criticism. They foster a heretical
doctrine of man, one at radical variance with the biblical view. For *Playboy's* man, others—especially women—are *for* him. They are his leisure

accessories, his playthings. For the Bible, man only becomes fully man by being *for* the other.

Moralistic criticisms of *Playboy* fail because its antimoralism is one of the few places in which *Playboy* is right. But if Christians bear the name of One who was truly man because He was totally *for* the other, and if it is in Him that we know who God is and what human life is for, then we must see in *Playboy* the latest and slickest episode in man's continuing refusal to be fully human.

Freedom for mature sexuality comes to man only when he is freed from the despotic powers which crowd and cower him into fixed patterns of behavior. Both Miss America and The Playboy illustrate such powers. When they determine man's sexual life, they hold him in captivity. They prevent him from achieving maturity. They represent the constant danger of relapsing into tribal thralldom which always haunts the secular society, a threat from which the liberating, secularizing word of the Gospel repeatedly recalls it.

**The American mess
is worse than any other**

Ian Nairn   **The American Landscape**   **49**

Ian Nairn, architect and editor, was born in England in 1930. After receiving a Bachelor's degree in mathematics from Birmingham University, and after three years of service as an R.A.F. jet fighter pilot, he decided to devote his time to architecture. He was a contributor to The Exploding Metropolis *(1958), has been an editor of* Outrage *and* Counter-attack, *and is presently the editor of* Architectural Review. *He is also architectural correspondent of* The Daily Telegraph. *In the following selection, the American environment is described as both destroyed and disregarded. Nairn's critique indicates what has become an important contemporary issue. Only recently have Americans become concerned with what Eric Hoffer has termed "grooming" the environment. For related ideas, see also Kouwenhoven, Cox, Carson, Galbraith.*

We have an empirical modern architecture based (ostensibly, anyway) on specific needs, individual solutions, the creation of a humane and exciting environment, but we have no modern townscape to go with it, nothing to join up the individual masterpieces into a corporate place. On Park Avenue, New York, two undoubted masterpieces nod at one another across the street, each elegantly and humanely designed within its boundaries. But separating the Lever and Seagram buildings are a rush of cars, browbeaten shrubs, dumb pavements—a chaos of nonrelation. They remain architectural gems; but as attempts to be anything more, any part of the total city, they are stillborn.

This chaos of nonrelation is probably worse in America than anywhere else in the world. And this is odd, because most of the fifty states have created for most of their members the world's richest society. Nowhere else, ever, has the man in the street had so much money and so much leisure in which to spend it. Everywhere, interest in the arts is booming: yet the most continuous, most down to earth, most easily apprehended art of all—the art of making a pattern in the environment—is entirely neglected. . . .

By an unhappy series of accidents, a lot of America has never really had any kind of man-made visual pattern and identity, in the sense in which English villages or German towns have. There is tremendous local feeling, but it is quite unexpressed in the shape of the place—or only expressed by functional accidents like the grain elevators and the water towers and the courthouse squares, grand though all these may be. With "the towns where the automobile got there first" there is not even that: around Van Horn in Texas, or in parts of the Deep South like Mobile, and of course in all the new settlements of the last twenty years. With exurbia it is a little more understandable: if you are way out on Long Island you do share, vicariously, a little of the identity of metropolitan New York. . . .

Goop, the goulash of environment, is not a simple thing due purely to the automobile or to exurbia or commercial pressures. The American mess is worse than any other mess in the world for a combination of reasons, all of which act together. Some of the reasons came over with Columbus, some are America's own contribution. They are like the components of an explosive that had been smoldering together for years and that finally went off after the Second World War. To get a cure, the disease needs a more detailed diagnosis.

So every man-made settlement in America was conscious and self-conscious. And self-conscious planning arrived in America in its most dogmatic and simple-minded form, the plane geometry of the Renaissance, the newfound simplicity which man thought was the key to the universe. Where better to demonstrate it than the New World? Now, Renaissance plans in Europe did not stay simple for very long: it was not, after all, the golden solution. And moreover, they were almost always next to or imposed upon medieval plans, so that the end result was not just formality, but formality plus informality, a very different thing. But in America the plans did not get more complex and more subtle: they got simpler. The progression was from the disarming strings of squares in Savannah and the quadrilateral of squares in Philadelphia to the single courthouse square of the Middle West and then, directly, to the straightforward gridiron. And at the gridiron, Renaissance aesthetic simplicity taken to its ultimate (rather like Malevich's white circle on a white square, alas), met land-surveyors' economic simplicity at its crudest. The grid was not only a kind of ideal, it was the cheapest and easiest way of carving up land. Like the Model T Ford, it ran its competitors out of business. But, unlike the Model T, its only virtue was commercial simplicity.

Like coexistence, the gridiron is now a loaded word. It has emotional overtones, it is supposed to be a typically American product like hominy grits or clam chowder, and it has the undoubted superficial virtue of being able to tell you in a strange town exactly how to get from Main and Seventh to Walnut and Sixteenth. Unfortunately, it is also the biggest agent in making all the blocks in between undistinguishable, because it has two incontrovertible drawbacks that are matters of optics, not of argument. . . .

There have been plenty of reactions against the gridiron, starting in the garden with Downing and the layout of Central Park, through the Greenbelt towns to the average big subdivision of today. But in many ways, to continue the metaphor, these plans are tease without strip. It is a tragedy that American towns should be all formality in the center where some informality would harmonize and give point to the genuinely formal occasions, and all informality in the suburbs where a little formality is desperately needed to give cohesion and pattern.

And if the street pattern has no continuity, neither have the buildings lining it. I am putting forward continuity of some kind as a *sine qua non:* all it really means is that when I write a sentence, I hope that the words in it will bear some relation to each other: and it is the same with the parts of a town. They must make sense of some kind—which does not in the least mean regimentation or monotony, for I could have written any sort of sentence I pleased: it just implies some kind, any kind, of meaning—or even of non-meaning or chaos, but only as a special case. Chaos occasionally is good fun and essential: every life should have—occasionally—the completely aimless week and the helpless drinking bout and the sexual orgy. But chaos all the time is just chaos. A town full of permanently chaotic people is given a special name: lunatic asylum. Yet what else is US 1 between New York and Philadelphia but a topographical loony bin? And, like it or not, over the years places do react on people.

Each building is treated in isolation, nothing binds it to the next one: there is a complete failure in relationship—odd, in a nation which has self-consciously exalted family relationship, i.e., relationship inside the isolated units, to a new consciousness of "togetherness," and exalted it alas by such means that togetherness itself has become a dirty word. Yet togetherness in the landscape or townscape, like the coexistence of opposites, is essential.

What is odder is that outside the town centers there never seems to have been relationship of man-made units. To take this at its most revealing, a New England village green is not simply an English village green transplanted. The individual units are bigger, which makes the job of relationship more difficult, and they are already formalized and isolated as though they were a late-nineteenth-century suburb. What binds them together— just as in a suburb—is the trees, and hence if they are seen in winter, even showplaces like Ipswich, Connecticut, or Salem, Massachusetts, or Hancock, New Hampshire, seem flavorless, standing around like plucked chickens. In an English green, if you took away all the foliage, the effect might be impaired but it would not be destroyed. Not that the New England villages are not delightful places; of course they are. But the point is that their charm is not really a man-made delight, that it is useless to go to New England for a solution even by analogy to our man-made problems. And what happened in the comparable parts of, say, Idaho was that the pattern was repeated first without the village green and then without the trees.

So, before the Industrial Revolution started and before it was possible to mass-produce houses or automobiles or anything else, the basic forces for non-relation and nonidentity were already there: a standardized community plan and lack of relationship between the parts. (I am trying to show just how the circumstances lined up to produce the catastrophic exploding metropolis of the last ten years in America. The explosion is purely a twentieth-century phenomenon, but the reasons why it was catastrophic go back much further.) . . .

The bald fact is that the last real pioneering inside America finished when the railroad reached the West Coast: 1869. *Ninety-five years ago,* time enough for a smaller band of pioneers with much less means at their disposal, to build all the Norman cathedrals in England. America as a pioneering country, careless of details, is simply a bolthole for complacency. And in particular the idea of America needing to prove its manhood and virility by stamping on Nature as hard as possible, as a child might pull off insects' legs, is contemptible and shaming.

The attitudes and the accidents were building up over the centuries. All that the situation needed now was the means for explosion. The twentieth century provided them, like a two-stage rocket, with the automobile around

1920 and with the possibility for cheap universal mobility after 1945. But to blame the automobile or the wish to live in a suburb for the mess is a monstrous injustice. The mess is in men's minds: the agents only make it capable of realization. Northern Switzerland, which is very nearly comparable to one of the "clean" industrial areas of America—say, exurban Boston or Palo Alto—has cars and suburbs, yet it is probably more exciting and interesting than it was half a century ago, rather than less. In other words, the products of technology have been used, not allowed to take command.

To all these factors there ought to be added one more. It is, I think, specifically American; and to an outsider it can only seem pointless and stupid. Its cause is natural and results from a misuse of the conception of freedom: its results are so patently absurd that any self-respecting society should have tried to control them. America is founded very properly on individual rights: the misuse is to assume that a business or corporation can act corporately as though it were, say, ten thousand individuals. It is not: it is another animal altogether, and one whose temper may be bad or good. If it is good, you get Olivetti of Milan; if it is bad, you get—well, take a walk down any highway. Because the billboards show the conflict between individual freedom and the common good at its crudest. Billboards, like the car and the FHA loan, are of course not bad things in themselves; they are just other means, to be used or misused. For man to put one sign outside his door is legitimate and logical (we in England have swung too far to the other extreme, and repress all such outdoor advertising that could enliven and humanize our urban streets). But for a company to act as ten thousand individuals and claim an equal right to put up ten thousand stereotyped signs in ten thousand different places is, literally, a perversion. It can be done, as the French do with St. Raphael or Dubonnet, by fitting each sign to the surroundings, by signing a contract with the site, as it were: by practicing the art of relationship. This can fairly claim the liberties of ten thousand individuals. But the same sign slapped down regardless of site from Oregon to Florida is just the blind, immature, unselective action of a spoiled child. And, which is doubtless more to the point, it doesn't even sell more X or Y or Z. (For me, and perhaps for more Americans than people realize, it sells less. I'm damned if I'm going to buy something that squats in front of my favorite view.) In Western Europe there is a wide variety of control over advertisements. Italy and Belgium are as bad as America; England and Switzerland have more or less stringent systems. Is anyone seriously going to say that the level of consumption of beer or gasoline, either over-all or of any particular brand, is less in England and Switzerland than in Italy or Belgium? Put in that way, the proposition is absurd. . . .

Looked at in another way, all this is an expression of conspicuous waste or the theory of obsolescence. And that in itself is another attitude which contributes to "the state of the nation"—the literal physical state of the nation's land surface—and why it is rapidly getting worse. Conspicuous waste, as applied in America, is a result of the misuse of mass production analogous to billboards resulting from the misuse of the idea of individual liberty. There are some things which are suited to rapid obsolescence and some which are not. In an economy which can make almost anything to any shape, size and degree of permanence, the dividing line is largely an emotional one. If a man is emotionally bound up with something, it is useless telling him that here is a brand-new XYZ and that his own XYZ is a heap of junk: he will continue to care for it long after it ought to have become a heap of junk, because it is part of himself. It applies to automobiles to some extent, depending on the quality of the excellence of the machinery (there is more feeling for and care of a ten-year-old car like the TD M.G. in America than in England) and it certainly applies to homes. To plan for an economy which replaces homes as one would replace electronic equipment is absurd because it ignores the emotional stake involved, something just as tangible as bricks and mortar. The moment a building is occupied it acquires—quite apart from its architectural quality—an emotional charge rather like an electric charge, something which in the end may be the most important thing about it. The continued existence of Carnegie Hall in New York, against all the odds, is an example of that. . . .

The misuse of liberty, the misunderstanding of mass production. There is a third element, more insidious, more American than either: the commercialization of emotional needs. In splitting and isolating in this way I am trying to make sense out of an imprecise but very tangible attitude that is a blend—often an indivisible blend, an amalgam—of all these and which is directly responsible for the look of the edges of Louisville or Cleveland. It is specifically American, but it is no more inherent or necessary or inevitable than the Prendergast political machine was to Kansas City. In its effects it is oddly similar to a corrupt city administration, and perhaps the same mixture of attitudes has produced both. What may seem to have been hopeless political morasses have in fact been cleaned up, usually by the efforts of one or two stubborn people. All that was needed was a starting point and an objective. The same is true of the visual morass. This book is an effort toward the creation of a lever: whether it can be applied to any fulcrum is a matter for America itself. And "cleaned up," of course, does not mean merely tidied up.

Of the three elements, the last is the worst. Its end result is that when you hear the words love or beauty or scenic splendor or elegance or charm you are sick to your guts. And that is a kind of living death, because all those words do in fact mean worth-while things. In visual terms it means that there is so much crap around that everything has to be super-marvelous to make up for it. As the next stage, the grafting on of emotional persuasion as a sales' gimmick (common enough from *New Yorker* advertising, evident also in the landscape)—feel as the Pilgrim Father did; take part vicariously in every kind of life—Indian, Mexican, eighteenth-century Virginian, imported European—but never take part in real life.

The end product is Disneyland, which is absolutely right where it is, i.e., as a fantasy world, a suspension of disbelief. The human mind and heart needs that, too. But in America, the attitude of Disneyland is being spread over the entire continent.

The coast is the line of bungalows that marks out America so frighteningly to the air-borne visitor, all the way down to New York from the coast of Maine. And to counteract, New Hampshire has to call itself a "Land of Scenic Splendor." It is, indeed, but it won't be for very long if it simply trots out the inflated words and doesn't do anything to preserve the scenery. The same is true at the other end of America of the overadvertised Indian rugs in the astounding visual chaos that seems to happen anywhere in New Mexico where more than two people and a car are in one place at a time. The same is true, changing the sense a little, of exalting Savannah and Charleston as the apogees of gracious Southern living when both have Negro slums which would be surprising even in Naples. In every case the reality has been too squalid, so people have turned their backs on it and erected a make-believe world. Squalor has been compounded with hypocrisy. . . .

The whole of America, from Pacific to Atlantic, could be built up organically and sensitively, just as a human body is made up of molecules making cells, making organs and limbs. At the moment America is a great big heap of artifacts—the most varied and exciting heap that the world has ever seen, dumped down in the most monotonous and dreary way that the world has ever seen. If they could be given pattern, the result would be the most varied, exciting and unregimented set of places that the world has ever seen, each with its own internal order coming out of its own specific needs; perhaps similar to the next place, perhaps completely different.

It is, frankly, a vision; there's no point in half measures. But it is a vision that could be carried out in a hundred million tiny stages. Any of them would be an improvement, any of them could be carried out independently of any others. That is part of the vision too: no grand superimposed plan, politically unworkable and temperamentally unpracticable, but a million gestures of self-help. As long as the gestures practice relationship and sequence and identity, they are bound to come out right, and the more disparate they are, the better. So the "how" by which this might be achieved is as empirical as the thing itself. Sometimes it might be a state planning commission, sometimes a group of citizens, sometimes a single property-owner who would make the first gesture in an area—a single piece of preserved countryside, a new subdivision, a courthouse square, an urban renewal project. If the idea has anything in it, then it will spread of its own. If not, then no amount of imposition will make it work, and there would be no point in trying.

One further step could be taken immediately, and that is a pilot scheme to look at a town and its countryside together, in terms of sorting out identities, defining boundaries, exploring townscape and landscape potentialities. There have been surveys galore, but never like this: a survey trying to give a character map of a whole region.

It would best be a medium-size town between 50,000 and a quarter of a million—Lancaster, Pennsylvania, or Muncie, Indiana (already famous for another sort of survey, Lynd's *Middletown*), or Albuquerque or San Diego or Lansing. It would have to be a rapid survey, sketching in rather than exploring street-by-street, it it is not to get bogged down in a welter of information. It must be as compelling as a novel, as persuasive as a political tract. It must have general application without losing the ability to solve particular cases. Above everything else, it must be fun—fun to do, fun to write, fun to read. It in many ways is the necessary sequel to this book. The job is necessary and urgent. If the face of America is not to disappear in a welter of nonidentity, the time to act is right now. The need for visual identity is there, the tools with which visual identity can be created are there. All that is lacking is the elementary know-how to make the tools express the needs. A whole new world of excitement and fulfillment is waiting, implicit in the wonderful variety of American sites and in the wonderful variety of material that the twentieth century has made available.

America is a managed society

50

Tom Hayden

The Ability to Face Whatever Comes

Tom Hayden, a recent graduate of the University of Michigan, is one of the founders of Students for a Democratic Society who presently works on the SDS Poverty Project in New Jersey. The following selection is one of a series which appeared in the New Republic *under the general title "Young Rebels Speak." Hayden, as a spokesman of the New Left, criticizes American society on a number of grounds. See also Whyte, Mills, Communist Party, U. S. A., Berle, Brooks.*

Most people think this is a healthy country, with a few isolated ailments. But the difficulties encountered in trying to cure those ailments persuade some of us that an epidemic has spread over America. Signs of it are everywhere. Three current ones are the Vietnam war, the reluctance of authorities to meet the needs of Negroes and poor people, and the furore over free speech in universities. In each case, the pattern is the same.

1. *People have little active control over decisions and institutions.* The Vietnam war is run from the LBJ ranch, the Pentagon, and the US Mission in Saigon, without any real participation by representatives of the American and Vietnamese people. In the same way, the Administration decided that the Mississippi Freedom Democrats, in their present radical form, have no "legal" right to a place in the Democratic Party and the Congress. So, too, are poor people kept out of the poverty program unless they behave properly. University students as well are excluded from decisions about the kind of education they pay for and need.

2. *When trouble breaks out, Americans blame frustrated minorities of agitators; the mainstream of America is accepted as good for everyone except psychological misfits and outside enemies.* It is unthinkable to most people that the Vietnamese peasantry is the backbone of the anti-colonial movement. In much the same way Southern Negroes are seen as the tools of SNCC; in fact this view is held by reputable Northern liberals almost as much as by diehard segregationists. Critics of the Berkeley Free Speech Movement attacked a "Maoist" fringe for the trouble, even though actual polls showed that a majority of students favored the civil disobedience tactics.

3. *Those actually responsible for the Vietnam war, segregation, poverty and university paternalism are not Birchite generals, Southern rednecks and old-fashioned college alumni. Instead they are powerful and respectable men whose type is now dominant throughout society.* The war is a product of Johnson, McNamara, Rusk and their glamorous National Club. The destiny of Mississippi's political economy is in the hands of national Democratic bureaucrats, bankers and policymakers. Life and labor are most exploited in the very cities which are centers of Democratic power and affluent liberalism. Berkeley is the most "advanced" public university; its administration is heralded widely for its application of industrial-relations concepts to organized education.

A civil rights worker in Mississippi can at least count on some Northern support; but what do you do if the whole country sees the Viet Cong guerrillas in the way white Mississippians see the civil rights movement? There is very little in American experience that would foster an identity between our people and the Vietnamese; there is at least a domestic tradition of support for racial equality and due process. There is no group in America which can directly press the case of the Vietnamese in the way that Negroes have pressed their case on white America. On the contrary, those Americans who stand for the Vietnamese have their message weakened or disqualified because they are students, professors or housewives. And people outside America who oppose the war are disqualified as Communists, narrow nationalists or both. The protest against the war almost seems to create a stronger patriotic current in the country. Where only the official versions of reality are generally accepted, how can a new reality break through the taboos? How can what is silenced by the established order make itself truly heard?

Yet even with this apparent perfection of social control, an uneasiness remains widespread. National consensus did not save Kennedy from violence, nor did it fully crush skepticism about the official stories of the murder. The civil rights bills did not prevent the ghetto rebellions of the last two summers. Neither did the poverty program, although it moved some of the rioting to Job Corps camps. Even LBJ's "guidelines" could not pacify the auto and steel workers during the last grievance negotiations. All our generals and counterguerrilla experts, plus our brute strength, can't teach those Asian peasants the American Way.

A Managed Society

The cause of this uneasiness traditionally has been the working class, more recently the Negroes, and nowadays it seems to be the youth. It is not simply the poor youth, those whom Labor Secretary Wirtz calls "the outlaws." The news from Darien is that the sons and daughters of chief executives are smoking pot. From Bronx High School of Science we hear that the college-bound kids tend to cheat the most. And, of course, there are those protest marchers everywhere. A decent citizen can't escape them by watching television; they're being interviewed as they burn draft cards. Nor the radio; all you get is Dylan, folk rock, protest songs. From the clubhouse at Augusta comes word that the General shares the distress of all parents; and down at Lake LBJ, the President, himself a family man, registers his surprise at this disinterest in the Great Society.

The cost of managing these conflicts is very high. A managed society is a paralyzed one, in which humane promises go unrealized, dreams die, people stop hoping for anything beyond the necessary evil. Depending on their social position, people act in variously impotent and damaging ways: delinquency, crime, narcotics, psychological failure, sexual insecurity, cheating, suicide.

Instead of workers driven into motion by class dynamics, the "proletarians" spawned in the paralyzed society are the various outcasts whose sense of reality cannot be adjusted completely to the dominant myths and given roles.

Many Negroes are outcasts in white society. Many working people are outcasts from business society, and most from union society as well. Many young people are outcasts because, if they are poor, they have no future within the existing system; and, if they are affluent, they cannot be fulfilled by endless striving for more of what they inherited at birth. Many professionals are outcasts because their talents are wasted by the Great Society. Housewives too.

These outcasts do not form an economic class; they share a common status. They are not unified by common places of work or living; they are isolated. They have no common set of immediate needs; their views of the world often clash. They seem to want only a modest freedom for themselves within a system they have no hope of changing. They flare into revolt now and then, but individually and indirectly; they appear more to be evading, perhaps mocking, the system while going along with its routines. The strain upon them comes from living with what they cannot accept but cannot change.

If neither a class crisis nor a genuine division of social opinion seems in the making, what can turn outcasts toward effective rebellion?

The problem is partially one of strategy and tactics, or building a movement; partially personal and existential, or finding a basis for radical work when there is very little hope for positive change within a lifetime. I offer only the most tentative and general ways to look at these problems, because I believe they will be settled, if at all, more by feel than theory and mostly in immediate specific situations.

"Building a movement" means that however alienated new radicals might be, they somehow work in existing American communities. If only to prevent the total closing of society, or to take real steps that create change, there must be community controversy inspired by an organized left. Without developing a human base, clearheaded about the way its needs are denied, the new radicalism will have neither leverage nor growth.

Points of departure for community work are nearly endless: organizing strong independent movements of the poor through protests, community centers and cooperatives, union organizing among low-income workers, and insurgent political campaigns; threading such neighborhood movements in coalition with similar forces around the country so that national movement and pressure is generated; connecting with the fresh radicalism on campuses, in the peace movement, and in professions wherever possible, so as to give all a broader vision, the reinforcement that comes with new energy, and a great popular base; deepening the work always to move new people out of silence and into active discovery of their own talents; going always below the existing leadership to keep insurgency growing at its root; keeping the issue of exclusion from the power structure in the fore always as the link between all parts of the movement.

A Five Point Program

Real accomplishments are possible. First, the movement can make modest gains which mean something to individuals and neighborhoods: rent control, play streets, apartment repairs, higher welfare payments, jobs. Second, democratic movements appear, giving people opportunities for decision-making, protest and program which are not available now. Third, existing coalitions begin to support the new movements, or are challenged by them, thus changing the focus of community controversy. Fourth, radical ideas become more visible, especially attacks on poverty and civil rights policy, because the ideas flow from an organized movement that can challenge local power. Fifth, the work is a crucial learning experience that can be used in many ways by the people who are participating.

Acting as a radical means far more than overcoming the orthodox pressures to conform, great as those are. It means, at this time, working with little belief in Utopia. There simply is no active agency of radical change — no race, class or nation — in which radicals can invest high hopes as they have in previous times. Nor is there much possibility, so damaged are we, of building a utopian community in the here and now, from which to gather strength, go forth and change the world. That "the people" often are brilliant and resourceful should not blind us to faults. At least some of the time, people fight each other when their "interest" is in uniting; respond fearfully when they should stand up; vote "wrong" when radical alternatives are put forward; lose spirit in the final rounds of battle; remain attracted privately to the system of manipulated authority they condemn in public. But if radicalism is unable to bank fully on history or morality, what is available?

This problem, however it is stated, is wearing down the strength of many people in the new movements. It causes students to withdraw into fatalism after one or two years in the field, and it causes equally heavy forms of weariness among community people, North and South, at the grass roots of the civil rights, peace and labor movements. The same crisis, I imagine, has withered past movements and led radicals, such as the current labor leadership, into sorry marriages with the system they once tried to overthrow.

Then is the only value in rebellion itself, in the countless momentary times when people transcend their pettiness to commit themselves to great purposes? If so, then radicalism is doomed to be extraordinary, erupting only during those rare times of crisis and upsurge which American elites seem able to ride.

The alternative, if there is one, might be for radicalism to make itself ordinary, patiently taking up work that has only the virtue of facing and becoming part of the realities which are society's secret and its disgrace. Radicals then would identify with all the scorned, the illegitimate and the hurt, organizing people whose visible protest creates basic issues: who *is* criminal? who *is* representative? who *is* delinquent? Radicals then would ask of the conventional majority: at what cost have we laid down these lines and rules? Who is victimized, enslaved, freed? What have we won and what have we lost as a people who, long seeking a Christian commonwealth, put our best talents into the extermination of redskins, wops, micks, krauts, nips, niggers, gooks and red revolutionaries?

Radicalism then would give itself to, and become part of, the energy that is kept restless and active under the clamps of a paralyzed imperial society. Radicalism then would go beyond the concepts of optimism and pessimism as guides to work, finding itself in working despite odds. Its realism and sanity would be grounded in nothing more than the ability to face whatever comes.

**A crisis has overtaken
the American labor movement**

Grant C. McConnell   **Private Power
and American Democracy**   **51**

Grant C. McConnell was born in Portland, Oregon, in 1915. He received his Bachelor's degree from Reed College in 1937, was a Rhodes scholar, and received his Ph.D. from the University of California at Berkeley in 1952. He is currently professor of political science at the University of Chicago. Among his other works are Decline of Agrarian Democracy *(1953) and* The Steel Seizure of 1952 *(1960). In the following selection, he de-*

scribes the crisis in the labor movement, including the decline in member-
ship and a decline in "dynamism." For related ideas, see Mills, Communist
Party, U.S.A., Henry, Blum.

By the 1960s a condition approaching crisis had overtaken the American
labor movement. That "crisis" is the appropriate term is sometimes dis-
puted, but certainly many observers and participants in the movement are
deeply troubled. With its apparent change of direction in the 1930s great
fervor developed and widespread hopes arose that the labor movement
was on its way to a transformation of American society. But as the greatly
enlarged movement gradually settled down to a bureaucratized existence,
the fervor abated and disillusionment took its place. It was a new illustration, perhaps, of the insight of Gompers when he spoke of the relegation
of "some idealism to movements which do not move to the dead ashes of
blasted hopes and promises."

Nevertheless, there were other signs of a more objective character that
all was not well with the American labor movement. The first was that the
growth of union membership had stopped. Following World War II union
membership had increased slightly more rapidly than the increase in the
civilian labor force, a growth that continued until 1953. In the following
year, however, union membership as a percentage of the labor force began
dropping. The decline has continued on a slow downward curve from 28
per cent in 1953 to a bare quarter. There has also been a decline in absolute numbers since 1957. Although these figures indicate no catastrophe,
they are not signs of good health in a movement that has always presumed
that ultimately it would include most of the working class.

This failure to grow is a reflection of a series of particular failures.
Thus it reflects the failure of a much-heralded campaign to organize in
the South. It reflects the similar collapse (or perhaps simple abandonment)
of a campaign to organize agricultural workers. More important than either
of these is the continuing lag in organization of white-collar workers during an era in which the ratio of white- to blue-collar workers is steadily
increasing.

There are other signs of the membership decline. Most apparent but also
most difficult to measure is the decline of dynamism in the labor movement. As the low attendance of members at local meetings reflects, it is
no longer possible to generate the enthusiasm of members. And union
leaders have only limited ability to gain the voting support of members in
public elections except where they can demonstrate that issues are of the
most immediate concern to labor. Various reasons have been offered in
explanation. Unions are much more efficient organizations than they were
in the 1930s, but they are also much more bureaucratic and impersonal.
And the leaders who formed the new industrial unions of the CIO have,

like their counterparts in the older AFL unions, grown older. With this bureaucratization and aging has come increasing attention to the problems of internal government in the unions. Intellectuals and liberals have been more and more articulate on this subject, and union members have themselves proved restive under their established regimes.

Some observers have also emphasized factors external to the unions. The most dramatic of these is automation (a term frequently used loosely to cover mechanization and improved technology). There is a sharp difference of opinion as to whether automation results in a net destruction of jobs, but it is clear that it does eliminate some jobs on which particular unions have relied for maintenance of their membership rolls in the past. The examples of the Mineworkers and the West Coast longshoremen support the argument that unions cannot handle the problem and at the same time maintain their membership. Automation has also been a factor tending to make strikes difficult or even, as in the telephone industry, nearly impossible. The availability of strikes as tools in collective bargaining has also been diminished by a strong and apparently growing public intolerance for strikes on any substantial scale. The continuation of a large pool of unemployed, the conviction of young workers "that union seniority systems and attrition programs for dealing with automation are conspiratorial devices foisted on industry by labor organizations, whose sole concern is to guard the vested rights of their own dues payers," and the hostility of Negroes to unions are among the factors that are claimed to have made both unions and collective bargaining obsolescent.

The implicit prediction is a gloomy one for the labor movement; nevertheless, if it is that unions are going to wither and die in America, it may be too far reaching. As Philip Taft has observed, crises for the labor movement have been heralded before and have in time proved exaggerated insofar as sheer organizational survival is concerned. Moreover, there are good reasons to believe that many unions of craft workers and many in the service trades may continue to go along much as they have in the past, bargaining to improve wages, hours, and working conditions for their limited constituencies. While some of these constituencies may shrink, others may grow to a limited extent. Even industrial unions such as those in mining, steel, oil and textiles, in which automation is a vivid prospect, will still have the same basis for existence, despite continually smaller memberships.

But to say all this, is not to deny the reality of a crisis. Whether or not this is the proper term, it is clear that a sharp reevaluation of the labor movement is under way in many circles. To no small degree this reevaluation is itself the crisis. Until comparatively recently the labor movement had the apparent stance of a challenger to the established order of things, speaking on behalf of men at the lower end of the social spectrum.

The voluntarism of Gompers and his successors belied this, but until World War II unions still had to fight for recognition and acceptance, although they accepted the economic and political order within which they existed. This struggle did much to disguise the nature of voluntarism. But recognition and acceptance have recently become general. One of the most striking facts about the labor movement today is that, as one close student puts it, employers do most of the work of maintaining union membership through enforcement of the union shop and deduction of union dues from wages. By 1960 almost three quarters of union members were covered by agreements providing for union shops; 78 per cent were under agreements with checkoff provisions. Some of the unions without such provisions are in the construction industry and control access to jobs through control of hiring. In short, unions need no longer engage in the struggle that has been their principal preoccupation in the past and which has given them the air of crusading organizations.

While unions were afflicted with deep insecurity and doubt whether they could survive in the face of the bitter hostility of employers and the erratic unreliability of members, it was understandable that maintenance of organization should be an ultimate consideration in union policy. This was a large part of the practical meaning of the old voluntarism, and it often gave a stern and bitter quality to industrial relations. With that issue now largely settled, the other qualities of voluntarism are returning to the surface, notably the tendency of unions to collaborate with employers in arrangements that are mutually gratifying but of doubtful advantage to those outside their respective constituencies. Although this tendency can occur under peaceful and friendly conditions, it can also appear, as in steel, where there is genuine hostility.

The willingness of certain unions to accept solutions that require a virtual casting out of some of their members (to say nothing of potential members) is equally striking. These solutions may well be justified in terms of abstract economic efficiency, and may even be forced upon the unions. Nevertheless, they are at odds with the aspirations for self-government and self-determination within unions. The democratic presumptions of the unions may have substance, but they are repudiated when the unions themselves participate in the liquidation of a part of their membership.

The issue of political action is obviously deeply troubling to union leaders today. Many labor publications are heavily given over to political news and political appeals. Much of the energy of prominent leaders goes to political matters, at local, national, or international levels. Some of the most vigorous leaders quite plainly wish for a greater role in politics for the labor movement. Thus, Joseph Beirne, President of the Communications Workers, has placed strong emphasis upon greater political participation by the labor movement. External observers, particularly those who are most troubled by the present situation of the labor movement, share the view that union goals are too narrowly economic.

Despite the frequently intense desire of some union leaders to enlarge the political and social horizons of their organizations, however, the labor movement is ill constituted to realize their hopes. The national unions remain the foci of power in the movement, and they are all founded on an exclusive basis. The constituency of each is narrow and more likely to be further narrowed than broadened. For such organizations the logic of voluntarism remains compelling. The evidence of attempts to achieve important results by political action is disappointing to those who would transform the labor movement by sheer political campaigning. The United Auto Workers have been in the best situation to achieve political results; nevertheless, even that union has had only limited success and has had to return to aggressive economic action as its principal tool. The difficulty has been stated by the then President of the United Steelworkers, David J. McDonald: "I firmly believe the type of unions which exist today will not suffice for the future." He asked for "entirely new ideas of organizing and different types of organization." Such new ideas of organization, if intended to achieve results upon the political scene, could only involve a broader constituency for the labor movement.

The break with voluntarism which came in the 1930s was real. It involved the labor movement in the creation of a greatly enlarged constituency and in political modes of action. If the voluntarism of Gompers and his associates and their immediate successors is regarded as at heart an antipolitical creed, then perhaps it is correct to say that the break with voluntarism was almost complete. Despite the doctrinaire quality of the rejection of political action in the old AFL, however, this rejection was probably never the heart of the matter. The autonomy of narrowly constituted organizations has always been more important, as could be seen in the apparent inconsistency of the craft unions' deep involvement in local politics at the same time they supported the Gompers antipolitical position nationally. More recently, labor has been willing to act in national politics, but most of its political involvement has been directed to the goal of organizational security. When legislation affected organizational matters, as with Taft-Hartley, or where appointed governmental officers had important powers over organizational issues, as with the National Labor Relations Board, organized labor willingly entered the political arena.

Just as large corporations secure in the exercise of their own market power have asserted the doctrine of *laissez faire,* whereas other business organizations have resorted to the use of governmental authority, organized labor has at different times and places either insisted on the wrongfulness of political involvement or engaged in legislative and political campaigns. To the extent that private economic power proves reliable, it may be expected that both business and labor will renounce politics and insist upon the antigovernmental strictures of *laissez faire* and voluntarism. To the extent that private economic power is unreliable, whether for purposes of internal discipline or defense against external influences on their spheres of interest, it may be expected that business and labor will seek the use of government.

Labor's deviation from voluntarism, then, has been less dramatic than it has seemed. Many labor leaders do indeed show a deep ambivalence on the issue of political participation. It is notable, however, that the historic goal of organizational security has to a very large degree been achieved for many unions. With this achievement, it is increasingly open to labor to conclude treaties of collaboration with industry in which the classically narrow goals of voluntarism are those of the labor movement. If there is a further step it is that units of government be used to enforce these ends along with those sought by industry in their collaboration. There are already signs of such a step.

A gap between potential and actual performance

52

New Program of the Communist Party U.S.A. (a draft)

In the following selection, the Communist Party criticizes American capitalism on the ground that the gap between capacity and performance reveals a contradiction between the social character of production and the private appropriation of its output. For related ideas, see Parkes, Berle, Galbraith, Brooks, Hayden.

The most conspicuous feature of American capitalist society is the gap between its potential and its actual performance. And this relationship is, after all, the most rational yardstick by which to judge a social order. It does no good to tell a poverty-stricken family today that it really is better off than the fabulously wealthy Pharaohs of ancient Egypt because it may own a television set whereas they could not. The family will judge its con-

New Program of the Communist Party U.S.A. (A draft) (N.Y.: Political Affairs Publishers, 1966), pp. 19-21. Reprinted by permission of the publisher.

dition, not by the standards of ancient Egypt, but by the standards that it knows, or senses, are within the capacity of contemporary American society.

By this common-sense measure American capitalism is the most delinquent social order in history. If in other lands poverty has been, or is, the condition of man because the capacity to produce wealth is inadequate, this is not so in the United States. Here the poverty and deprivation that afflict 70 million Americans by one authoritative count are not the consequences of scarcity. They are indictments of a social order that possesses more than ample means to remedy these conditions but does not.

In an economy of scarcity an inequitable social organization can affect only the degree and distribution of poverty, but poverty itself is endemic. In an economy of abundance only social inequity can produce poverty. In this sense the very achievements of American capitalism rise up to accuse it. Here each malnourished child, each substandard dwelling is a witness to the defects of the social system because the capacity to produce food and shelter is so abundant.

The gap between capacity and performance is a manifestation of what Karl Marx, the founder of scientific socialism, revealed as the primary contradiction of capitalist society—the contradiction between the social character of production and the private appropriation of its output. To be sure, as we are constantly reminded, capitalism has changed since Marx's day. It certainly has changed in this respect: the contradiction has become immeasurably more intense.

In the United States the process of production in vast industrial plants and complexes is a marvel of social, collective effort, with the labors and skills of thousands embodied in each finished product. This social effort exceeds in scale anything done or contemplated in Marx's day. But the finished product of this effort still is the private property of the corporate owners, motivated by the quest for profit, just as it was in his day. The difference is that the empires of wealth controlled by today's corporate owners make the largest capitalist enterprises of Marx's time seem trivial. In short, the production is more social, the appropriation is no less private.

The contradiction between production and appropriation is a corrosive source of the moral crisis in society. Liberal critics deplore the discrepancy between inadequate expenditures of society for its public sector (low-cost housing, health, education, recreational facilities, and so on) and the lavish expenditures for the chrome and tail fins of automobiles, for so-called status symbols, for advertising and packaging. They are inclined, however, to attribute this to a perverse quirk of values. But is it simply a matter of moral values? Is it not true that if there were as substantial a profit to be made from low-cost housing or public playgrounds as there is from automobiles, investment capital would flock to such socially necessary projects and fat advertising budgets would proclaim their virtues? Basic human wants are neglected because there is little profit in satisfying them; artificial needs are created and stimulated because there is much profit in doing so. The root immorality is in the built-in supremacy of private profit over human need. Thus, a whole set of false moral values arises like a malodorous belch from the economic bowels of society.

The immorality is aggravated because socialized production is so incredibly prolific, and to make private appropriation profitable to the maximum requires an ever more monstrous apparatus of sales, credit and advertising to induce people to buy things they either truly do not need or really cannot afford. And side by side with such apparent gluttony there is a famine in the things that millions of Americans desperately need — homes, schools, hospitals and other social services. For the many millions living in poverty and deprivation the famine embraces the most elemental human necessities. Is it possible for a society to so abuse its resources and energies without creating a pervasive moral crisis?

In Marx's classical analysis the contradiction between socialized production and private appropriation must reach a breaking point when the method of appropriation (with all the corresponding social relations) becomes an intolerable barrier to the further development of the means of production. In the United States there is a latent and growing anxiety about such a breaking point. The problem is dramatized by nuclear energy, a prodigious source of power, and by automation, a new dimension in productive capacity. To leave these productive means in the hands of monopoly, with no pilot for their use except the extraction of maximum profit, is to court catastrophe. These means are so revolutionary that their orderly introduction, without wrenching economic dislocation and social havoc, can only be effected with social planning. And for social planning there must be social ownership. Without this, the prospect is for haphazard, piecemeal introduction of more automation and atomic power installations, with consequent evil economic effects.

Competition among monopolies to keep unit labor costs down is responsible for much technical progress since World War II. But this is marked by two deformities:

1. The progress has been uneven and chaotic, and has not fully developed to its overall potential. The very planlessness of capitalist society, the extensive unused plant capacity, and vested interests in older techniques protected by rigged monopoly prices are among factors that act as a brake on technical advance.

2. The harmful social effects of automation under capitalism, expressed most drastically in growing unemployment, create a barrier to the translation of the technical progress which occurs into the social progress that is attainable.

In short, the development of productive means strains increasingly at the social relations that encase it. The incompatibility between monopoly capitalism and economic and social advance reaches a point where society can no longer defer the choice between one or the other, except at its own gravest peril.

**Purposeful, pragmatic,
and prosperous**

Editors of Newsweek　　　　　　　　**The Teen-Agers**　　**53**

In this selection, the editors of Newsweek *magazine analyze the actions, attitudes, and problems of American adolescents. Their conclusions are based on surveys conducted for* Newsweek. *For related ideas, see Cox, Hayden, Goodman.*

Everyone knows all about them. To Eastern Europeans, the teen-agers of California, cavorting on their surfboards or burning on their beaches, seem a shimmering vision of the true capitalist paradise. In Japan, a generation of adolescent kids imitate the typical American teen-ager by drinking *remon*—lemon pop—singing protest songs and strumming *ereki*—electric–guitars.

Reporting to Italian readers, the magazine L'Europeo recently concluded: "America's teen-agers make up, as we shall see, the most pitiless, irreducible, indestructible dictatorship in the world." And Manuel Maloof, an Atlanta tavern keeper, says he can "pick 'em up around the eyes, the wrinkles around the eyes, and the way they wear their hair and the way they talk. It's hard to define, but it's the challenge they give you." Of course, Maloof admits, the older he gets the harder it is to tell: "Sometimes it looks like everybody's under 21."

It does indeed. The American population has found the fountain of youth and, swimming in it, grows younger. The nation's official median age is 27.9 and declining. There are some 17.9 million Americans between 13 and 17, the high-school years. At times the world they inhabit seems strange and remote, more exotic than the mythic glades of Ponce de León's Florida. Even those adults who share living space with them are baffled by their tribal ways, secret passwords and ritualistic songs and dances. . . .

Teen-age years are social years, with a bewildering gradation of clubs, cliques, castes and accompanying forms of untouchability. "There are few periods of life," according to sociologist James S. Coleman, "in which associations are so strong, intimate and all-encompassing as those that develop during adolescence." No wonder, then, that today's teen-agers value the social arts above all others.

Asked by the *Newsweek* survey what they like best about themselves, almost one in every three said they were friendly ("I have a nice smile") and well-adjusted ("I get along fine with people"). Almost all (90 per cent) feel that they have a lot of friends, more than half wish they had more. What do they like least? Their own appearance, for 26 per cent — and in the same self-critical vein, their tempers, which 16 per cent tend to lose. Their sense of groupness, if not necessarily togetherness, is confirmed by 77 per cent who say they are the same as others their age (the figure rises to 79 per cent for suburban children and 82 per cent for those in the crowded industrial East). . . .

Though the greatest problem in an adolescent's life is himself, the teen-age generation sees clearly enough that the principal problems confronting the nation are avoiding war (58 per cent) and eliminating racial discrimination (16 per cent). Even more clearly — and candidly — they see how they differ from previous generations. They value their freedom, mobility and improved education. Most voluntarily acknowledge the benefits of "a better standard of living." This generation lives the good life, likes it and wants more. A graduating senior declares his ambition "To be rich, happy, healthy and famous rather than poor, sad, sick and insignificant.". . .

With a flourishing economy, their nation can afford to keep a large part of its potentially productive population inside classrooms through high school, basking in the warmth of a social incubator. And in the citadel of conspicuous consumption there is no consumer group quite so conspicuous as the teen-agers, whom Harvard's David Riesman has called "consumer trainees." What wonderful games they play! Big business urges them to get out and do what they love to do anyway — buy.

Only 21 per cent say they don't much care for shopping. Three per cent aren't sure. Seventy-six per cent regard it as one of the experiences they most enjoy: not so much for what they buy — they are fickle and their attachments shallow — but for a sense of independence and possession. Knowledge is power, but so is buying power.

At home, where the heart is, the nation's adolescents have every good reason to be heartened by their parents' spirit of fair play. Neither age group calls the tune but both carry it. A heavy majority of teen-agers get along just fine with their parents. Only 12 per cent think their parents try to run their lives. Eighty-six per cent in the survey say the folks at home mind their own business.

Inevitably there are conflicts. Of 17 per cent who admit they smoke (as much as a pack a day among 17-year-old boys), 82 per cent say their parents know it, 85 per cent say their parents disapprove of it. Fourteen per cent believe their parents should be more understanding. Girls also feel slightly less understood than boys. "My parents don't like me to run around with boys, and I think I should be able to," says a Tulsa, Okla., teen-ager. She is 13.

Since privilege and mobility are two of the teen-age generation's hallmarks, it follows that the most prevalent form of parental punishment should be the withholding of privilege: more specifically, "grounding" — keeping the junior birdman in his hangar or taking away the car keys. Grounding is especially popular (or unpopular) in the lone, flat expanses of the Midwest (40 per cent) and the West (45 per cent) where wheels are not only an essential for getting around but also the center of social life and a major source of status. . . .

To their dismay, parents increasingly find themselves low bidder for their children's confidence and attention. Home life is being preempted by the high school, where the kids spend most of their day (8 a.m. to 4 or 5 p.m. by the time the after-class activities and the bus ride home are added). At school, they make most of their friends, learn most of their lessons and are advised, encouraged, analyzed, consoled and profoundly influenced by specialists in surrogate parenthood, the guidance counselors.

What is school? It is an edifice, occasionally majestic, a single, brooding Victorian pile or a cluster of sunny bungalows connected by breezeways, in which classes are taught, clubs convened, records kept, tests graded, teachers tested, rules ruled, cheats cheated, newspapers published, tales told, hands held, smokes smoked, dances danced, drills drilled, sports played, games played, plays played, bells rung and yells yelled. For the student, the best part of school is friends (38 per cent), followed by social life (16 per cent) and learning (16 per cent) in a dead heat.

High school also separates the teen-ager's world as cleanly as if the United States were riven by the Grand Canyon instead of the Continental Divide. On one side are the blessed, who have earned the right to go on to college and probable prosperity. On the other are the damned, who drop out, stop short or, at best, go on to vocational training schools and sharply circumscribed earning potential. "High school," says a boy in Poughkeepsie, N.Y., "is either the beginning or the end."

Separation between the groups is almost complete. Neither has a bed of roses. The college-bound may have hopes of beating the draft temporarily, but they work under crushing pressure for grades if they want to get into a competitive college.

In the second of the two cultures, teen-agers may feign indifference to higher education or feign faint-hearted ambitions to give it a whirl, but "we know, and deep down they know," says Albany (Calif.) High School principal Harry J. Price, "that they won't be successful." . . .

Performance in school can change the course of a life. Demands are stringent. The book strap of yesteryear could never go round today's bulky curriculum. "There is more pressure on us to accept adult responsibilities than ever before," says Suzanne Slayden, 17, of Knoxville, Tenn. "The school program is much harder and more advanced." Each year brings more new things to learn in the same number of weeks. Exams, therefore, become hurdles that must be negotiated: over the bar, by knowing, or under it, by cheating.

Columbia University's Dr. Allen Barton, who supervised a study of 99 colleges that concluded half the students in the sample had cheated, believes high-school cheating is even more prevalent "because college is usually more dedicated to ideas and learning." By teachers' and administrators' reports and their own admissions, high-school students copy one another's homework, plagiarize from critical essays, carry crib notes into class and swipe exam questions from teachers' offices. . . .

"Sex is the biggest topic in any high school and you can't tell me it isn't," said one of the young seminarists. In considering adolescence, says University of California sociologist Edgar Z. Friedenberg in his influential book "The Vanishing Adolescent," sexuality "must be regarded in somewhat the same light as photosynthesis in the study of ecology—as the penultimate source of all energy."

As the sea can be seen in a drop of water, the change in teen-age social patterns can be seen in a single word-ending: "going steadily" as opposed to "going steady." It used to be steady, in word if not in deed, and the relationship was given all the solemn trappings of a demi-marriage. At the United Nations, a former guide recalls, teen-agers going steady would insist on squeezing into the same quadrant of a revolving door because "we're a unit."

Now the going is "steadily" because socially mobile teen-agers are wary of entangling alliances and increasingly convinced that a relationship depends on what emotions its partners invest in it, not on what term they agree to call it by. Sociologist Friedenberg finds and applauds a growing sense of "erotic authenticity" among America's adolescents, an ability to rejoice in their whole physical self, to love openly and respond warmly without a neurotic preoccupation with sexual love. "Girls," he says, "don't look so much like flaming hors d'oeuvres and more like girls."

"Can you imagine making sex education a compulsory thing?" asks a Nevada girl. "The parents and the church groups would scream and jump up and down." But a good deal of screaming is being done without the facts. Not even those who are studying the question have much information on the actual content of high-school "sex education" courses; many of the courses tender only cautious, academic information on the biological aspects of reproduction. One thing seems certain. America's high schools have not yet acknowledged a revolutionary change in sexual relations. In the words of William Denham, associate professor at Howard University's School of Social Work, "We continue to perpetuate beliefs of a pre-contraceptive era in a contraceptive age."

Today's teen-agers, to put it bluntly but accurately, want to know the how, and their parents want to know the how-much; they want to know if premarital sex is really on the increase among the younger generation.

The *Newsweek* survey questionnaire did not deal with sex habits, partly because the legality of such inquiries among minors is in doubt, and also because such questions evoke an often meaningless jumble of wishes, facts, and boasts. Some sources, however, indicate that increasing numbers of teen-agers engage in premarital sex, at least in certain areas and among certain social strata. A New York City boy is convinced that "the majority of teen-age girls sleep with the boy they're going with, from 14 up. It's part of the times." And two obstetric residents at the Emanuel Hospital in Portland, Ore., assert that pregnancy is the leading cause of the city's high-school dropouts.

Across the U.S., illegitimate live births among mothers aged 15 to 19 were 40,000 in 1940, and climbed to more than 101,000 out of 4 million births in 1963. In a recent report, the Connecticut Health Department estimates that one of six teen-age girls in the state was illegitimately pregnant last year.

Yet those who have been involved in the precious few systematic studies of the subject counsel calm. Ira Reiss, a University of Iowa sociologist, believes "there is no indication" that younger teen-agers "are indulging in indiscriminate sex practices." He is joined by Paul Gebhard, an associate on the pioneer Kinsey report and now head of the Institute for Sex Research at Indiana University. Among younger teen-agers, Gebhard says, "there hasn't been any real increase in premarital coitus in recent years. The great liberalization has been in the ability to talk freely about sex." Many authorities say the public has confused a demonstrable increase in premarital sex among college students with increased sex in high schools. . . .

Negro teen-agers in the *Newsweek* survey set themselves apart with consistent, usually cautious but occasionally astonishing expressions of faith in the future. They have no illusions about life today. Twenty-two per cent say they are less happy now than at 8 or 9, compared with 8 per cent of the group as a whole. Thirty-one per cent of Negroes think life will be worse when they reach 21, against 25 per cent in the entire group.

Yet 26 per cent of Negroes believe their generation has "more freedom" than other generations, vs. 22 per cent over-all. One-third of the Negro youngsters think racial discrimination will still be a problem for their generation, compared with 44 per cent in the over-all sample.

Most striking is the Negroes' attitude toward college. Forty-one per cent feel "certain to go to college." While 18 per cent of the entire group say their parents exert "a lot of pressure" on them to go to college, the figure rises to 38 per cent among Negroes, suggesting more parental pressure for higher education among Negroes than among any other geographic, chronological or economic group in the country.

In Watts, the Los Angeles slum district torn apart by Negro violence last year, a 16-year-old Negro boy—call him Bruce (not his real name)—attends Jordan High School, almost entirely Negro except for a few Mexican-Americans. Subdued, bored ("There's nothin' to do. There's no place to go"), he has never been out of Los Angeles and has no car to get him out. A smile comes to his face when he talks of the riot. "Yeah, I was in it," he says happily. "I didn't do none of the burnin' but I was lootin'."

Bruce is a "B" student but isn't sure he can get into college. He wants a good summer job and can't find one. On winter weekends he earns extra money shining shoes at a downtown parlor. He is "scared" by his future. Yet even Bruce, with nothing going for him but his own determination and the sun through the smog, has not given up. He still believes white employers will treat him fairly if he is "qualified." He is not bitter. "I'm not gonna drop out. If I can't get into college I'll probably go out and get a job." Bruce's parents share his timid hope. "If he is prepared," his mother says, "he will have an equal break."

Still other teen-agers are not merely hopeful outsiders. They are outlaws, the violent minority, Negro and white, with vast capacities for destruction and a need to turn these capacities to action. Teen-age crime rates are rising. Over the last decade they have risen more than 100 per cent while the corresponding population increase has been 45 per cent. Children 13 to 17, 9 per cent of the total population, account for 18 per cent of all arrests. Most are for larceny and auto theft, though 15 per cent of their infractions are violations of curfew and loitering laws.

This is the segment of America's teen-age population that dwells on the dark side of a waxing moon, that gets the headlines, terrorizes the gentry and lives in terror itself. In Boston, a juvenile delinquent with a prison record talks into a tape recorder in the Streetcorner Research program organized by Harvard's Ralph Schwitzgebel: "Whenever I get in a fight or anything I'm shaking like a leaf . . . I'm just plain scared . . . scared to walk the streets, scared to go out of my house, scared to stay there."

"The long-term problem is failure," says Wayne County (Detroit) Probate Judge James H. Lincoln. "The doorways of opportunity have been pretty much slammed in everyone's face unless they have first walked through the doors of education."

Nevertheless, Lincoln believes there is "too much stress on the behavior problems of juveniles. We should talk more about achievement." Any juvenile "can get into trouble. Most do, but they will work out of any problem if they have any degree of success in their lives.". . .

In contrast to the troubled minority, most teen-agers seem docile indeed. They criticize themselves sternly: drinking, smoking, long hair, hot rods, eye make-up, net stockings, eccentric clothes. In Salt Lake City, Mormon teen-agers seem uniformly to abhor beards, connecting them with left-wing politics, liquor, licentiousness and dope. Brigham Young wore a beard, but at the right time.

Teen-agers prefer heroes to political issues. Fifty-eight per cent consider John F. Kennedy a "great" President. ("He gave us a young attitude.") LBJ ranks "fair" with 39 per cent, "good" with 41 per cent and "great" with only 9 per cent (though "great" with 25 per cent among Negroes). President Johnson, a New York City boy complains, "goes around dragging cars, cutting across fields, things the President shouldn't do."

Political apathy is the rule among adolescents, with a generally hawkish stance in their attitude toward Vietnam, but tiny pockets of revolt are visible. The cause célèbre is rarely international, usually local, but the significant thing is that the youngsters take action. Teen-agers marched around the Memphis courthouse last week protesting a judge's campaign to close three teen-age "Go-Go" clubs because they supposedly had gone-gone too far toward dim lights and smuggled-in booze. . . .

Youngsters endorse the broad outlines of adult society and adults smile wryly over the Dictatorship of the Teen-ager. Yet the coin has a less shiny side. In the opinion of prominent educators and psychologists, the teen-age population, instead of riding roughshod over helpless adults, is actually being segregated, shunned, manipulated, discriminated against and forced to live in a deluxe ghetto where tastes and mores of a distinct subculture flourish only for lack of meaningful integration into a stable adult society.

"These youngsters," says Frank Brown, principal of the adventurous and widely admired Melbourne (Fla.) High School, "feel that nobody listens to them, that they have no friend at court. Certainly they're not listened to in the schools, because the schools are in a serious state of intellectual disrepair." Adolescents are "discriminated against by the parents, by the schools, by all of society." Social institutions, Brown contends, "have always been against young people."

Many major U.S. cities and suburbs have teen-age curfew laws which assume a youngster guilty as soon as he appears on a street without a "responsible adult" after the witching hour. Other cities, such as Richmond, New Haven, Cleveland, Omaha and Hallandale, Fla., have curfew laws on the books but do not enforce them. Why? "We just thought we ought to have one," one mayor says.

Spies and junior informers infiltrate teen-age nightclubs. Pedagogues dictate hair styles and anathematize granny dresses. Adolescents beg for responsible work in the adult world and find little or none. "I think life is rotten," says a 17-year-old in South Bend. "Man has to have a place in society but some of the places I just couldn't take." Adults, agrees sociologist Coleman, "have shut him out of the job market, have told him, in effect, to go off to school and not bother them."

Until they reach 18, teen-agers have almost no civil rights. Courts act as their prosecutor and protector. Teen-agers, says John A. Schulz, associate professor of psychology at Portland (Ore.) State College, are excluded from the family and forced to create a culture of their own. Different patterns prevail abroad. "I'll never forget the shock of walking into a Dutch tavern," recalls Schulz, "and seeing an entire family enjoying a beer together."

California's Friedenberg is a leading authority on adolescents and one of their most spirited defenders. His iconoclasm ranges far and wide. He compares the role teachers play to that of a doctor who might enter a home to treat a patient and begin to criticize the wallpaper in the patient's bathroom. Friedenberg also thinks teen-agers don't get enough money. "Kids still have very little to spend. They should have money. They should have cars. It's the one basis of their social order. Cars are important. They are for all America. There's no other privacy."

Looking ahead. Shunned or sheltered, adjusted or manipulated, teen-age America carries on. *Newsweek's* survey finds the youngsters optimistic about ameliorating disease, urban problems, college crowding and depressions, confident that creative talents will be used better in the future and that outer space will successfully be explored.

They are rather less optimistic about poverty, the threat of war, highway accidents, racial discrimination, moral standards and crime. But their own attitudes and openness to new ideas may be more potent than they think.

Nearly half their parents in a previous *Newsweek* survey, for instance, said they would object to a Negro family as next-door neighbors, but just over a quarter of the teen-agers feel the same way. Overwhelming majorities of the youngsters have no objection to sharing classrooms or churches with Negroes. Even in the South 62 per cent have no objection to sitting next to a Negro in school.

Enthralled by the marvel of themselves, the young know not what the future holds, but they think they know who holds the future. Some of the shaggier types will be shorn of their locks and will not, like Samson, lose too much strength. Steadily they will expand to keep pace with their expanding universe, tasting, trying, flying or falling, getting to do what they are now only yearning to do. On the last page of Chicago's Senn High School 1965 yearbook, a poem by Karen Miyake concluded:

Oh how
I want to be a Bob Dylan, a Pete Seeger, a Peter, Paul and Mary,
an Illya Kuryakin, a Peter O'Toole, a Seymour Glass, a City seeker,
a gate builder, a lemon flower, an umbrella mender, a roof beam
raiser, a ball in the valley, a free, whole human.
I think I'll go eat a bananafish
It's a hard rains a-gonna fall.

And this year a 17-year-old New York City boy, Steve Anderson, looks into the future and beyond. "I hope there is a hereafter because it's something else to do." . . .

**The dominant value in American
culture is personal independence**

Lawrence H. Fuchs   **John F. Kennedy
and American Catholicism**

54

Lawrence H. Fuchs was born in New York in 1927 and received his Ph.D. from Harvard in 1955. He is currently a professor of American politics and Director of Faculty at Brandeis University. He has also served as the Director of the U.S. Peace Corps in the Philippine Islands. His works include The Political Behavior of American Jews *(1955) and* Hawaii Pono: A Social History *(1961). The following selection describes John F. Kennedy as a symbol of the interaction of the Catholic religion and American society. For related ideas, see Herberg, Cox, Gabriel, Warner, Baltzell.*

The culture-religion of Americans is more than its Protestant inheritance but it cannot be understood apart from it. American Protestants have revealed a pronounced and distinctive unity (when compared to other world religions) in the belief that God must be experienced immediately and directly and that conceptualization of that experience is a task for the

From *John F. Kennedy and American Catholicism* by Lawrence H. Fuchs, pp. 225-231, 235-240, 242-252, by permission of Meredith Press. Copyright, 1967, by Lawrence H. Fuchs.

believer alone, checked only against the biblical text. This has been the central belief of most American Protestants regardless of whether they belong to the Lutheran, Reform, or other churches of the sixteenth-century Reformation, the churches of the seventeenth-century Puritan Revolution, such as Congregationalist and Quaker, the churches of the eighteenth-century Awakening, such as Methodist, Baptist, or Unitarian, or the churches of the nineteenth-century revivals, such as Disciples of Christ and Seventh-day Adventists. It has been a belief which, when mixed with other elements of the American environment, has affected the values, behavior, and psychological style of all Americans in contrast to Europeans and Asians; but is originally and remains essentially a Protestant belief.

Clash of Styles

The psychological style of a people (psycho-cultural might be the best word) describes their *ways* of perceiving, understanding, believing, feeling, and communicating. Americans, and especially Protestant Americans, have a distinctive psychological style as foreign observers from the eighteenth century to the present have observed consistently. It is a style which rests to a considerable degree on the Protestant principle of an empirical God-encounter (as seen most dramatically at revival meetings), whether it is called conversion, faith, or a decision for Christ. The Protestant emphasis on the individual's unassisted encounter with God in the American environment has promoted an empirical, intuitive, subjective (as opposed to theoretical, deductive, and authoritative) psychological style which not only divides Americans from other cultures but which, to a lesser extent, has separated Protestants from Catholics in America. The archetypal Protestant, in insisting that the individual stands alone in relationship to God and opposing metaphysical intellectualism, tradition, and authority, has recoiled from Catholic indulgences, confession, dependency on priests, the distinction between mortal and venial sins, and the Catholic emphasis on mercy and forgiveness.

Against this style is the Catholic style, which rests on the belief that man must be incorporated into God's visible society called the Church to share the life of Christ who is God as well as man. Except for the mystics, Catholics do not experience God immediately in the simple direct way described by Protestants. The truth of his revelations is in the possession of the Church, and its divinely empowered organs will express it. Religion may be personal, but it is complicated and mysterious and not something that can be intuited by the individual. That is why Latin has been important to the liturgy and why Communion is a vital sacrament. It is why the religious wear special clothes, and why important distinctions are made between the sacred and profane, as in the creation of religious orders with special vows. Moral questions are seen as complicated, requiring authoritative interpretation and guidance. The Bible says that thou shalt not kill, but how does that answer the questions of war, abortion, or euthanasia? Salvation requires the avoidance of sin, but who decides which sins are mortal and which are not? Out of such beliefs has emerged a psychological style emphasizing mystery, tradition, obedience, devotion, and the need for coherence and order. To Catholics, it sometimes seems that the Protestant view of man veers crazily from one extreme to the other. Fundamentalists and Puritans emphasize man's utter sinfulness; liberal Protestants talk of man as no less perfect (or at least perfectible) than God himself. Thus, while some Protestants, obsessed by man's depravity, lurch off on crusades against drinking, gambling, and sex, others, imbued with hope for man's perfection on earth, attempt to engineer utopian communities such as Oneida, Brook Farm, and New Harmony.

While the Protestant style, and the beliefs and values from which it sprang, has dominated in America, important value differences remained between Catholics and non-Catholics, at least through the 1950's. One study in 1958 revealed that a significantly higher proportion of Jews and Protestants than Catholics valued intellectual autonomy above obedience in the raising of children. There were differences between Protestants and Catholics in each socioeconomic class, the largest at the highest level. A 1953 survey showed that Protestant and Jewish children were expected by their parents to display more independence and assume greater responsibility at an earlier age than Catholic children. A 1958 study revealed that a much higher proportion of Protestant clergymen and laymen than Catholics in the same categories believed they had a right to question what their churches teach.

The culture-religion of Americans has gone beyond Protestantism in emphasizing personal independence and achievement, and American Catholics from John Carroll on have had to confront a transmogrified Protestantism in America which European Catholics traditionally have seen as a liberal secular anathema to the Church. But Carroll and large numbers of American Catholics, particularly those from the middle and upper classes, and most especially those from English backgrounds, have always disagreed with the European continental view. They have promoted encounter with, and adaptation to, the American environment without fearing the loss of their Catholicism. They have become thoroughly Americanized with respect to ideology and psychological style while maintaining their own identity as communicants of the Roman Catholic Church.

Probably the most important leader the forces of encounter have ever had was John F. Kennedy. He came on the national political scene at a time when the spirit of encounter among American Catholics was relatively subdued and Catholic spokesmen of parochial defensiveness seemed to many

Protestants and Jews to be unusually active. There were exceptions, in the editorials and articles of *Commonweal* and *Cross Currents* (a Catholic-sponsored journal dedicated to fostering a Protestant-Catholic dialogue), the serious intellectual scholarship of *Thought* (Fordham University) and *Theological Studies* (Woodstock College), in the theology of John Courtney Murray, in the writings of Father Ong, Monsignor Ellis, and Father Weigel, in the liberal statements of Cardinal Cushing, Bishops Sheil and John J. Wright, and in the ecumenical action of leading Catholic governors and United States senators. The forces of encounter also could assert that most American Catholic leaders did not accept the dominant European Catholic view of church-state relations, as promulgated most recently and systematically by Pope Leo XIII. Regardless of these signs of encounter in the Church in America, most Jews and Protestants writing on Catholicism in the United States stressed their fear that Catholics, whatever their country, were bound to believe in one true Church and would impose their view of faith and morals on others wherever they had power. They pointed to a statement in the Jesuit journal, *La Civiltá Cattolica,* which appeared in 1948 and which argued that the Roman Catholic Church, being the only true Church, could adopt toleration of other forms of worship only as a matter of necessity. Everyone should understand, the article maintained, "that the Catholic Church would betray her trust if she were to proclaim, theoretically and practically, that error can have the same rights as truth." Non-Catholics decried Catholic persecution in Spain and in certain Latin-American countries, and more important, they complained of the imposition of Catholic truth in matters of faith and morals on local communities through pressure tactics, as in the Margaret Sanger case in Holyoke, and with respect to legislation affecting education, censorship, divorce, and sterilization in several states.

Winds of Change

Within a few years after the election of Kennedy, Catholicism in America was to erupt with a new vigor and diversity and the forces of encounter would become dominant. Before half of the decade of the 1960's was over, it became clear that the culture-religion of Americanism had profoundly affected American Catholics, even as it had influenced Jews, Buddhists, and Protestants themselves. To a considerable extent, John Kennedy was a symbol of the dynamic impact of the American environment on Catholicism. Like many Catholics of his generation, he esteemed not the virtues of humility, mortification, penance, chastity, poverty, and abnegation, but those values of independence and achievement which Americans have cherished since the eighteenth century. If the real difference between the Catholic and Protestant communities lay in their distinctive conceptions of virtue, as some Catholic writers maintained, Kennedy made clear that the American experience had blurred the difference. Between the supernatural and the natural, the theoretical and the empirical, the traditional and the new, the authoritative and the subjective, there was no doubt as to where Kennedy fit. He was the antithesis of the stereotyped separatist, parochial, anti-intellectual, superstitious, tribalistic, and fatalistic Catholic of Protestant literature and conversation. But the stereotype, while based on a core of reality, never suited hundreds of thousands of Catholics from Carroll to Spalding to Kennedy.

The 1960's saw an outbreak of Catholic activity and self-criticism which would have been unthinkable ten years before. A vast range of questions were suddenly wide open for debate: the relationship of the laity within the Church; the problem of self-determination or conscience for the individual Catholic; and the relationship of Catholic dogma to democratic values. No subject was immune from scrutiny, including birth control, divorce, parochial schools, and even the papacy itself. In addition to *Commonweal* and *Cross Currents,* articles challenging basic assumptions appeared in *America, The Sign, Ave Maria, Jubilee, Perspectives,* and a new weekly newspaper, the *National Catholic Reporter.* (Most avant-garde and irreverent of the publications was *Ramparts,* edited by Catholic laymen.)

The *National Catholic Reporter* was typical of the winds of change (a favorite Kennedy phrase) blowing through the Church in America. Its editors gave writers freedom to question every conceivable issue, including the celibacy of priests and nuns, the validity of the ban on mixed marriages, and the value of private confession. Its weekly circulation during the first year of publication (October, 1964 — October, 1965) jumped from eleven thousand to more than fifty thousand. A survey of its readers revealed that the new Catholic emphasis on self-criticism appealed especially to upper-class and upper-middle-class parishioners in the Middle West and Middle Atlantic states. Only 6 percent of its readers came from New England, America's most solidly Catholic region. Its lay audience — 30 percent of its readers were individual clergymen or sisters — was highly educated and well to do, 71 percent of all readers being college graduates and 34 percent having master's degrees. Nearly all heads of households were business or professional men with an average income of nearly fourteen thousand dollars.

Separatism was far from dead. Only in the Middle West could it be said that vigorous lay activity was an important feature of life in the Church. Elsewhere, particularly in Kennedy's New England, laymen were more passive. On some issues, such as racial segregation in the schools, the clerics of New England, led by Richard Cardinal Cushing, were much more willing to risk encounter than a majority of their parishoners. Many priests and nuns complained that there were far too many laymen suspi-

cious of change in the status quo in 'America and within the Church.
Other key members of the hierarchy were less open to encounter than
Cushing. Los Angeles' James Francis Cardinal McIntyre and, to a lesser
extent, New York's Francis Cardinal Spellman looked suspiciously at the
new ferment within the Church.

*   *   *

Kennedy as Symbol and Catalyst of Change

What, if anything, did the resurgence of the forces of encounter and the
new existential ferment in American Catholicism have to do with John F.
Kennedy? Even if Kennedy had been a school-teacher or a journalist, the
new breed of American Catholics probably would have appeared in the
1960's. Many factors were at work to break down the walls of Catholic
separatism in the United States and elsewhere. The most important was
the election of Pope John XXIII and his two extremely influential encyclicals, *Mater et magistra* and *Pacem in terris* and the convocation of the
Vatican Council. Also important was the profoundly penetrating self-criticism and ecumenism of several important European theologians such as
Henri de Lubbec and Yves Congar and the extremely significant work of
the French Jesuit philosopher and paleontologist, Teilhard de Chardin.
The very social changes in America which produced a Kennedy — social
class mobility for Catholics, the growing influence of secular education,
the spreading encounter of Catholics with non-Catholics in war and work
— were also factors in the growing strength of advocates of self-criticism
encounter.

Kennedy was mainly a symbol of change among Catholics in America,
but he was also a catalyst. Although he represented an old and significant
response of American Catholics to the environment of the New World
and the challenge of new Jerusalem, Kennedy, by becoming the most influential lay Catholic in American history, made the path of the new
breed and the generation of the third eye much easier. Because no one
in American history had ever become so completely identified with inter-
religious encounter as Kennedy, his election gave hope to the forces of
encounter. As a culture-hero, Kennedy could not help but inspire other
lay Catholics to identify with him, and he undoubtedly gave many of the
laity the courage to voice their doubts. Here was a layman who was not
only occasionally flip and irreverent toward the clergy, but he seemed
certain of his own positions in opposition to members of the hierarchy,
and was admired all over the world as the most representative American
of his time.

Without Kennedy, the forces of American pluralism, the rapidly developing thought of Catholic theologians, and the influence of Pope John

would have stimulated the American laity to new introspection anyway. With Kennedy, questions and doubts were brought more rapidly and forcefully into the open. Kennedy was a sign but he was also a stimulus who made it easier for Catholics to peel away their defenses both in and outside the Church. Young men and women who had never heard of de Lubbec or Congar or who had not even read *Mater et magistra* could see in the great respect accorded President Kennedy a sanction for self-criticism and encounter. Studies made by my students at Brandeis University of the opinion of Catholic instructors and students at Catholic and non-Catholic universities in the Boston area revealed that Kennedy spoke to their needs and aspirations as Catholics to a considerable extent. In praising him, they said repeatedly that the President represented the ecumenical conviction that, as one of them put it, "truth can be found in many places." Kennedy spoke for them, they maintained, in implicitly attacking the ghetto mentality that had separated Catholics from their fellow Americans. Because Kennedy was a culture-hero—millions mourning him watched his funeral on television and knew that Mass was said in the White House for the first time in history—Catholics could be more self-confident than at any time since the Revolution.

For many non-Catholics, John F. Kennedy made it clear that Catholicism was not incompatible with freedom. He maintained his own position on social and political questions in the face of strong opposition in the episcopacy, making the doctrine of papal (usually read by non-Catholics as priestly or episcopal) infallibility seem as irrelevant to the issue of personal freedom as Al Smith always said it was. Actually, the Catholic Church was still authoritarian, as even the new breed acknowledged in submitting to its doctrines and rituals, in the sense that the source of authority given to the bishops and the Pope is God. Logically, America's culture-religion and the Roman Catholic Church were as uncongenial as ever. In reality, John F. Kennedy revealed the extent to which personal freedom for Catholics is consistent with their view of loyalty to an authoritarian Church.

Evidence of such freedom abounded everywhere in the 1960's. Studies showed that at least 30 percent of married Catholics in the United States practiced birth control. There were no violent Catholic protests against the allocation of antipoverty funds for birth control or even against the more activist proposals being studied by the United States Senate. An increasing number of Catholics challenged the desirability of parochial schools, and in 1962 the St. Louis archdiocese placed a ban on the building of schools and recommended that parents vote for bond issues to expand the public school system. Although movies and books were much more explicit on sex in the 1960's than they were in the 1940's, Catholic pressure for censorship slackened considerably, and hundreds of thousands of Catholics paid scant attention to the censorship of books and motion pictures by NODL.

Catholic Adaptation

Did this mean that American Catholicism was somehow less Catholic than that of Italy, France, or the Philippines? Clearly, it was different. Wherever the Church has gone, each national culture has stamped its values on Catholicism. Only because Europe has gone through the agony of the Protestant Reformation do we find in France and Germany profound dogmatic and speculative theological discussion. The colonial style of Catholicism in Latin America was essentially pre-sixteenth-century Catholicism imposed primarily by the sword and mission on top of Indian and Malayan folk religions which were adaptable. Catholicism in those countries shows the effects of Spanish Catholicism prior to the Council of Trent (1543–63) and the convulsions of the Reformation. It has produced an anticlerical tradition in reaction to medieval Catholicism comparable to Europe's but virtually no sophisticated theological thought.

The conditions of the Church in America have been radically different from those found in Europe or in colonial outposts. In the United States, Catholicism has been a minority religion in an overwhelmingly Protestant but pluralistic society held together by a culture-religion inspired by the dogma of eighteenth-century liberalism emphasizing the possibilities of human nature; in addition, Catholicism in America has been the religion of immigrants, particularly the Irish who came from the northernmost corner of Europe where they had been relatively untouched by the influence of the Enlightenment, and where religion had been their major defense against English oppression.

These two factors account for the recurring tension within American Catholicism between the forces of encounter and separatism. Most immigrants wanted to become Americans and remain Catholics too. They wanted to share the promise of a new Jerusalem without repudiating altogether the traditions of the old country and the authority of their Church. From a European point of view, reconciliation was impossible. Even the most brilliant of all European observers on American life, Alexis de Tocqueville, predicted in the 1830's that either all Americans would become Catholic or Catholic Americans would abandon their religion. It is easy to excuse de Tocqueville's mistake. No one before or since has better understood the tendencies and implications of democracy in America; it was not democracy which de Tocqueville saw as uncongenial to Catholicism, it was the emphasis in America's culture-religion on personal independence. It has been the genius of American history to defy even de Tocqueville's logic. Catholics such as England, Ireland, and Gibbons saw that Catholicism could flourish under these new and peculiar conditions, but it is not surprising that Rome and even many priests and parishioners had a difficult time understanding their attitudes.

To the extent that adaptation to the culture-religion is crucial to the Americanization process and to the degree that the culture-religion represents a transmogrified Protestantism, the character of American Catholics has been affected by the psychological implications of Protestant principles. This was what the controversy over Americanism in the Church at the turn of the century was about as it applied to Americans. Because the errors Pope Leo XIII condemned were stated as hypothetical positions, it was possible for American Catholic leaders to disassociate themselves explicitly from the heresies under attack, and to act as if they applied to Europeans only. Had the Pope named names and cases, a schism might have followed. Instead, the Church in America continued to produce men who were loyal to it, but whose actions and stated convictions often seemed to illustrate the condemned heresies. Finally, Pope John and the Second Vatican Council—without explicitly rejecting the utterance of any previous Pope—endorsed doctrines associated sixty years before with the errors of Americanism.

History confounded the logic not just of de Tocqueville and the clerics of nineteenth-century Rome but of self-appointed spokesmen for America's culture-religion. To see American Catholicism, as Blanshard did in the late 1940's, primarily in terms of unrefuted encylicals and canon laws produced in the European environment was to miss the point of the uniqueness of the American experience. Logically, one can still find much in Catholic dogma and law which would justify the destruction of American civil liberties, but in history experience usually triumphs over logic, and that probably has been more true in the United States of America, whose people have defied tradition and exalted experience, than elsewhere. American Catholics have been gripped by the experience of American history, shaped and transformed by it, while, in the main, remaining true to the Church. They have been able to drink deeply of the wine of freedom and prosper within the Church of Rome.

*   *   *

Religion in America

If the test of religiosity in any society is theological preoccupation backed by sectarian intensity, then Americans have failed ever since they stopped hanging heretics in the seventeenth century. Both European and Oriental critics of religious life in America find it wanting. The Europeans stress the absence of sectarian convictions; Asians observe the absence of mysticism. Both point out that religious life in the United States is social and practical, although they often fail to notice the intensity of commitment which Americans make to their culture-religion and the extent to which its principles have infused sectarian religious life.

From Tom Paine, who explained that he wrote his *Age of Reason* to preserve "true theology" from the destruction of the French Revolution, through the Second Great Awakening, when Protestant ministers were imbued with Jeffersonian and Jacksonian ideals, to the post-Kennedy writings of Callahan and Novak, Americans—more than any other people in history—have believed in the capacity of man to fulfill the will of God. To the Puritans, the Arminian heresy lay primarily in its optimistic judgments of man's capacity to choose goodness. This too was the essence of St. Augustine's criticisms against Pelagius and of the orthodox Catholic judgment on what came to be known as the heresy of Pelagianism. One can quarrel with Jeffersonian optimism as being shallow and mischievous without denying that it is at the heart of the American culture-religion or failing to see that it is grounded in metaphysical presuppositions.

Several spokesmen for traditional Protestantism, Catholicism, and Judaism have complained of the pervasive Arminianism-Pelagianism (without calling it that) of America's culture-religion as an insufficient explanation of and an inadequate weapon to deal with the complexly tragic questions of human existence. They have seen the backlash of frustrated utopian Arminian-Pelagian dreams result in vigilantism or isolationism; but the most penetrating of critics have not failed to see that Americans, as much as any modern nation, have been true believers. Their culture-religion has had its prophets (Emerson), philosophers (Jefferson), poets (Whitman), and heroes, including John F. Kennedy.

Oliver Wendell Holmes once said, "We are the Romans of the modern world . . . a great assimilating people," but he also said that we are all tattooed in our cradle with the beliefs of our tribe. In America, the beliefs of many tribes have been tolerated and even welcomed. The Buddhists in Hawaii prosper; Mormons in Utah thrive; Jews in New York flourish; and forty million Catholics win increased respect and recognition. The price has been acceptance of other religions as having equally valid rights, the minimization of forms and rituals, considerable indifference to theology, and endorsement of a humanistic culture-religion which emphasizes man's capacity for choice based on experience.

America is the meeting ground where different cultures encounter each other, and in the process of confrontation, the characteristics of some of them persist and influence the others; but not all cultures are equally influential. Americans, including Catholics, have been enveloped by the dominant values of our culture-religion. Immigrants have been permitted to continue their traditions with respect to food, music, and art, and to have their own newspapers, languages, and churches. In the process of encounter, they change the customs of their hosts, as Catholics did in promoting the celebration of Christmas in the United States, but they are

acculturated to the fundamentals of Americanism. No metaphor yet invented describes the process: neither a melting pot, pressure cooker, nor
rainbow.

The dominant value of American culture is personal independence—the
right and ability to choose without external restraint—and American Catholics, while not expecting their children to show as much independence as
Protestants or Jews and not valuing intellectual autonomy above obedience
as much as non-Catholics, have embraced that value to a considerable extent. Although the 1958 study referred to above revealed that a significantly
higher proportion of Jews and Protestants than Catholics valued intellectual
autonomy above obedience in the raising of children, perhaps the most remarkable finding was the degree to which American Catholics did choose
intellectual autonomy. Some 70 percent of the upper-middle-class white
Catholics, 63 percent of those in the lower-middle-class, and even 51 percent in the upper-working-class Catholic group preferred the value of autonomy. While a significantly higher proportion of Protestants than Catholics believed they had the right to challenge what their church teaches, a
surprising 67 percent of active Catholic laymen also asserted that right.
The studies, made by sociologist Gerhard Lenski in Detroit, while revealing that many Catholics were still tattooed with the beliefs of their tribe,
showed also the assimilative power of America's culture-religion.

Lenski's most startling finding was that third-generation Catholics were
in many respects more typically Catholic than their parents and grandparents. Middle-class Catholics, for example, showed a smaller proportion of
the third generation committed to the principle of intellectual autonomy
than in the first and second generations. From such statistics, Lenski concluded that the nation would become more Catholic in many ways, including a declining emphasis on intellectual independence, a slowing rate of
material progress, rising birth rates, a narrowing of the latitude for the
exercise of the right of free speech and increased restraints on Sunday
business, divorce, and possibly birth control.

The opposite has happened in every respect since the book was published
in 1961, indicating that either the concept of intellectual autonomy has a
much more complex meaning to middle-class third-generation Catholics
than it had to their parents or grandparents or Catholics in the working
classes, or that John F. Kennedy and the Second Vatican Council have
stimulated profoundly the tendencies toward autonomy which did exist
among Catholics of all generations, especially those with more education.
This particular finding by Lenski was contradicted implicitly by two other
sociological studies published in 1964 and 1965, and based on later surveys
than the one made in Detroit. One of them, by Father Joseph H. Fichter,
found the older generation conservative (as measured by views on public
policy questions) and less critical of the Church than the younger parish-

oners. The other, by Father Andrew Greeley, showed on the basis of a large sample of college graduates in 1961 that Catholic anti-intellectualism had sharply declined by the early 1960's. Statistics aside, by 1966 an increasing number of younger Catholics tended to prize their personal independence and believed as much as Protestants and Jews that spiritual self-direction was indispensable to genuine religious commitment. They insisted, as Gary MacEoin put it in *New Challenges to American Catholics,* that "the Church must be a society of freedom."

The process of Americanization or adaptation to the culture-religion of America is often deplored by respected religious leaders such as Reinhold Niebuhr, Robert McAfee Brown, Father Gustave Weigel, and Rabbi Will Herberg. Even when they grant that the blunting of sectarian differences helps to promote vital unity in a pluralistic society, they sometimes see the process as compromising traditions and practices long associated with deep concern for the ultimate questions of human existence. Americans are charged not just with merging their transcendental concerns with those of the secular culture, but as lacking in spiritual or religious concerns.

There is no question that religion has often been subsumed by national patriotism in America, but it is doubtful if transcendental religion was more of a check on the worldly goals of sixteenth-century Catholic Spain or is currently more of a test of the national foreign policy of Moslem Pakistan than it has been in the United States. By valuing personal independence, Americans may burden themselves with vicious status competition and deep psychological isolation, but they have not been prevented from recognizing the claims of individual conscience. Probably no religious group so well exemplifies traditional American values as the Quakers, who have given a higher proportion of conscientious objectors to participation in American wars than any other group.

The accusation that spiritual life in America is often banal, and religious commitment often superficial because the culture-religion has blurred sectarian differences, can be analyzed only in terms of some standard of spirituality and religious commitment. If ritual is an important index of spiritual life, then Americans are not as spiritual as Filipinos or Columbians. If the passive virtues of obedience, piety, and austerity are the primary measures of transcendental concern, then most Hindus and Buddhists are far more religious than Americans. If theological preoccupation is the test, the Germans and French are certainly more religious. The obvious and more traditional indexes of religiosity indicate a decline in America in recent decades. Studies show that per capita contributions to Protestant churches over the past twenty-five years have been declining. The ratio of clergymen to the general population in the past hundred years has gone down, the number of church seats available in proportion to the population has declined, and even reports of church attendance by the

Gallup poll show a drop over the past twenty years. Among Protestants there is probably less doctrinal orthodoxy and devotionalism than at any time since the Revolution.

Yet it was only a few decades ago that ministers and priests were congratulating themselves on the so-called "religious revival" in America. Then, climbing church attendance may have been little more than a function of suburbanization with its demand for a church-centered social life. In retrospect, it seems to me that no genuine religious revival could have permitted the vigilantism of McCarthy, the platitudes of Eisenhower, and the moralisms of Dulles. By contrast, the marching nuns, priests, and rabbis in Selma, Alabama, the extraordinary emphasis on renewal in Protestant churches, the accelerated activity in evangelical sects such as the Jehovah's Witnesses or the Seventh-day Adventists, and the deep soul-searching reported by group leaders, psychiatrists, and college teachers indicate that religion is far more a vital force in the 1960's than it was in the two previous decades.

But these developments have been accompanied by a rising agnosticism and widespread assumption that religion is less a force than it used to be. Studies have shown that a higher percentage of college students in the 1960's professed agnosticism than in the 1950's, and that there were proportionately more agnostics in college in the 1950's than in 1913. A 1965 Gallup poll revealed that the percentage of Americans who see religion as losing influence had more than tripled since 1957. But do statistics that show that 52 percent of the college students believe that religious influence is losing ground actually demonstrate that religion is losing ground? Or do they signify a deepening awareness of the vulnerability of the human condition and a profound feeling of dissatisfaction with the answers provided by sectarian religion to questions of ultimate concern?

The growing opposition to automated faith and the commitment to the value of personal choice rather than militating against religion may be a prelude to a deeper, more complex spirituality than Americans have known before. Paul Tillich's assertion that salvation can be located in "the courage to be" has been embraced by new-breed Catholics, Jews, Protestants, agnostics, and atheists on college campuses all over the country. His definition of religion as "ultimate concern" is not only compatible with a culture which emphasizes personal responsibility for choice but which has been called the most secular civilization in a secular age.

Secularism — which is characterized by neutrality of the state with respect to religion, tolerant attitudes toward religious differences, and an assessment of men in terms of how they function — is incompatible with extreme sectarianism; but it is not necessarily antagonistic to profound and complex religious commitment unless one defines religion in purely sectarian terms. Many Catholic and some Protestant writers have equated secular religion with materialism, assuming that the advance of secularism would mean the corruption of spiritual values, but Protestant theologian Harvey Cox has argued that secularism should be welcomed by believing Christians and Jews precisely because it makes possible a greater range of freedom and responsibility for man. It tests his spiritual resources more sharply and disturbingly than they have been challenged before.

Secularism makes war on parochialism, but not necessarily on religion. Are Jews more religious if they insist on their chosenness to live according to the moral law? Are Catholics more religious if they maintain that non-believers are eternally damned? Are Protestants more religious if they hold to a belief in the predestination of the elect? Parochialism says not just "Here I stand," but "There you must stand." It is often a defensive re-action to fear that puts up walls and signs that read: "Be careful," "Whites only," "No Irish need apply."

An Ecumenical Man

John F. Kennedy represented an antithetical approach to parochialism in human affairs. For him, life was not to be feared but affirmed. Ex-perience was not to be avoided but courted. Cardinal Cushing has quoted the President as saying, "We must esteem other religious faiths" (not tolerate, but "esteem"). Kennedy had the capacity to expose himself to differences, even to reach out to understand them, and yet remain true to his own convictions. He wanted it absolutely clear that he was against religious extremism and intolerance from whatever source. When he talked to the United Nations in September, 1963, just two months before his death, he protested that human rights "are not respected when a Buddhist priest is driven from his pagoda," a not very subtle reference to alleged Catholic persecution of Buddhists in Vietnam. Then, to make it clear that no group is immune from the fault of intolerance, religious or racial, he pointed out that human rights are attacked "when a synagogue is shut down, when a Protestant church cannot open a mission [something Protes-tants have complained against Catholics in Latin America for years], when a cardinal is forced into hiding, or when a crowded church service is bombed [as had happened recently to a Negro church in Alabama]."

Kennedy's broad ecumenism — his desire for encounter with others — was not incompatible with a deepening sense of ultimate concern or growing identification with Catholicism. For Kennedy, as he told the students and faculty of Boston College in April, 1963, the importance of Pope John and his farsighted encyclicals was that "we are learning to talk the lan-guage of progress and peace across the barriers of sect and creed." Follow-ing the Pope's death, Kennedy pointed out that while John had been "the chosen leader of world Catholicism, . . . his concern for the human spirit transcended all boundaries of belief or geography." Three weeks later, the

President told the Irish Parliament: "The supreme reality of our time is
our indivisibility as children of God and our common vulnerability on this
planet . . . we must remember there are no permanent enemies." Because
that was Pope John's belief too, Kennedy was able to say, after reading
Pope John's remarkable encyclical *Pacem in terris:* "As a Catholic I am
proud of it; and as an American I have learned from it." Pope John had
made Kennedy proud to be a Catholic exactly because John himself was
not prideful. Kennedy praised *Pacem in terris* but pointed out to his
Catholic audience that it was not uniquely Catholic and "that it closely
matches notable expressions of convictions and aspirations from churchmen
of other faiths, as in recent documents of the World Council of Churches,
and from outstanding world citizens with no ecclesiastical standing."

Only a few weeks before he died, John F. Kennedy spoke to the Protestant Council of New York City. In this speech, Kennedy went beyond
not only his sectarian origins but the culture-religion of Americanism too.
Although he saw the mission of Americans as the promotion of the family
of man, he did not define progress in terms of the spread of American
values. He pointed out that most of the world knew nothing about free
enterprise, due process of law, or the Australian ballot, and asserted that
the family of man could accept differences of ideology, politics and economics and transcend differences of race and religion. He reminded his audience
that most members of the family are not white and most of them are not
Christian, but all of them share the desire to survive in dignity. Warning
that the family of man could not survive a nuclear war or endure the
growing gap between the rich and the poor, he hoped that man would
prevail, not just Catholicism, or America, or even political freedom or
personal independence, as Americans have known them, but man. To judge
from the worldwide reaction to Kennedy's death, this secular President
from a secular country spoke to the spiritual needs of men everywhere.
This man who wore his religion so lightly communicated his sense of ultimate concern.

The culture-religion of America can be faulted on many grounds. At its
worst, it has been no less ethnocentric than any other religion, and even
more intolerant than the absorptive, flexible philosophies and religions of
the East. By its insistence on personal independence, it has often inhibited
mutuality and love in personal relationships. It has helped to promote a
kind of competitiveness and loneliness unknown to the more traditional
cultures of Asia. It has torn at traditions, burdening Americans, especially
Protestants, with the need to find· meaning from one's naked existence
rather than as a member of a family, tribe, church, or historic community.
The response of Americans often has been a weak, other-directed conformism to the values of the Rotary and to the standards of the market-
place, or an avoidance of a crisis of personal decision, but there also has
been a response of Lincoln and Kennedy.

If Americans have lived with alienation longer than most people, it is mainly because they are a nation of uprooted Europeans and Asians held together partly by the customs and loyalties of their subcultures but also by a commitment to a culture-religion which in its emphasis on independence often confines them, in de Tocqueville's words, to the solitude of their own hearts. Americans took from Luther and Calvin those Protestant principles which had the most meaning for their unique historical experience. Whatever in the new theology of Protestantism promoted self-sufficiency was grasped before the turn of the eighteenth century. Protestantism thus became both a result and a cause of psychic isolation. For Luther, a representative of the new breed of his time, there was one way to know God's word: "Thou must thyself decide. Thy life is at stake. Therefore must God say unto thee in thy heart, 'This is God's word,' else it is still undecided."

Until the election of John F. Kennedy, the Catholic Church, more than any other single institution, and Catholics more than any other group of Americans, were viewed as hostile to the American insistence on personal independence. Kennedy was President for less than three years and the Roman Catholic Church still asserts its claim to truth through authoritative spokesmen commissioned by God beginning with the Pope of Rome. Yet the Church both in America and the world has embraced the value of individual choice long associated with the civilization of North America. It is a powerful and explosive value, creating technology which expands the aesthetic and intellectual dimensions of human personality and builds friendships across traditional barriers, but which also destroys traditions which have enabled men for centuries to find themselves in others and in nature. It is a dangerous value which has often led to pride, willfulness, and hatred; but it is a value which can also lead to commitments to love God and to care for man, as well as self-centeredness devoid of either. It is a value which may be muted or even radically altered with the passage of time as Americans encounter Asians, Latin Americans, and Africans in mutually enriching relationships. But it is the value of our time and culture, of Protestants and Jews, and increasingly of Catholics, Western Europeans, and peoples in large cities everywhere, forcing them to think with Luther that "everyone must do his own believing as he will have to do his own dying." Or was it John F. Kennedy who said that?

Topical Index by Author

The American

Selections in this section deal primarily with problems of identity, role, and interpersonal relations. Matters of "maleness," "femaleness," race, and nationality, among other things, are discussed by these writers. Selections are arranged in chronological order; the number in parentheses after the author's name designates the number of the selection in the book.

The American Manner

Selections in this section deal with the style and mode of being American. They attempt to get at uniquely American characteristics as they are revealed in a wide range of beliefs, behaviors, and creative endeavors.

American Values

Selections in this section are concerned with the beliefs of Americans in a wide range of areas, including the religious, economic, political, and social.

American Social Organization and Institutions

Selections in this section, as the title indicates, deal with the institutional and social organizational forms which Americans have constructed. These include such institutions as the religious, educational, and political.

The Arts

Selections in this section are concerned with the fine and popular arts in America, including architecture, literature and belles lettres, and painting.

The Physical Environment

Selections in this section deal with the natural and man-made environment in which Americans live, work, and play, including the city, suburb, and country.